悠 UQ HOLDER!

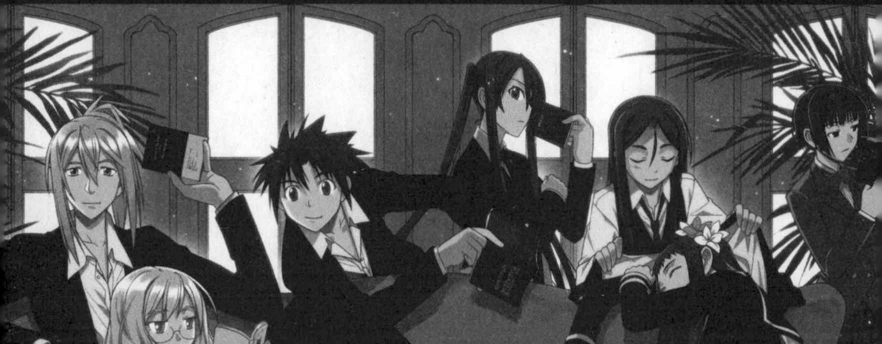

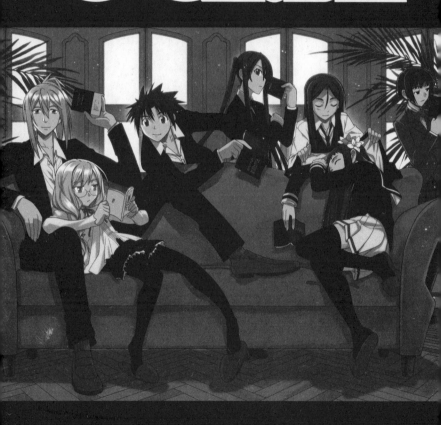

KEN AKAMATSU

vol.6

CHARACTERS

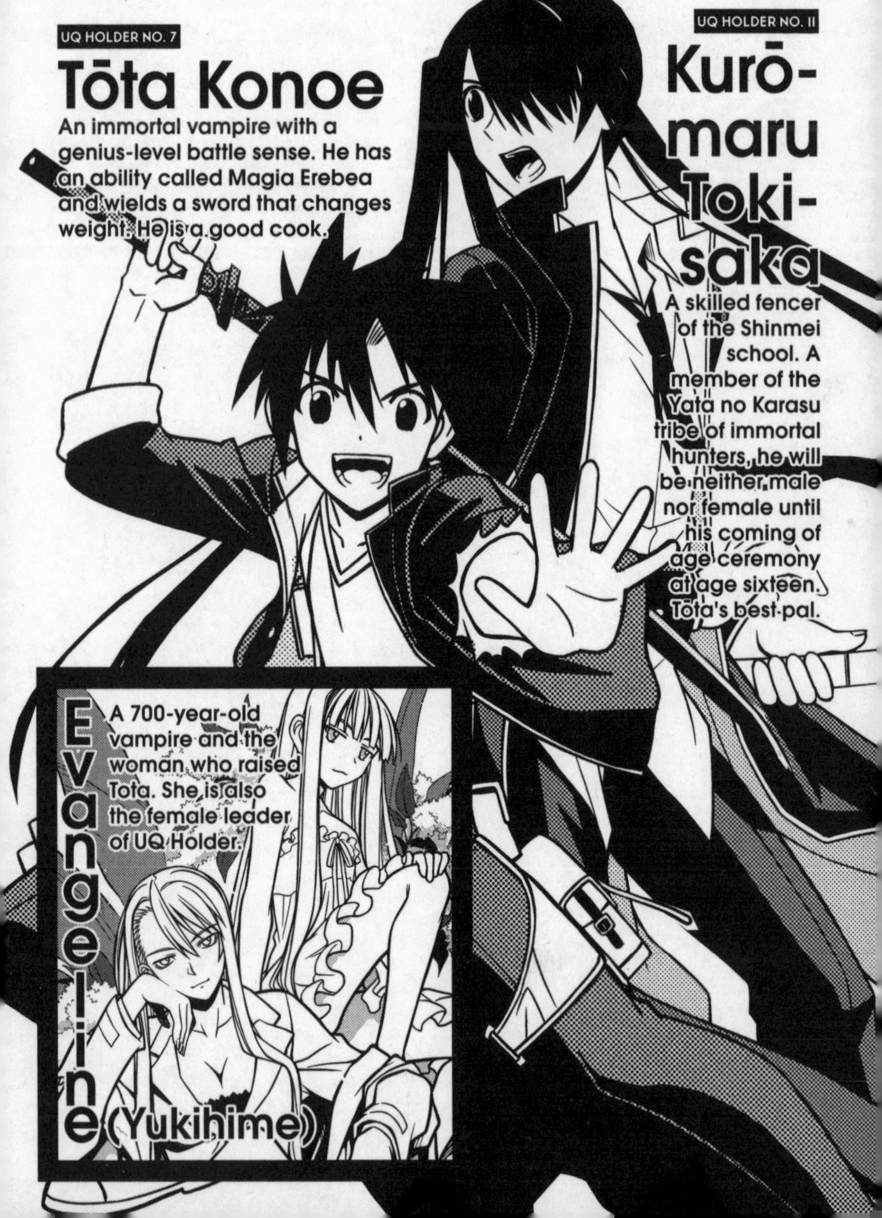

UQ HOLDER NO. 7

Tōta Konoe

An immortal vampire with a genius-level battle sense. He has an ability called Magia Erebea and wields a sword that changes weight. He is a good cook.

UQ HOLDER NO. 11

Kurōmaru Tokisaka

A skilled fencer of the Shinmei school. A member of the Yata no Karasu tribe of immortal hunters, he will be neither male nor female until his coming of age ceremony at age sixteen. Tota's best pal.

Evangeline (Yukihime)

A 700-year-old vampire and the woman who raised Tota. She is also the female leader of UQ Holder.

UQ HOLDER!

Ken Akamatsu Presents

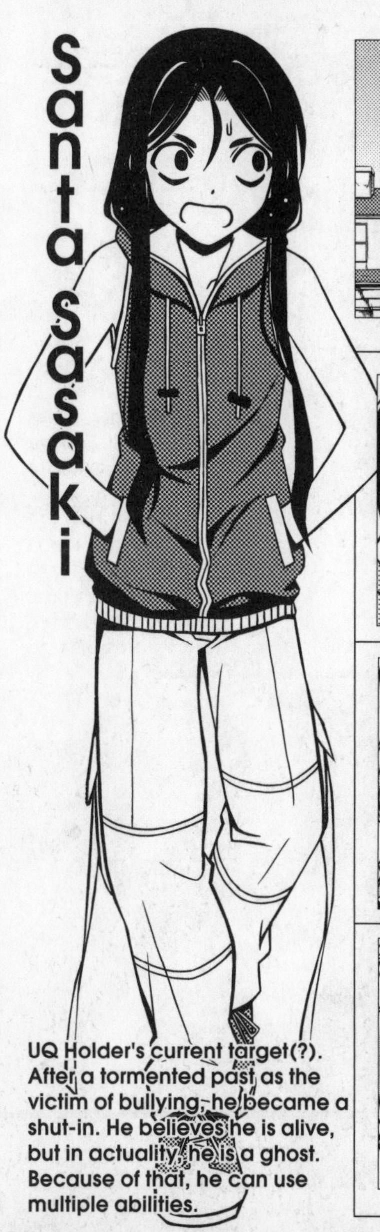

Santa Sasaki

UQ Holder's current target(?). After a tormented past as the victim of bullying, he became a shut-in. He believes he is alive, but in actuality, he is a ghost. Because of that, he can use multiple abilities.

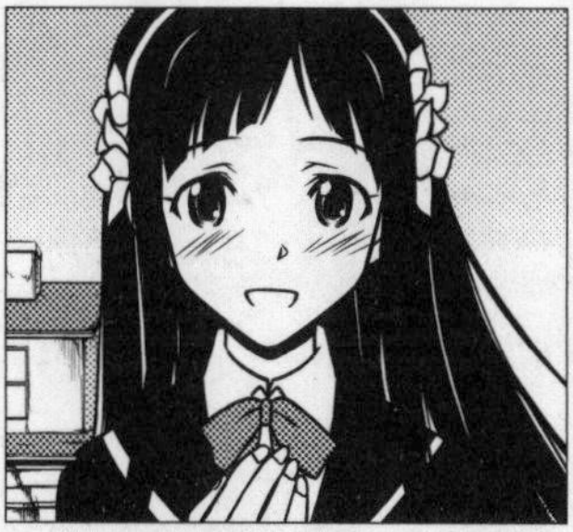

Sayoko

Bound Santa's spirit to this world eight years ago. Is she the mastermind behind the series of bizarre murders?

UQ HOLDER NUMBERS

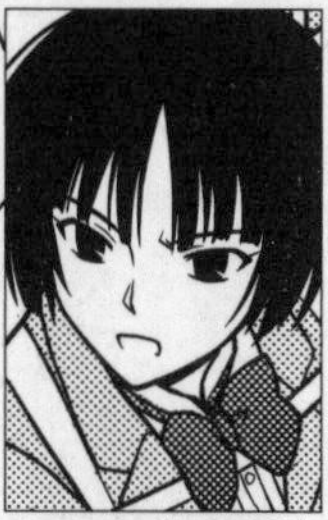

UQ HOLDER NO. 4

Karin

Cool-headed and ruthless. Her immortality is S-class. Also known as the Saintess of Steel. Loves Eva.

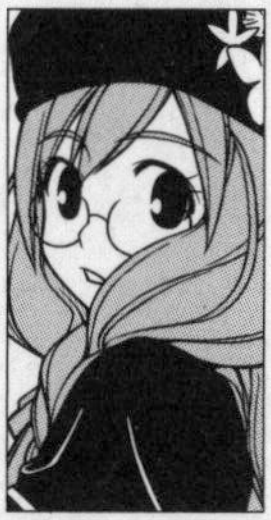

UQ HOLDER NO. 9

Kirië Sakurame

The greatest financial contributor to UQ Holder, who constantly calls Tōta incompetent. Her ability is "Reset and Restart."

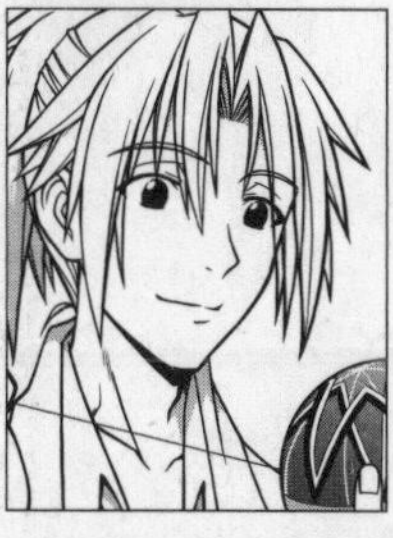

UQ HOLDER NO. 10

Ikkū Ameya

Looks young, but is an 85-year-old full-body cyborg. Very good with his hands.

THE STORY SO FAR

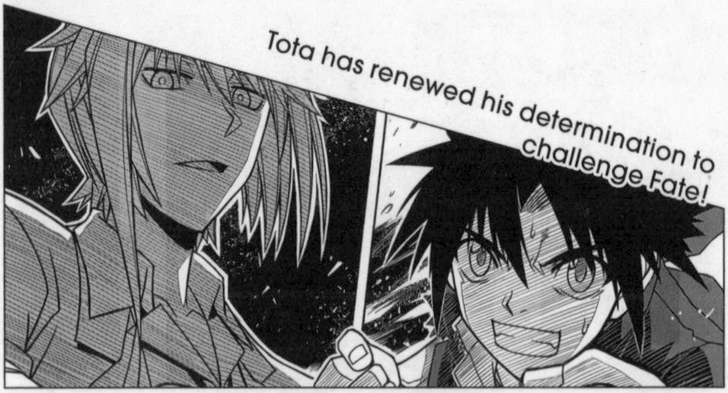
Tota has renewed his determination to challenge Fate!

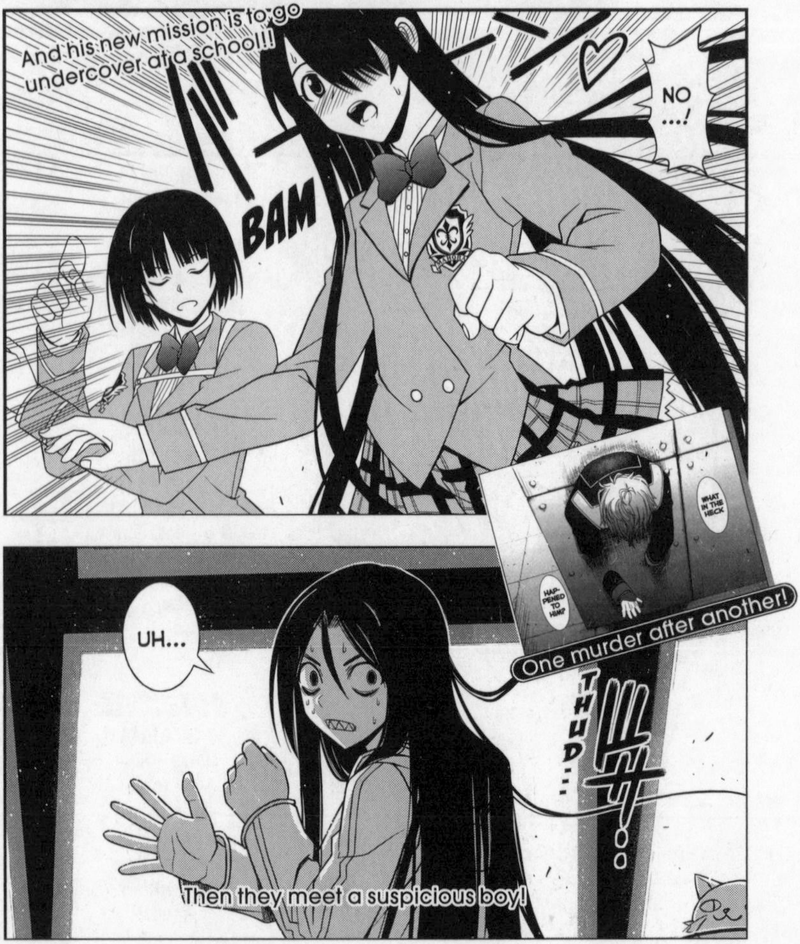
NO ...!
BAM
And his new mission is to go undercover at a school!!
WHAT IN THE HECK
HAPPENED TO HIM?
One murder after another!
THUD...
UH...
Then they meet a suspicious boy!

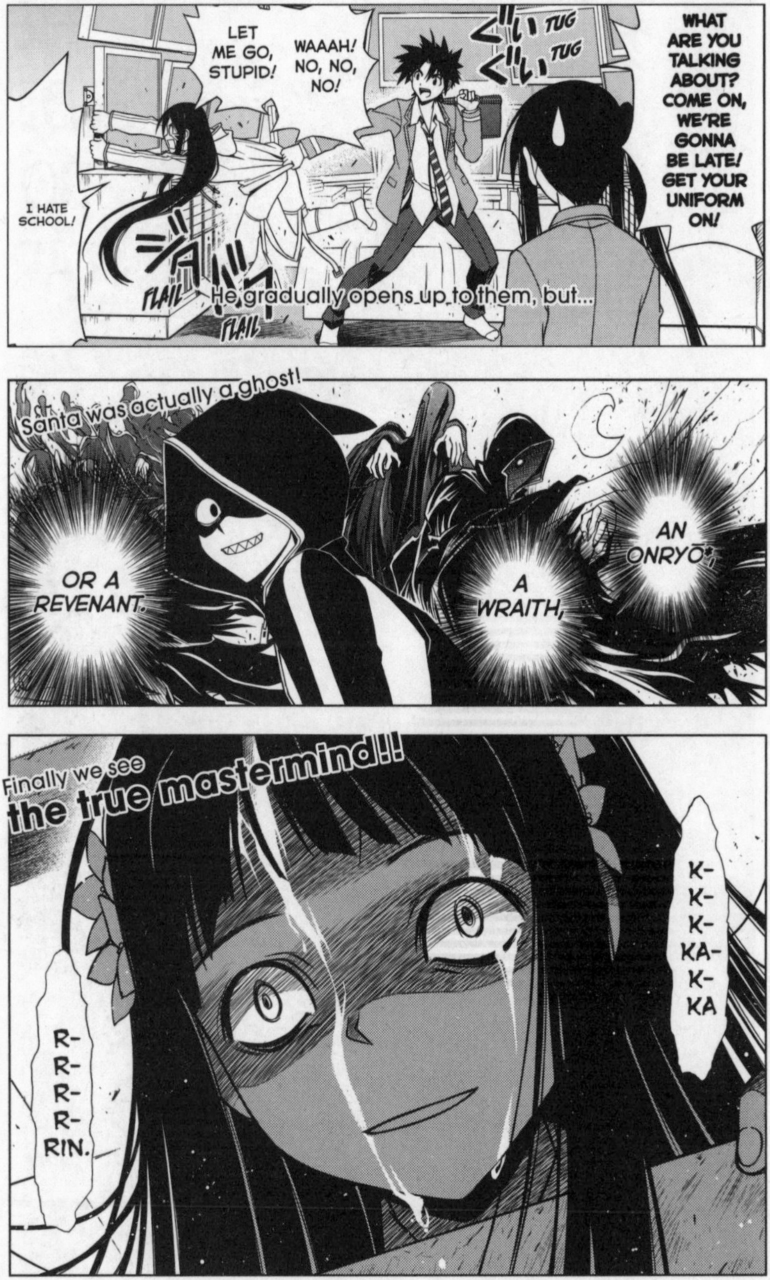
WHAT ARE YOU TALKING ABOUT? COME ON, WE'RE GONNA BE LATE! GET YOUR UNIFORM ON!
TUG
TUG
WAAAH! NO, NO, NO!
LET ME GO, STUPID!
I HATE SCHOOL!
FLAIL
FLAIL
He gradually opens up to them, but...
Santa was actually a ghost!
AN ONRYŌ*,
A WRAITH,
OR A REVENANT.
Finally we see the true mastermind!!
K-K-K-KA-K-KA
R-R-R-R-RIN.

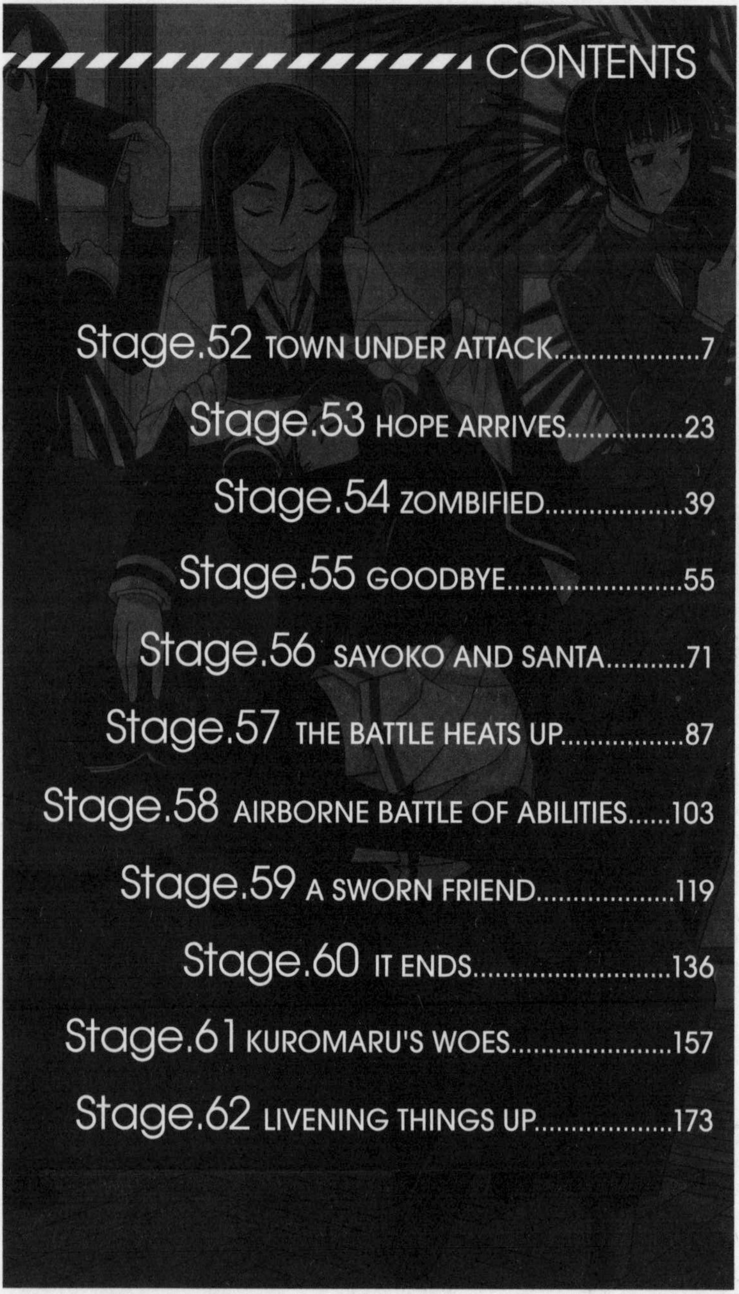

CONTENTS

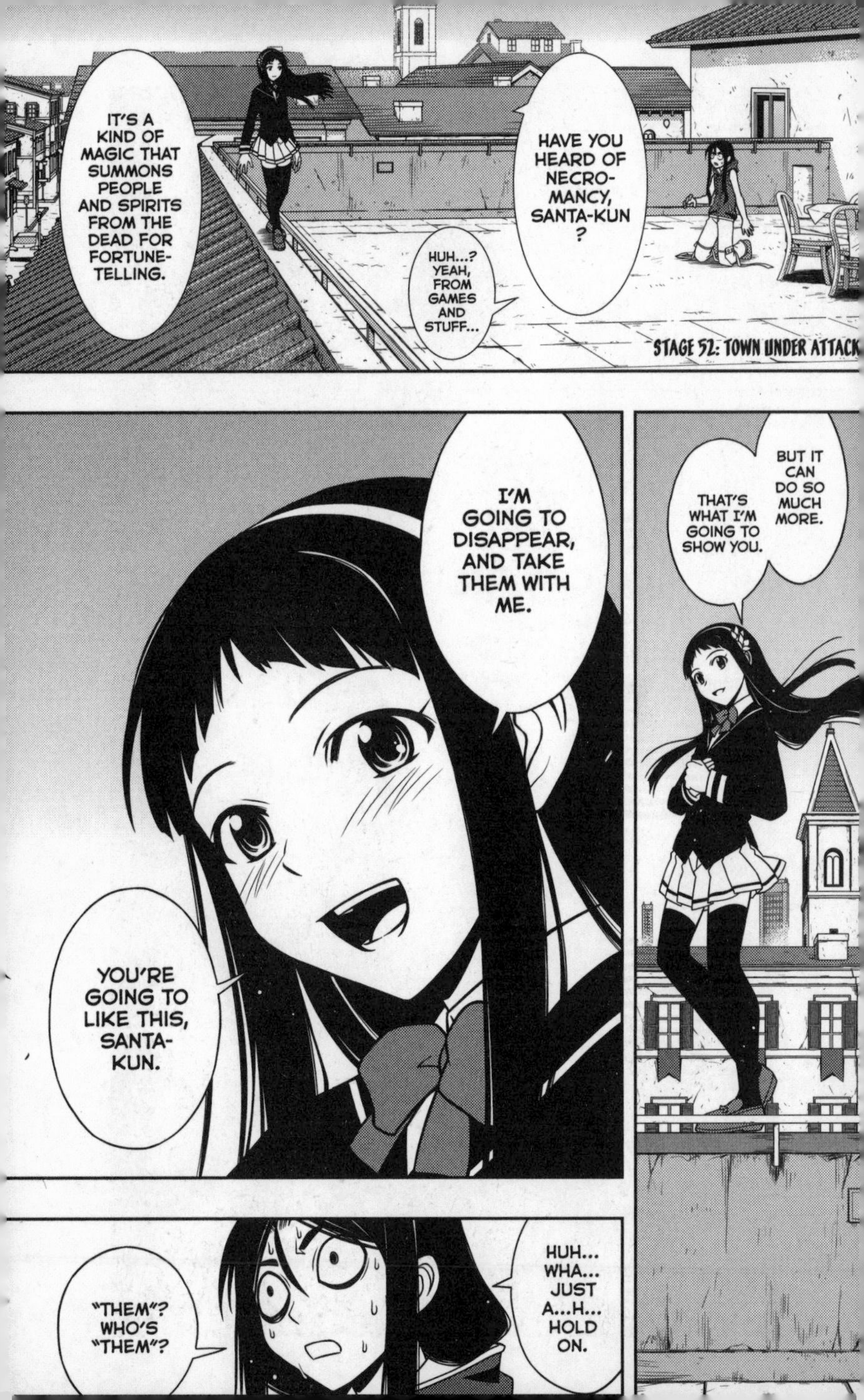
STAGE 52: TOWN UNDER ATTACK
HAVE YOU HEARD OF NECROMANCY, SANTA-KUN?
HUH...? YEAH, FROM GAMES AND STUFF...
IT'S A KIND OF MAGIC THAT SUMMONS PEOPLE AND SPIRITS FROM THE DEAD FOR FORTUNE-TELLING.
BUT IT CAN DO SO MUCH MORE.
THAT'S WHAT I'M GOING TO SHOW YOU.
I'M GOING TO DISAPPEAR, AND TAKE THEM WITH ME.
YOU'RE GOING TO LIKE THIS, SANTA-KUN.
HUH... WHA... JUST A...H... HOLD ON.
"THEM"? WHO'S "THEM"?

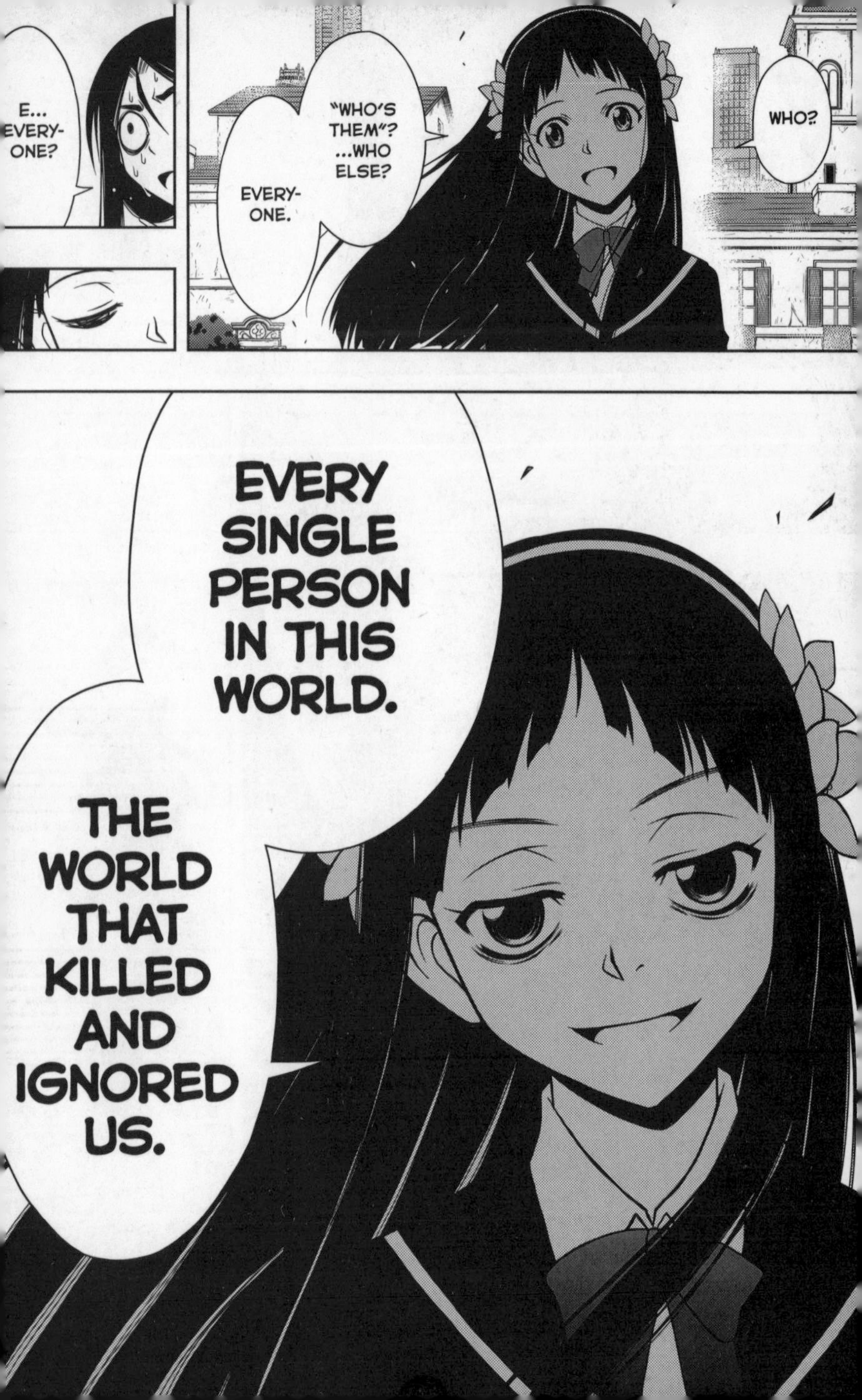
WHO?
"WHO'S THEM"? ...WHO ELSE?
EVERY-ONE.
E... EVERY-ONE?
EVERY SINGLE PERSON IN THIS WORLD.
THE WORLD THAT KILLED AND IGNORED US.

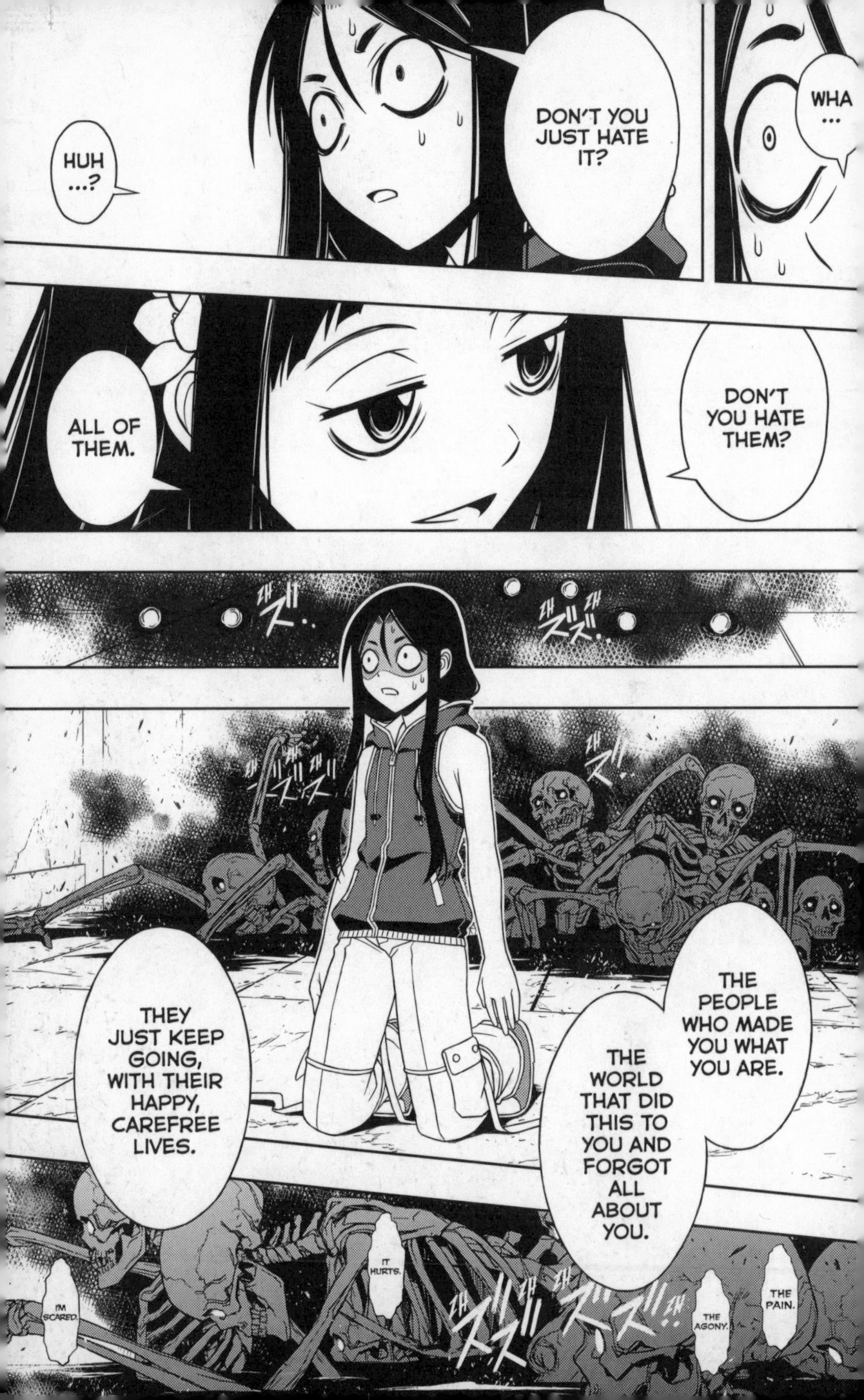
WHA...
DON'T YOU JUST HATE IT?
HUH...?
DON'T YOU HATE THEM?
ALL OF THEM.
THE PEOPLE WHO MADE YOU WHAT YOU ARE.
THE WORLD THAT DID THIS TO YOU AND FORGOT ALL ABOUT YOU.
THEY JUST KEEP GOING, WITH THEIR HAPPY, CAREFREE LIVES.
THE PAIN.
THE AGONY.
IT HURTS.
I'M SCARED.

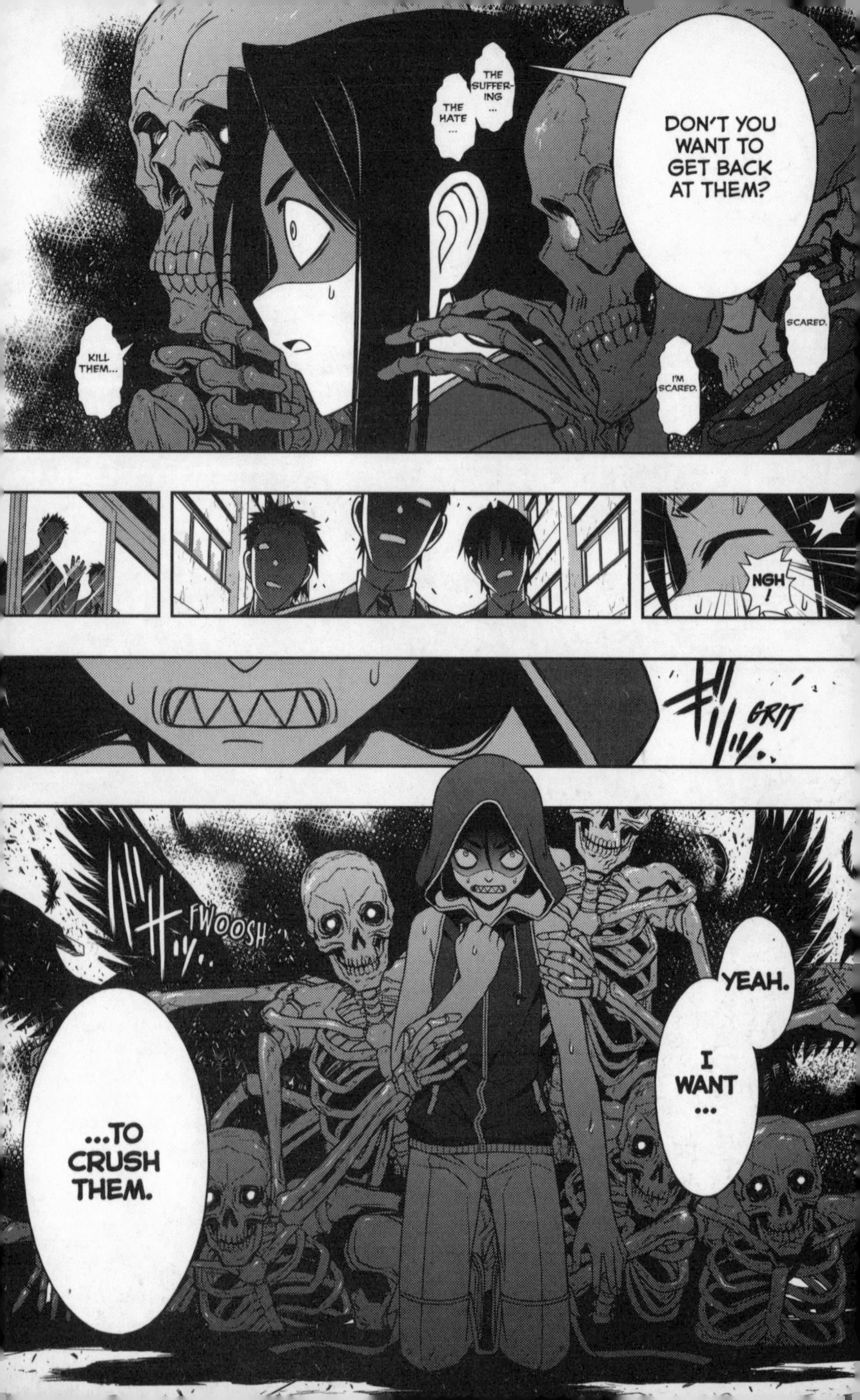
DON'T YOU WANT TO GET BACK AT THEM?
THE SUFFER-ING ...
THE HATE ...
SCARED.
I'M SCARED.
KILL THEM...
NGH!
GRIT
YEAH.
I WANT ...
FWOOSH
...TO CRUSH THEM.

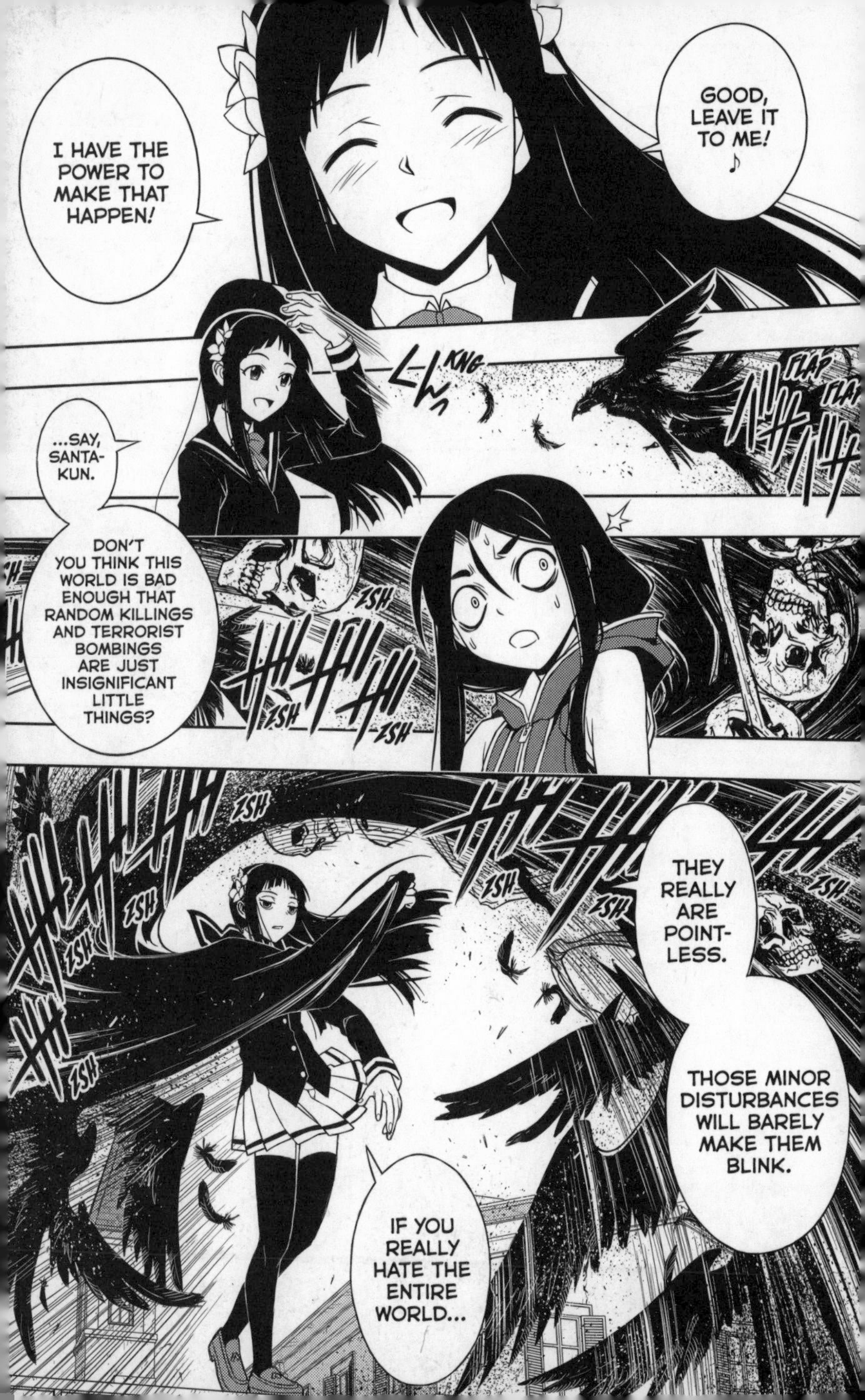
GOOD, LEAVE IT TO ME! ♪
I HAVE THE POWER TO MAKE THAT HAPPEN!
FLAP FLAP
KNG
...SAY, SANTA-KUN.
ZSH
ZSH
ZSH
DON'T YOU THINK THIS WORLD IS BAD ENOUGH THAT RANDOM KILLINGS AND TERRORIST BOMBINGS ARE JUST INSIGNIFICANT LITTLE THINGS?
ZSH
ZSH
ZSH
THEY REALLY ARE POINT-LESS.
THOSE MINOR DISTURBANCES WILL BARELY MAKE THEM BLINK.
ZSH
ZSH
ZSH
ZSH
IF YOU REALLY HATE THE ENTIRE WORLD...

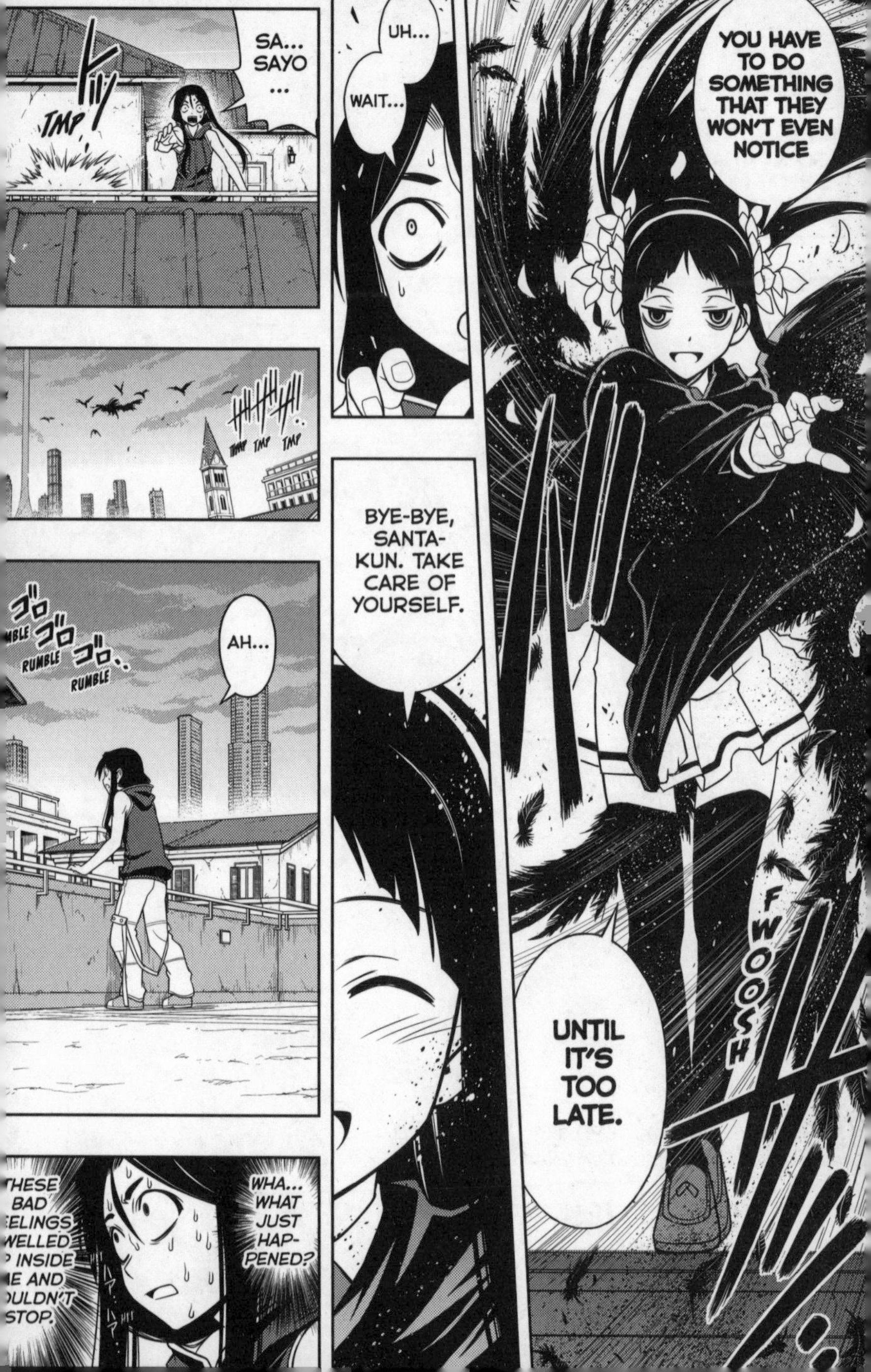

YOU HAVE TO DO SOMETHING THAT THEY WON'T EVEN NOTICE
UNTIL IT'S TOO LATE.
FWOOSH
UH...
WAIT...
BYE-BYE, SANTA-KUN. TAKE CARE OF YOURSELF.
SA... SAYO ...
TMP
TMP TMP TMP
ゴロ RUMBLE ゴロ RUMBLE ゴロ.. RUMBLE
AH...
WHA... WHAT JUST HAP-PENED?
THESE BAD EELINGS WELLED P INSIDE E AND OULDN'T STOP.
ハァ ハァ

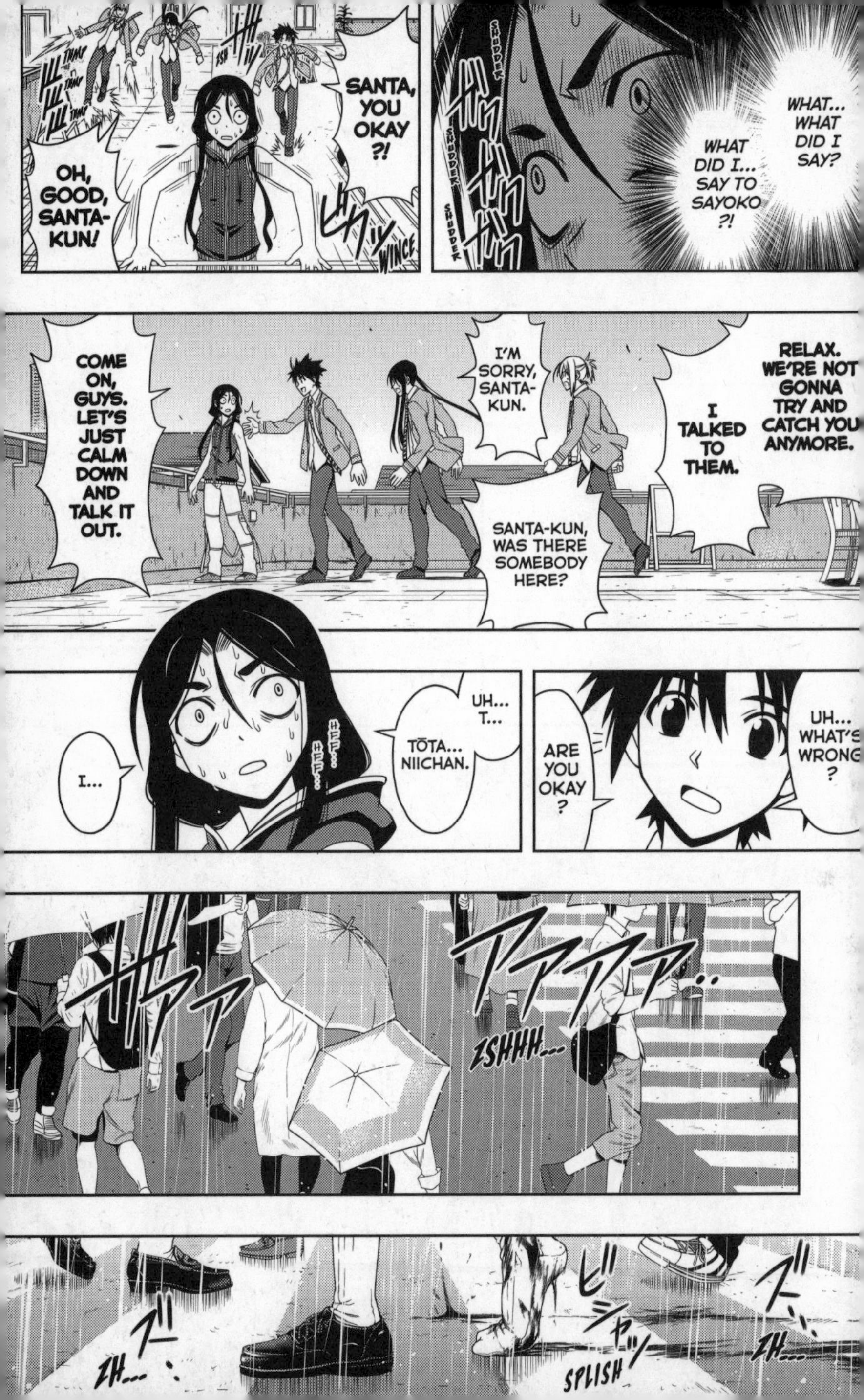
WHAT... WHAT DID I SAY?
WHAT DID I... SAY TO SAYOKO ?!
SHUDDER
SHUDDER
SHUDDER
SHUDDER
THMP
THMP
THMP
TSH
SANTA, YOU OKAY ?!
OH, GOOD, SANTA-KUN!
WINCE
RELAX. WE'RE NOT GONNA TRY AND CATCH YOU ANYMORE.
I TALKED TO THEM.
I'M SORRY, SANTA-KUN.
SANTA-KUN, WAS THERE SOMEBODY HERE?
COME ON, GUYS. LET'S JUST CALM DOWN AND TALK IT OUT.
UH... WHAT'S WRONG ?
ARE YOU OKAY ?
UH... T...
TŌTA... NIICHAN.
HFF...
HFF...
I...
ZSHHH...
ZH...
SPLISH
ZH...

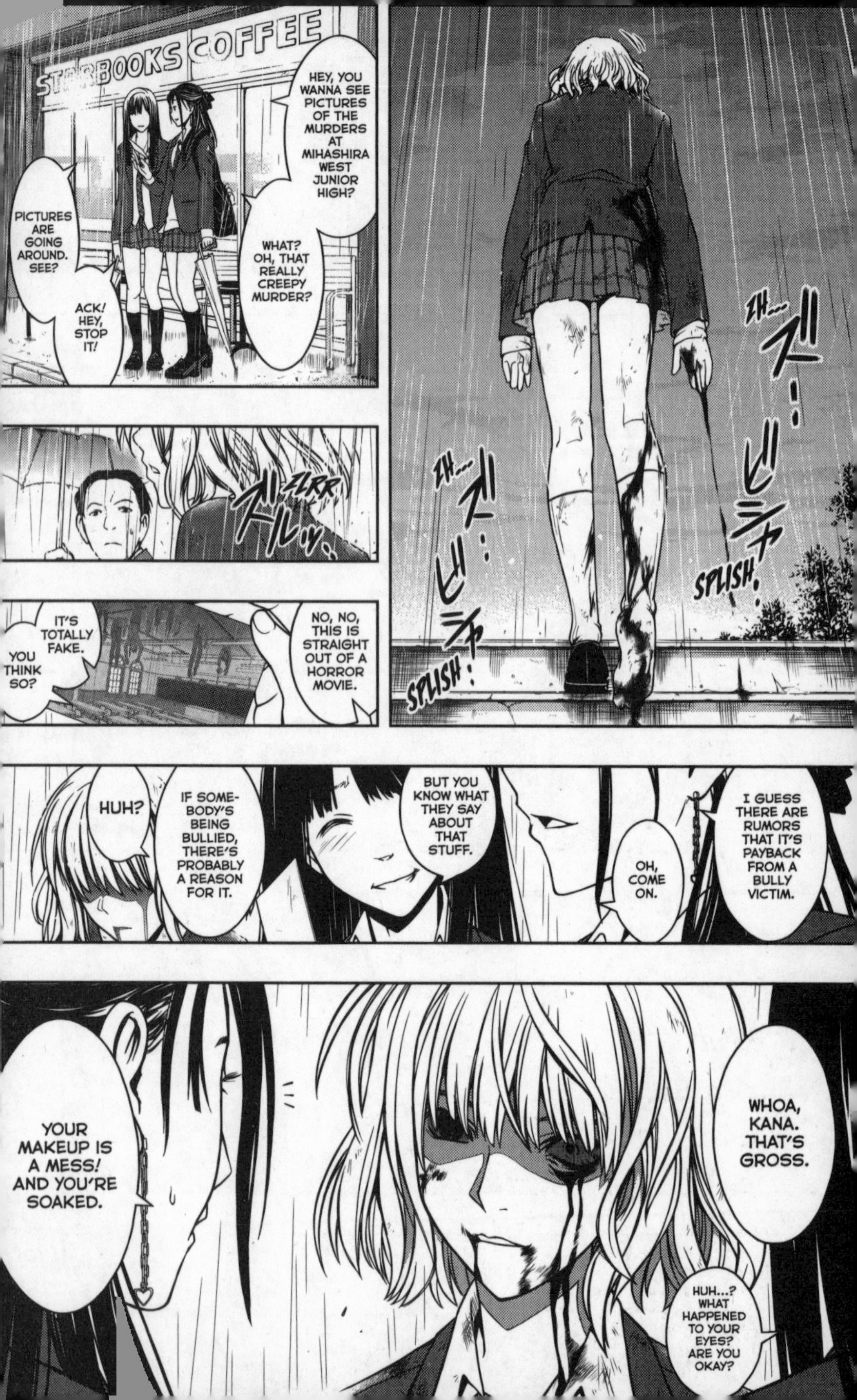
ZH...
SPLISH!
ZH...
SPLISH!
BOOKS COFFEE
HEY, YOU WANNA SEE PICTURES OF THE MURDERS AT MIHASHIRA WEST JUNIOR HIGH?
WHAT? OH, THAT REALLY CREEPY MURDER?
PICTURES ARE GOING AROUND. SEE?
ACK! HEY, STOP IT!
ZLRR
NO, NO, THIS IS STRAIGHT OUT OF A HORROR MOVIE.
IT'S TOTALLY FAKE.
YOU THINK SO?
I GUESS THERE ARE RUMORS THAT IT'S PAYBACK FROM A BULLY VICTIM.
OH, COME ON.
BUT YOU KNOW WHAT THEY SAY ABOUT THAT STUFF.
IF SOMEBODY'S BEING BULLIED, THERE'S PROBABLY A REASON FOR IT.
HUH?
WHOA, KANA. THAT'S GROSS.
HUH...? WHAT HAPPENED TO YOUR EYES? ARE YOU OKAY?
YOUR MAKEUP IS A MESS! AND YOU'RE SOAKED.

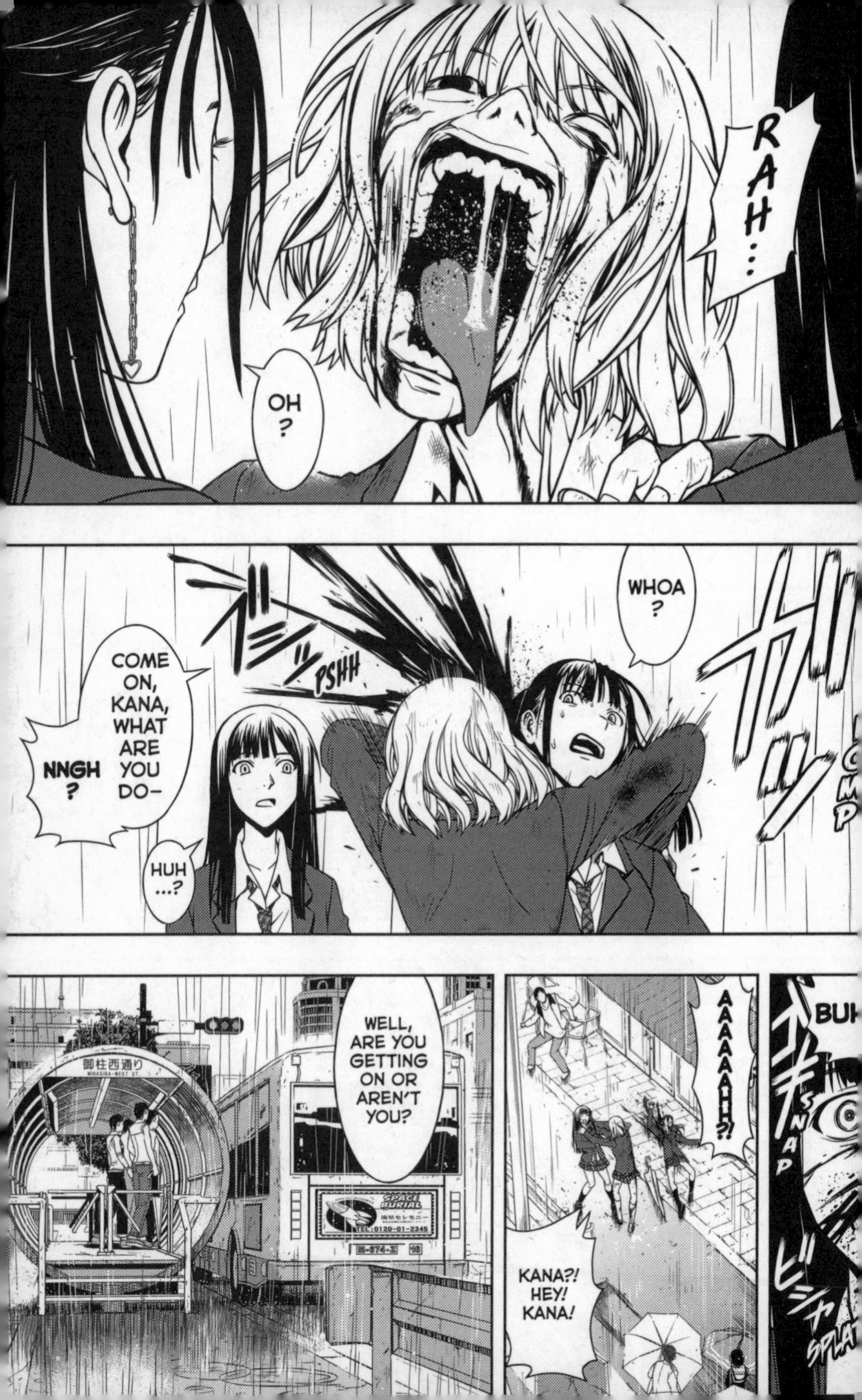
RAH…
OH?
WHOA?
PSHH
COME ON, KANA, WHAT ARE YOU DO-
NNGH?
HUH…?
SNAP
AAAAAAAHH?!
KANA?! HEY! KANA!
御柱西通り
MIHASIRA-WEST ST.
WELL, ARE YOU GETTING ON OR AREN'T YOU?
SPACE BURIAL

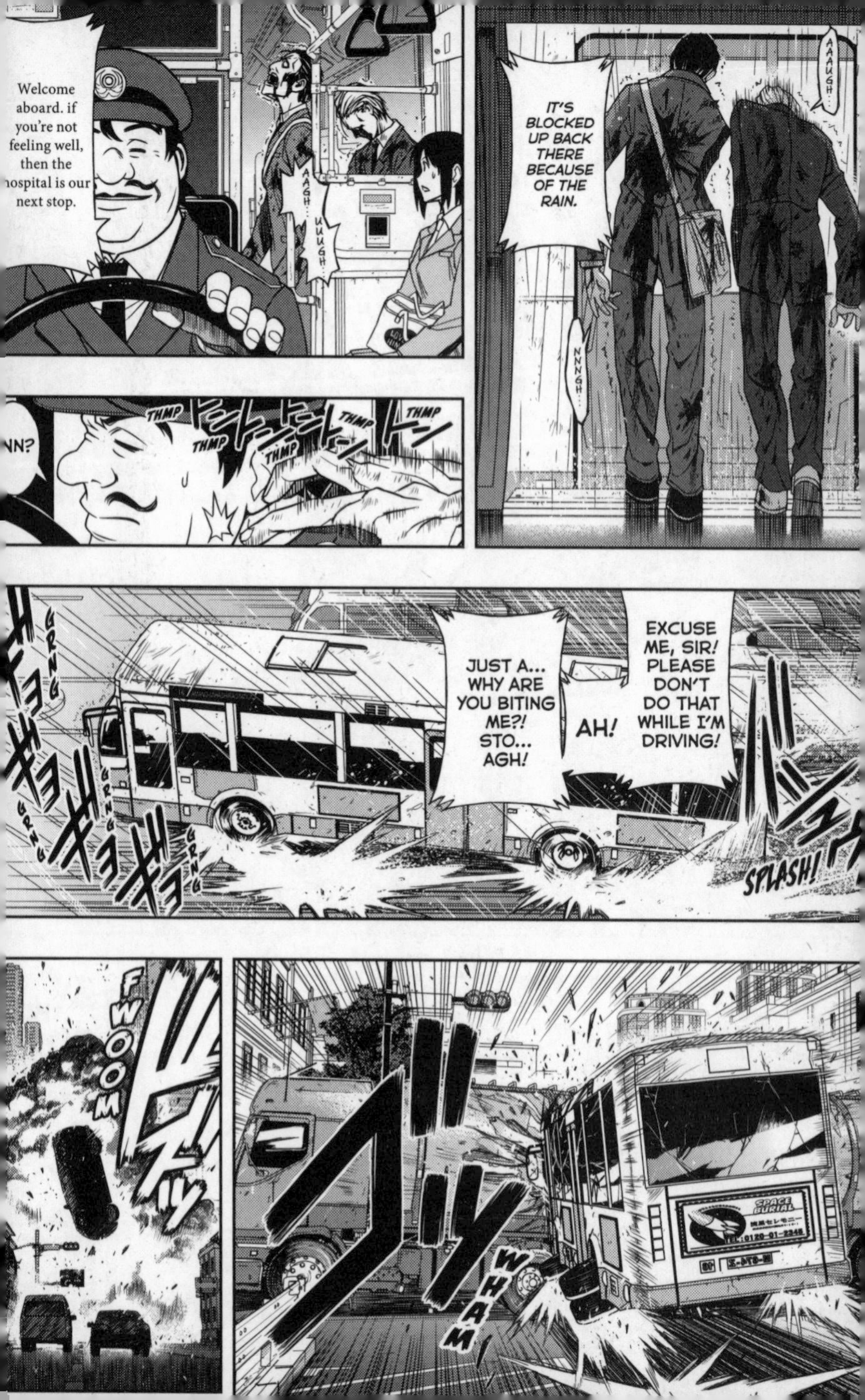
IT'S BLOCKED UP BACK THERE BECAUSE OF THE RAIN.
AAAUGH...
NNNGH...
Welcome aboard. if you're not feeling well, then the hospital is our next stop.
AAGH...
UUUGH...
NN?
THMP
THMP
THMP
THMP
THMP
EXCUSE ME, SIR! PLEASE DON'T DO THAT WHILE I'M DRIVING!
AH!
JUST A... WHY ARE YOU BITING ME?! STO... AGH!
SPLASH!
GRNG
GRNG
GRNG
GRNG
SPACE BURIAL
WHAM
FWOOOM

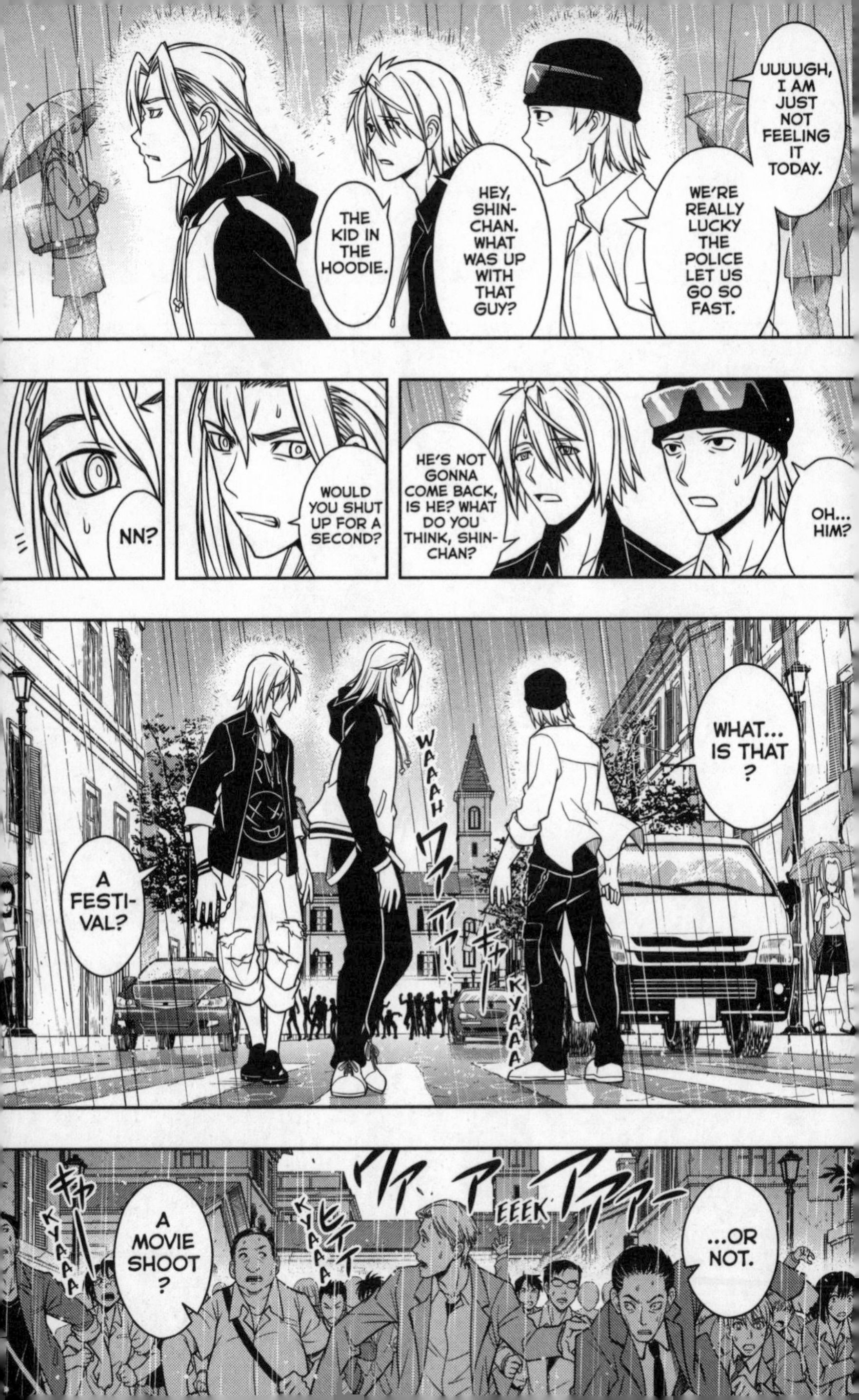
UUUUGH, I AM JUST NOT FEELING IT TODAY.
WE'RE REALLY LUCKY THE POLICE LET US GO SO FAST.
HEY, SHIN-CHAN. WHAT WAS UP WITH THAT GUY?
THE KID IN THE HOODIE.
OH... HIM?
HE'S NOT GONNA COME BACK, IS HE? WHAT DO YOU THINK, SHIN-CHAN?
WOULD YOU SHUT UP FOR A SECOND?
NN?
WHAT... IS THAT ?
KYAAAA
WAAAAH
A FESTI-VAL?
...OR NOT.
EEEK
KYAAAA
A MOVIE SHOOT ?
KYAAAA

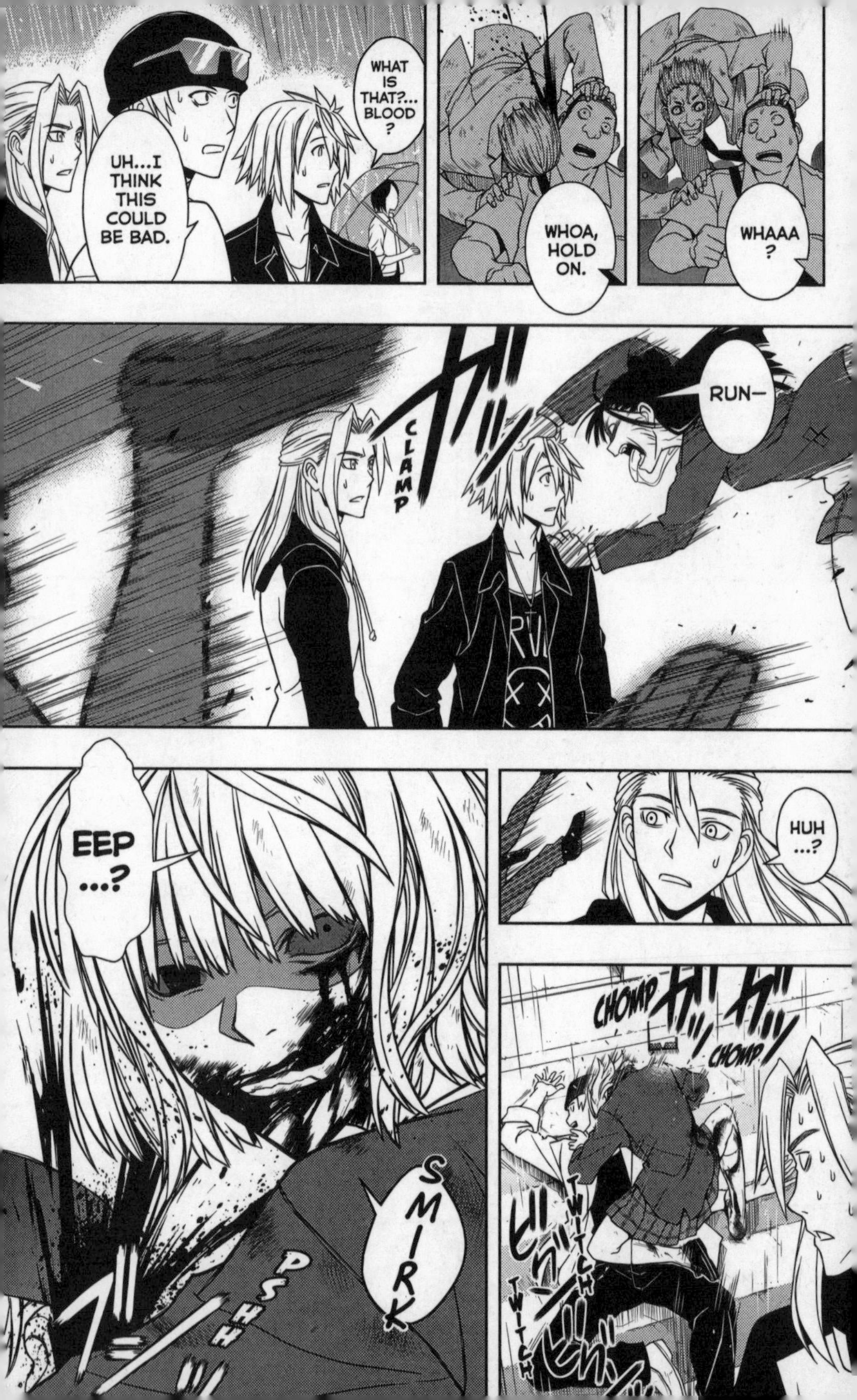
WHAAA ?
WHOA, HOLD ON.
WHAT IS THAT?... BLOOD ?
UH...I THINK THIS COULD BE BAD.
RUN—
CLAMP
HUH ...?
CHOMP
CHOMP
TWITCH
TWITCH
EEP ...?
SMIRK
PSHH

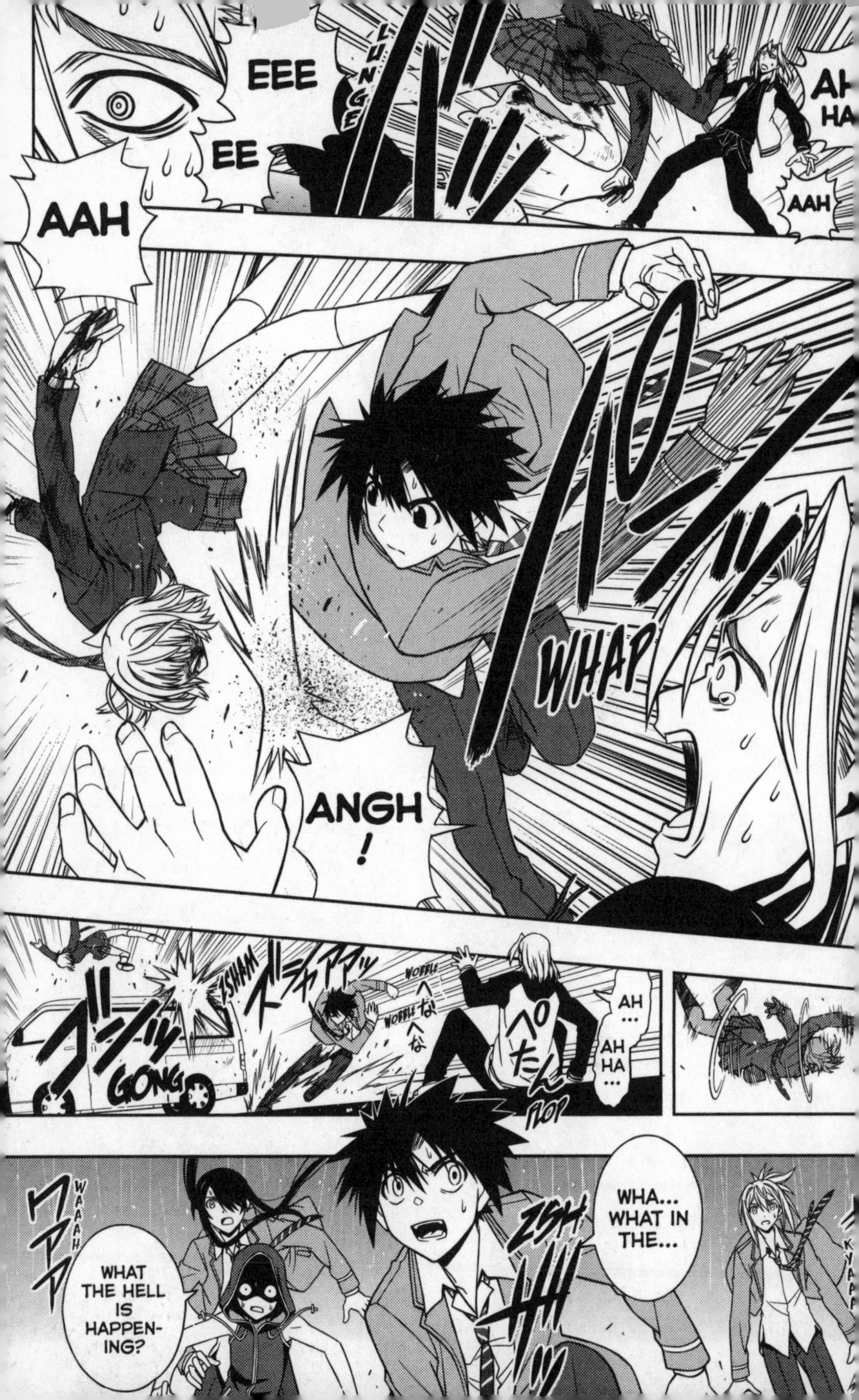
AH HA
AAH
LUNGE
EEE
EE
AAH
WHAP
ANGH !
AH ... AH HA ...
FLOP
WOBBLE
WOBBLE
ZSHAM
GONG
KYAA
WHA... WHAT IN THE...
ZSH
WHAT THE HELL IS HAPPEN-ING?
WAAAAH

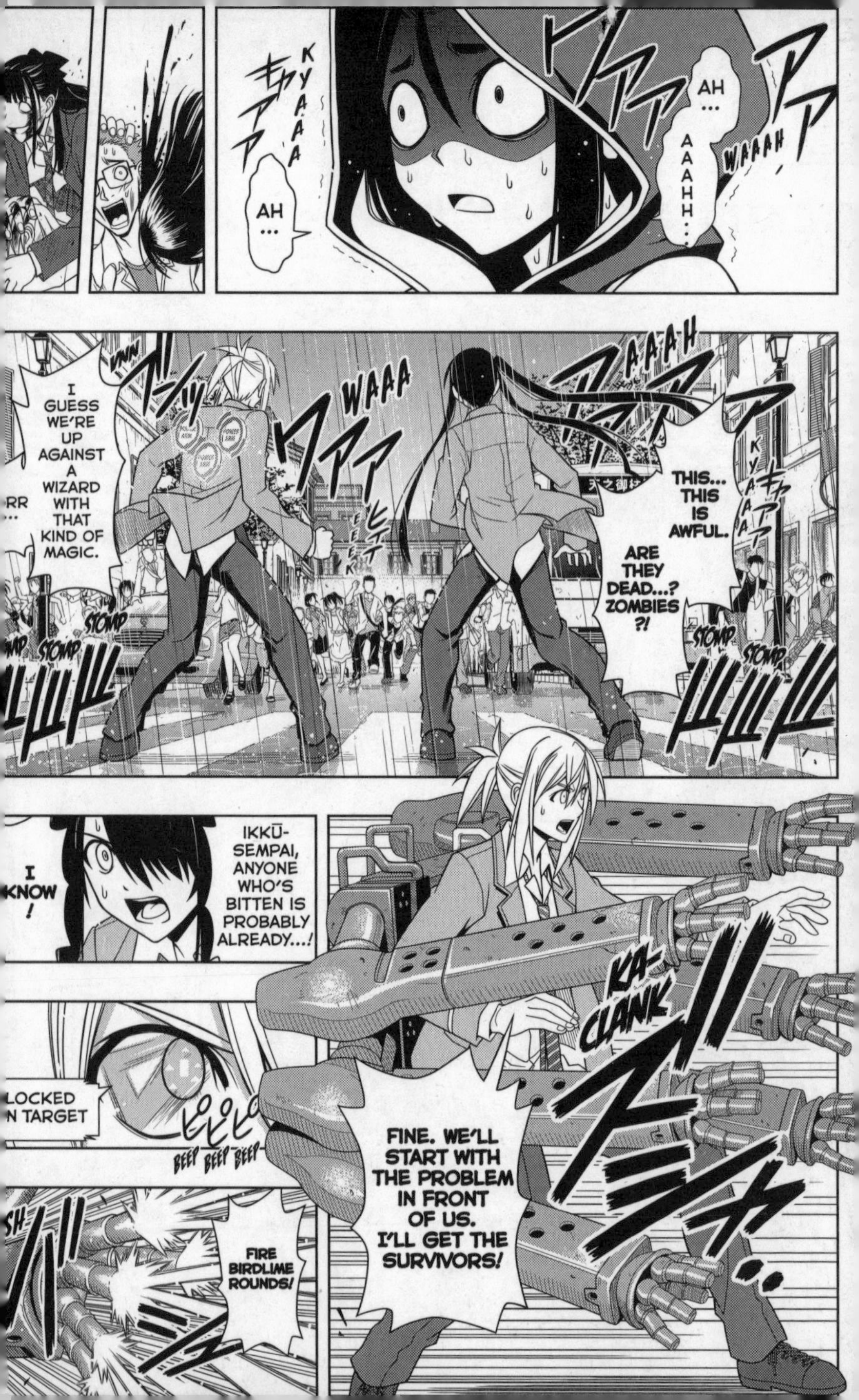
AH... AAAAHH...
WAAAH
KYAAAA
AH...
AAAAH
KYAAAA
THIS... THIS IS AWFUL.
ARE THEY DEAD...? ZOMBIES?!
STOMP
STOMP
WAAA
EEEEK
VNN
I GUESS WE'RE UP AGAINST A WIZARD WITH THAT KIND OF MAGIC.
STOMP
STOMP
KA-CLANK
FINE. WE'LL START WITH THE PROBLEM IN FRONT OF US. I'LL GET THE SURVIVORS!
IKKŪ-SEMPAI, ANYONE WHO'S BITTEN IS PROBABLY ALREADY...!
I KNOW!
LOCKED ON TARGET
BEEP BEEP BEEP
FIRE BIRDLIME ROUNDS!

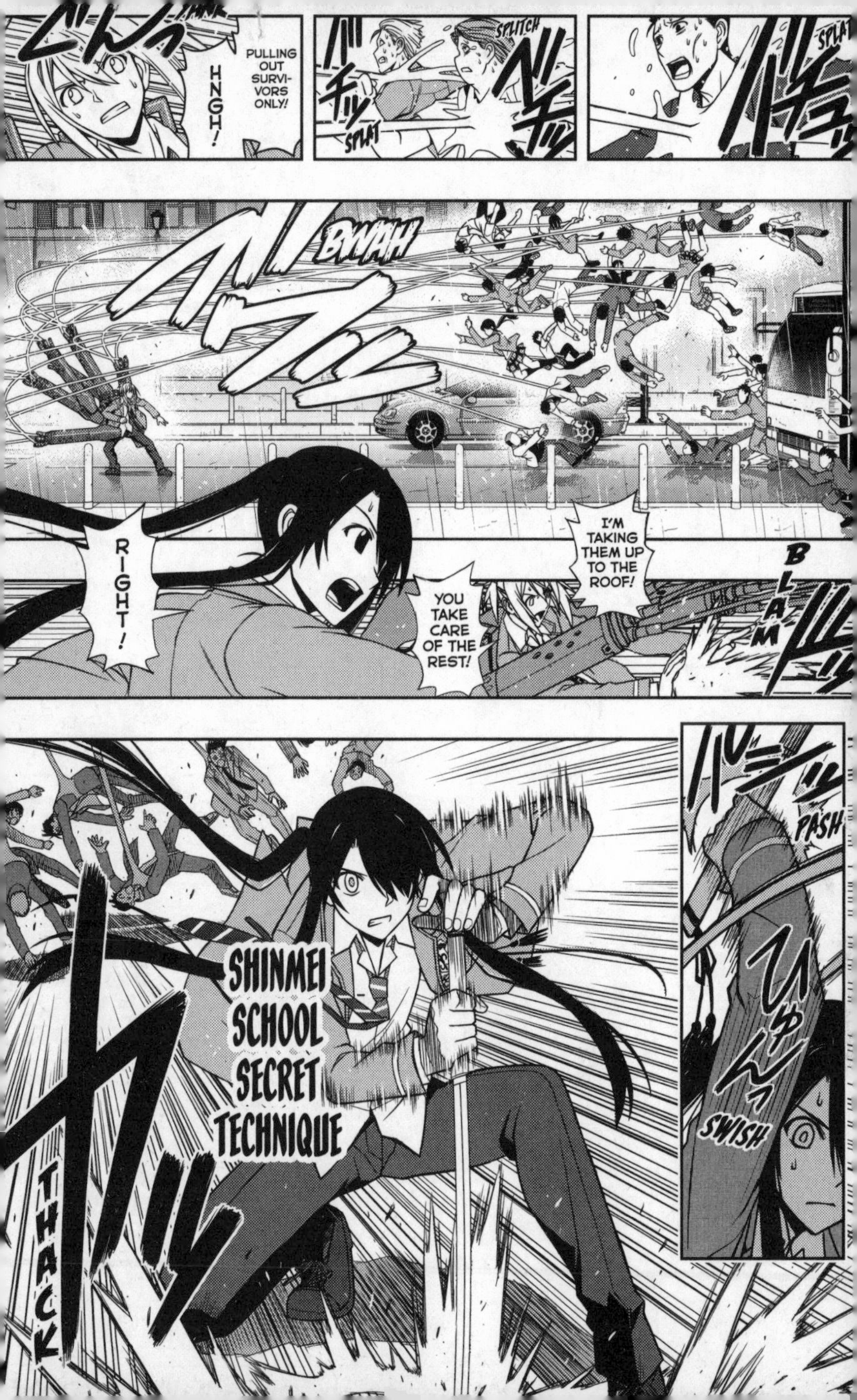
SPLAT
SPLITCH
SPLAT
PULLING OUT SURVIVORS ONLY!
HNGH!
BWAH
BLAM
I'M TAKING THEM UP TO THE ROOF!
YOU TAKE CARE OF THE REST!
RIGHT!
PASH
SWISH
SHINMEI SCHOOL SECRET TECHNIQUE
THACK

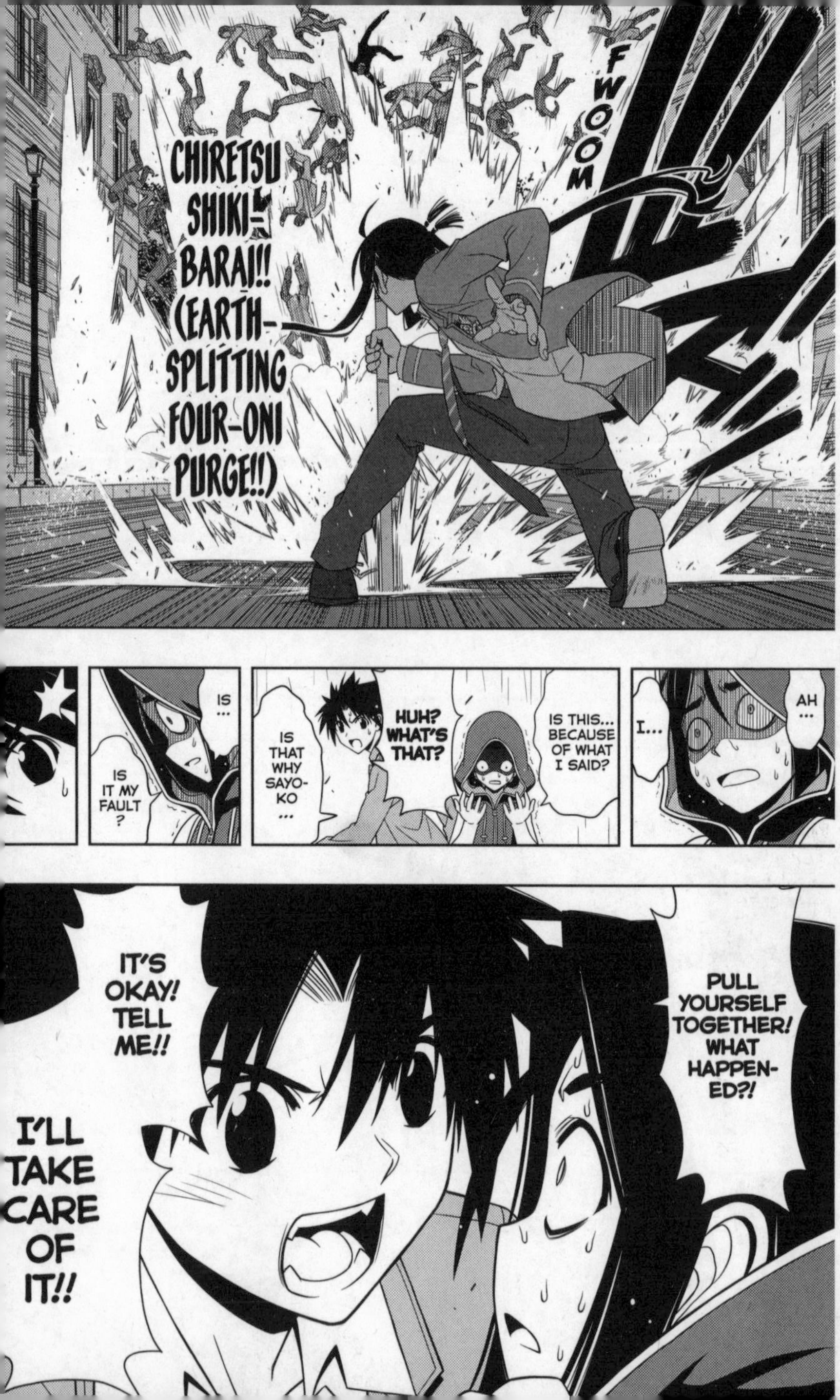
FWOOOM
CHIRETSU SHIKI-BARAI!! (EARTH-SPLITTING FOUR-ONI PURGE!!)
AH ...
I...
IS THIS... BECAUSE OF WHAT I SAID?
HUH? WHAT'S THAT?
IS THAT WHY SAYO-KO ...
IS ...
IS IT MY FAULT ?
PULL YOURSELF TOGETHER! WHAT HAPPEN-ED?!
IT'S OKAY! TELL ME!!
I'LL TAKE CARE OF IT!!

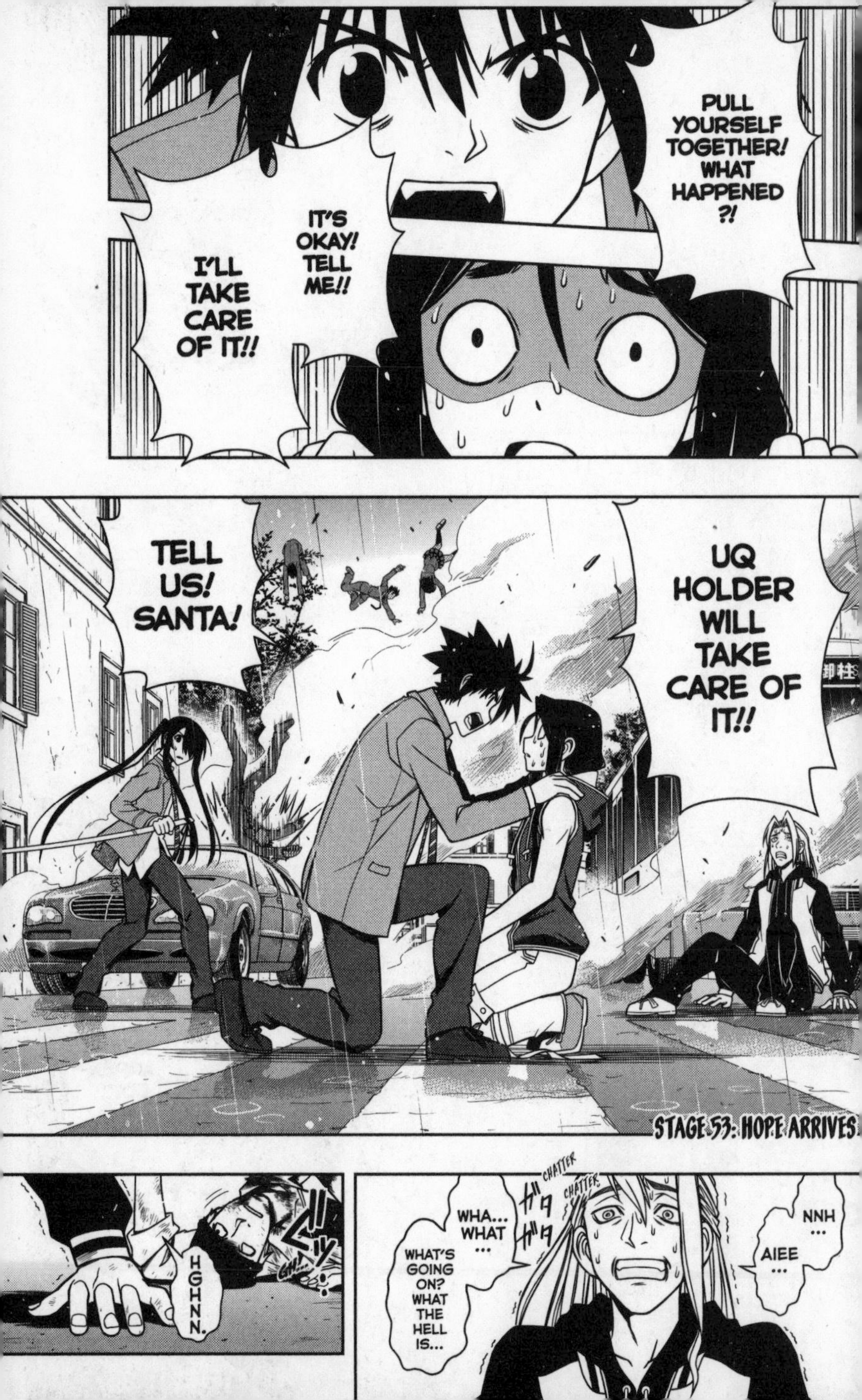
PULL YOURSELF TOGETHER! WHAT HAPPENED?!
IT'S OKAY! TELL ME!!
I'LL TAKE CARE OF IT!!
UQ HOLDER WILL TAKE CARE OF IT!!
TELL US! SANTA!
STAGE 53: HOPE ARRIVES
NNH ... AIEE ...
CHATTER
CHATTER
WHA... WHAT ...
WHAT'S GOING ON? WHAT THE HELL IS...
HGHNN.
GH!...

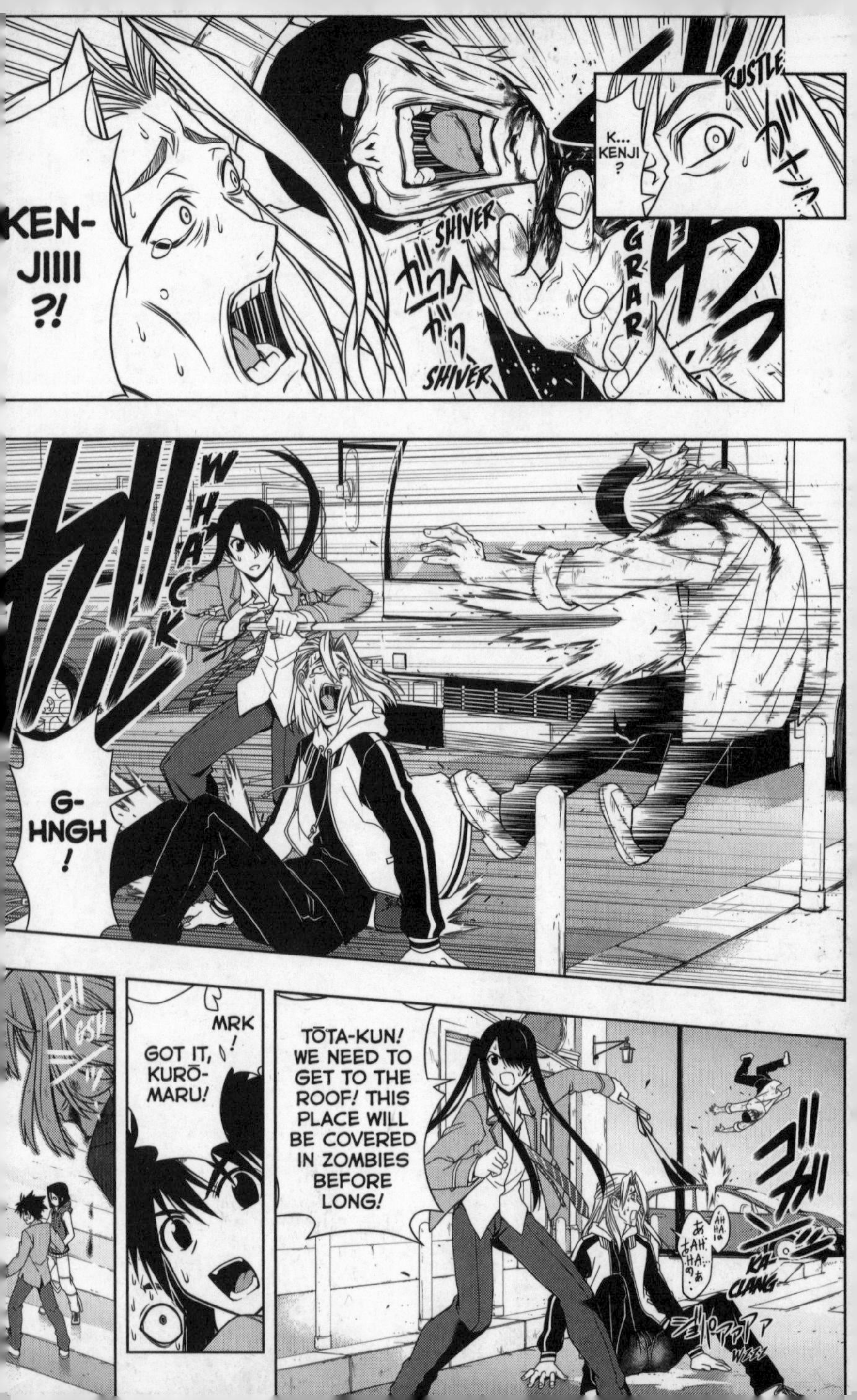
RUSTLE
K... KENJI?
SHIVER
GRAR
SHIVER
KEN-JIIIII?!
WHACK
G-HNGH!
KA-CLANG
TŌTA-KUN! WE NEED TO GET TO THE ROOF! THIS PLACE WILL BE COVERED IN ZOMBIES BEFORE LONG!
MRK!
GOT IT, KURŌMARU!

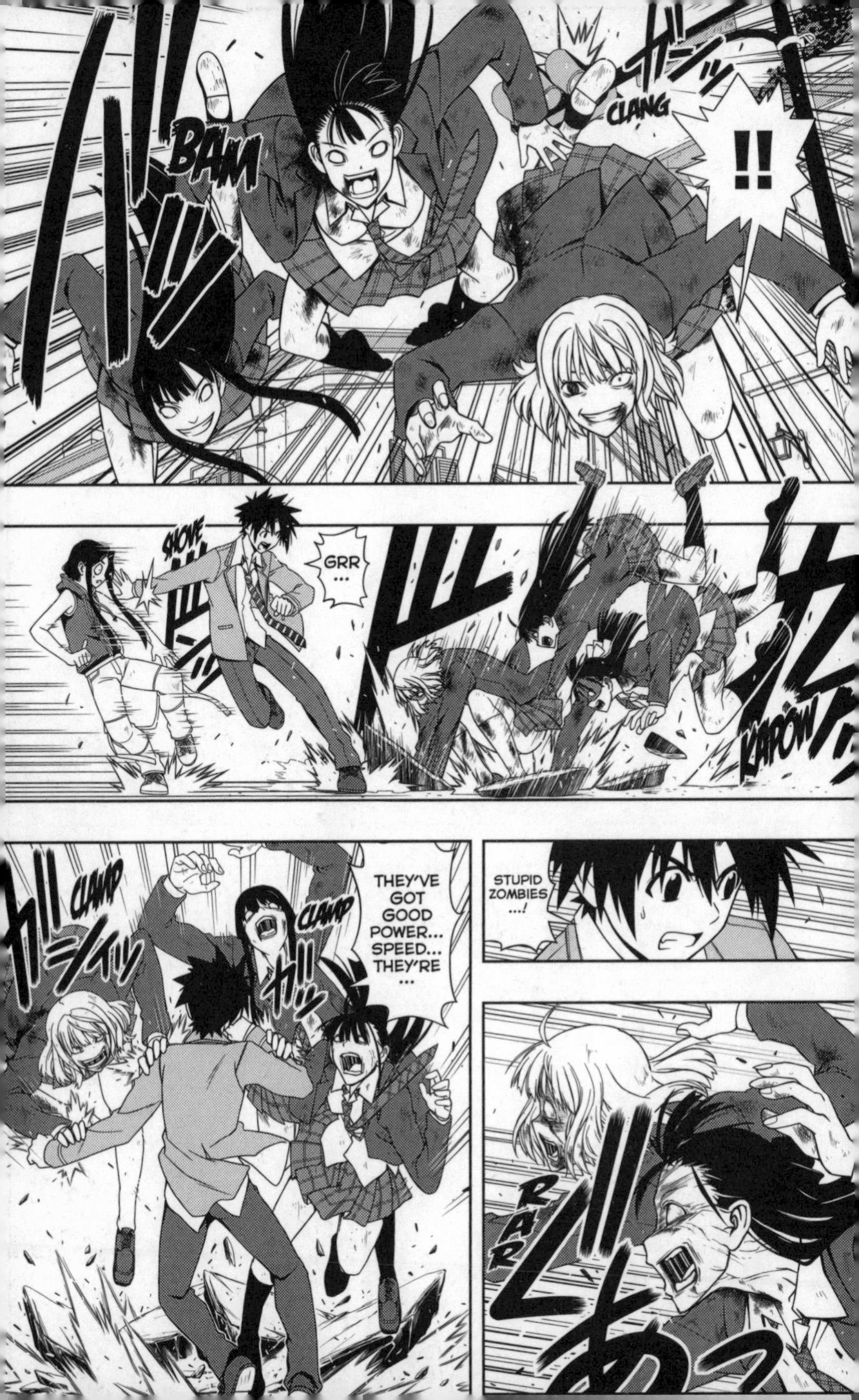
CLANG
!!
BAM
KAPOW
GRR ...
SHOVE
STUPID ZOMBIES ...!
RAR
THEY'VE GOT GOOD POWER... SPEED... THEY'RE ...
CLAMP
CLAMP

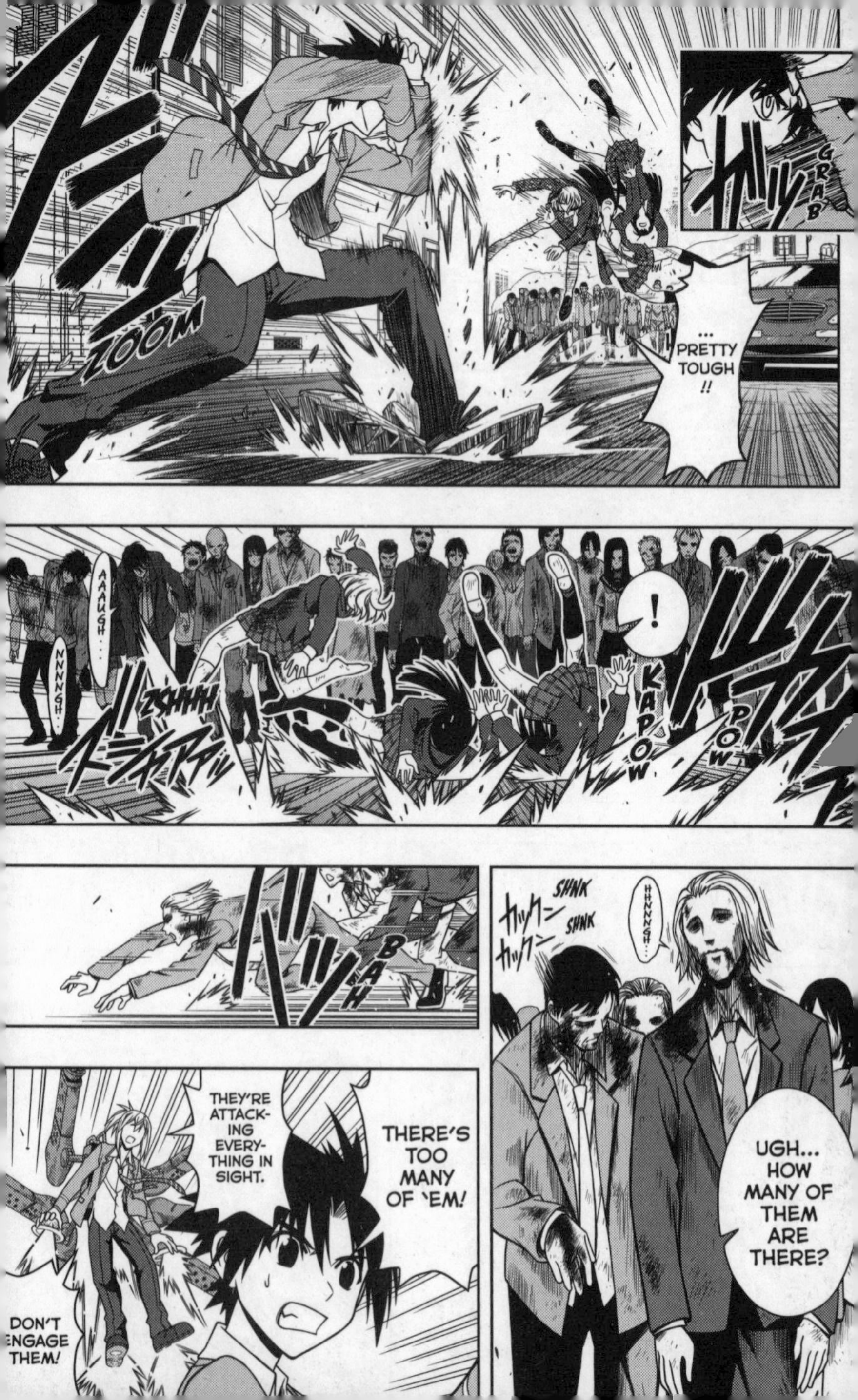
GRAB
ZOOM
... PRETTY TOUGH !!
POW
!
KAPOW
ZSHHH
AAAUGH...
NNNNGH...
SHNK
SHNK
HNNNNGH...
UGH... HOW MANY OF THEM ARE THERE?
BAAH
THERE'S TOO MANY OF 'EM!
THEY'RE ATTACKING EVERYTHING IN SIGHT.
DON'T ENGAGE THEM!

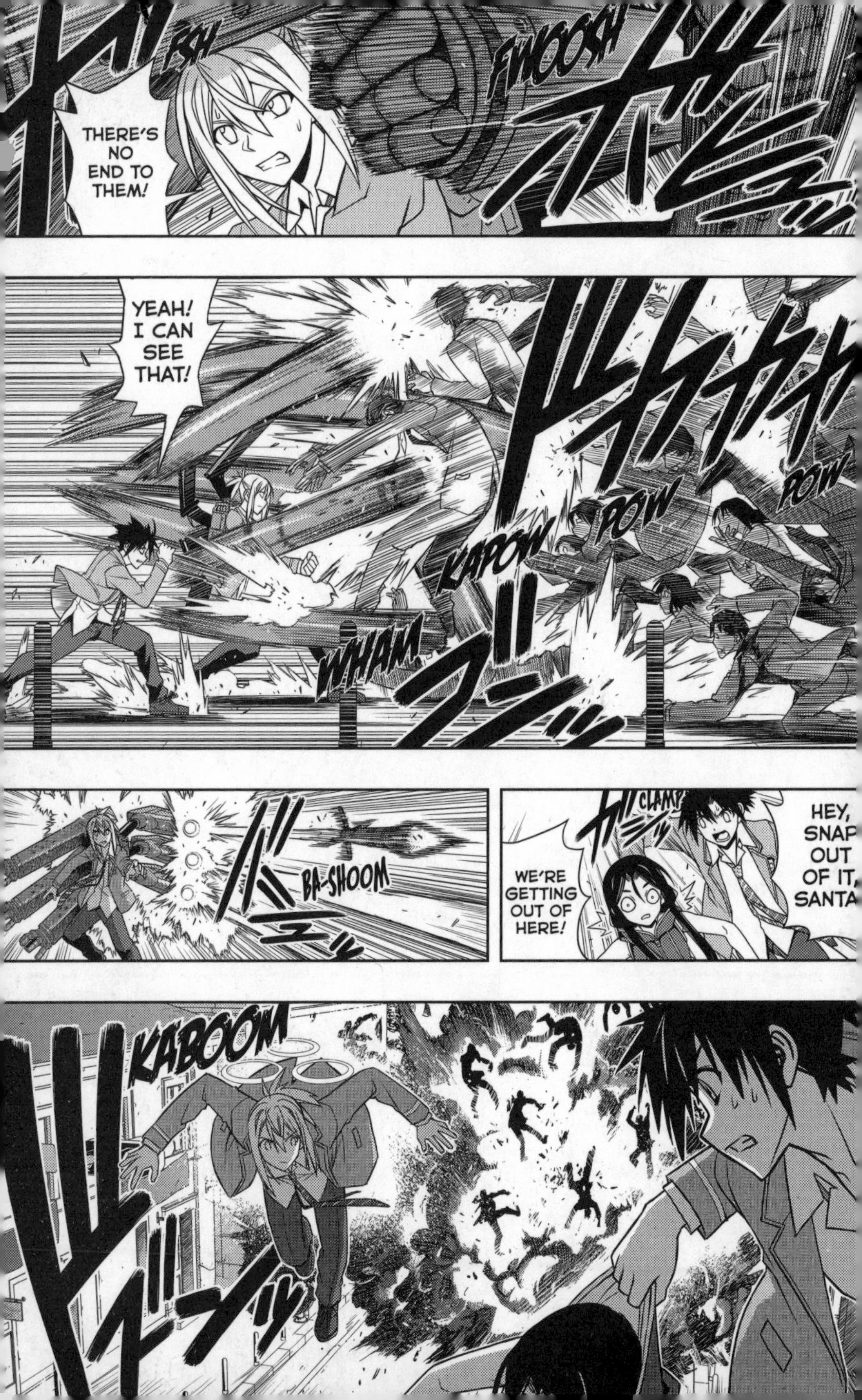
FWOOSH
FSH
THERE'S NO END TO THEM!
POW
POW
YEAH! I CAN SEE THAT!
KAPOW
WHAM
HEY, SNAP OUT OF IT, SANTA
CLAMP
WE'RE GETTING OUT OF HERE!
BA-SHOOM
KABOOM

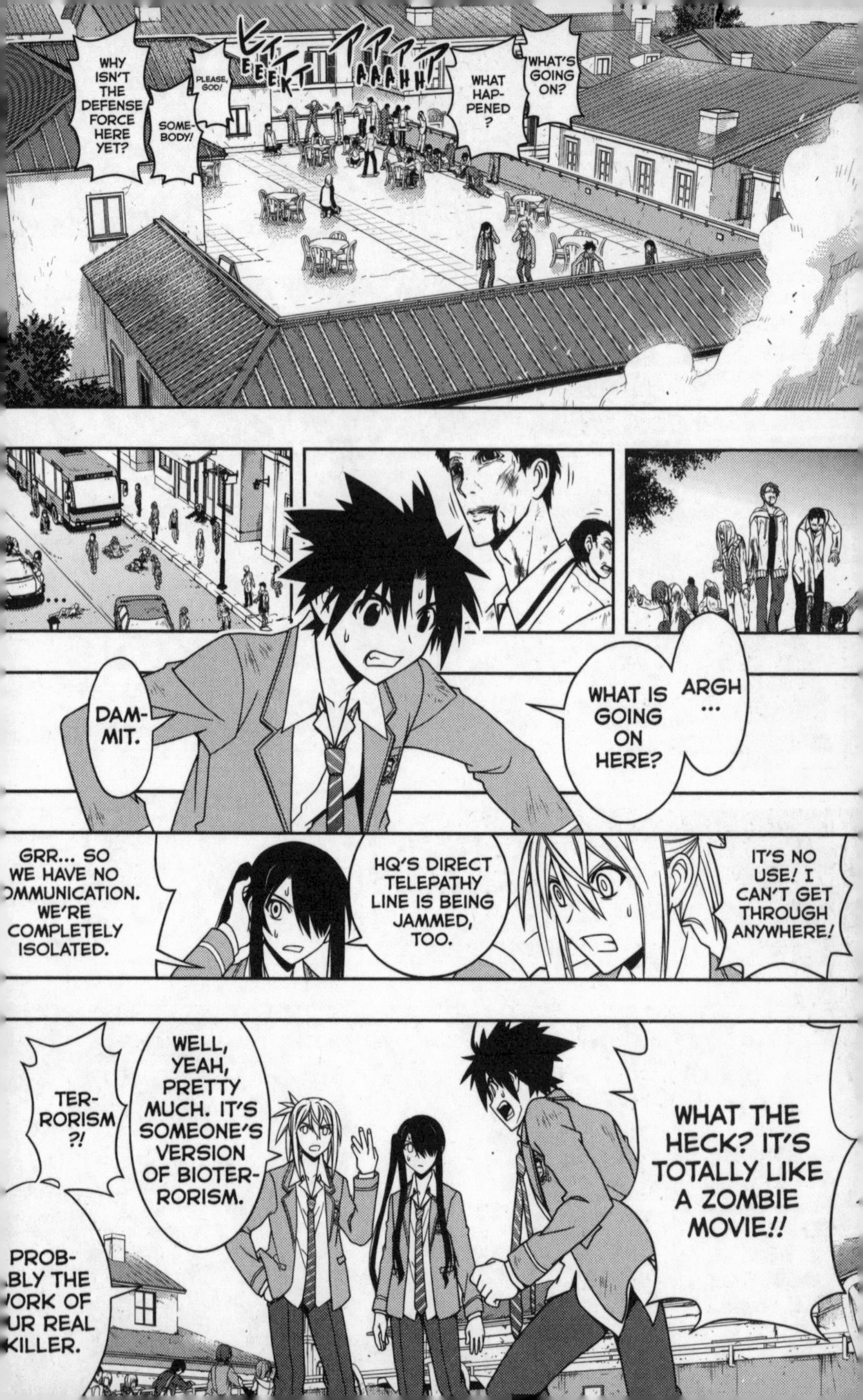
WHAT'S GOING ON?
WHAT HAPPENED?
EEEKK
AAAHH
PLEASE, GOD!
SOMEBODY!
WHY ISN'T THE DEFENSE FORCE HERE YET?
...
ARGH ...
WHAT IS GOING ON HERE?
DAMMIT.
IT'S NO USE! I CAN'T GET THROUGH ANYWHERE!
HQ'S DIRECT TELEPATHY LINE IS BEING JAMMED, TOO.
GRR... SO WE HAVE NO MMUNICATION. WE'RE COMPLETELY ISOLATED.
WHAT THE HECK? IT'S TOTALLY LIKE A ZOMBIE MOVIE!!
TERRORISM?!
WELL, YEAH, PRETTY MUCH. IT'S SOMEONE'S VERSION OF BIOTERRORISM.
PROB- BLY THE ORK OF UR REAL KILLER.

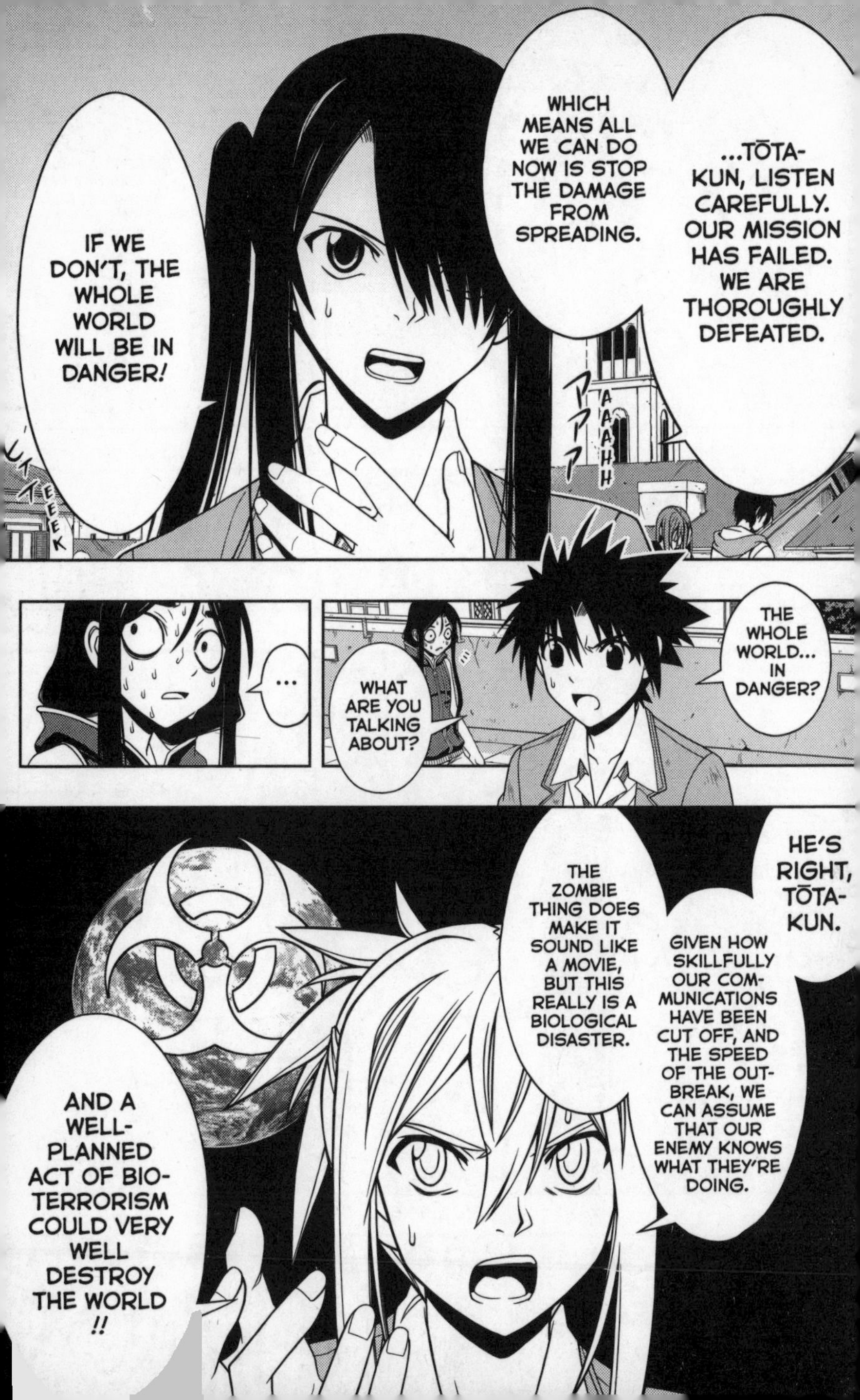
...TŌTA-KUN, LISTEN CAREFULLY. OUR MISSION HAS FAILED. WE ARE THOROUGHLY DEFEATED.
WHICH MEANS ALL WE CAN DO NOW IS STOP THE DAMAGE FROM SPREADING.
AAAHH
IF WE DON'T, THE WHOLE WORLD WILL BE IN DANGER!
EEEK
THE WHOLE WORLD... IN DANGER?
WHAT ARE YOU TALKING ABOUT?
...
HE'S RIGHT, TŌTA-KUN.
THE ZOMBIE THING DOES MAKE IT SOUND LIKE A MOVIE, BUT THIS REALLY IS A BIOLOGICAL DISASTER.
GIVEN HOW SKILLFULLY OUR COMMUNICATIONS HAVE BEEN CUT OFF, AND THE SPEED OF THE OUTBREAK, WE CAN ASSUME THAT OUR ENEMY KNOWS WHAT THEY'RE DOING.
AND A WELL-PLANNED ACT OF BIO-TERRORISM COULD VERY WELL DESTROY THE WORLD!!

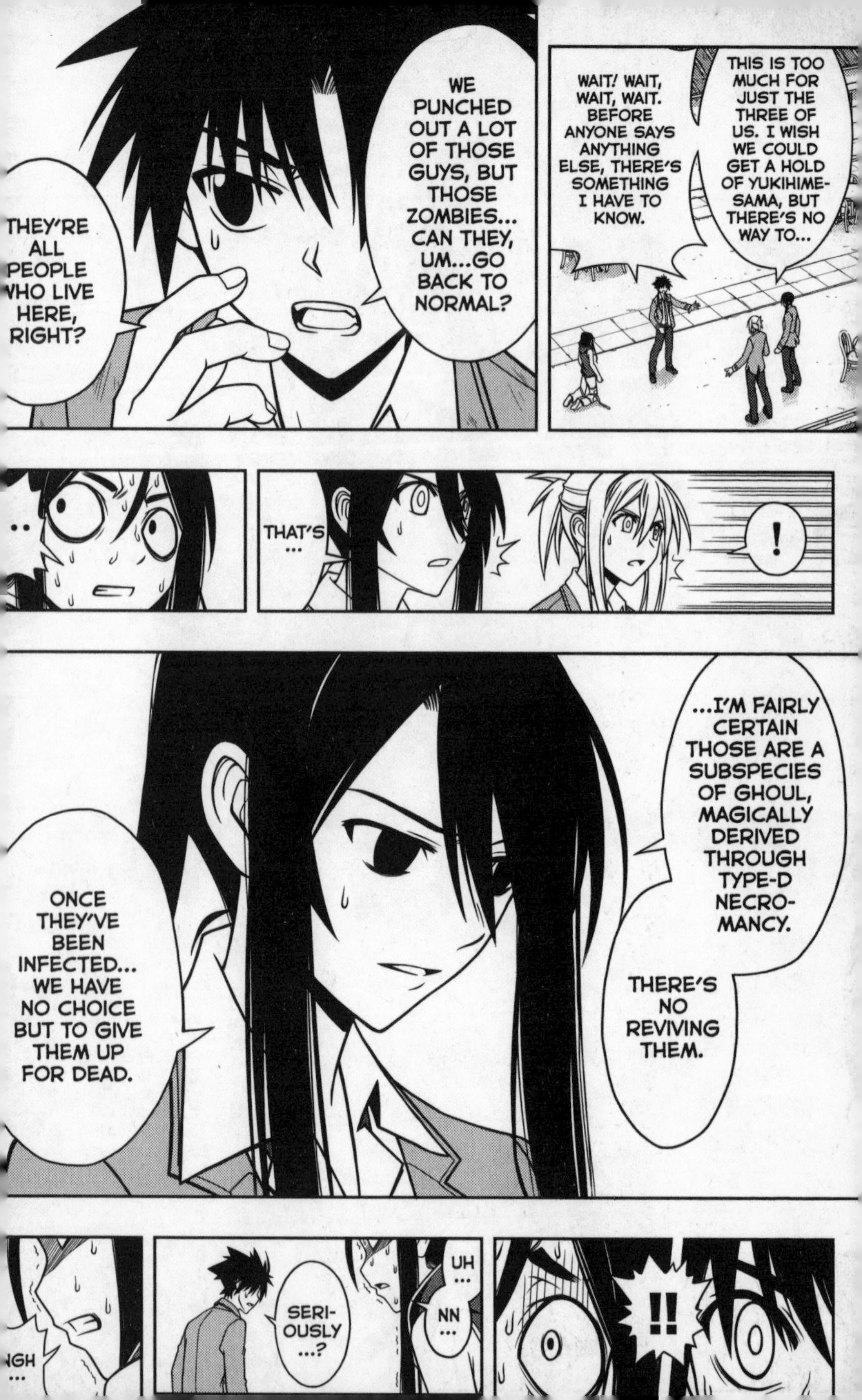
THIS IS TOO MUCH FOR JUST THE THREE OF US. I WISH WE COULD GET A HOLD OF YUKIHIME-SAMA, BUT THERE'S NO WAY TO...
WAIT! WAIT, WAIT, WAIT. BEFORE ANYONE SAYS ANYTHING ELSE, THERE'S SOMETHING I HAVE TO KNOW.
WE PUNCHED OUT A LOT OF THOSE GUYS, BUT THOSE ZOMBIES... CAN THEY, UM...GO BACK TO NORMAL?
THEY'RE ALL PEOPLE WHO LIVE HERE, RIGHT?
!
THAT'S ...
..
...I'M FAIRLY CERTAIN THOSE ARE A SUBSPECIES OF GHOUL, MAGICALLY DERIVED THROUGH TYPE-D NECRO-MANCY.
THERE'S NO REVIVING THEM.
ONCE THEY'VE BEEN INFECTED... WE HAVE NO CHOICE BUT TO GIVE THEM UP FOR DEAD.
!!
UH ...
NN ...
SERI-OUSLY ...?
NGH ...

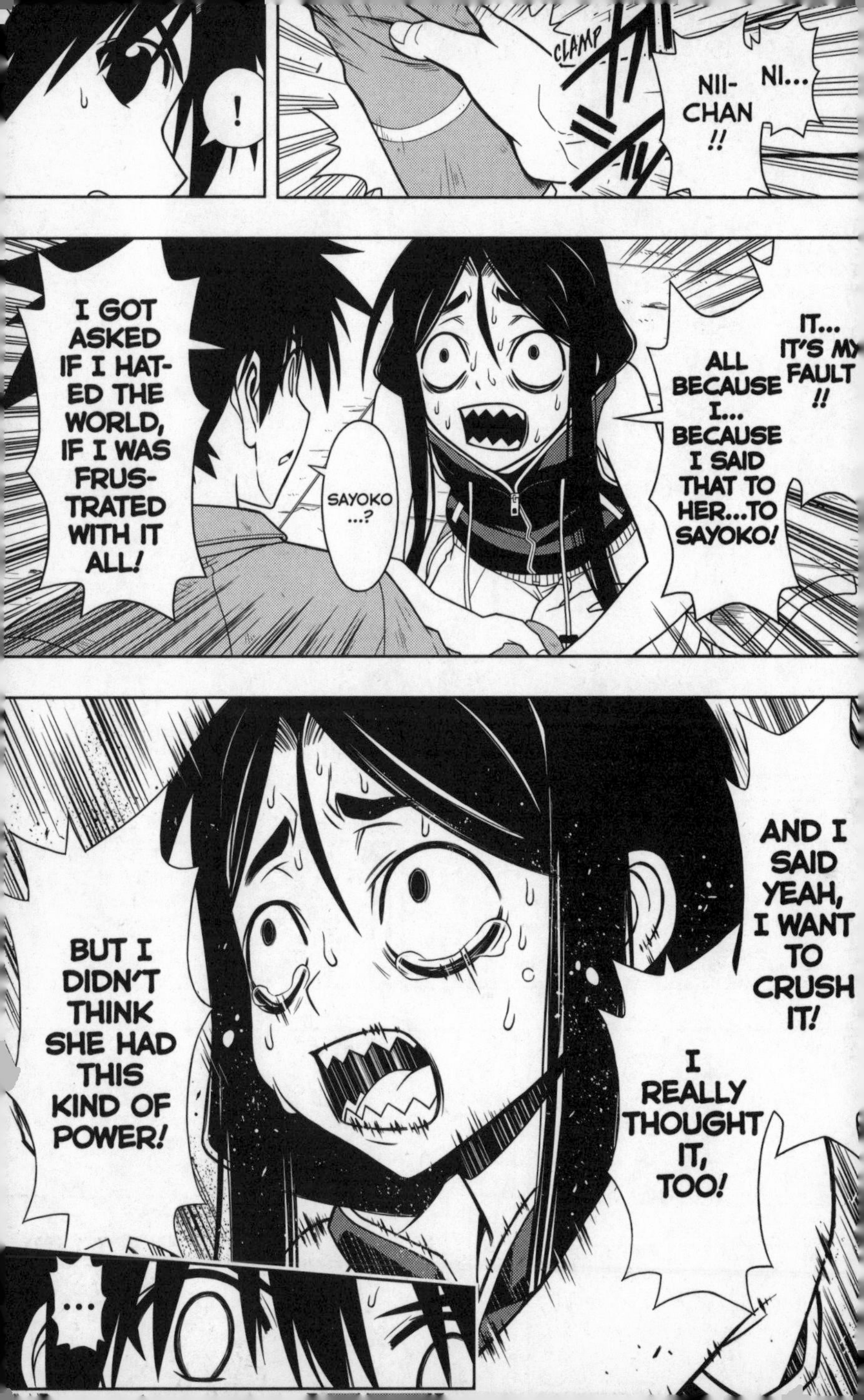CLAMP
NI...
NII-CHAN!!
!
IT... IT'S MY FAULT!!
ALL BECAUSE I... BECAUSE I SAID THAT TO HER...TO SAYOKO!
SAYOKO...?
I GOT ASKED IF I HATED THE WORLD, IF I WAS FRUSTRATED WITH IT ALL!
AND I SAID YEAH, I WANT TO CRUSH IT!
I REALLY THOUGHT IT, TOO!
BUT I DIDN'T THINK SHE HAD THIS KIND OF POWER!
...

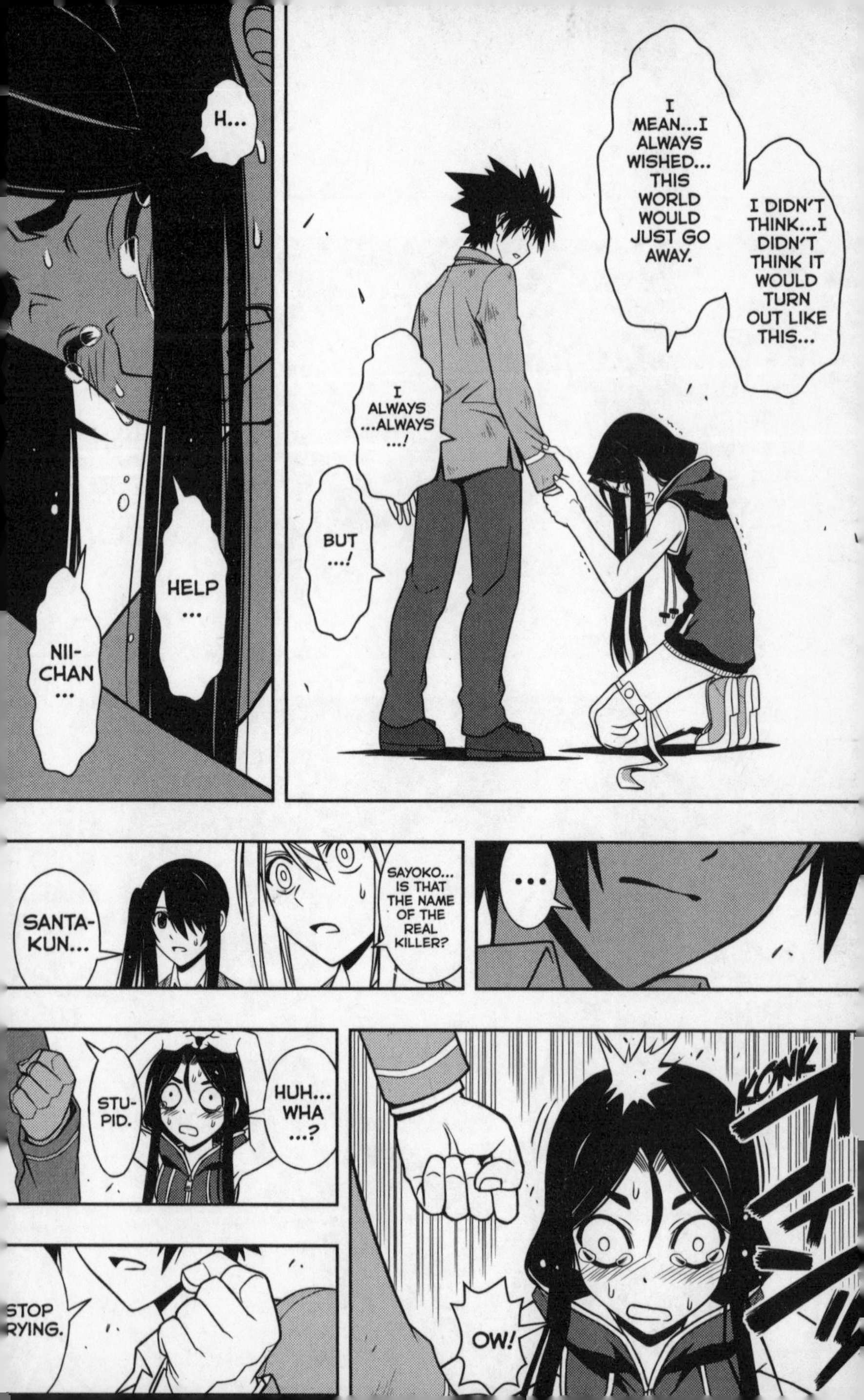
I DIDN'T THINK...I DIDN'T THINK IT WOULD TURN OUT LIKE THIS...
I MEAN...I ALWAYS WISHED... THIS WORLD WOULD JUST GO AWAY.
I ALWAYS ...ALWAYS ...!
BUT ...!
H...
HELP ...
NII-CHAN ...
...
SAYOKO... IS THAT THE NAME OF THE REAL KILLER?
SANTA-KUN...
KONK
OW!
HUH... WHA ...?
STU-PID.
STOP RYING.

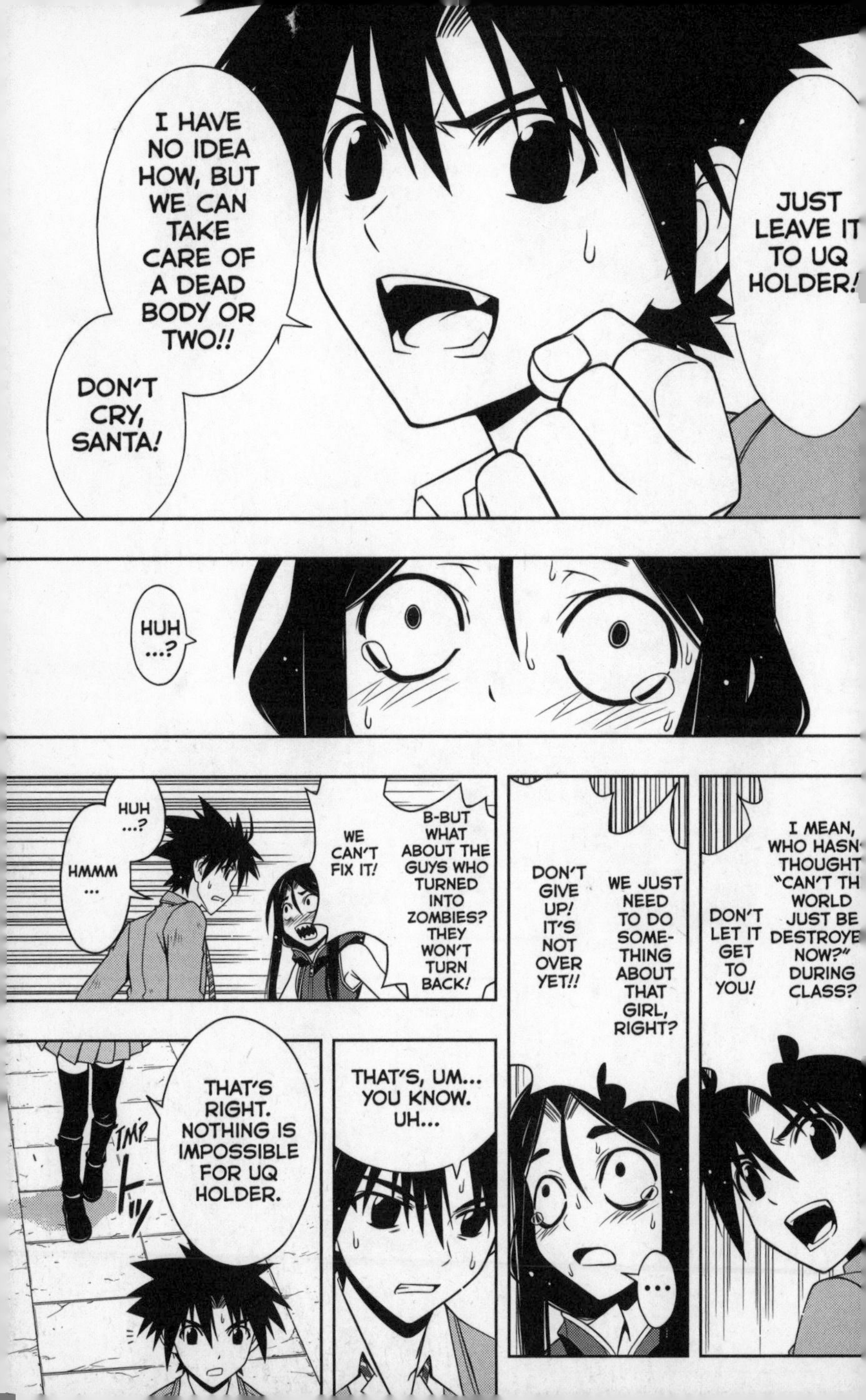
JUST LEAVE IT TO UQ HOLDER!
I HAVE NO IDEA HOW, BUT WE CAN TAKE CARE OF A DEAD BODY OR TWO!!
DON'T CRY, SANTA!
HUH ...?
I MEAN, WHO HASN THOUGHT "CAN'T TH WORLD JUST BE DESTROYE NOW?" DURING CLASS?
DON'T LET IT GET TO YOU!
WE JUST NEED TO DO SOME-THING ABOUT THAT GIRL, RIGHT?
DON'T GIVE UP! IT'S NOT OVER YET!!
...
B-BUT WHAT ABOUT THE GUYS WHO TURNED INTO ZOMBIES? THEY WON'T TURN BACK!
WE CAN'T FIX IT!
HUH ...?
HMMM ...
THAT'S, UM... YOU KNOW. UH...
THAT'S RIGHT. NOTHING IS IMPOSSIBLE FOR UQ HOLDER.
TMP

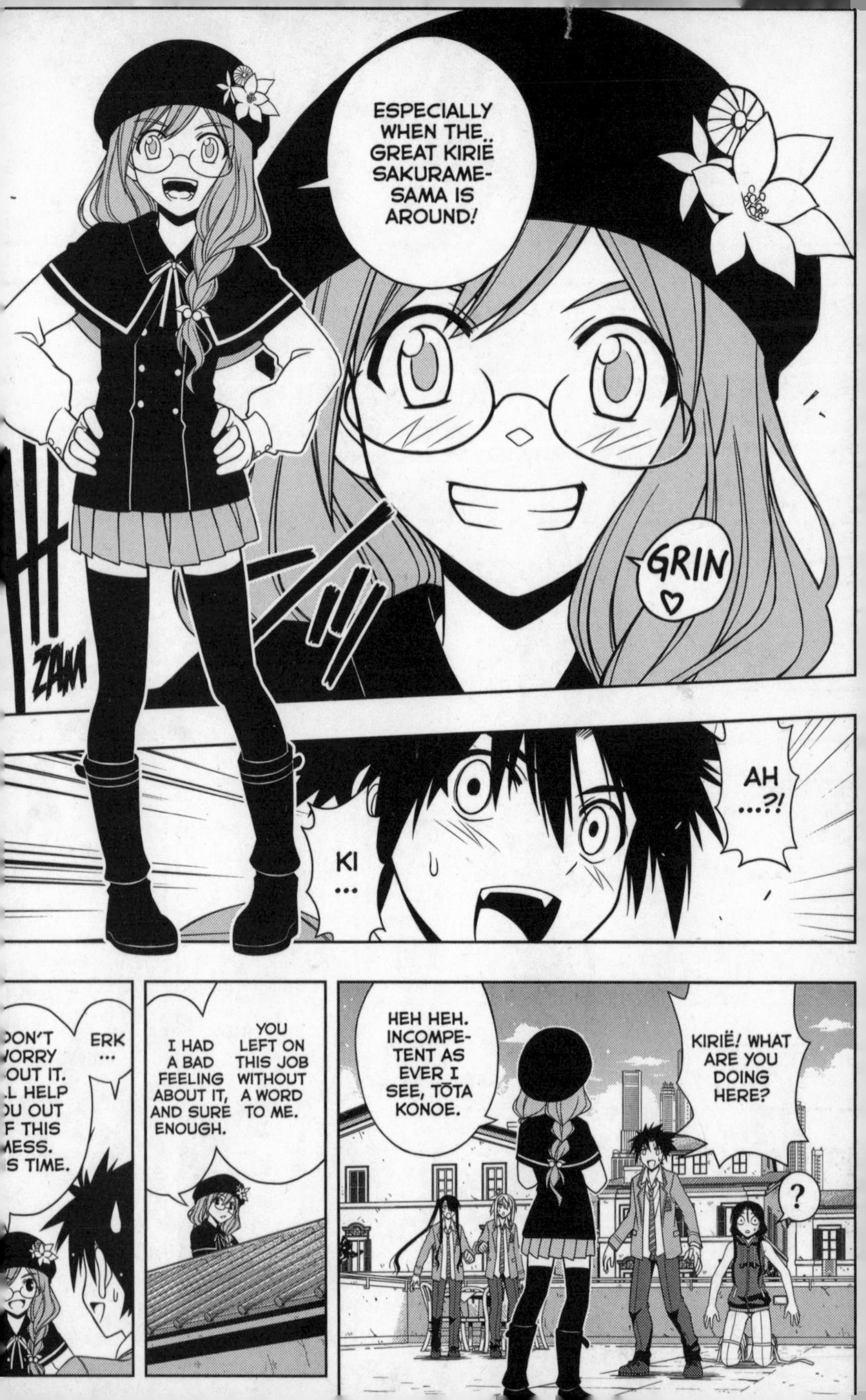
ESPECIALLY WHEN THE GREAT KIRIË SAKURAME-SAMA IS AROUND!
GRIN ♡
AH ...?!
KI ...
ZAM
KIRIË! WHAT ARE YOU DOING HERE?
?
HEH HEH. INCOMPETENT AS EVER I SEE, TŌTA KONOE.
YOU LEFT ON THIS JOB WITHOUT A WORD TO ME.
I HAD A BAD FEELING ABOUT IT, AND SURE ENOUGH.
ERK ...
DON'T WORRY OUT IT. L HELP OU OUT F THIS MESS. S TIME.

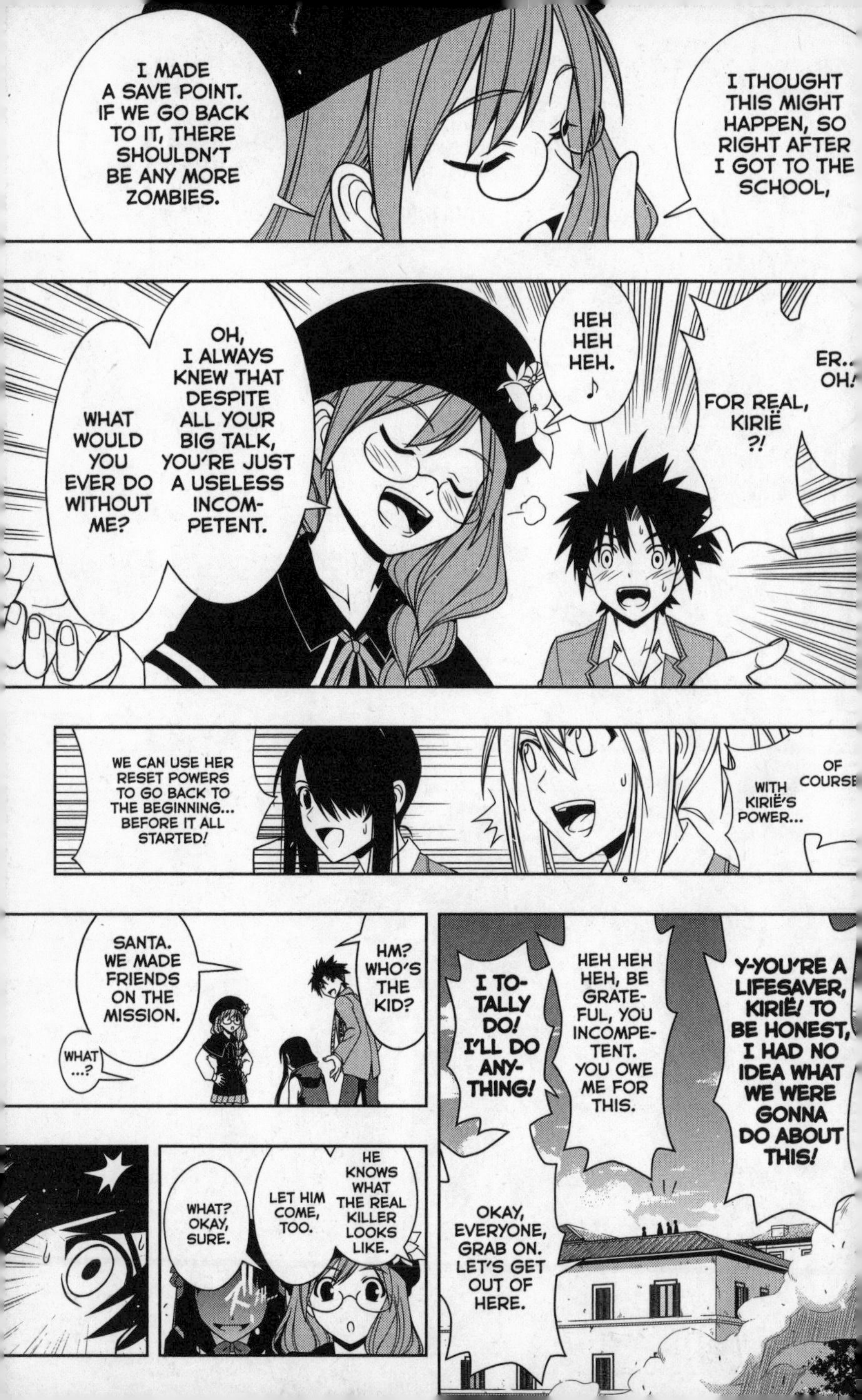
I THOUGHT THIS MIGHT HAPPEN, SO RIGHT AFTER I GOT TO THE SCHOOL,
I MADE A SAVE POINT. IF WE GO BACK TO IT, THERE SHOULDN'T BE ANY MORE ZOMBIES.
ER... OH!
FOR REAL, KIRIË?!
HEH HEH HEH. ♪
OH, I ALWAYS KNEW THAT DESPITE ALL YOUR BIG TALK, YOU'RE JUST A USELESS INCOMPETENT.
WHAT WOULD YOU EVER DO WITHOUT ME?
OF COURSE
WITH KIRIË'S POWER...
WE CAN USE HER RESET POWERS TO GO BACK TO THE BEGINNING... BEFORE IT ALL STARTED!
Y-YOU'RE A LIFESAVER, KIRIË! TO BE HONEST, I HAD NO IDEA WHAT WE WERE GONNA DO ABOUT THIS!
HEH HEH HEH, BE GRATEFUL, YOU INCOMPETENT. YOU OWE ME FOR THIS.
I TOTALLY DO! I'LL DO ANYTHING!
OKAY, EVERYONE, GRAB ON. LET'S GET OUT OF HERE.
HM? WHO'S THE KID?
SANTA. WE MADE FRIENDS ON THE MISSION.
WHAT ...?
HE KNOWS WHAT THE REAL KILLER LOOKS LIKE.
LET HIM COME, TOO.
WHAT? OKAY, SURE.

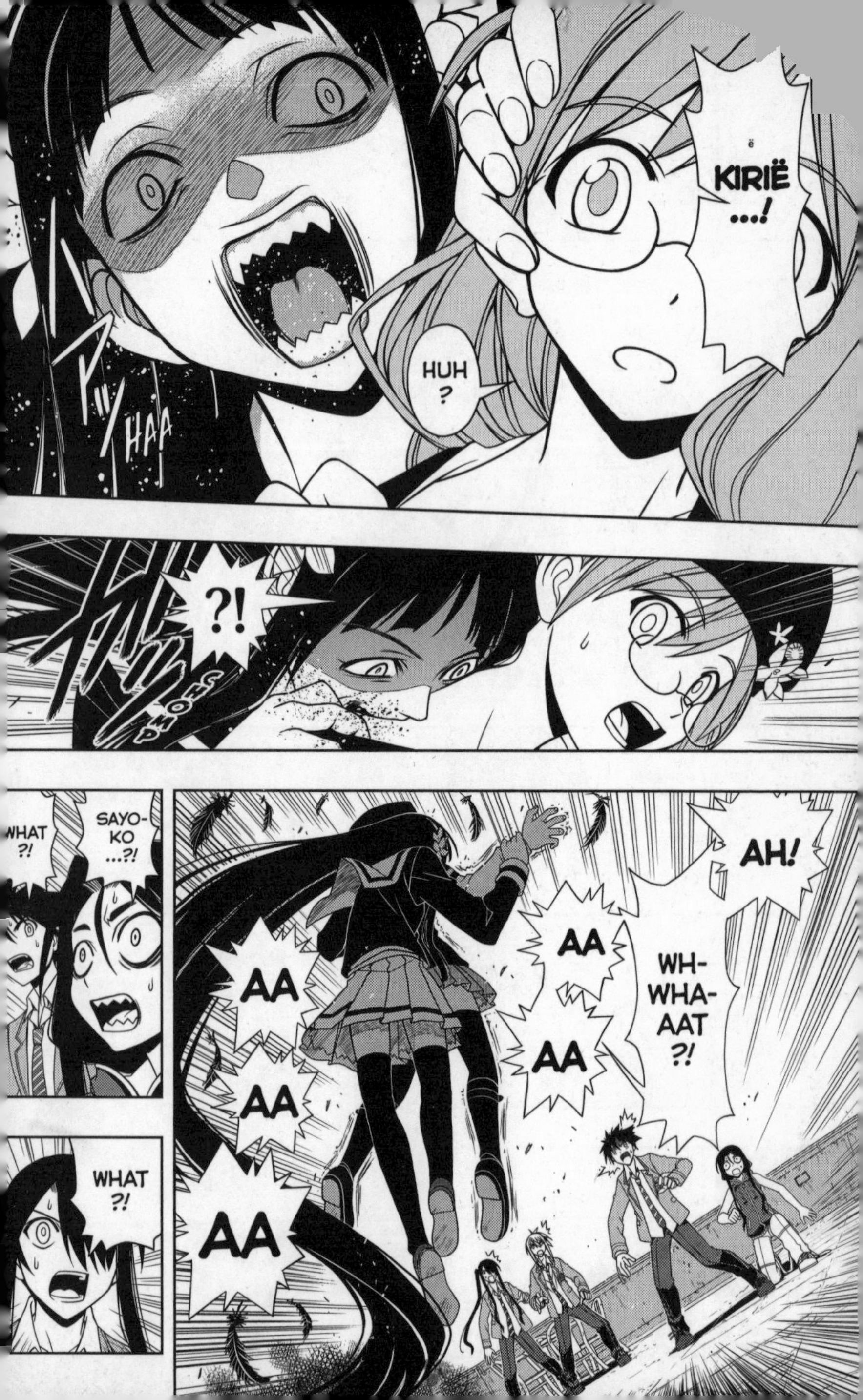
KIRIË ...!
HUH ?
HAA
?!
CHOMP
AH!
WH- WHA- AAT ?!
AA
AA
AA
AA
AA
SAYO- KO ...?!
WHAT ?!
WHAT ?!

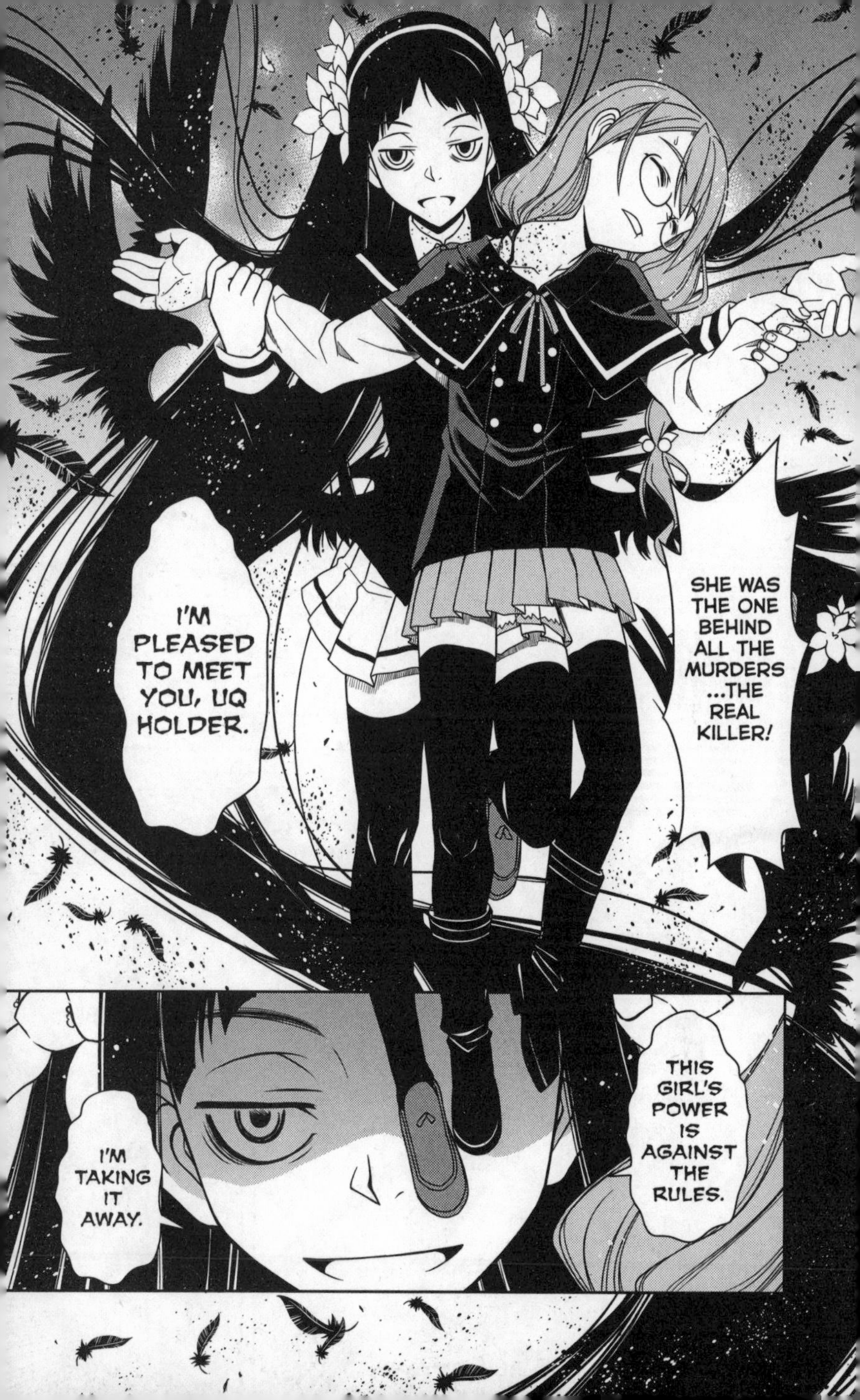
SHE WAS THE ONE BEHIND ALL THE MURDERS ...THE REAL KILLER!
I'M PLEASED TO MEET YOU, UQ HOLDER.
THIS GIRL'S POWER IS AGAINST THE RULES.
I'M TAKING IT AWAY.

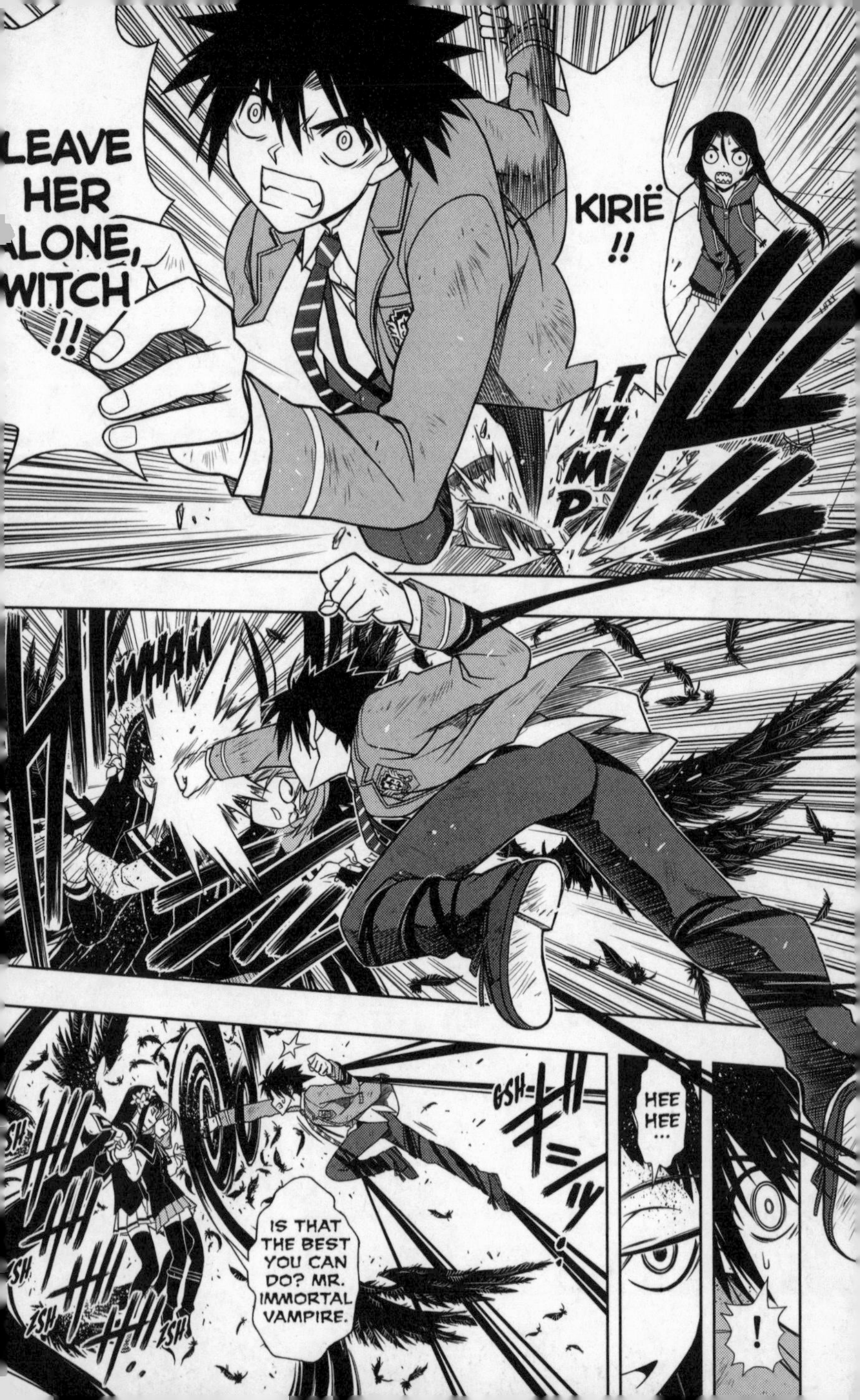
KIRIË !!
THMP
LEAVE HER ALONE, WITCH !!
WHAM
HEE HEE ...
!
GSH
IS THAT THE BEST YOU CAN DO? MR. IMMORTAL VAMPIRE.

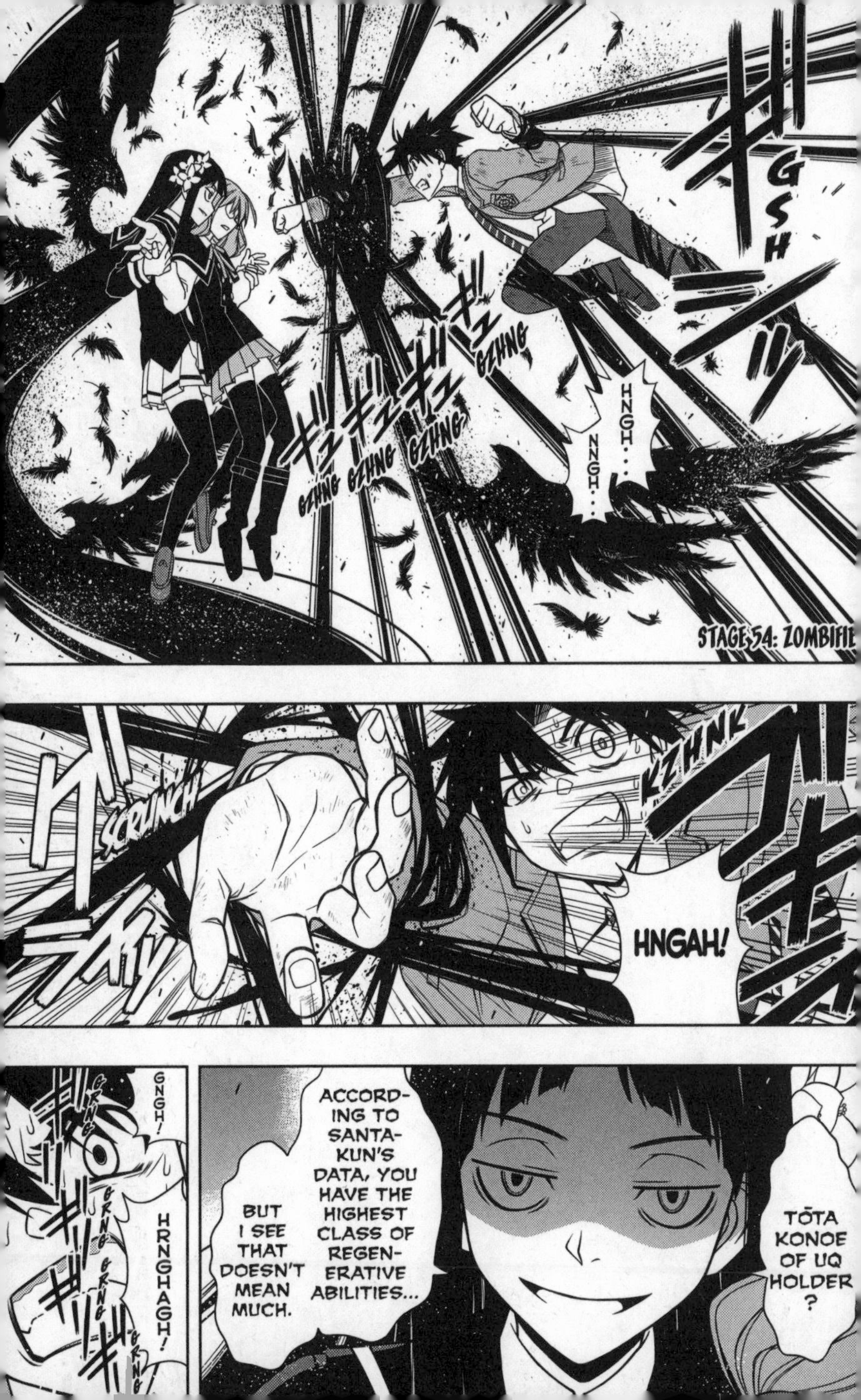
GSH
HNGH...
NNGH...
GZHNG
GZHNG GZHNG GZHNG
STAGE 54: ZOMBIFIE
KZHNK
HNGAH!
SCRUNCH
TŌTA KONOE OF UQ HOLDER?
ACCORDING TO SANTA-KUN'S DATA, YOU HAVE THE HIGHEST CLASS OF REGENERATIVE ABILITIES...
BUT I SEE THAT DOESN'T MEAN MUCH.
GNGH!
GRNG GRNG GRNG GRNG GRNG
HRNGHAGH!

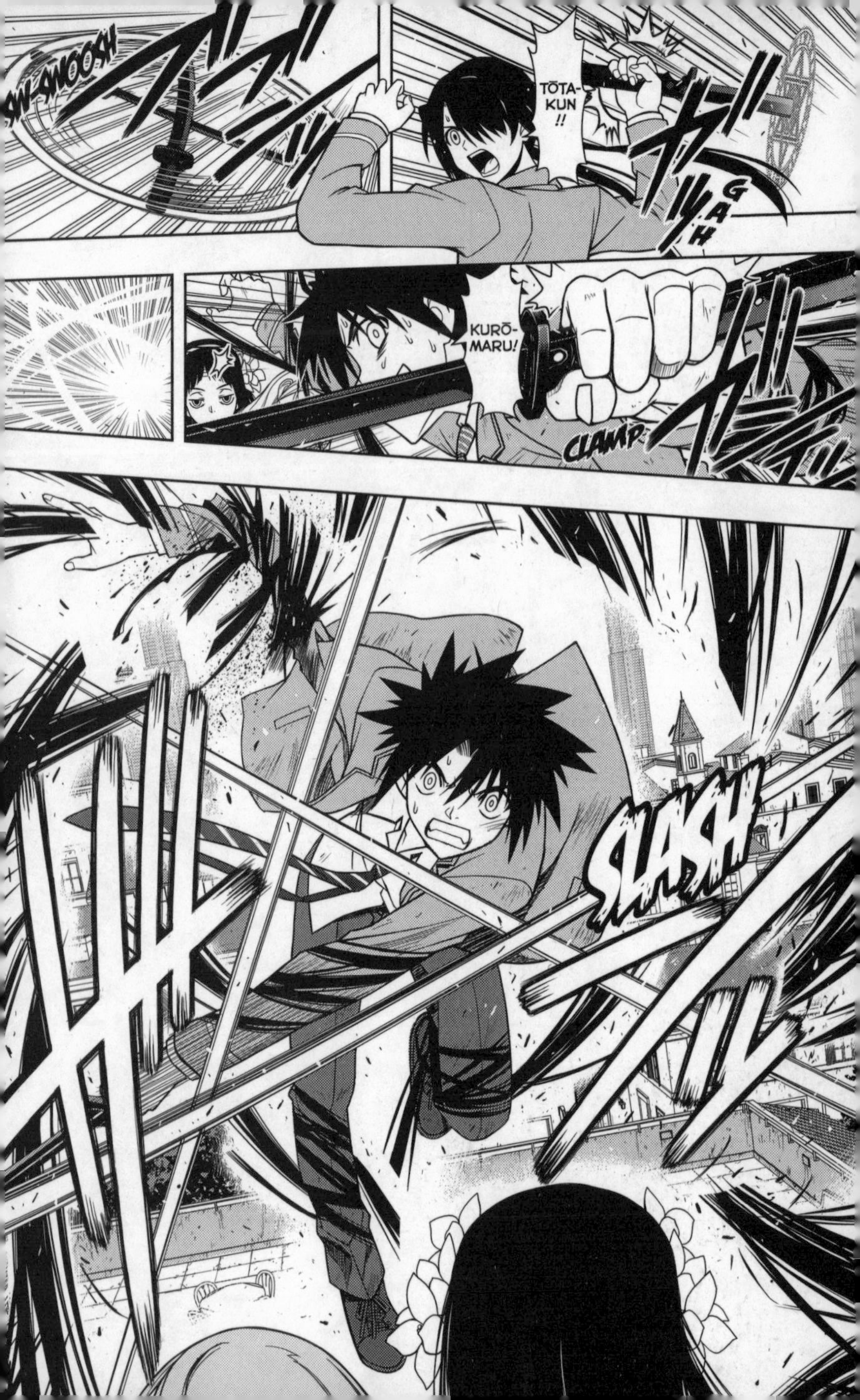
TŌTA-KUN!!
GAH
SW-SWOOSH
KURŌ-MARU!
CLAMP
SLASH

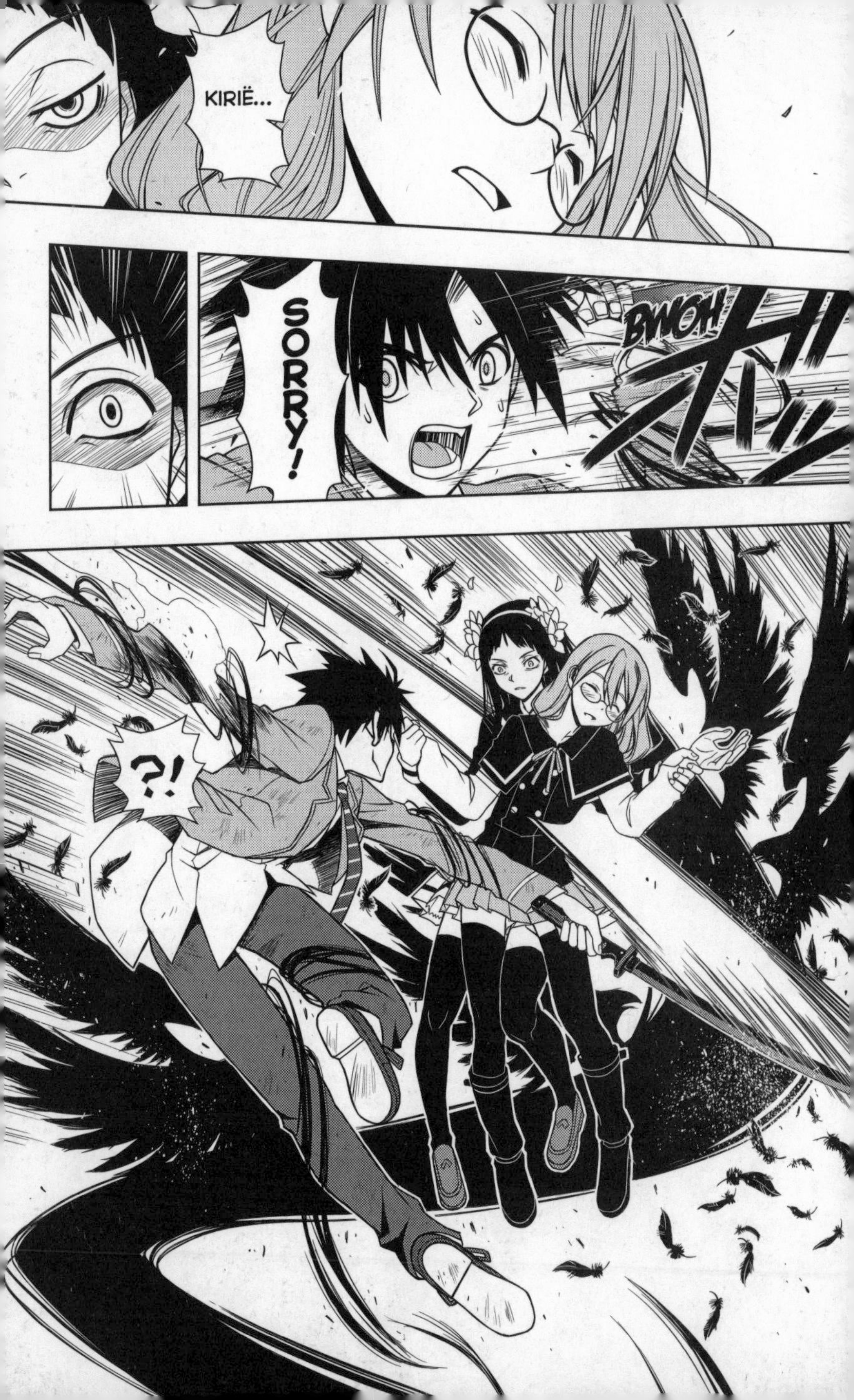
KIRIË...
BWOH
SORRY!
?!

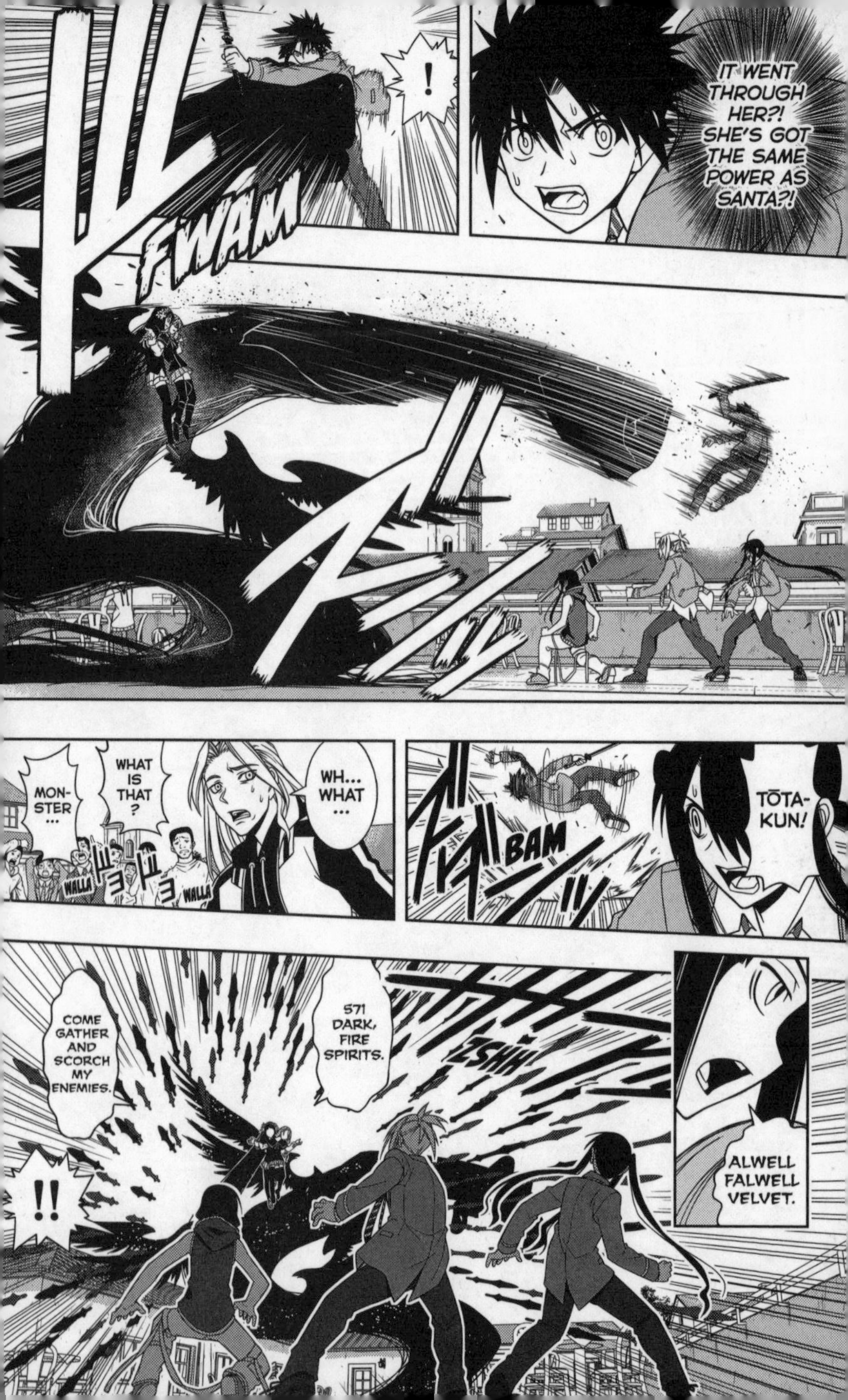
IT WENT THROUGH HER?! SHE'S GOT THE SAME POWER AS SANTA?!
!
FWAM
TŌTA-KUN!
BAM
WH... WHAT ...
WHAT IS THAT ?
MON-STER ...
WALLA
WALLA
ALWELL FALWELL VELVET.
571 DARK, FIRE SPIRITS.
COME GATHER AND SCORCH MY ENEMIES.
ZSHH
!!

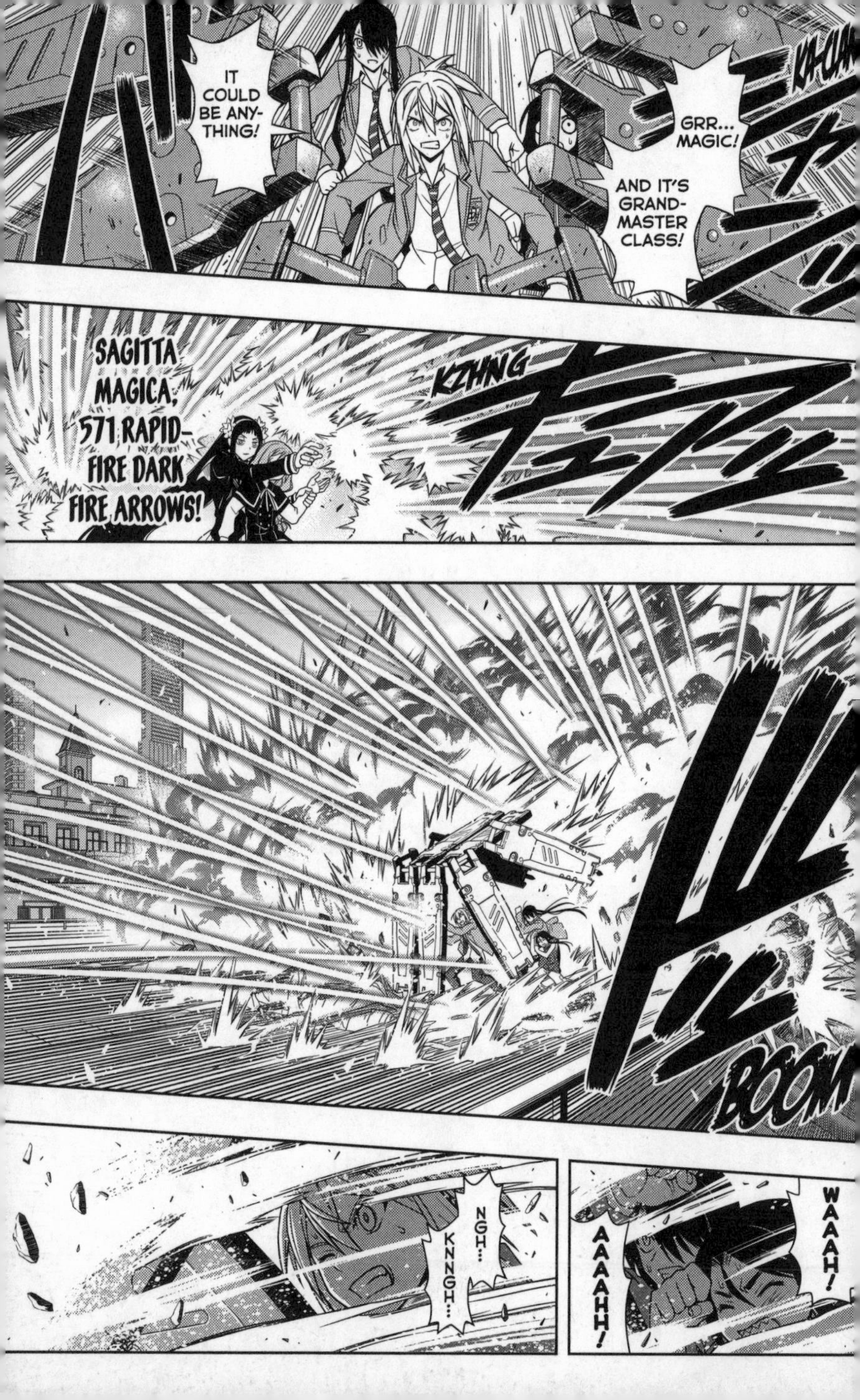
GRR... MAGIC!
AND IT'S GRAND-MASTER CLASS!
IT COULD BE ANY-THING!
KZHNG
SAGITTA MAGICA, 571 RAPID-FIRE DARK FIRE ARROWS!
BOOM
WAAAH!
AAAAHH!
NGH...
KNNGH...

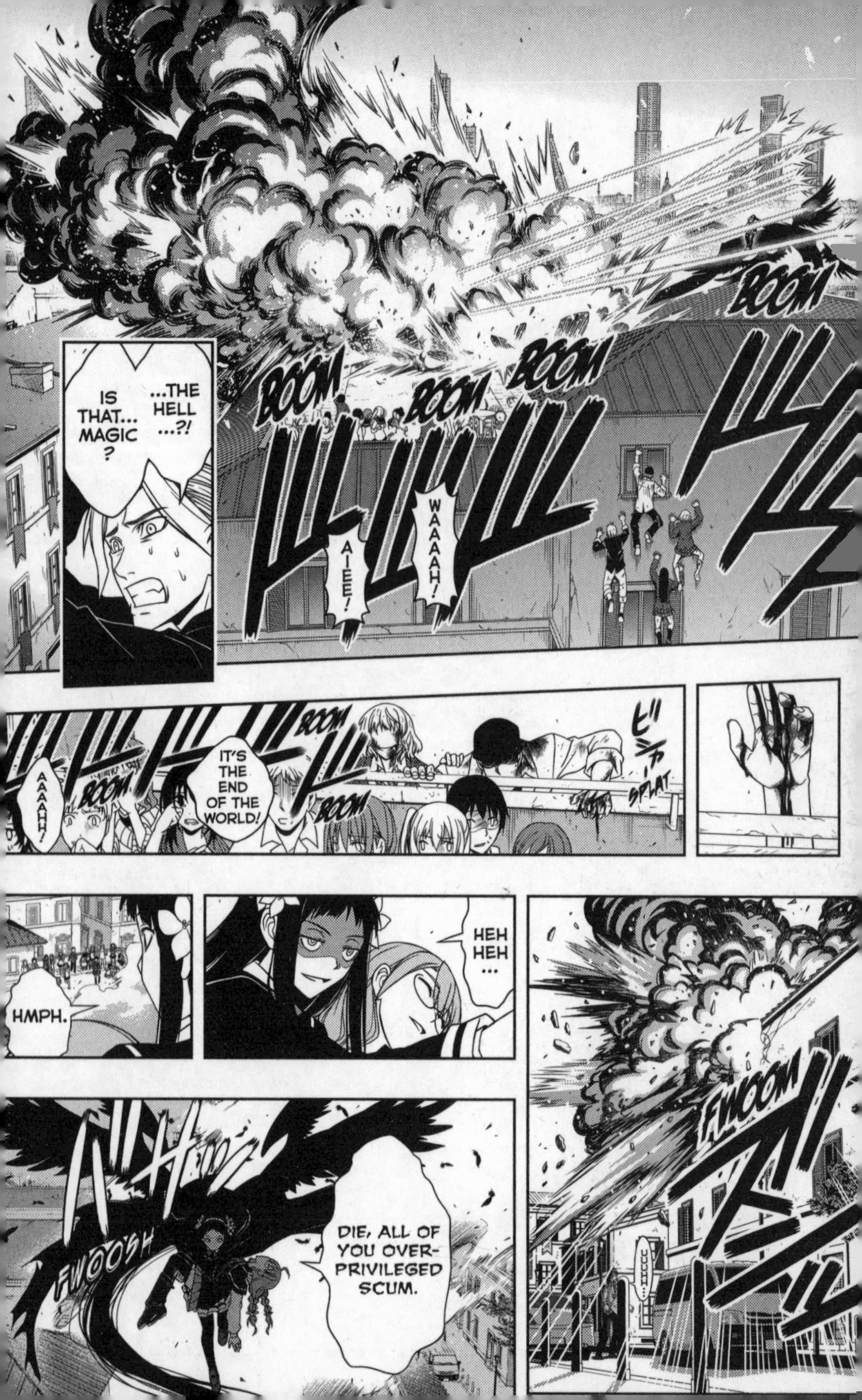
BOOM
BOOM
BOOM
BOOM
WAAAAH!
AIEE!
...THE HELL...?!
IS THAT... MAGIC?
ビシャ!
SPLAT
BOOM
BOOM
BOOM
IT'S THE END OF THE WORLD!
AAAAH!
FWOOM
UUUH...
HEH HEH...
HMPH.
DIE, ALL OF YOU OVER-PRIVILEGED SCUM.
FWOOSH

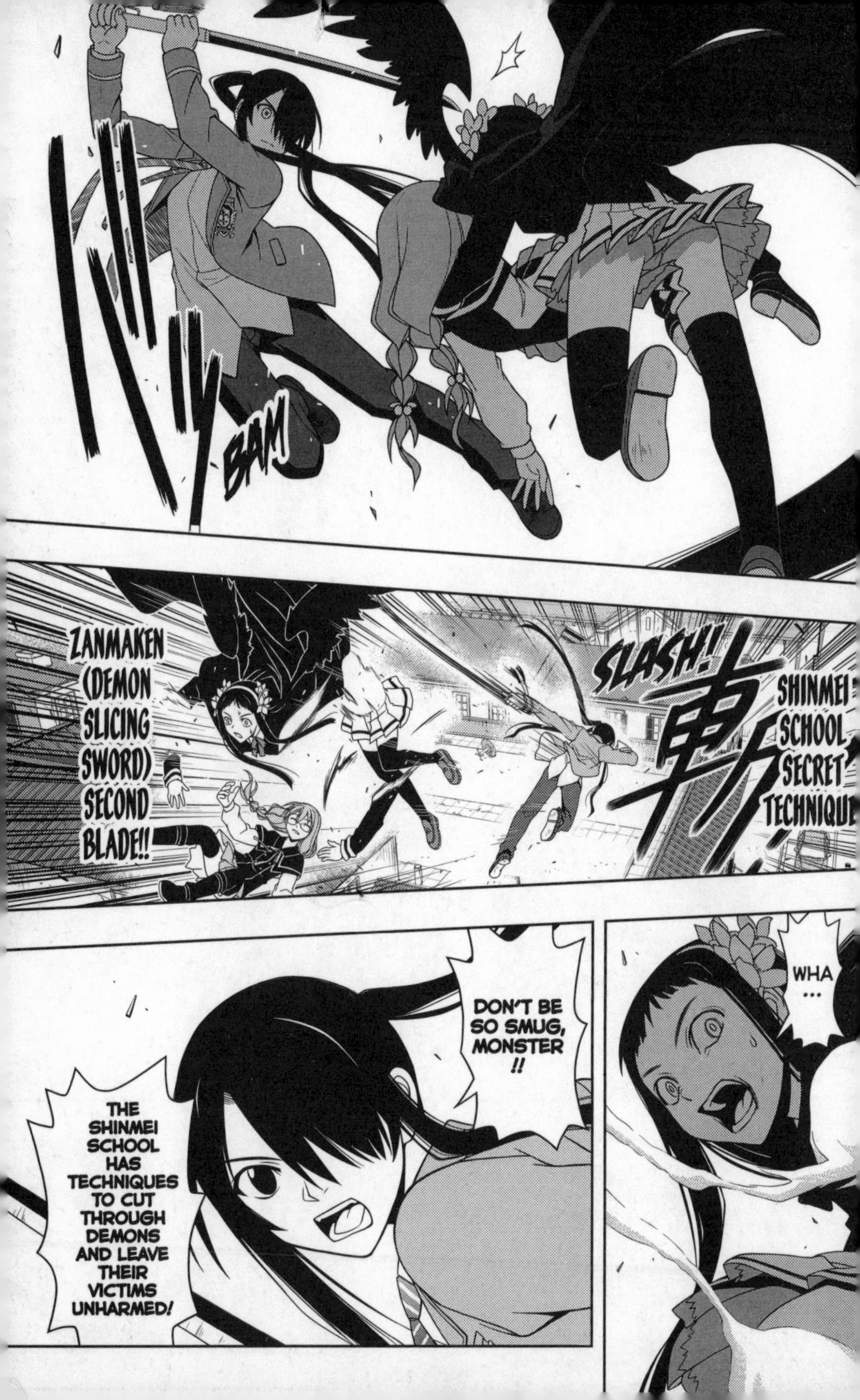
BAM
SHINMEI SCHOOL SECRET TECHNIQUE
斬
SLASH!
ZANMAKEN (DEMON SLICING SWORD) SECOND BLADE!!
WHA...
DON'T BE SO SMUG, MONSTER!!
THE SHINMEI SCHOOL HAS TECHNIQUES TO CUT THROUGH DEMONS AND LEAVE THEIR VICTIMS UNHARMED!

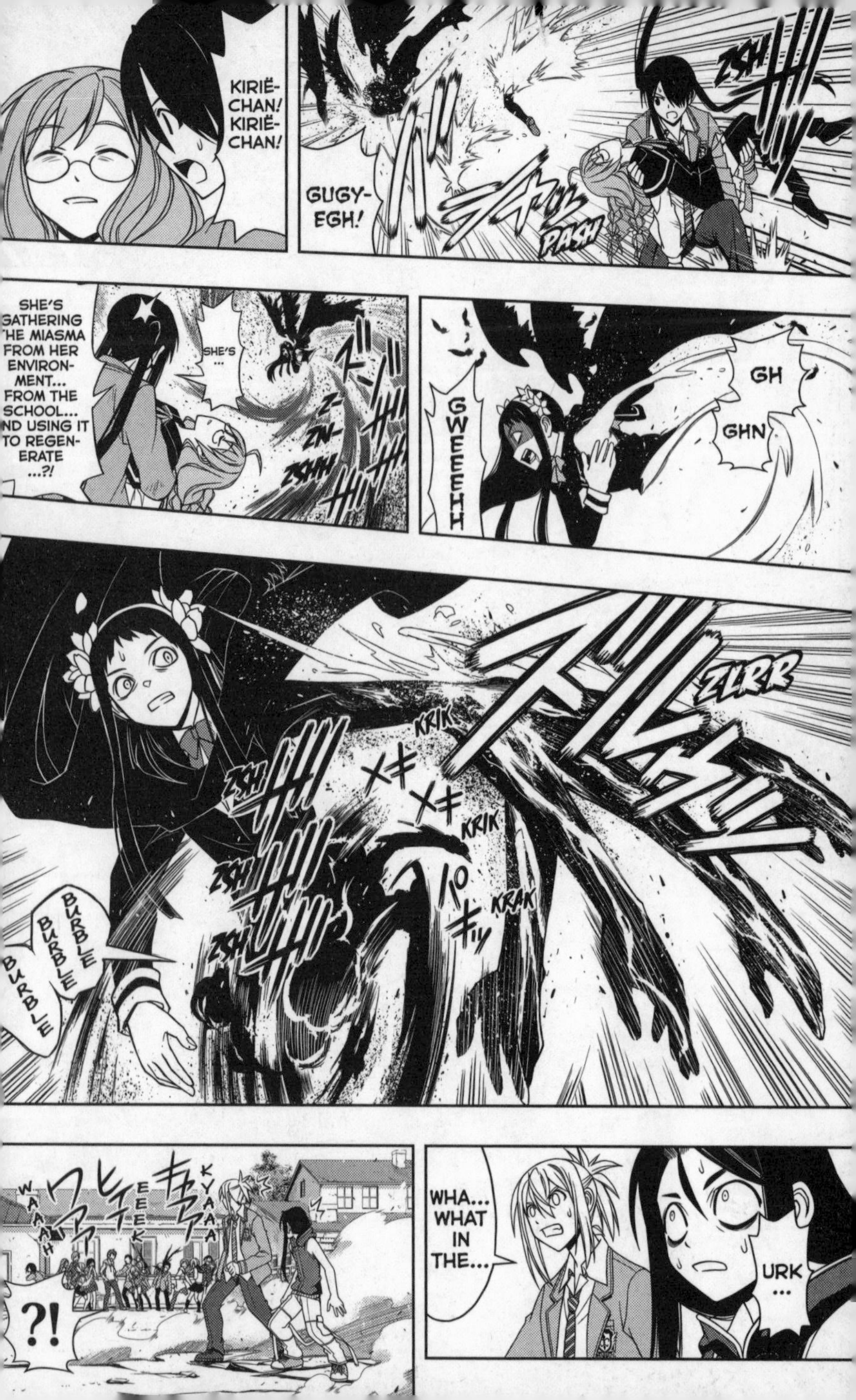
ZSH
PASH
GUGY-EGH!
KIRIË-CHAN! KIRIË-CHAN!
GWEEEEHH
GH
GHN
SHE'S...
Z-ZN-
ZSHH
SHE'S GATHERING HE MIASMA FROM HER ENVIRONMENT... FROM THE SCHOOL... ND USING IT TO REGENERATE ...?!
ZLRRR
KRIK
KRIK
KRAK
ZSH
ZSH
ZSH
BURBLE BURBLE BURBLE BURBLE
WHA... WHAT IN THE...
URK...
KYAAA
EEEK
WAAAH
?!

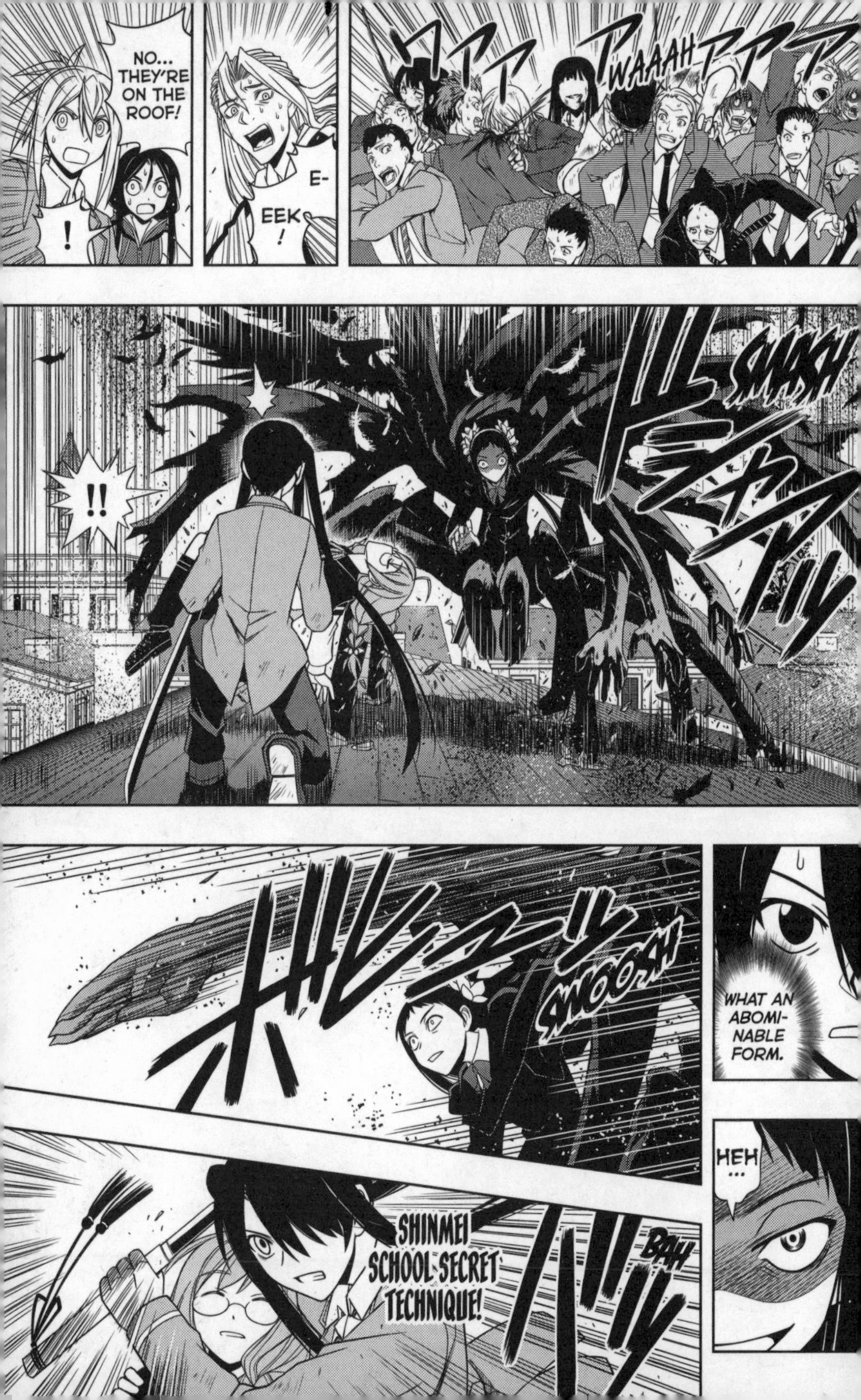
WAAAH
E-EEK!
NO... THEY'RE ON THE ROOF!
!
SMASH
!!
WHAT AN ABOMINABLE FORM.
SWOOOSH
HEH...
SHINMEI SCHOOL SECRET TECHNIQUE!
BAH

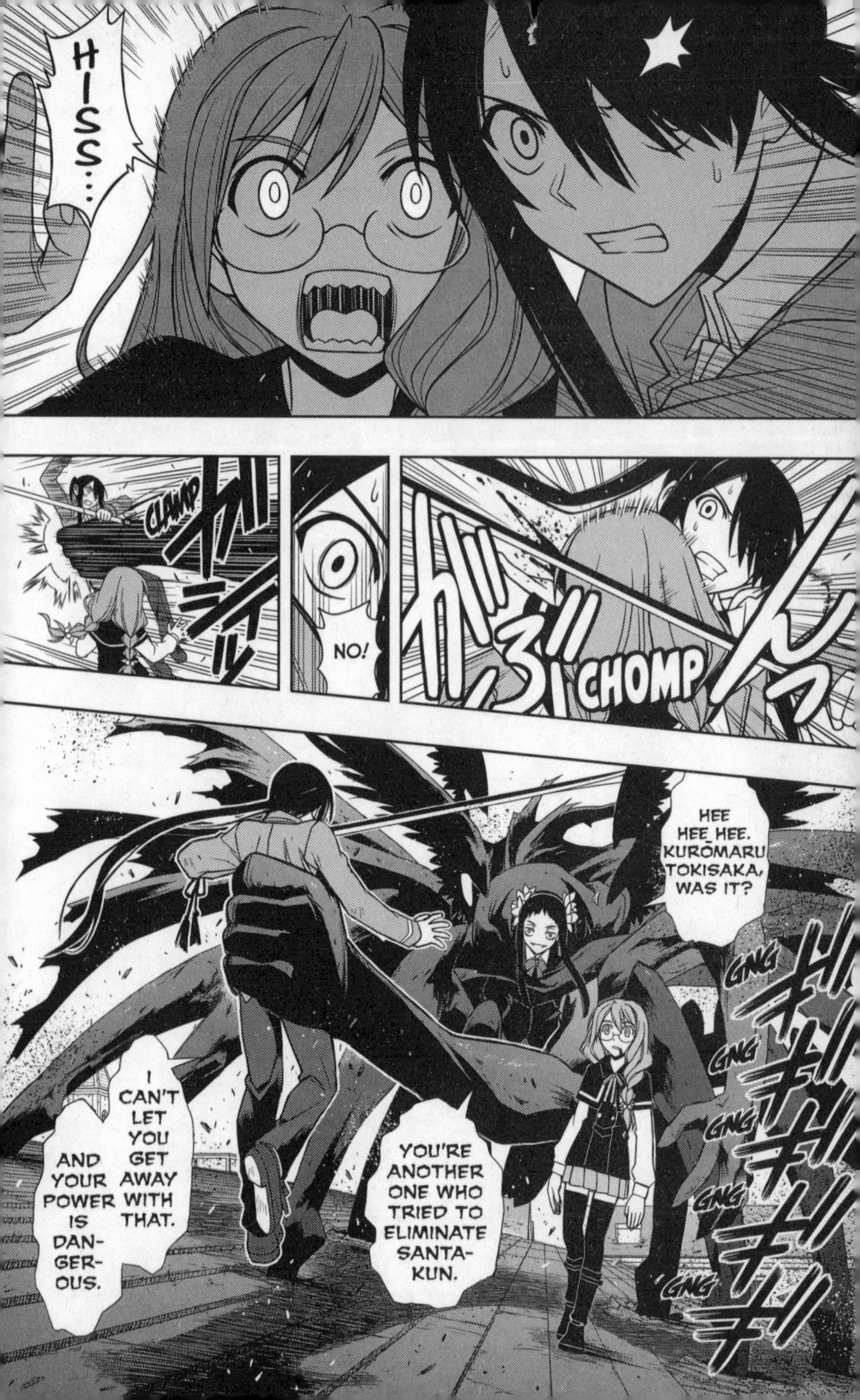
HISS...
CHOMP
NO!
CLAMP
HEE HEE HEE. KUROMARU TOKISAKA, WAS IT?
GNG GNG GNG GNG GNG
YOU'RE ANOTHER ONE WHO TRIED TO ELIMINATE SANTA-KUN.
I CAN'T LET YOU GET AWAY WITH THAT.
AND YOUR POWER IS DANGEROUS.

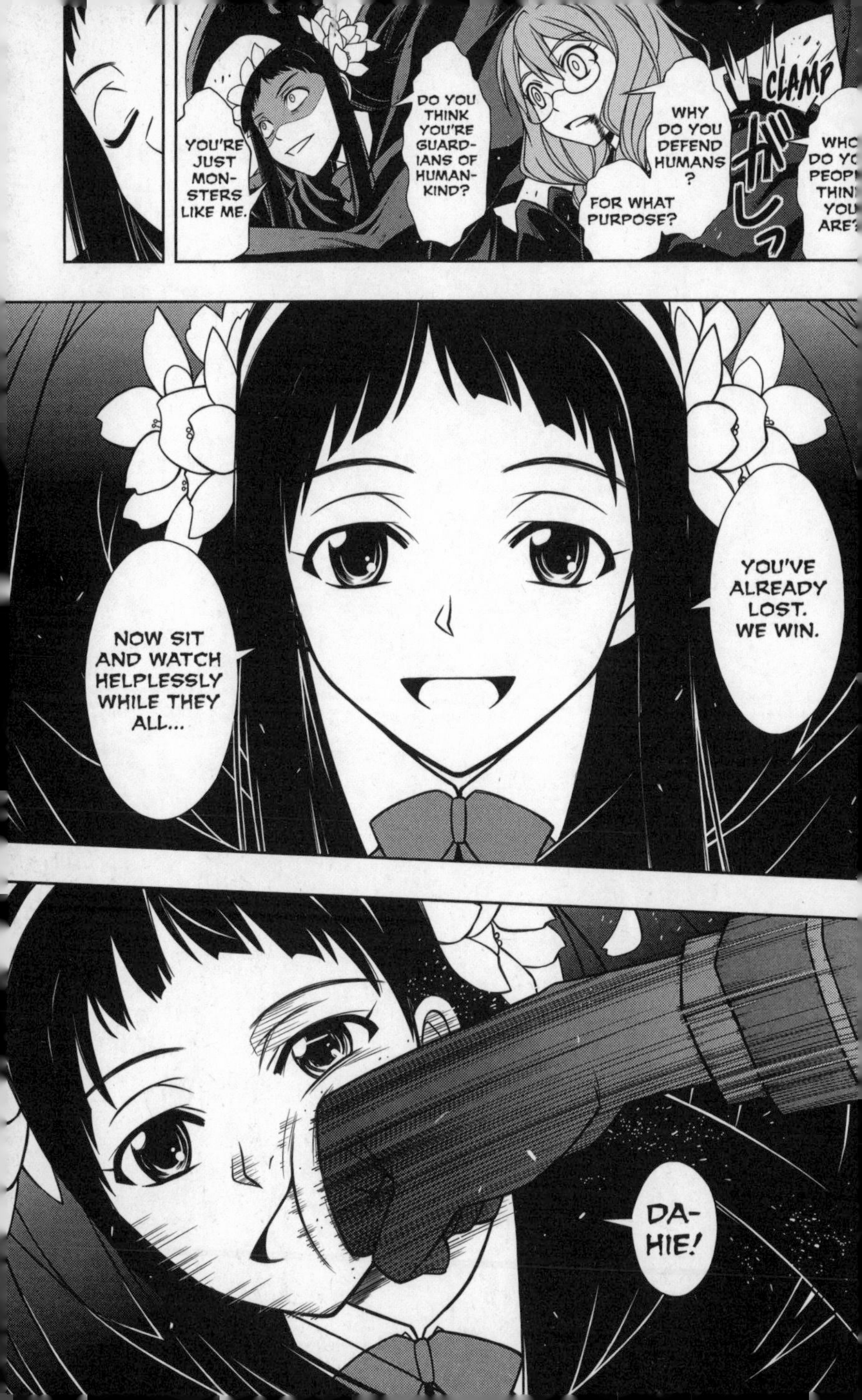
WHO DO YO PEOP THIN YOU ARE?
CLAMP
WHY DO YOU DEFEND HUMANS?
FOR WHAT PURPOSE?
DO YOU THINK YOU'RE GUARDIANS OF HUMANKIND?
YOU'RE JUST MONSTERS LIKE ME.
YOU'VE ALREADY LOST. WE WIN.
NOW SIT AND WATCH HELPLESSLY WHILE THEY ALL...
DA-HIE!

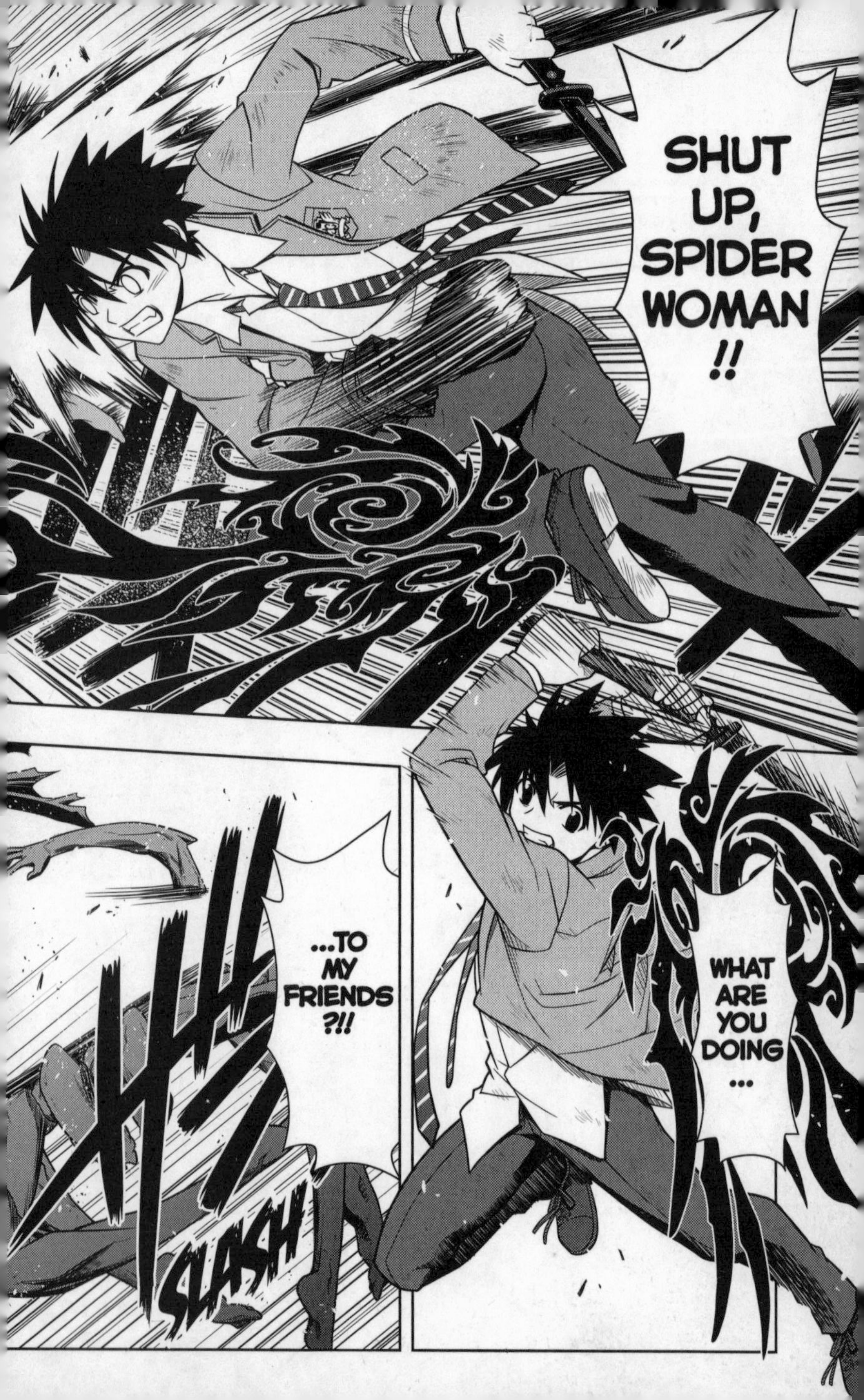
SHUT UP, SPIDER WOMAN!!
WHAT ARE YOU DOING...
...TO MY FRIENDS?!!
SLASH

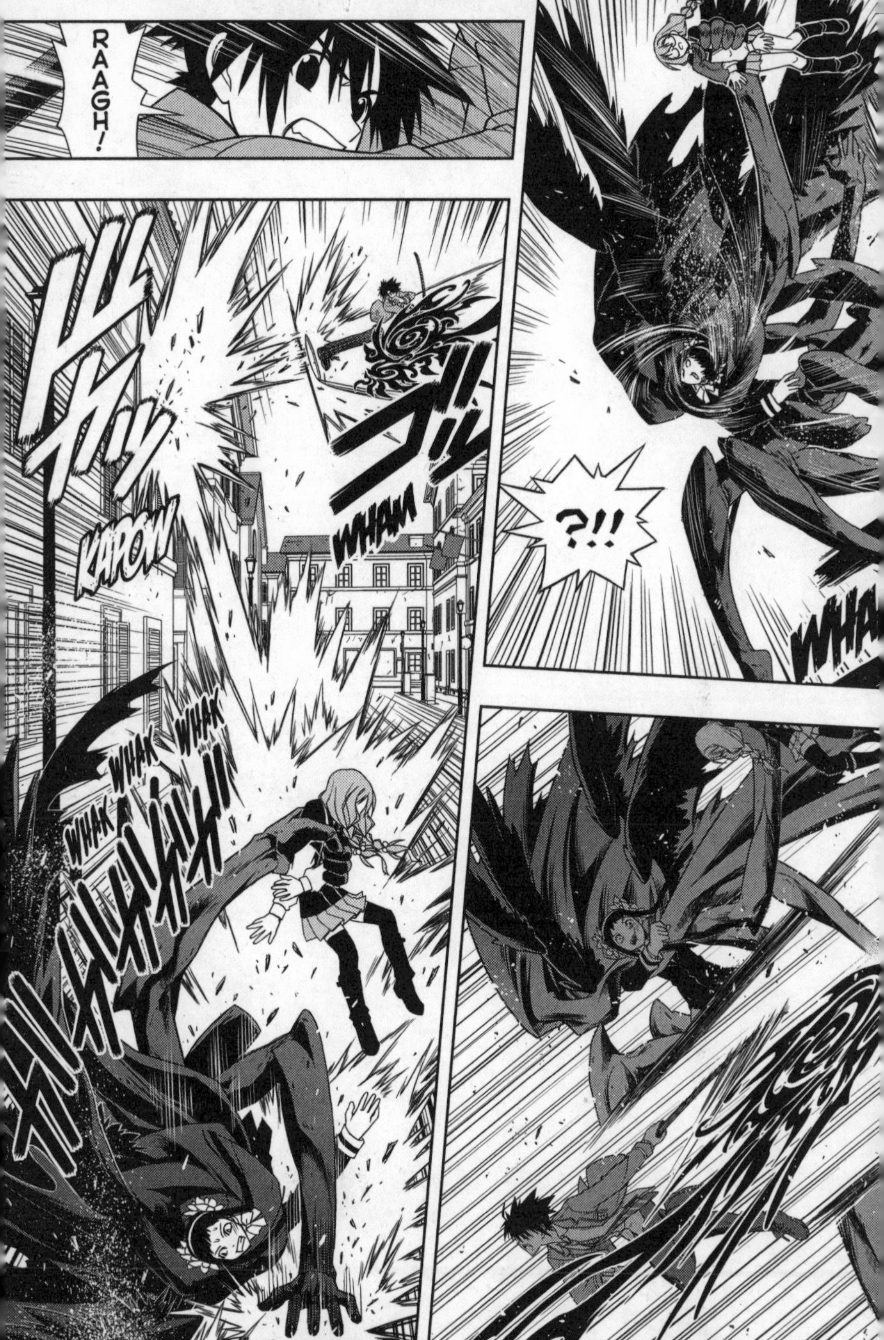
?!!
WHA
RAAGH!
WHAM
KAPOW
WHAK
WHAK
WHAK
WHAK

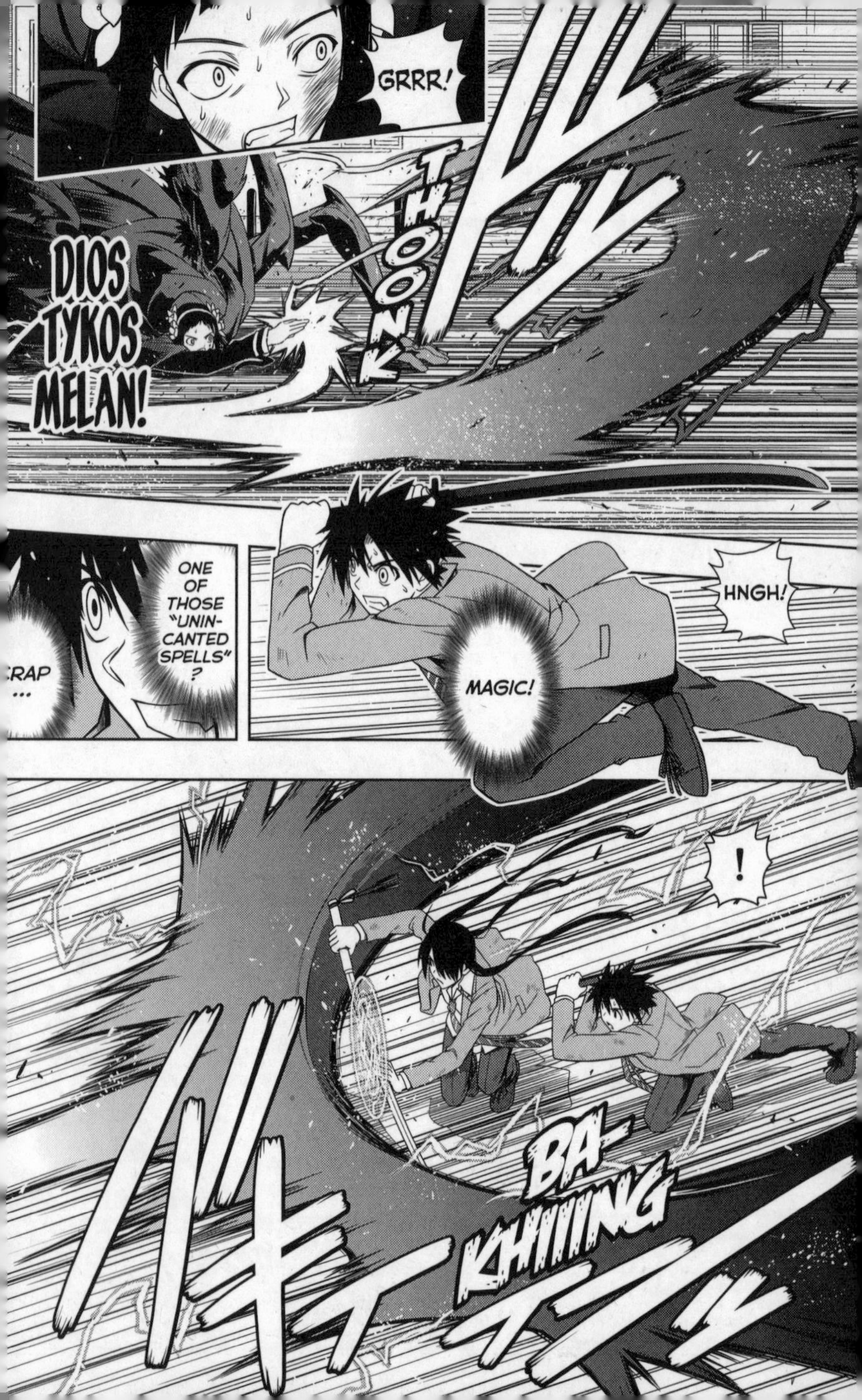
GRRR!
THOONK
DIOS TYKOS MELAN!
HNGH!
MAGIC!
ONE OF THOSE "UNIN-CANTED SPELLS"?
CRAP ...
!
BA-KHIIING

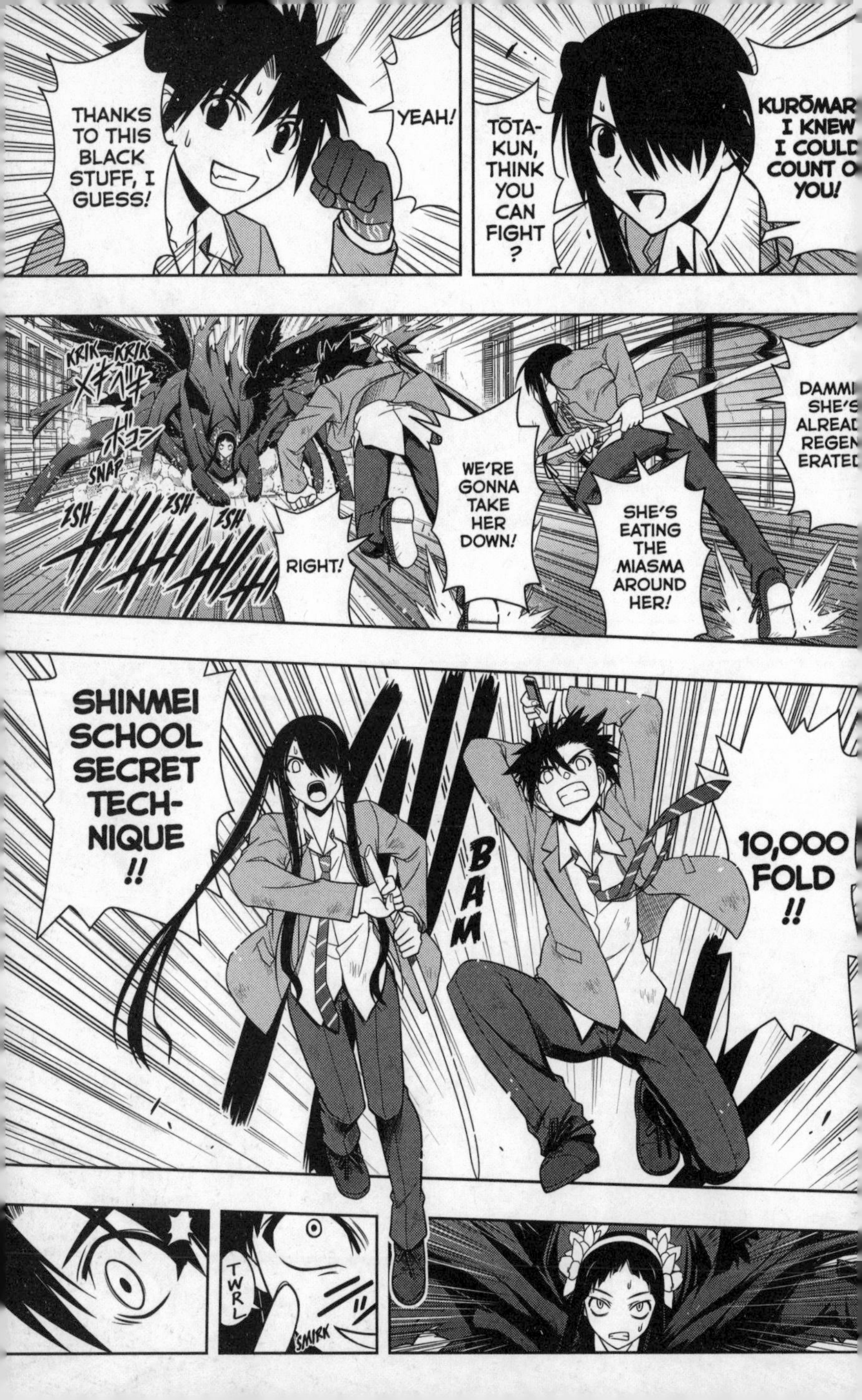
KURŌMAR I KNEW I COULD COUNT O YOU!
TŌTA-KUN, THINK YOU CAN FIGHT ?
YEAH!
THANKS TO THIS BLACK STUFF, I GUESS!
DAMMI SHE'S ALREAD REGEN ERATED
SHE'S EATING THE MIASMA AROUND HER!
WE'RE GONNA TAKE HER DOWN!
RIGHT!
KRIK KRIK
メキベキ
ボゴン
SNAP
ZSH ZSH ZSH
SHINMEI SCHOOL SECRET TECH- NIQUE !!
10,000 FOLD !!
BAM
TWRL
SMIRK

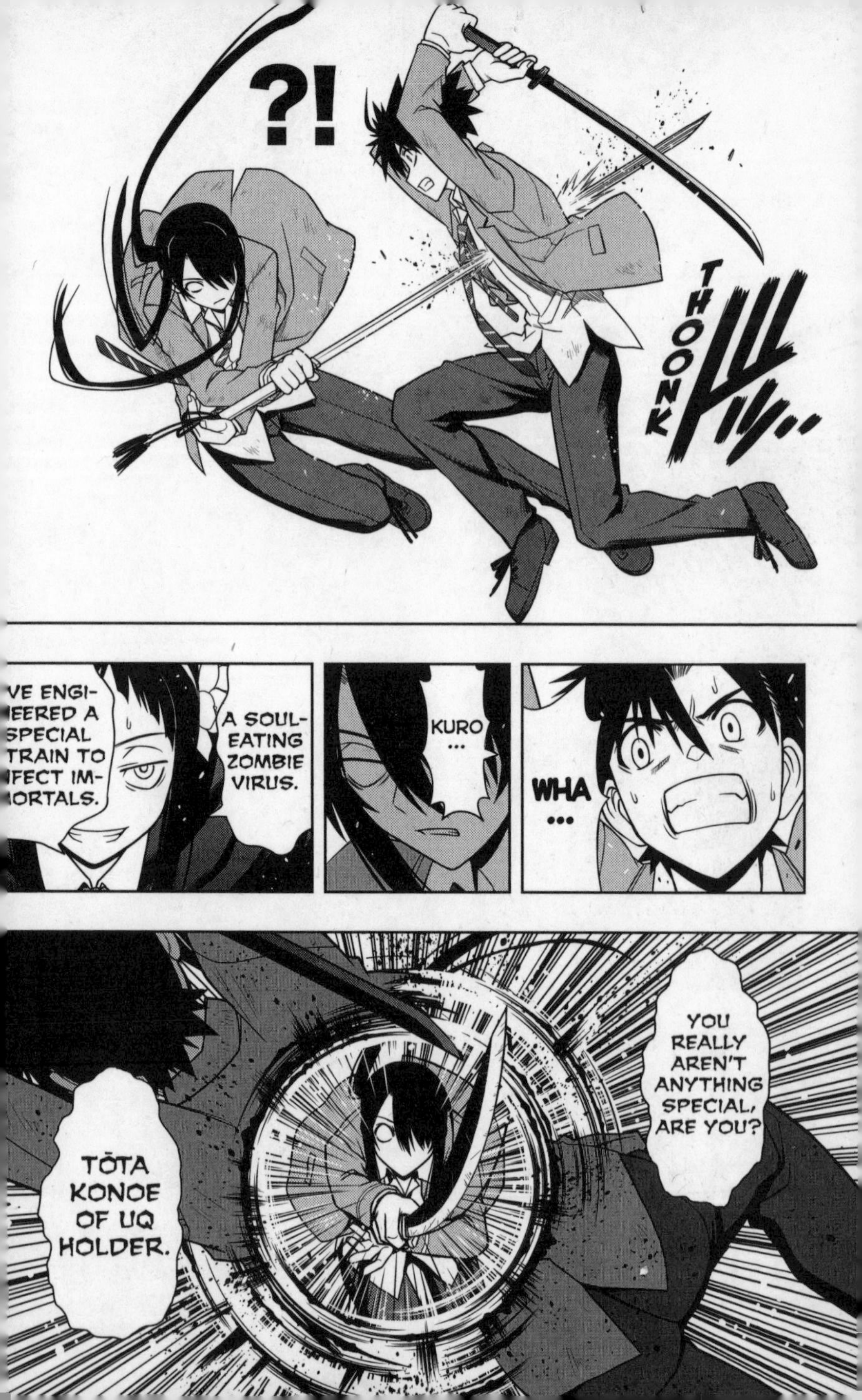
THOONK
?!
WHA...
KURO...
A SOUL-EATING ZOMBIE VIRUS.
VE ENGI-IEERED A SPECIAL TRAIN TO IFECT IM-IORTALS.
YOU REALLY AREN'T ANYTHING SPECIAL, ARE YOU?
TŌTA KONOE OF UQ HOLDER.

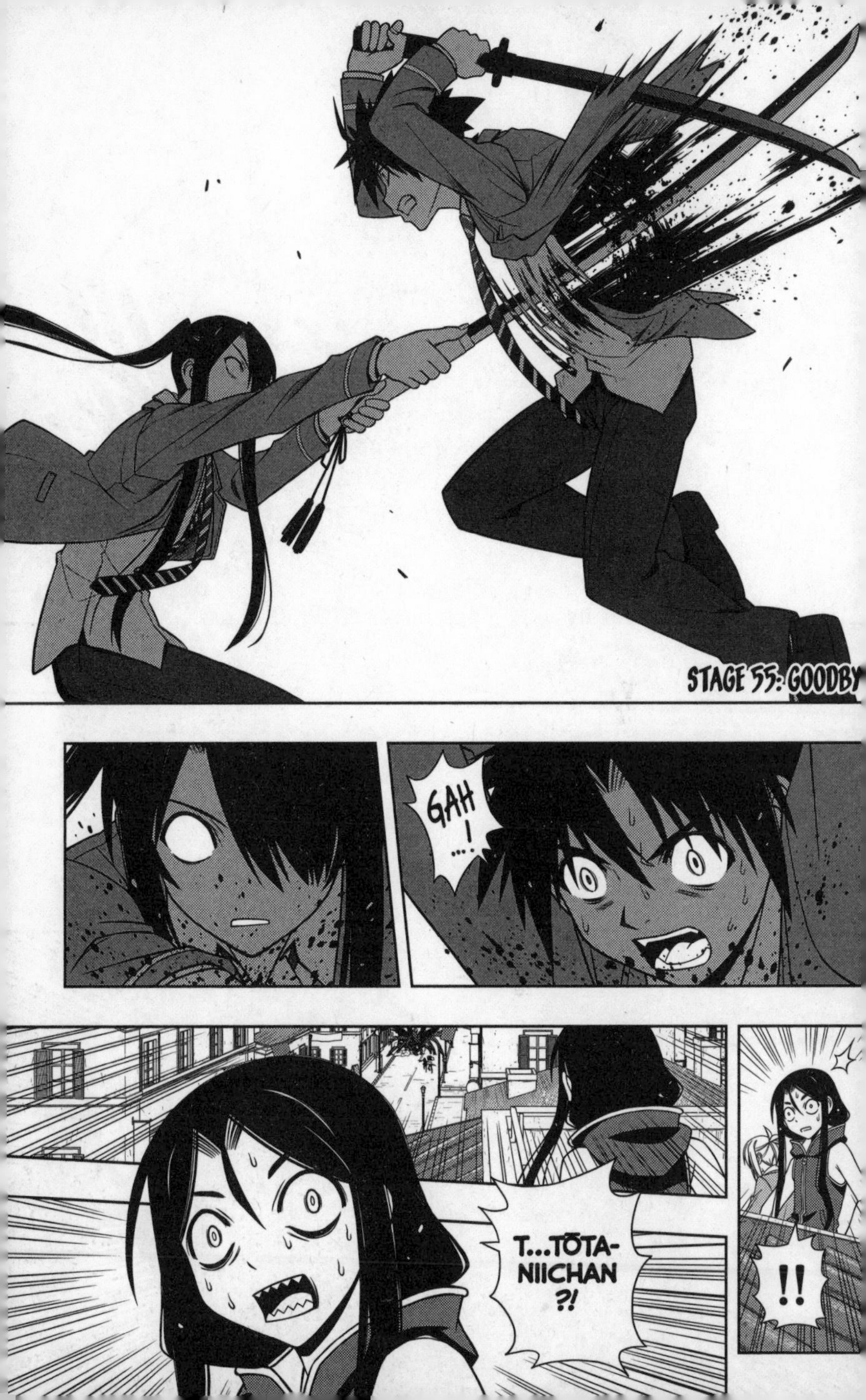
STAGE 55: GOODBY
GAH! ...!
!!
T...TŌTA-NIICHAN?!

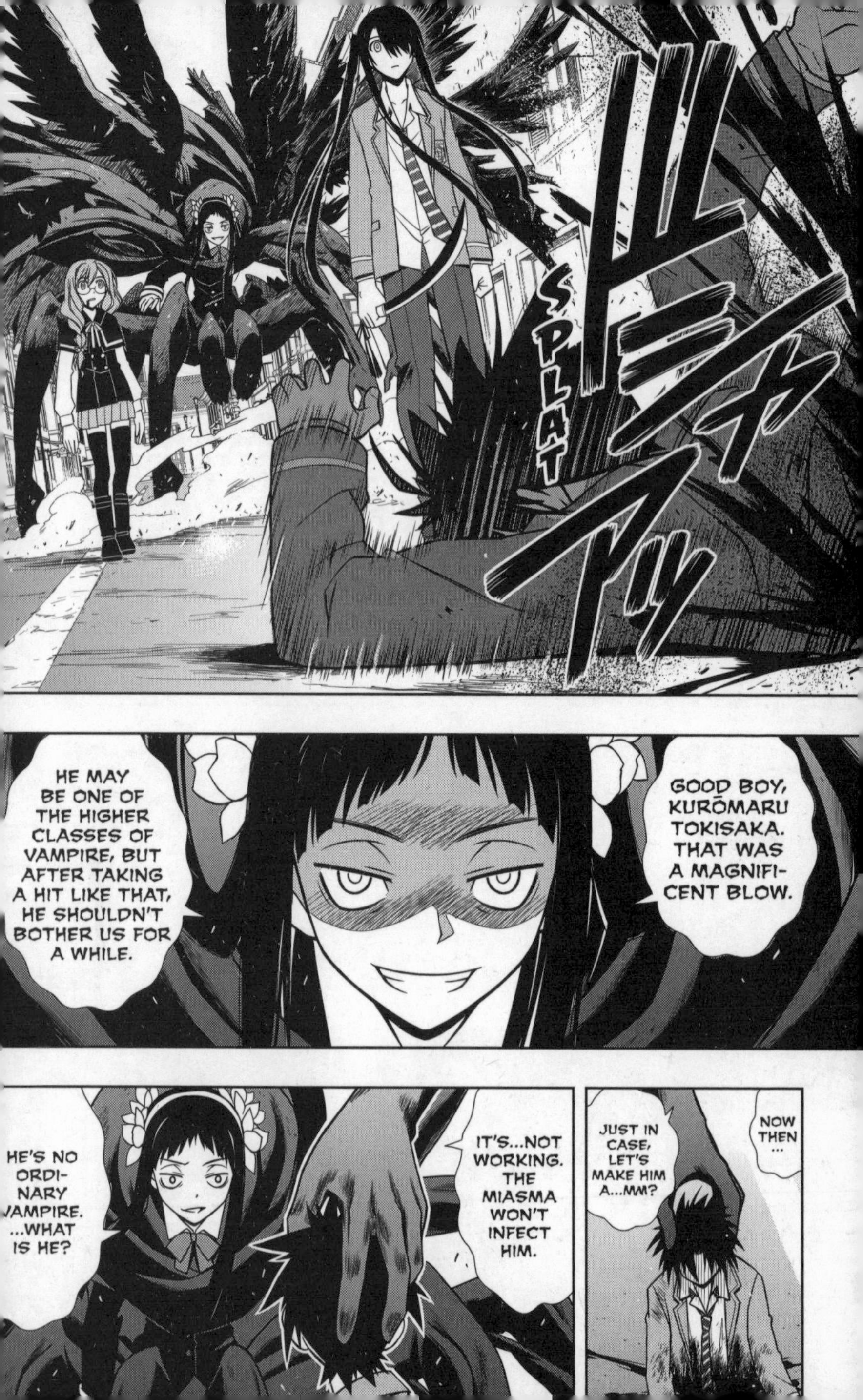
SPLAT
GOOD BOY, KURŌMARU TOKISAKA. THAT WAS A MAGNIFICENT BLOW.
HE MAY BE ONE OF THE HIGHER CLASSES OF VAMPIRE, BUT AFTER TAKING A HIT LIKE THAT, HE SHOULDN'T BOTHER US FOR A WHILE.
NOW THEN...
JUST IN CASE, LET'S MAKE HIM A...MM?
IT'S...NOT WORKING. THE MIASMA WON'T INFECT HIM.
HE'S NO ORDINARY VAMPIRE. ...WHAT IS HE?

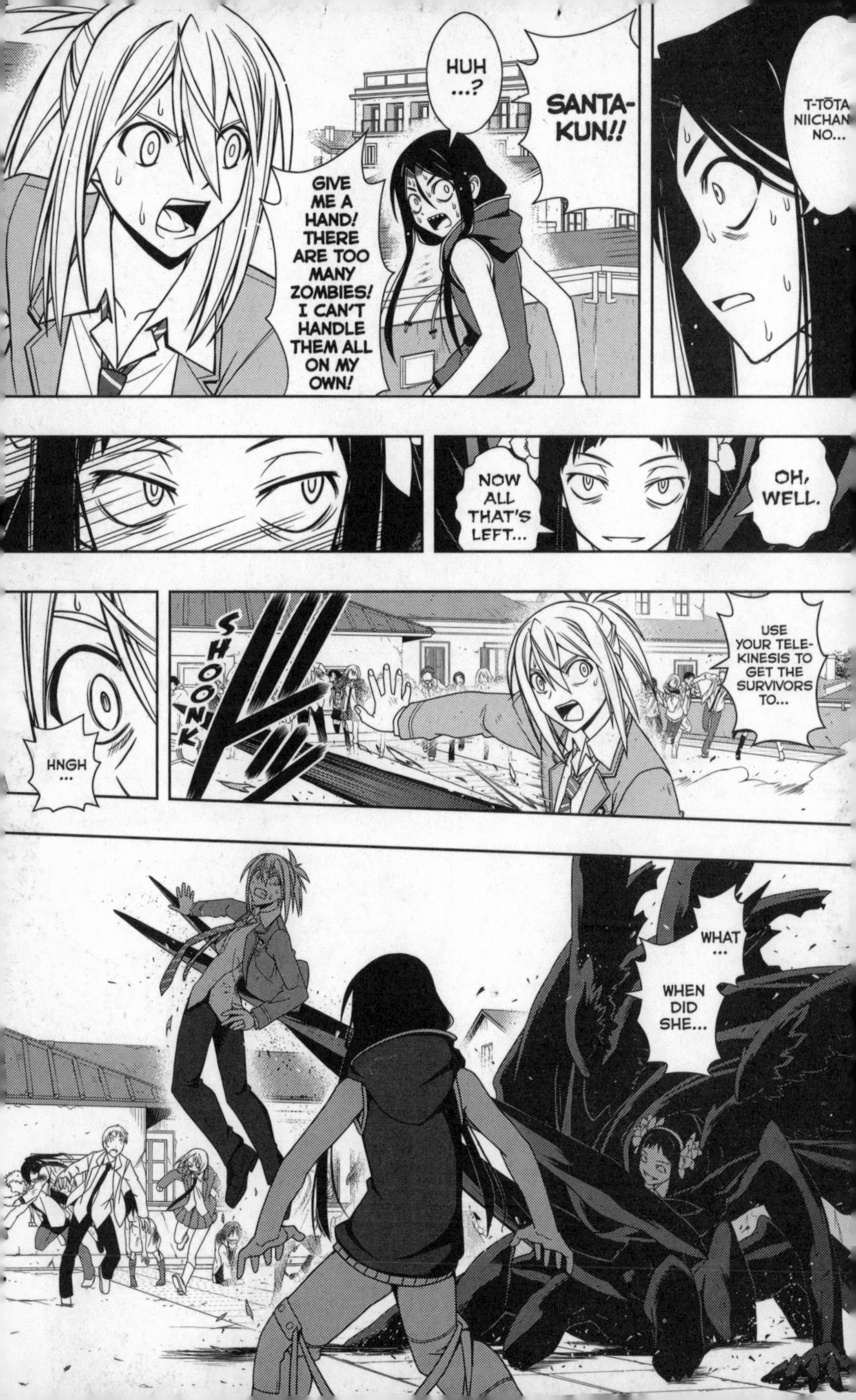
T-TŌTA NIICHAN NO...
SANTA-KUN!!
HUH ...?
GIVE ME A HAND! THERE ARE TOO MANY ZOMBIES! I CAN'T HANDLE THEM ALL ON MY OWN!
OH, WELL.
NOW ALL THAT'S LEFT...
USE YOUR TELE-KINESIS TO GET THE SURVIVORS TO...
SHOOONK
HNGH ...
WHAT ...
WHEN DID SHE...

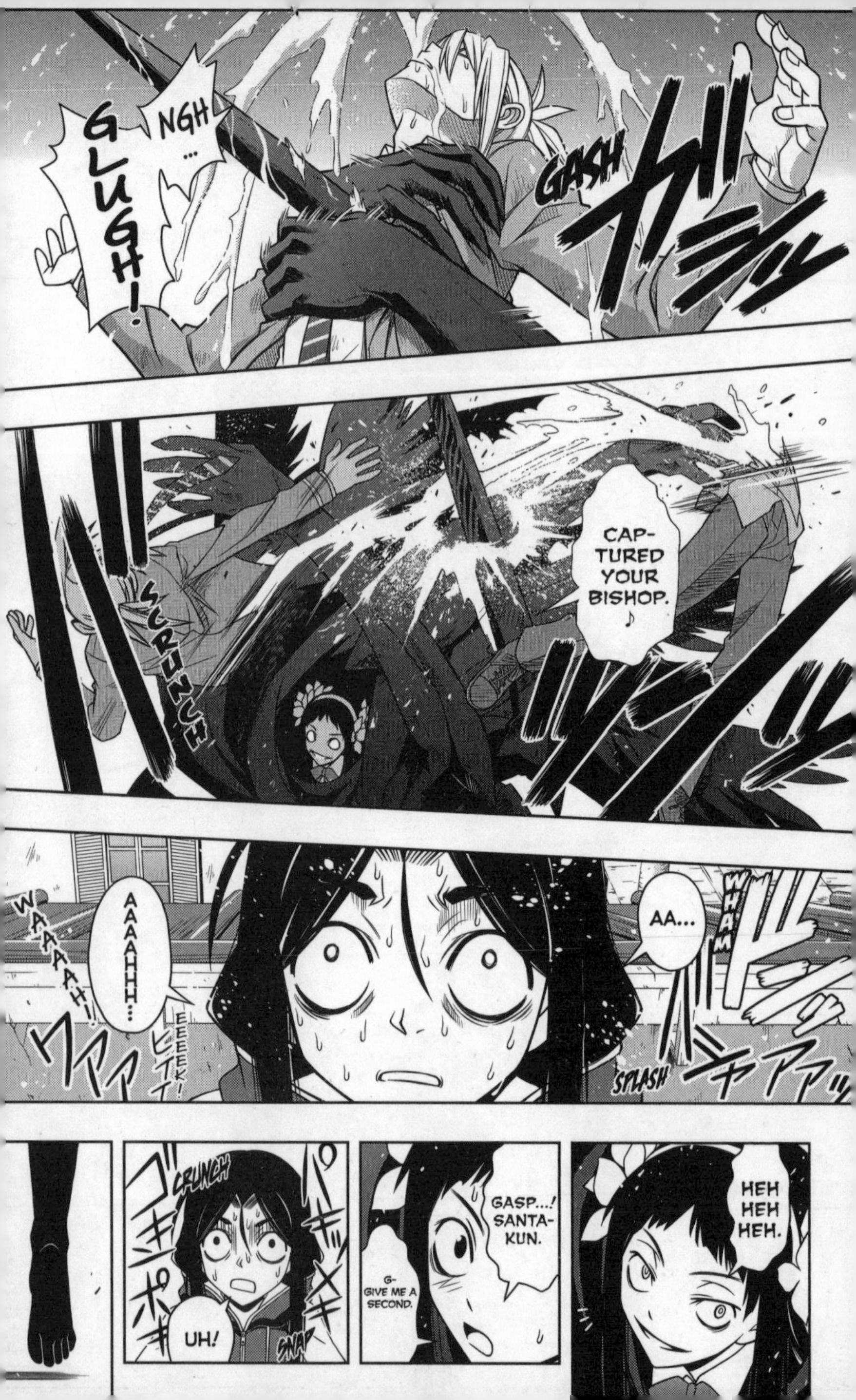
GASH
NGH...
GLUGH!
CAP-TURED YOUR BISHOP. ♪
SCRUNCH
WHAM
SPLASH
AA...
AAAAAHHH...
EEEEEK!
WAAAAAH!
HEH HEH HEH.
GASP...! SANTA-KUN.
G- GIVE ME A SECOND.
CRUNCH
UH!
SNAP

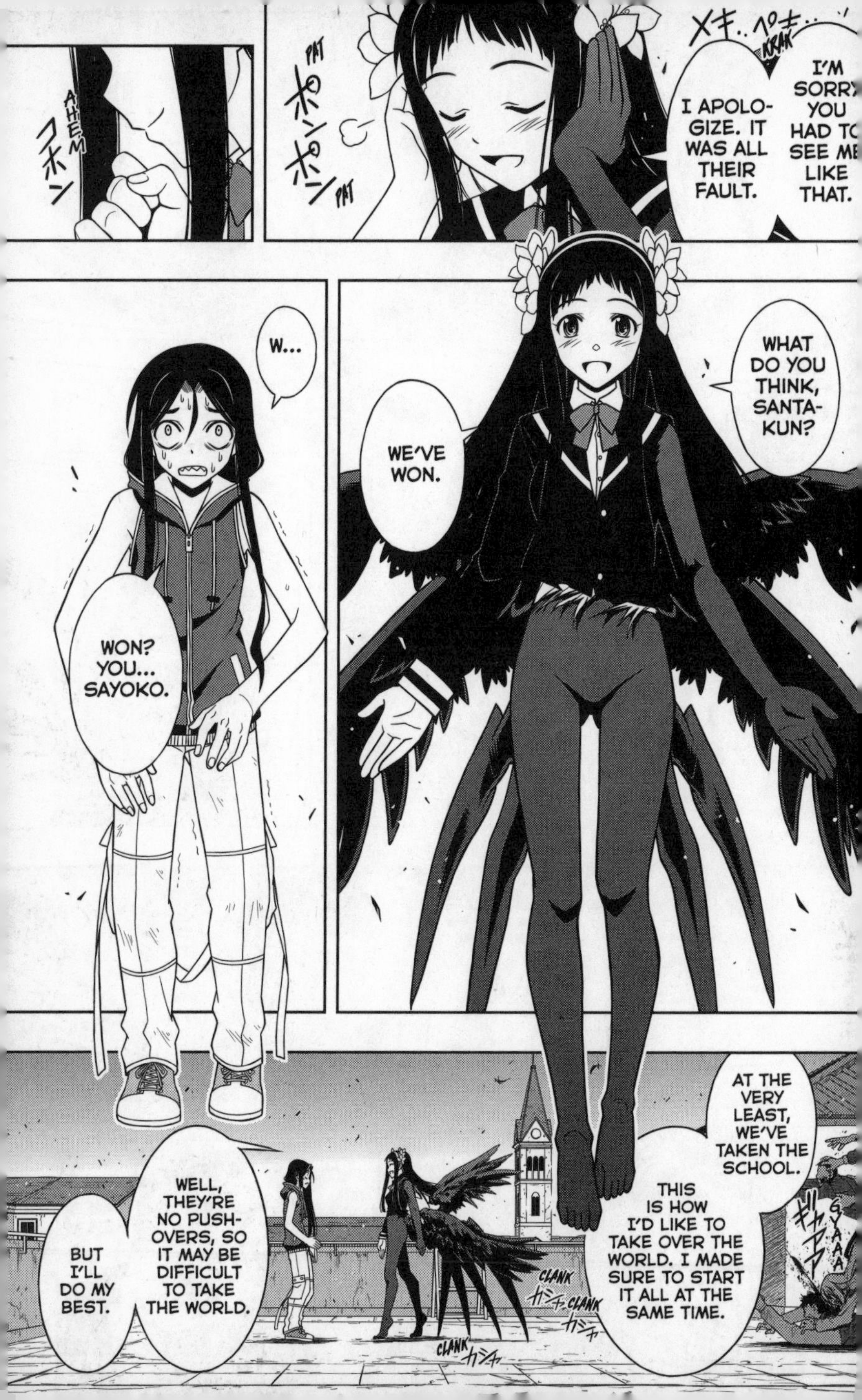
KRAK
I'M SORRY YOU HAD TO SEE ME LIKE THAT.
I APOLOGIZE. IT WAS ALL THEIR FAULT.
PAT PAT
AHEM
WHAT DO YOU THINK, SANTA-KUN?
WE'VE WON.
W...
WON? YOU... SAYOKO.
AT THE VERY LEAST, WE'VE TAKEN THE SCHOOL.
THIS IS HOW I'D LIKE TO TAKE OVER THE WORLD. I MADE SURE TO START IT ALL AT THE SAME TIME.
GYAAA
CLANK CLANK CLANK
WELL, THEY'RE NO PUSHOVERS, SO IT MAY BE DIFFICULT TO TAKE THE WORLD.
BUT I'LL DO MY BEST.

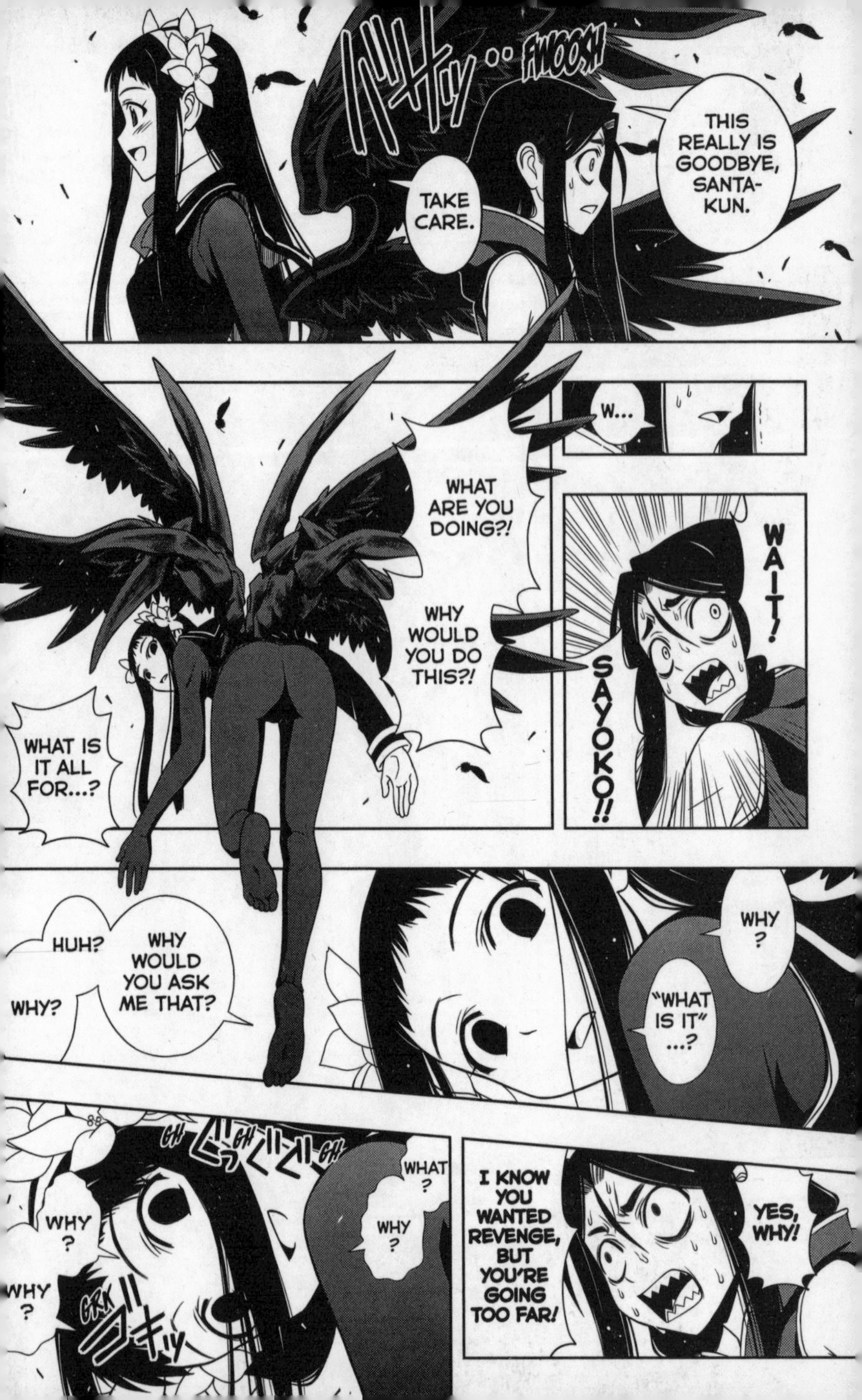
FWOOSH
THIS REALLY IS GOODBYE, SANTA-KUN.
TAKE CARE.
W...
WAIT!
SAYOKO!!
WHAT ARE YOU DOING?!
WHY WOULD YOU DO THIS?!
WHAT IS IT ALL FOR...?
WHY?
"WHAT IS IT" ...?
WHY WOULD YOU ASK ME THAT?
HUH?
WHY?
YES, WHY!
I KNOW YOU WANTED REVENGE, BUT YOU'RE GOING TOO FAR!
WHAT?
WHY?
GH
GH
GH
WHY?
WHY?
GRK

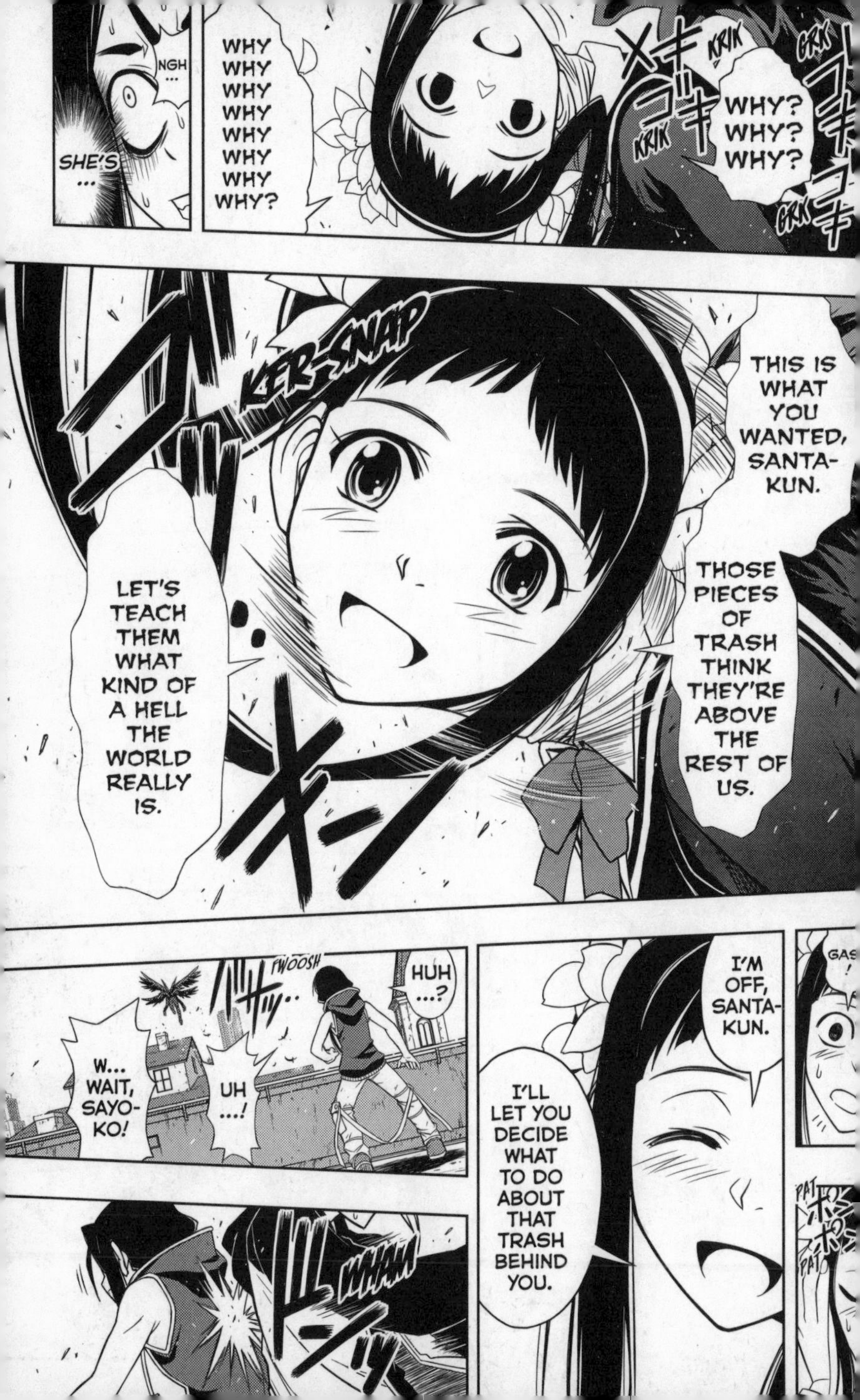
KRIK
KRIK
WHY? WHY? WHY?
GRK
GRK
WHY WHY WHY WHY WHY WHY WHY WHY?
NGH ...
SHE'S ...
THIS IS WHAT YOU WANTED, SANTA-KUN.
THOSE PIECES OF TRASH THINK THEY'RE ABOVE THE REST OF US.
KER-SNAP
LET'S TEACH THEM WHAT KIND OF A HELL THE WORLD REALLY IS.
GAS
PAT
PAT
I'M OFF, SANTA-KUN.
I'LL LET YOU DECIDE WHAT TO DO ABOUT THAT TRASH BEHIND YOU.
HUH ...?
FWOOSH
UH ...!
W... WAIT, SAYO-KO!
WHAM

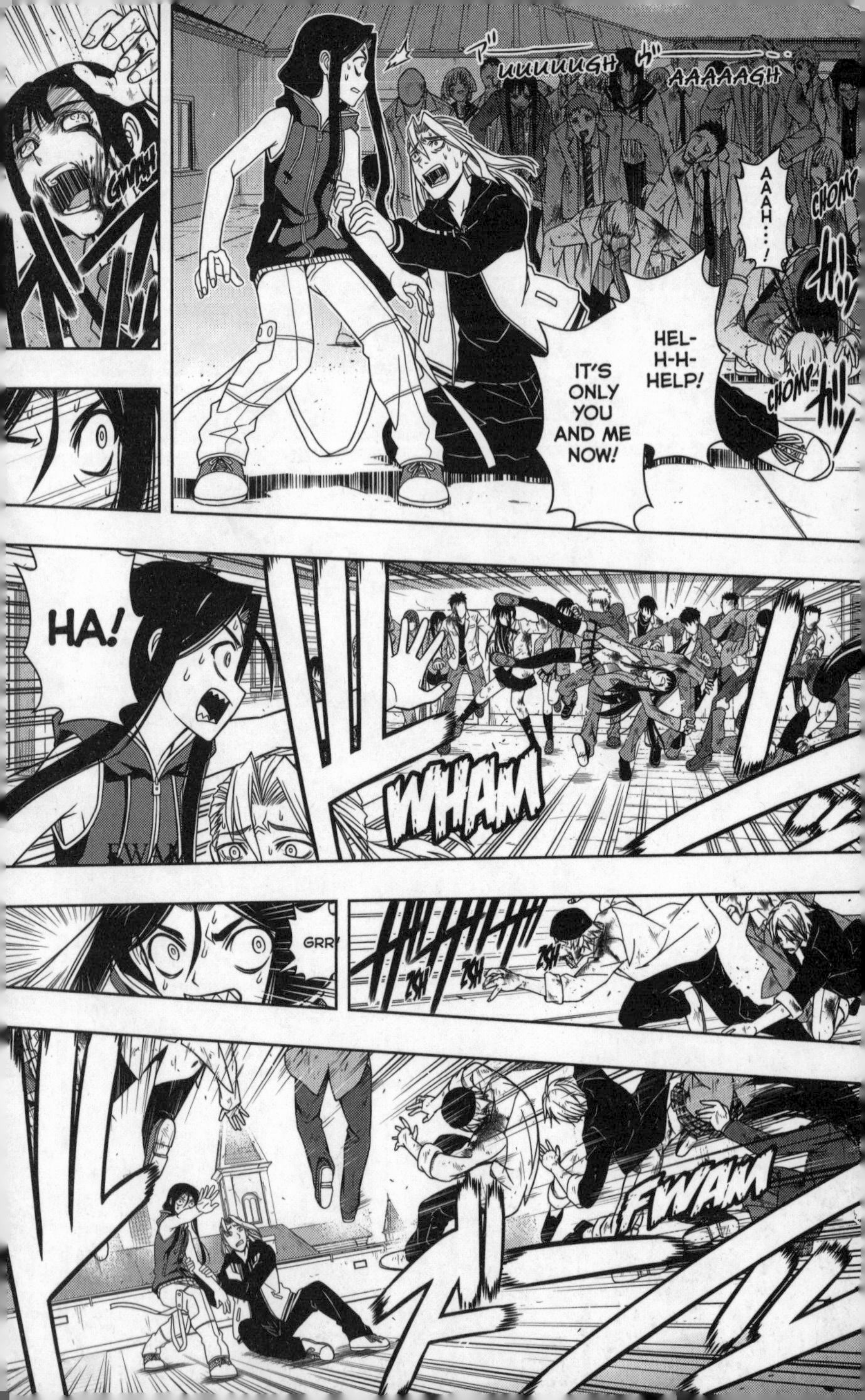

UUUUUUGH
AAAAAGH
AAAH...!
CHOMP
HEL-H-H-HELP!
IT'S ONLY YOU AND ME NOW!
CHOMP
GWAH
WHAM
HA!
FWAM
ZSH
ZSH
ZSH
GRR
FWAM

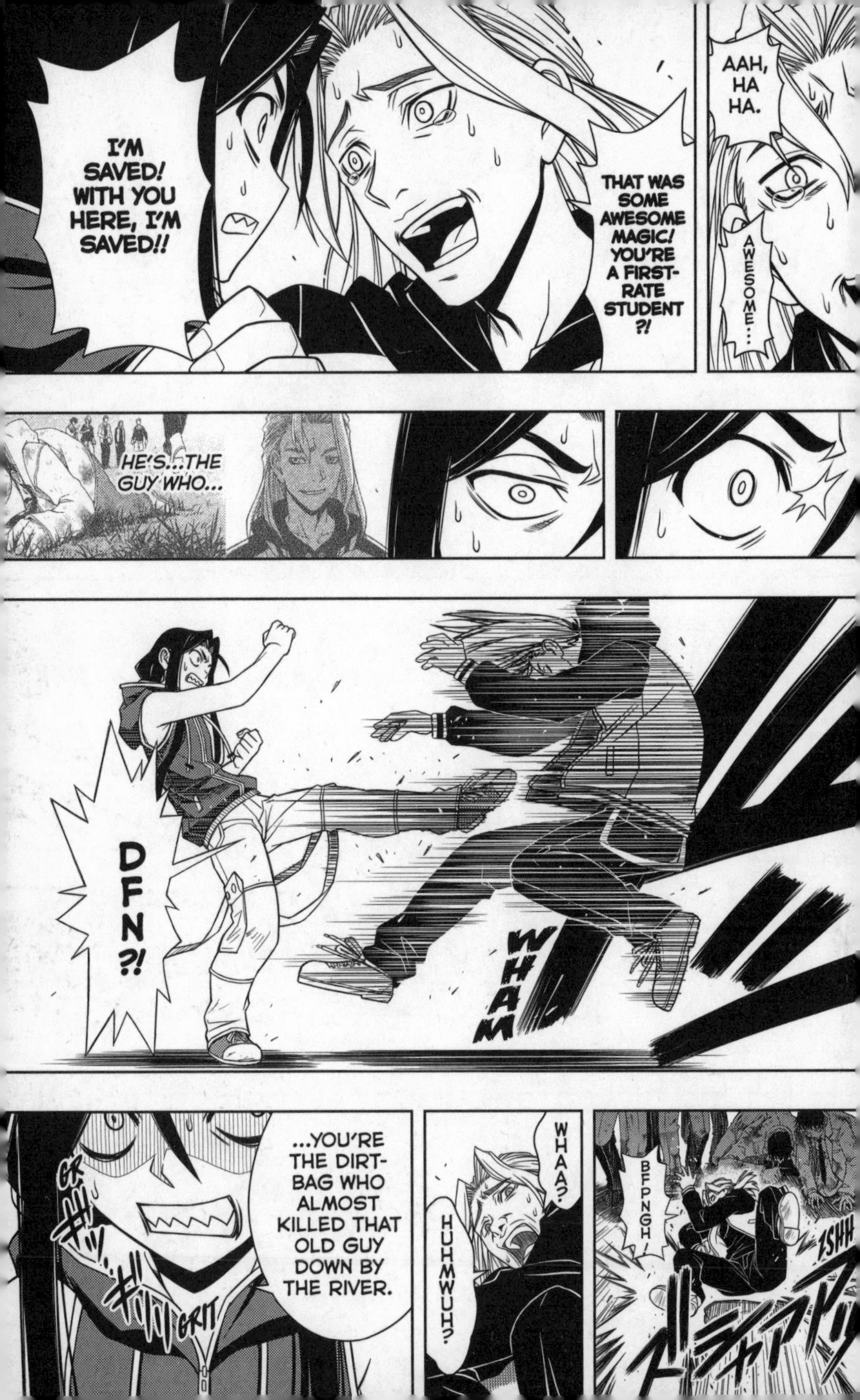
AAH, HA HA.
AWESOME...
THAT WAS SOME AWESOME MAGIC! YOU'RE A FIRST-RATE STUDENT?!
I'M SAVED! WITH YOU HERE, I'M SAVED!!
HE'S...THE GUY WHO...
DFN?!
WHAM
BFPNGH!
ISHH
WHAA?
HUHMWUH?
...YOU'RE THE DIRT-BAG WHO ALMOST KILLED THAT OLD GUY DOWN BY THE RIVER.
GR
GRIT

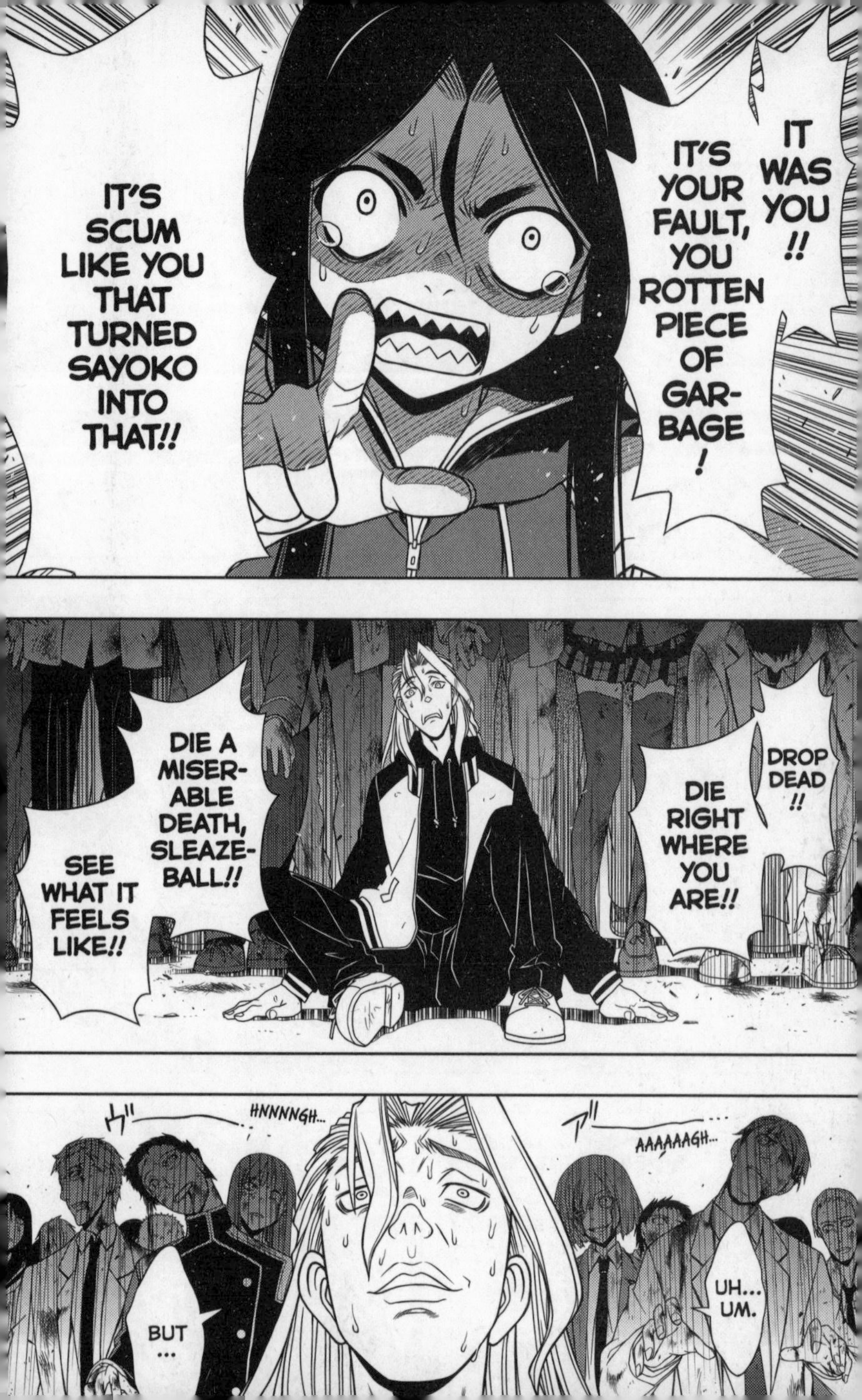
IT WAS YOU!!
IT'S YOUR FAULT, YOU ROTTEN PIECE OF GAR-BAGE!
IT'S SCUM LIKE YOU THAT TURNED SAYOKO INTO THAT!!
DROP DEAD!!
DIE RIGHT WHERE YOU ARE!!
DIE A MISER-ABLE DEATH, SLEAZE-BALL!!
SEE WHAT IT FEELS LIKE!!
AAAAAAGH...
UH... UM.
HNNNNGH...
BUT...

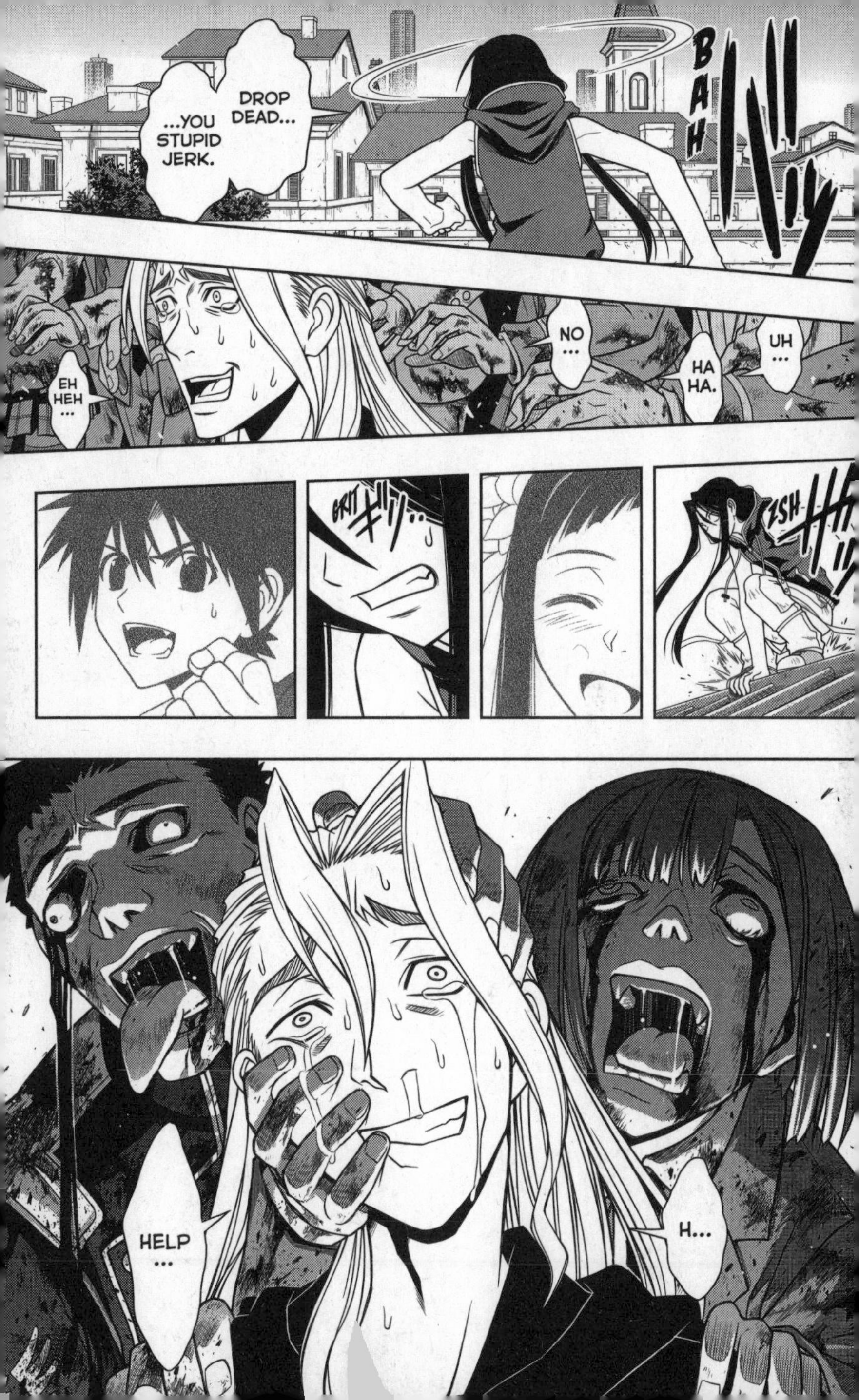
BAH
DROP DEAD...
...YOU STUPID JERK.
UH ...
HA HA.
NO ...
EH HEH ...
ZSH
GRIT
H...
HELP ...

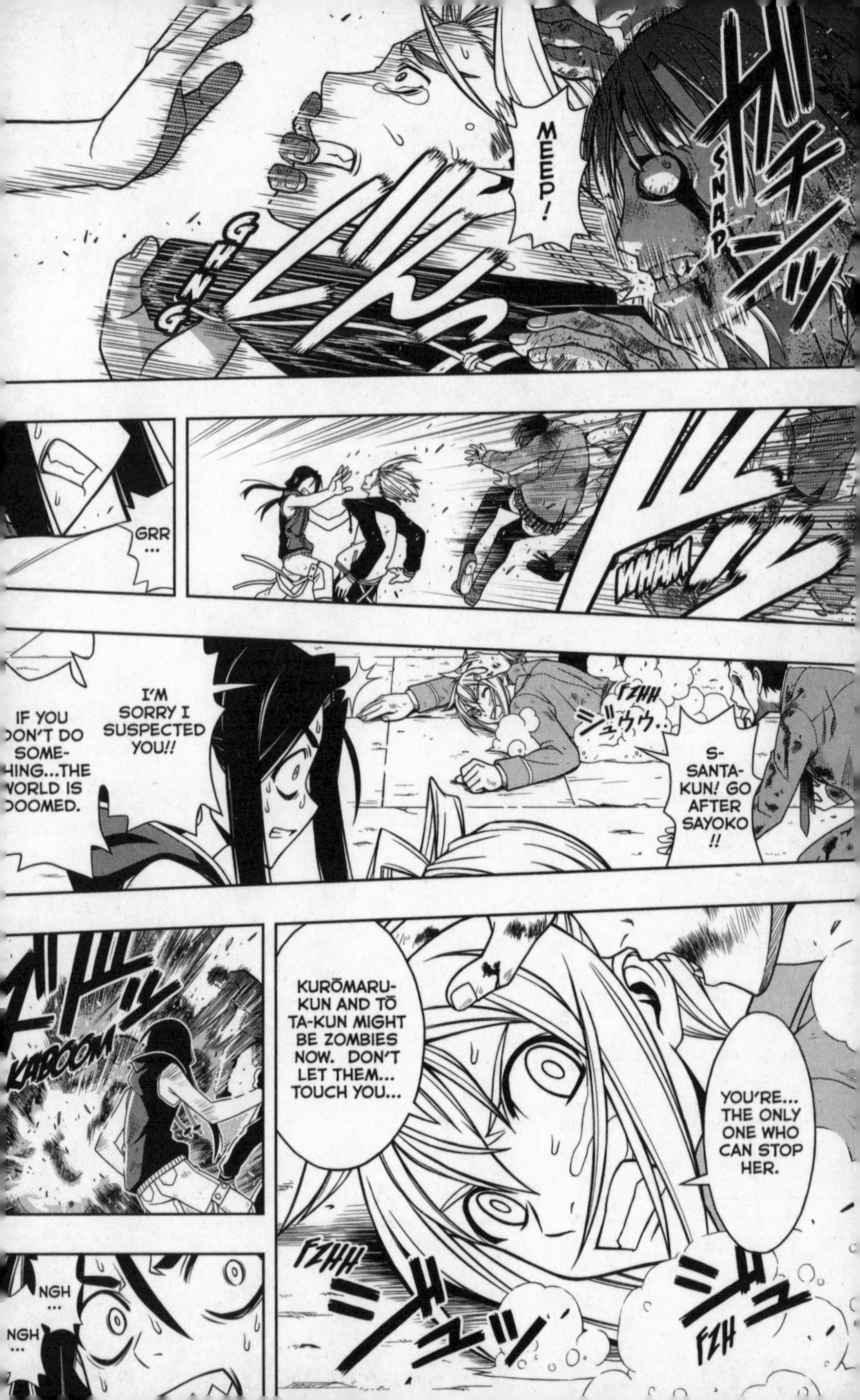
SNAP
MEEP!
GHNG
WHAM
GRR...
S-SANTA-KUN! GO AFTER SAYOKO!!
FZHH
I'M SORRY I SUSPECTED YOU!!
IF YOU ON'T DO SOME-HING...THE ORLD IS OOMED.
YOU'RE... THE ONLY ONE WHO CAN STOP HER.
KURŌMARU-KUN AND TŌTA-KUN MIGHT BE ZOMBIES NOW. DON'T LET THEM... TOUCH YOU...
FZHH
FZH
KABOOM
NGH... NGH...

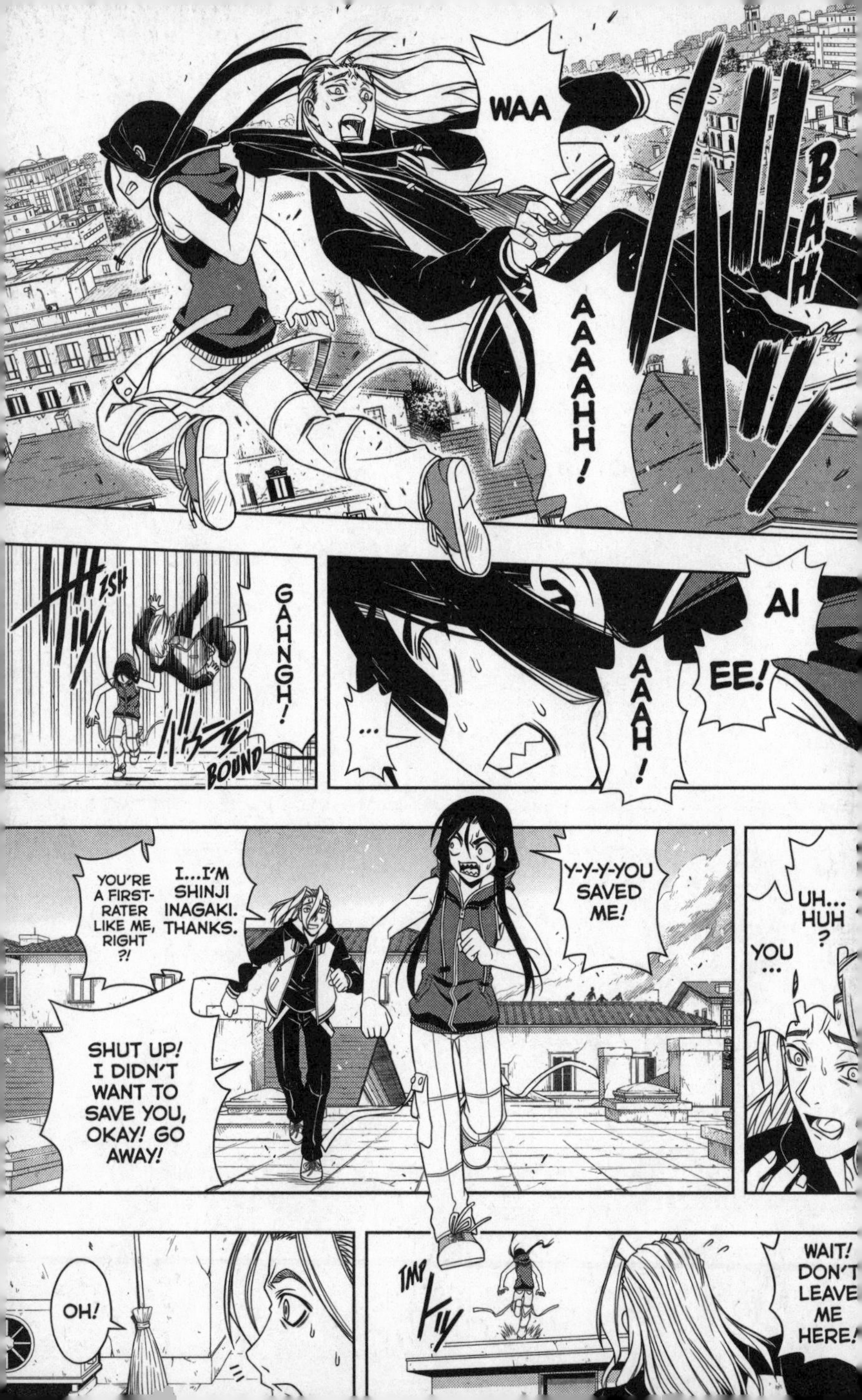
WAA
AAAAAHH!
BAH
AI
EE!
AAAH!
...
GAHNGH!
ISH
BOUND
UH... HUH?
YOU...
Y-Y-Y-YOU SAVED ME!
I...I'M SHINJI INAGAKI. THANKS.
YOU'RE A FIRST-RATER LIKE ME, RIGHT?!
SHUT UP! I DIDN'T WANT TO SAVE YOU, OKAY! GO AWAY!
WAIT! DON'T LEAVE ME HERE!
TMP
OH!

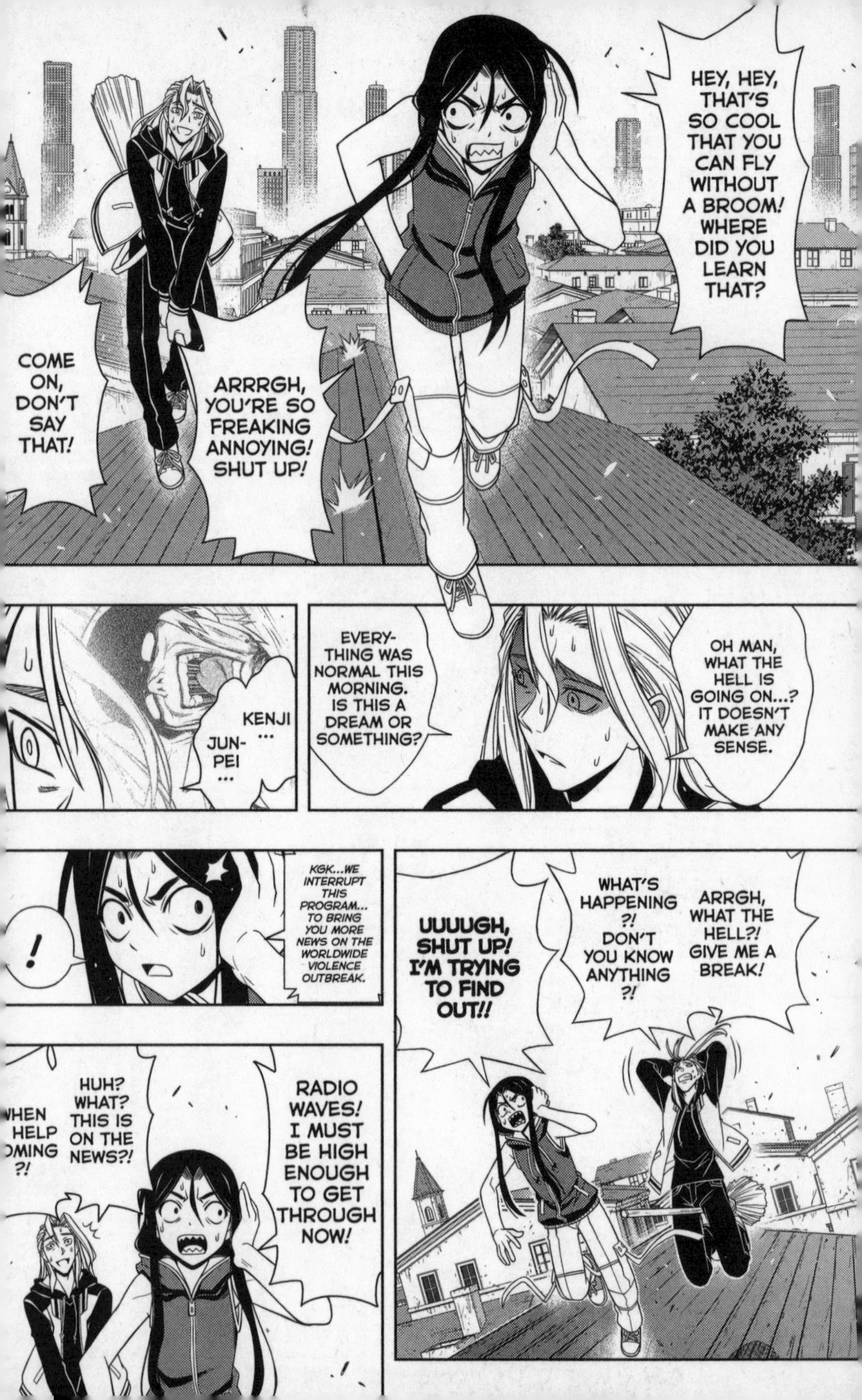
HEY, HEY, THAT'S SO COOL THAT YOU CAN FLY WITHOUT A BROOM! WHERE DID YOU LEARN THAT?
ARRRGH, YOU'RE SO FREAKING ANNOYING! SHUT UP!
COME ON, DON'T SAY THAT!
OH MAN, WHAT THE HELL IS GOING ON...? IT DOESN'T MAKE ANY SENSE.
EVERYTHING WAS NORMAL THIS MORNING. IS THIS A DREAM OR SOMETHING?
KENJI ...
JUN-PEI ...
KGK...WE INTERRUPT THIS PROGRAM... TO BRING YOU MORE NEWS ON THE WORLDWIDE VIOLENCE OUTBREAK.
!
RADIO WAVES! I MUST BE HIGH ENOUGH TO GET THROUGH NOW!
HUH? WHAT? THIS IS ON THE NEWS?!
ARRGH, WHAT THE HELL?! GIVE ME A BREAK!
WHAT'S HAPPENING?! DON'T YOU KNOW ANYTHING?!
UUUUGH, SHUT UP! I'M TRYING TO FIND OUT!!

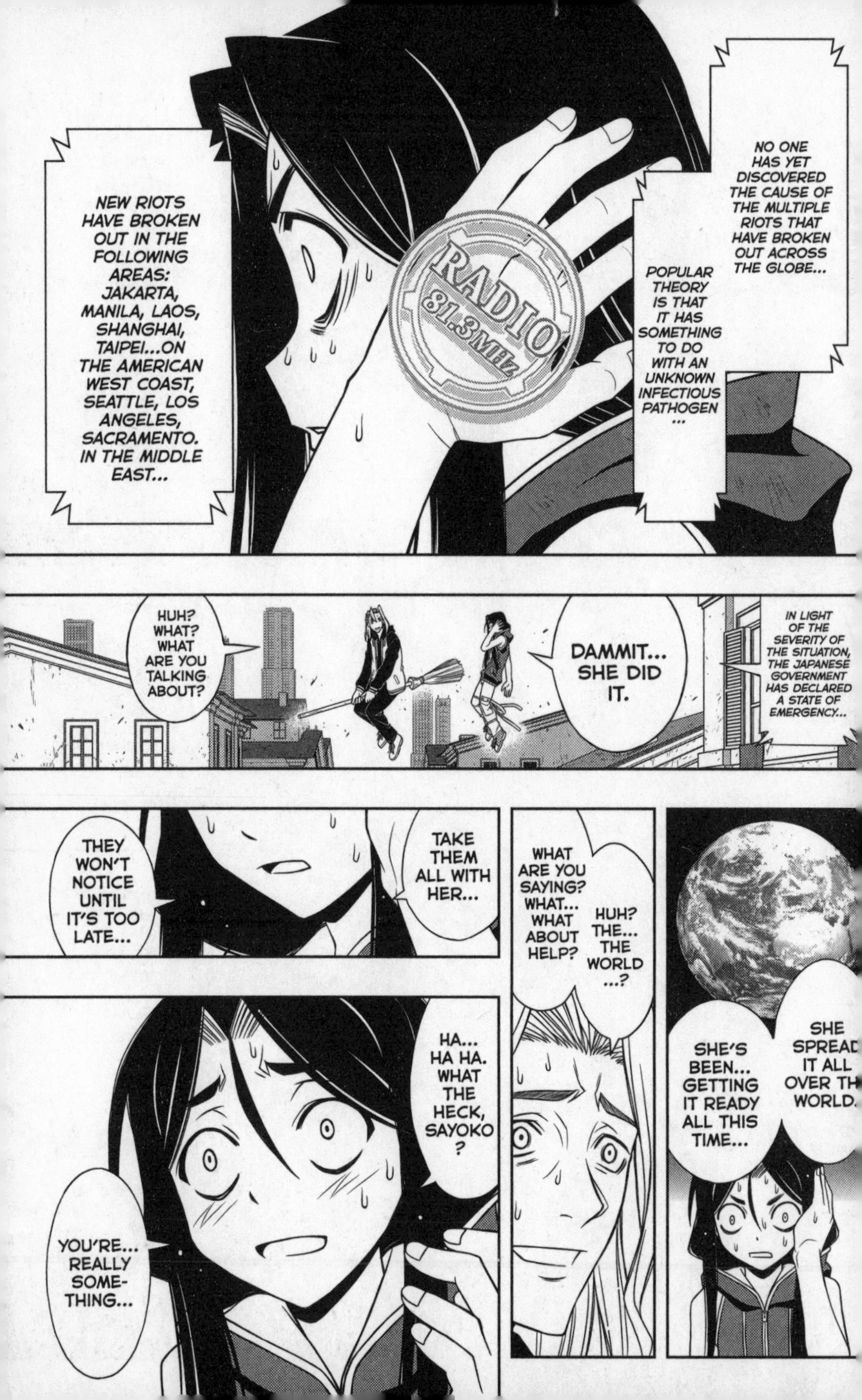
NO ONE HAS YET DISCOVERED THE CAUSE OF THE MULTIPLE RIOTS THAT HAVE BROKEN OUT ACROSS THE GLOBE...
POPULAR THEORY IS THAT IT HAS SOMETHING TO DO WITH AN UNKNOWN INFECTIOUS PATHOGEN...
RADIO 81.3 MHz
NEW RIOTS HAVE BROKEN OUT IN THE FOLLOWING AREAS: JAKARTA, MANILA, LAOS, SHANGHAI, TAIPEI...ON THE AMERICAN WEST COAST, SEATTLE, LOS ANGELES, SACRAMENTO. IN THE MIDDLE EAST...
IN LIGHT OF THE SEVERITY OF THE SITUATION, THE JAPANESE GOVERNMENT HAS DECLARED A STATE OF EMERGENCY...
DAMMIT... SHE DID IT.
HUH? WHAT? WHAT ARE YOU TALKING ABOUT?
SHE SPREAD IT ALL OVER TH WORLD.
SHE'S BEEN... GETTING IT READY ALL THIS TIME...
HUH? THE... THE WORLD ...?
WHAT ARE YOU SAYING? WHAT... WHAT ABOUT HELP?
TAKE THEM ALL WITH HER...
THEY WON'T NOTICE UNTIL IT'S TOO LATE...
HA... HA HA. WHAT THE HECK, SAYOKO?
YOU'RE... REALLY SOME-THING...

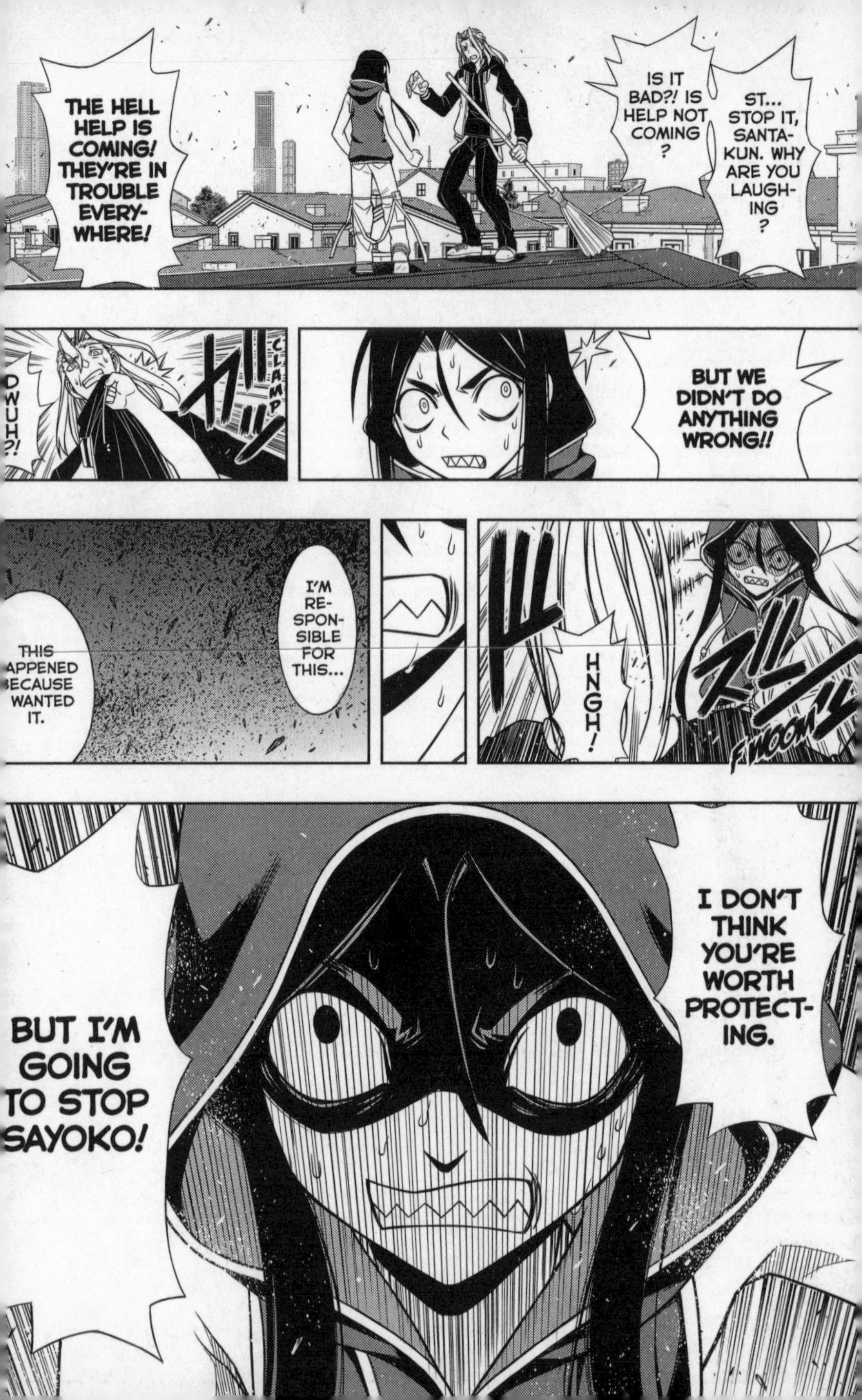
ST... STOP IT, SANTA-KUN. WHY ARE YOU LAUGHING?
IS IT BAD?! IS HELP NOT COMING?
THE HELL HELP IS COMING! THEY'RE IN TROUBLE EVERYWHERE!
BUT WE DIDN'T DO ANYTHING WRONG!!
CLAMP
DWUH?!
FWOOM
HNGH!
I'M RESPONSIBLE FOR THIS...
THIS APPENED ECAUSE WANTED IT.
I DON'T THINK YOU'RE WORTH PROTECTING.
BUT I'M GOING TO STOP SAYOKO!

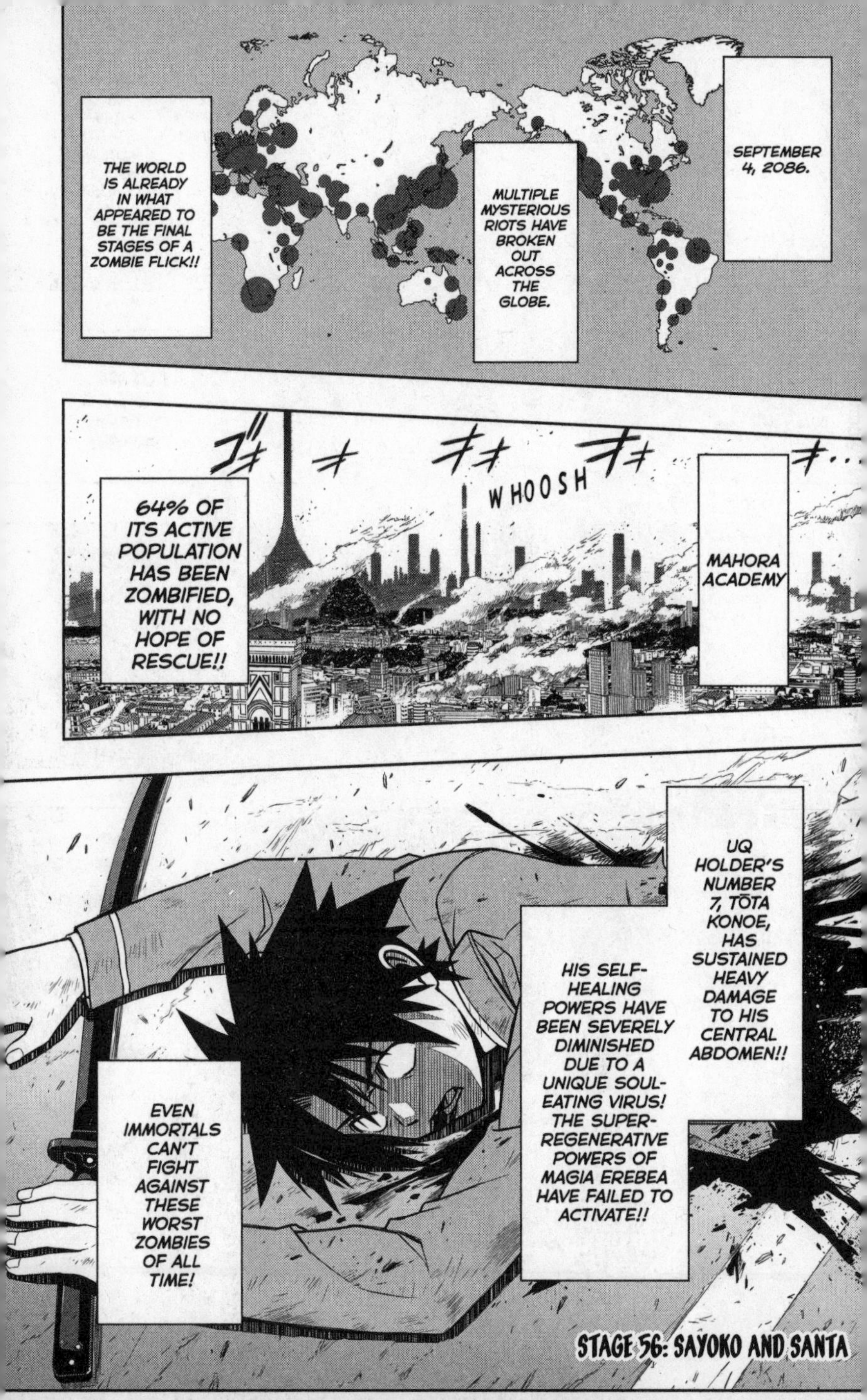
SEPTEMBER 4, 2086.
MULTIPLE MYSTERIOUS RIOTS HAVE BROKEN OUT ACROSS THE GLOBE.
THE WORLD IS ALREADY IN WHAT APPEARED TO BE THE FINAL STAGES OF A ZOMBIE FLICK!!
MAHORA ACADEMY
WHOOSH
64% OF ITS ACTIVE POPULATION HAS BEEN ZOMBIFIED, WITH NO HOPE OF RESCUE!!
UQ HOLDER'S NUMBER 7, TŌTA KONOE, HAS SUSTAINED HEAVY DAMAGE TO HIS CENTRAL ABDOMEN!!
HIS SELF-HEALING POWERS HAVE BEEN SEVERELY DIMINISHED DUE TO A UNIQUE SOUL-EATING VIRUS! THE SUPER-REGENERATIVE POWERS OF MAGIA EREBEA HAVE FAILED TO ACTIVATE!!
EVEN IMMORTALS CAN'T FIGHT AGAINST THESE WORST ZOMBIES OF ALL TIME!
STAGE 56: SAYOKO AND SANTA

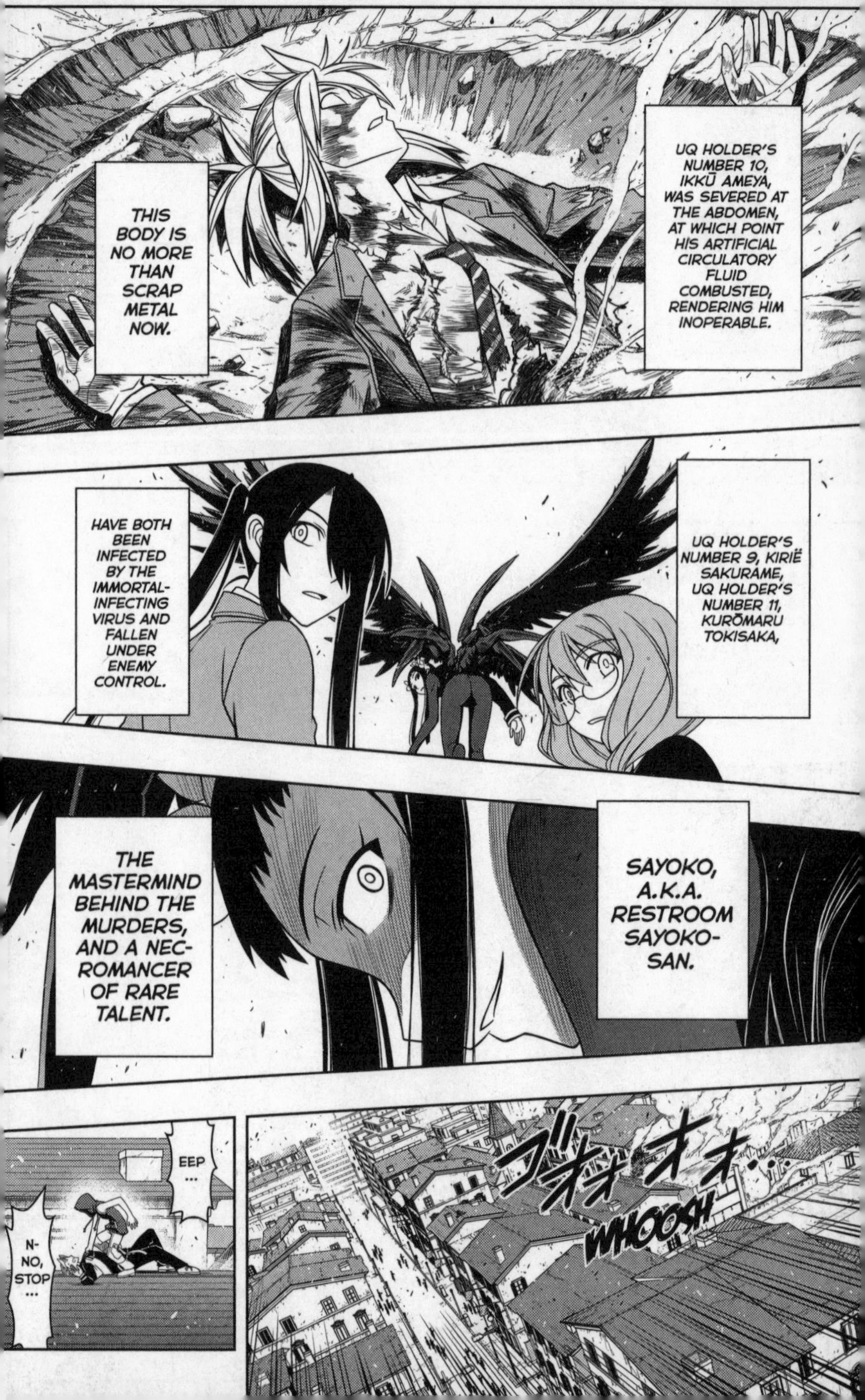
UQ HOLDER'S NUMBER 10, IKKŪ AMEYA, WAS SEVERED AT THE ABDOMEN, AT WHICH POINT HIS ARTIFICIAL CIRCULATORY FLUID COMBUSTED, RENDERING HIM INOPERABLE.
THIS BODY IS NO MORE THAN SCRAP METAL NOW.
UQ HOLDER'S NUMBER 9, KIRIË SAKURAME, UQ HOLDER'S NUMBER 11, KURŌMARU TOKISAKA,
HAVE BOTH BEEN INFECTED BY THE IMMORTAL-INFECTING VIRUS AND FALLEN UNDER ENEMY CONTROL.
SAYOKO, A.K.A. RESTROOM SAYOKO-SAN.
THE MASTERMIND BEHIND THE MURDERS, AND A NECROMANCER OF RARE TALENT.
ゴオオオオ…
WHOOSH
EEP...
N-NO, STOP...

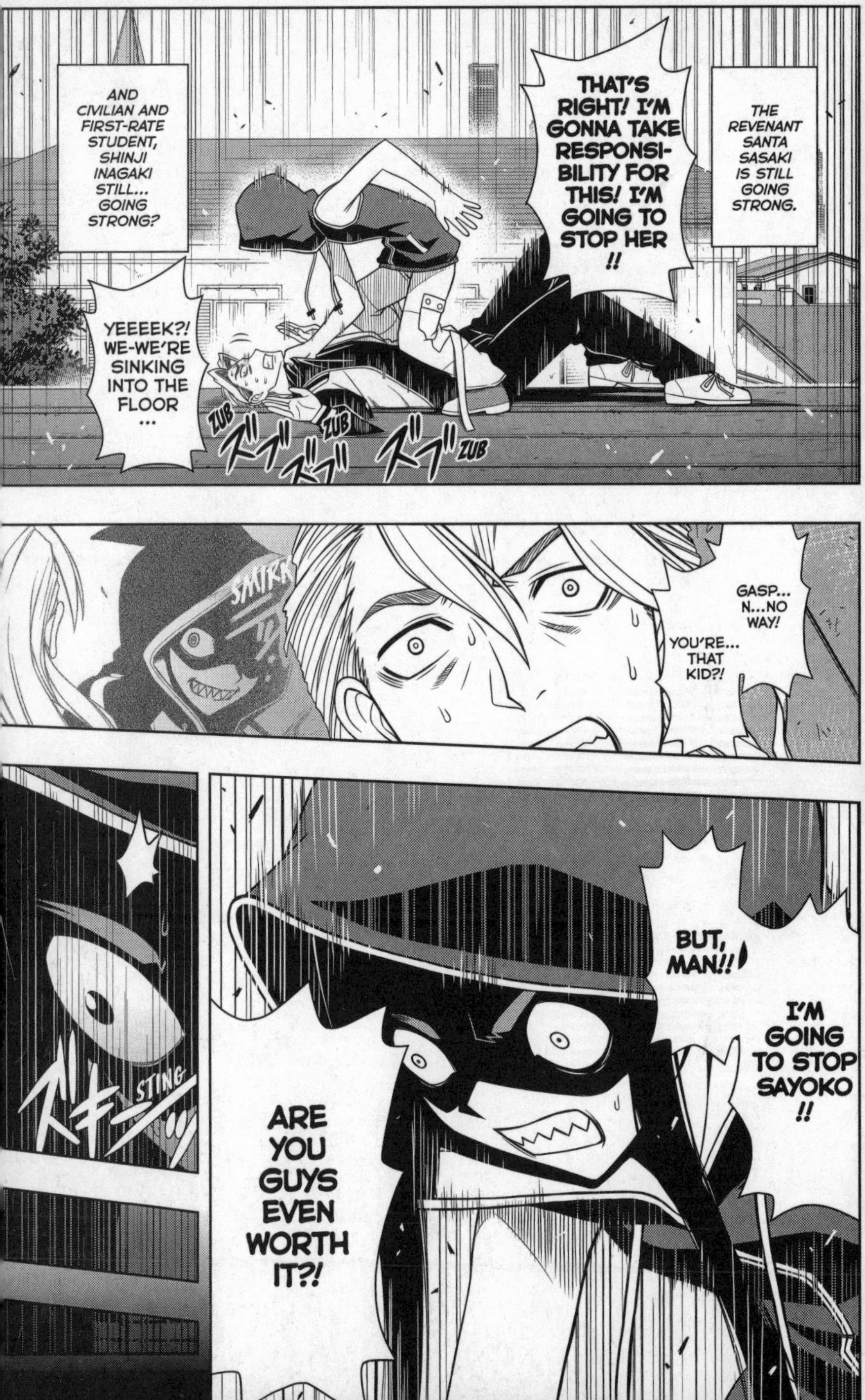
THE REVENANT SANTA SASAKI IS STILL GOING STRONG.
THAT'S RIGHT! I'M GONNA TAKE RESPONSIBILITY FOR THIS! I'M GOING TO STOP HER!!
AND CIVILIAN AND FIRST-RATE STUDENT, SHINJI INAGAKI STILL... GOING STRONG?
YEEEEK?! WE-WE'RE SINKING INTO THE FLOOR...
ZUB ZUB ZUB
GASP... N...NO WAY!
YOU'RE... THAT KID?!
SMIRK
BUT, MAN!!
I'M GOING TO STOP SAYOKO!!
ARE YOU GUYS EVEN WORTH IT?!
STING

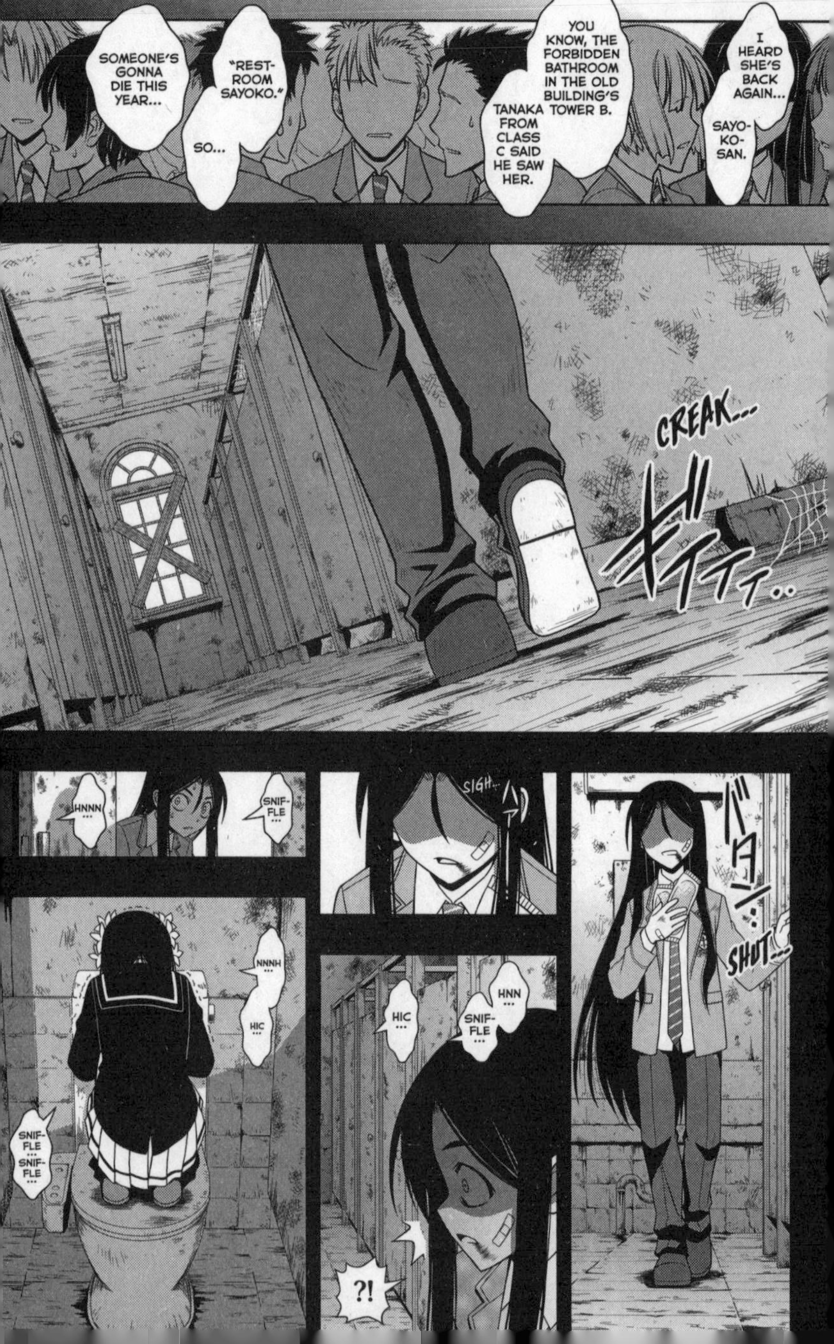

I HEARD SHE'S BACK AGAIN...
SAYO-KO-SAN.
YOU KNOW, THE FORBIDDEN BATHROOM IN THE OLD BUILDING'S TOWER B.
TANAKA FROM CLASS C SAID HE SAW HER.
"REST-ROOM SAYOKO."
SO...
SOMEONE'S GONNA DIE THIS YEAR...
CREAK...
SHUT...
SIGH...
HNN...
SNIF-FLE...
HIC...
?!
SNIF-FLE...
HNNN...
NNNH...
HIC...
SNIF-FLE... SNIF-FLE...

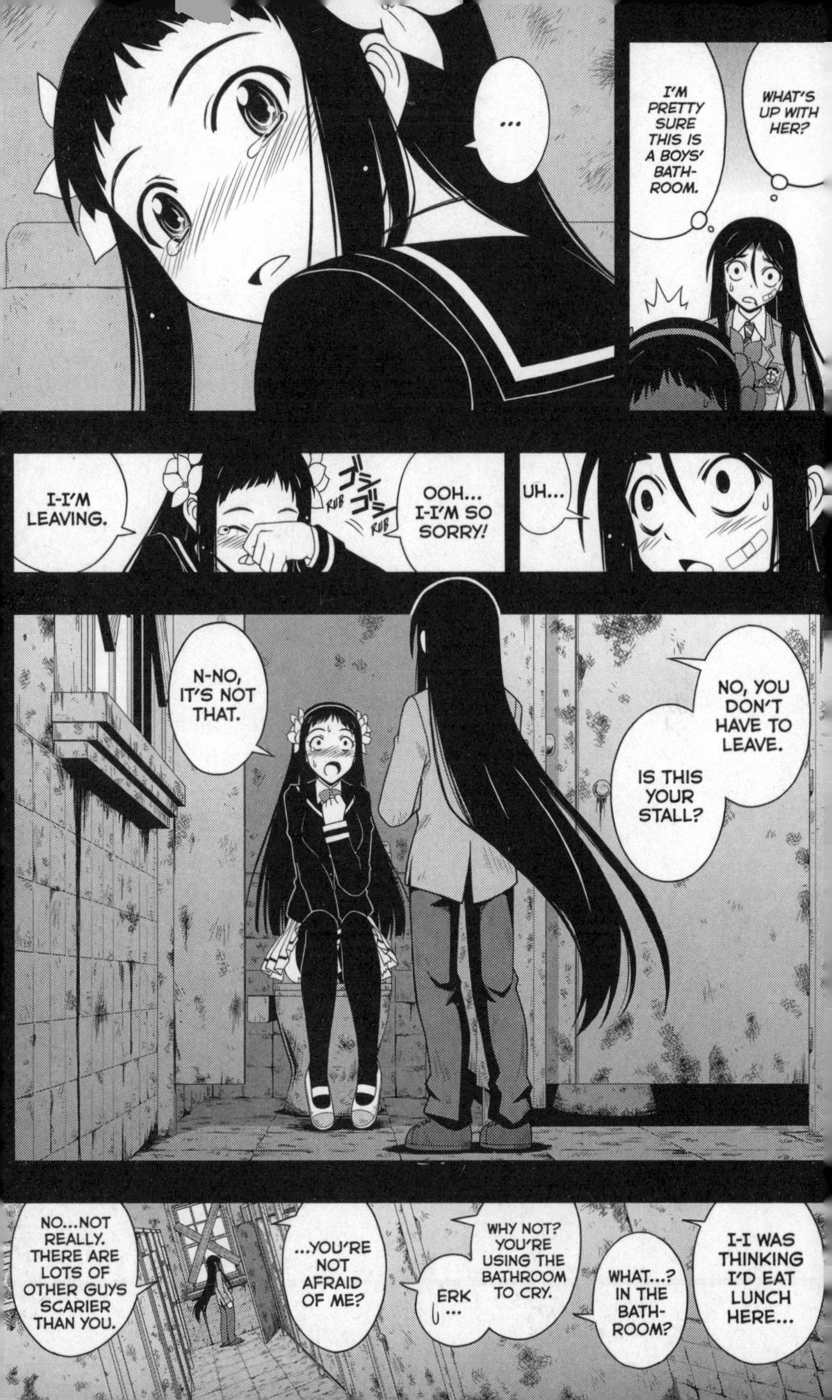
WHAT'S UP WITH HER?
I'M PRETTY SURE THIS IS A BOYS' BATHROOM.
...
UH...
ゴシゴシ RUB RUB
OOH... I-I'M SO SORRY!
I-I'M LEAVING.
NO, YOU DON'T HAVE TO LEAVE.
IS THIS YOUR STALL?
N-NO, IT'S NOT THAT.
I-I WAS THINKING I'D EAT LUNCH HERE...
WHAT...? IN THE BATHROOM?
WHY NOT? YOU'RE USING THE BATHROOM TO CRY.
ERK...
...YOU'RE NOT AFRAID OF ME?
NO...NOT REALLY. THERE ARE LOTS OF OTHER GUYS SCARIER THAN YOU.

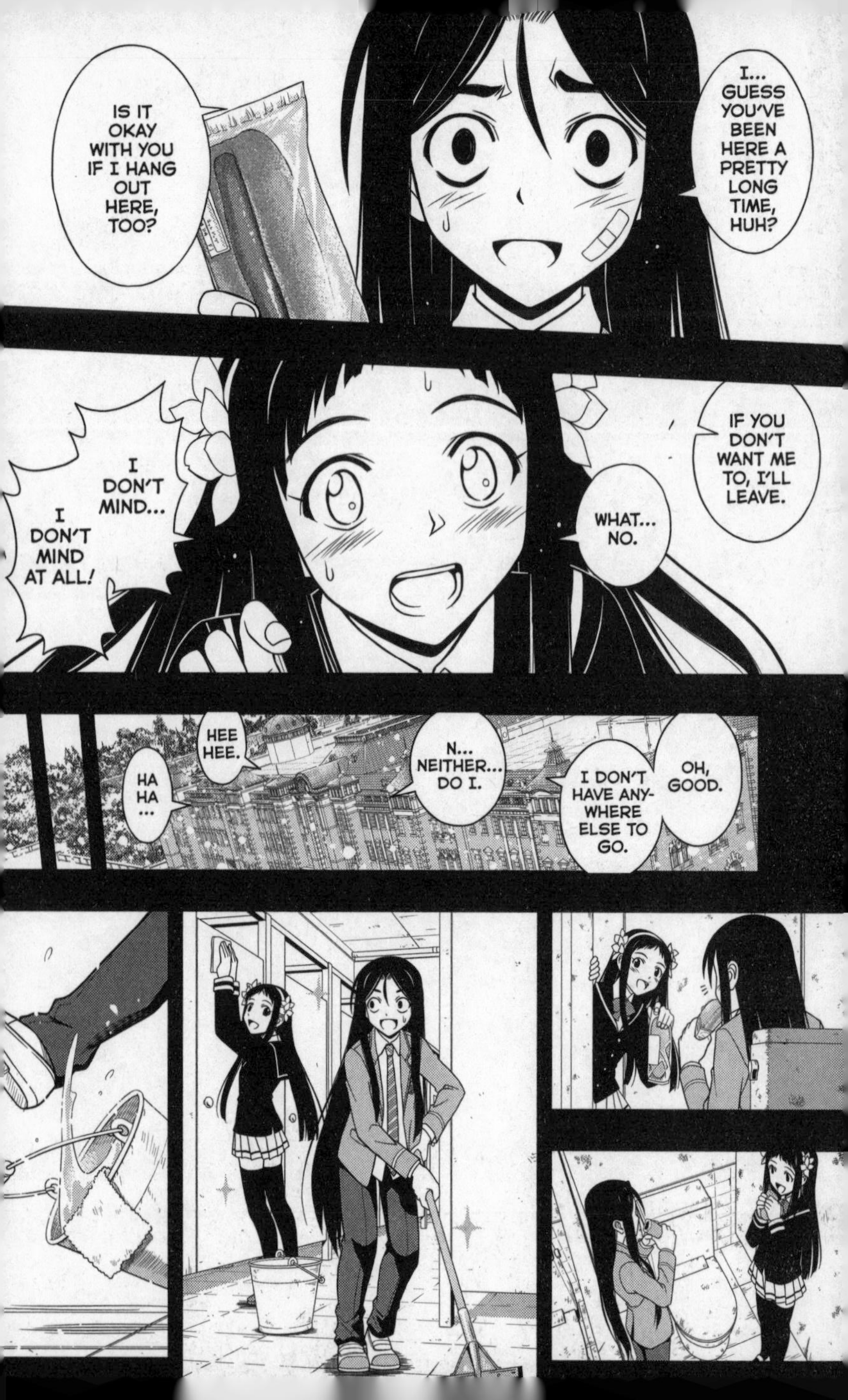
I... GUESS YOU'VE BEEN HERE A PRETTY LONG TIME, HUH?
IS IT OKAY WITH YOU IF I HANG OUT HERE, TOO?
IF YOU DON'T WANT ME TO, I'LL LEAVE.
WHAT... NO.
I DON'T MIND...
I DON'T MIND AT ALL!
OH, GOOD.
I DON'T HAVE ANY-WHERE ELSE TO GO.
N... NEITHER... DO I.
HEE HEE.
HA HA ...

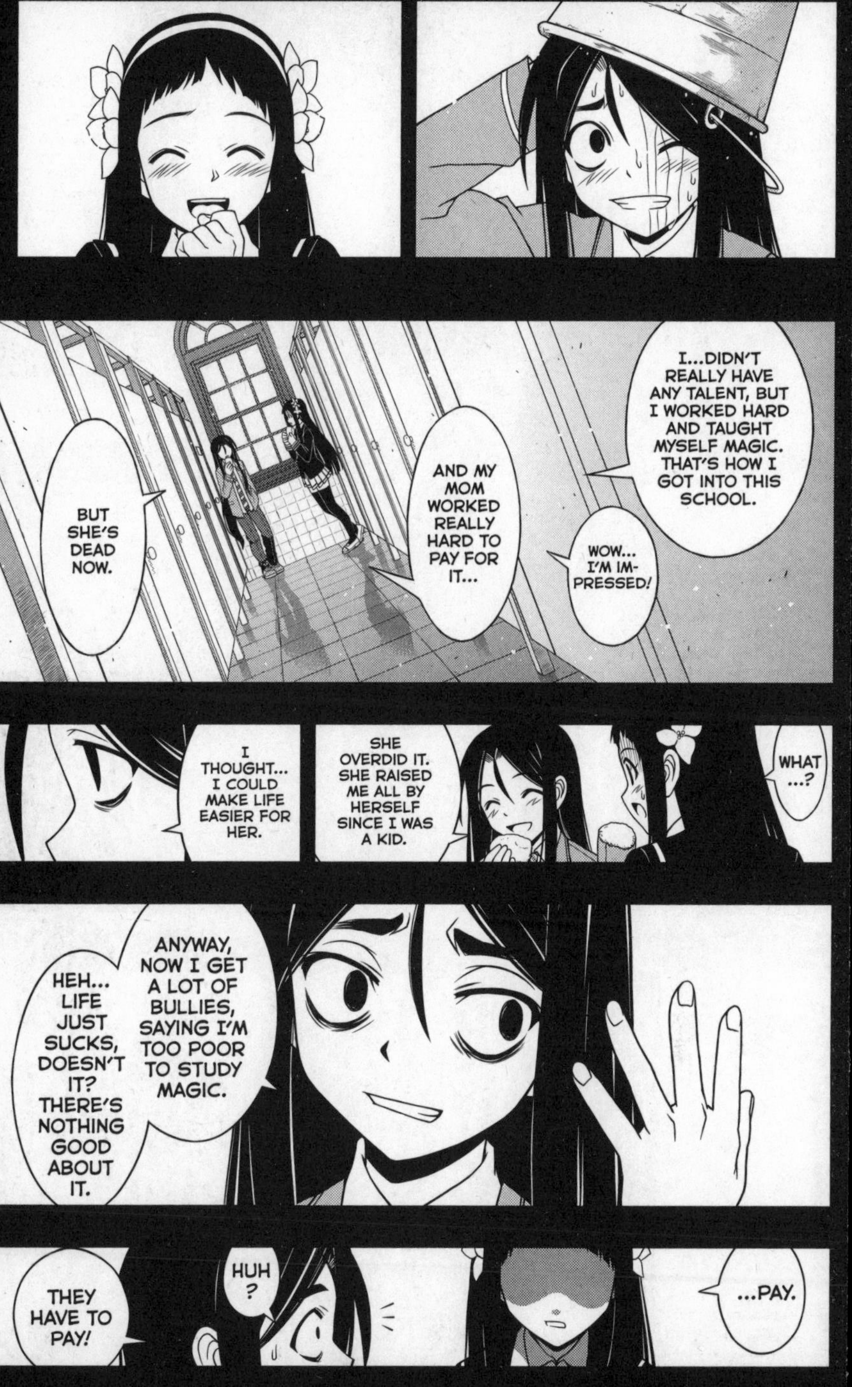
I...DIDN'T REALLY HAVE ANY TALENT, BUT I WORKED HARD AND TAUGHT MYSELF MAGIC. THAT'S HOW I GOT INTO THIS SCHOOL.
WOW... I'M IM-PRESSED!
AND MY MOM WORKED REALLY HARD TO PAY FOR IT...
BUT SHE'S DEAD NOW.
WHAT ...?
SHE OVERDID IT. SHE RAISED ME ALL BY HERSELF SINCE I WAS A KID.
I THOUGHT... I COULD MAKE LIFE EASIER FOR HER.
ANYWAY, NOW I GET A LOT OF BULLIES, SAYING I'M TOO POOR TO STUDY MAGIC.
HEH... LIFE JUST SUCKS, DOESN'T IT? THERE'S NOTHING GOOD ABOUT IT.
...PAY.
HUH?
THEY HAVE TO PAY!

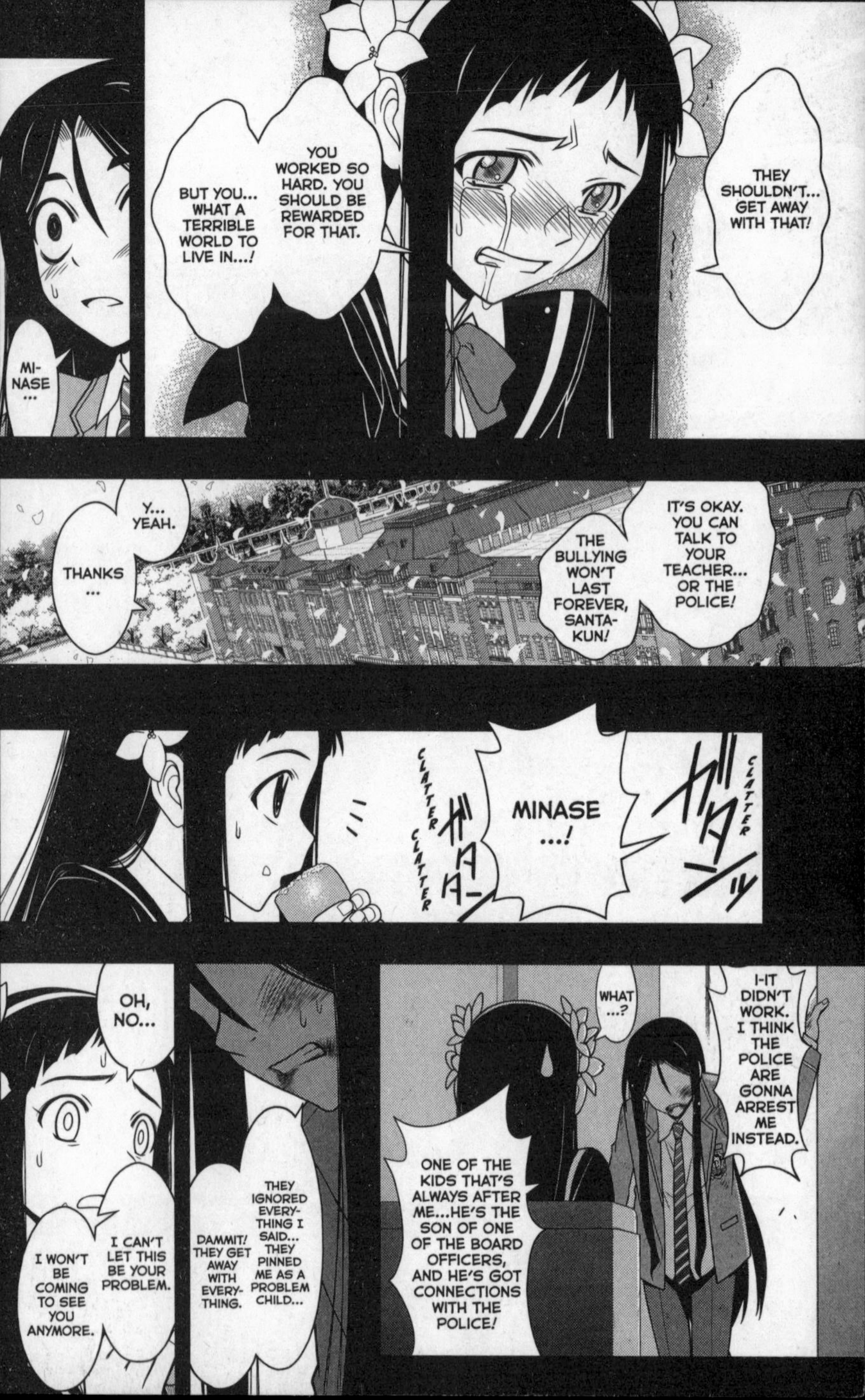
THEY SHOULDN'T... GET AWAY WITH THAT!
YOU WORKED SO HARD. YOU SHOULD BE REWARDED FOR THAT.
BUT YOU... WHAT A TERRIBLE WORLD TO LIVE IN...!
MI-NASE...
IT'S OKAY. YOU CAN TALK TO YOUR TEACHER... OR THE POLICE!
THE BULLYING WON'T LAST FOREVER, SANTA-KUN!
Y... YEAH.
THANKS...
CLATTER
MINASE...!
CLATTER CLATTER
I-IT DIDN'T WORK. I THINK THE POLICE ARE GONNA ARREST ME INSTEAD.
WHAT...?
ONE OF THE KIDS THAT'S ALWAYS AFTER ME...HE'S THE SON OF ONE OF THE BOARD OFFICERS, AND HE'S GOT CONNECTIONS WITH THE POLICE!
THEY IGNORED EVERY-THING I SAID... THEY PINNED ME AS A PROBLEM CHILD...
DAMMIT! THEY GET AWAY WITH EVERY-THING.
OH, NO...
I CAN'T LET THIS BE YOUR PROBLEM.
I WON'T BE COMING TO SEE YOU ANYMORE.

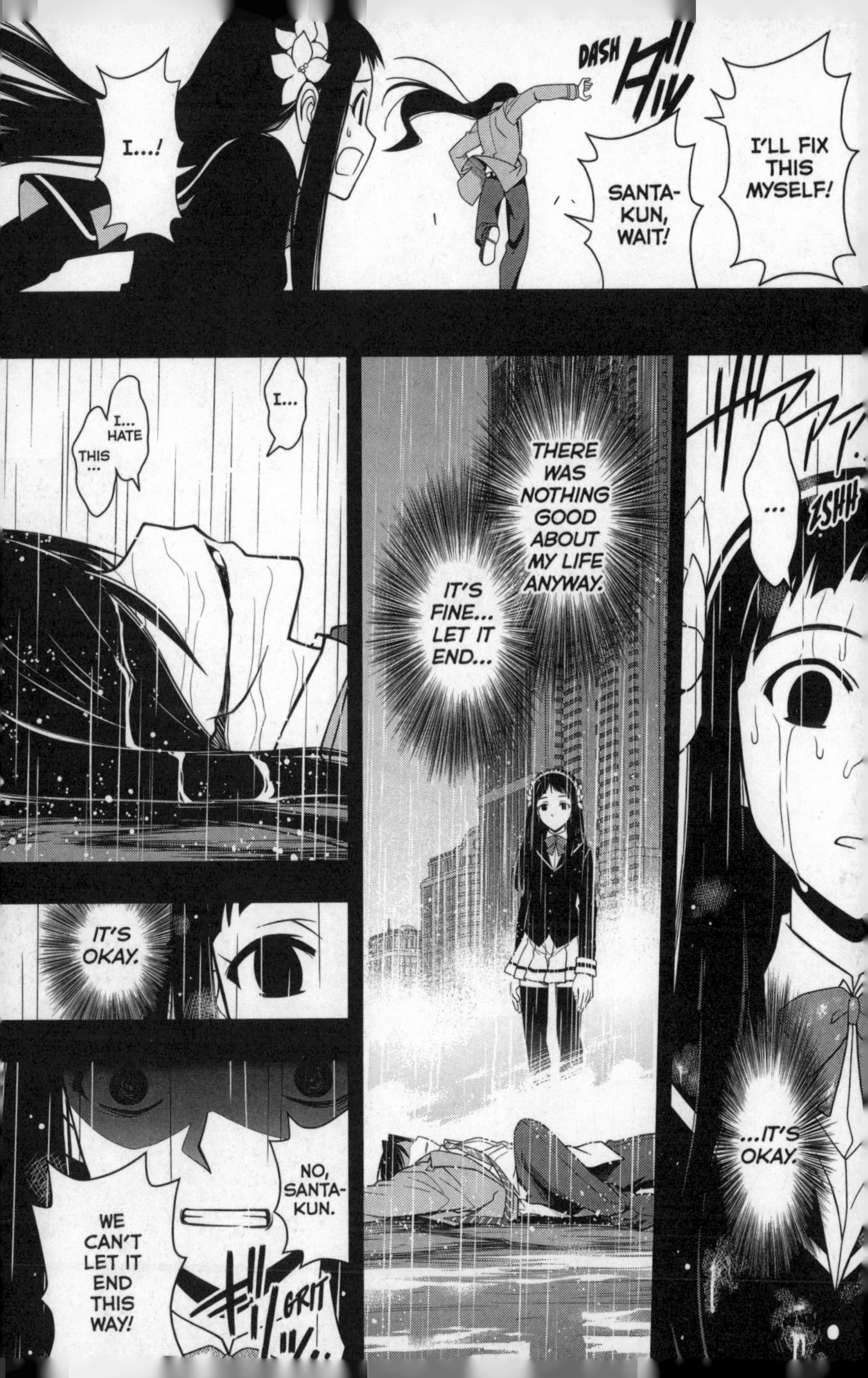
I'LL FIX THIS MYSELF!
DASH
SANTA-KUN, WAIT!
I...!
...
FSHH
...IT'S OKAY.
THERE WAS NOTHING GOOD ABOUT MY LIFE ANYWAY.
IT'S FINE... LET IT END...
I...
I... HATE THIS...
IT'S OKAY.
NO, SANTA-KUN.
WE CAN'T LET IT END THIS WAY!
GRIT

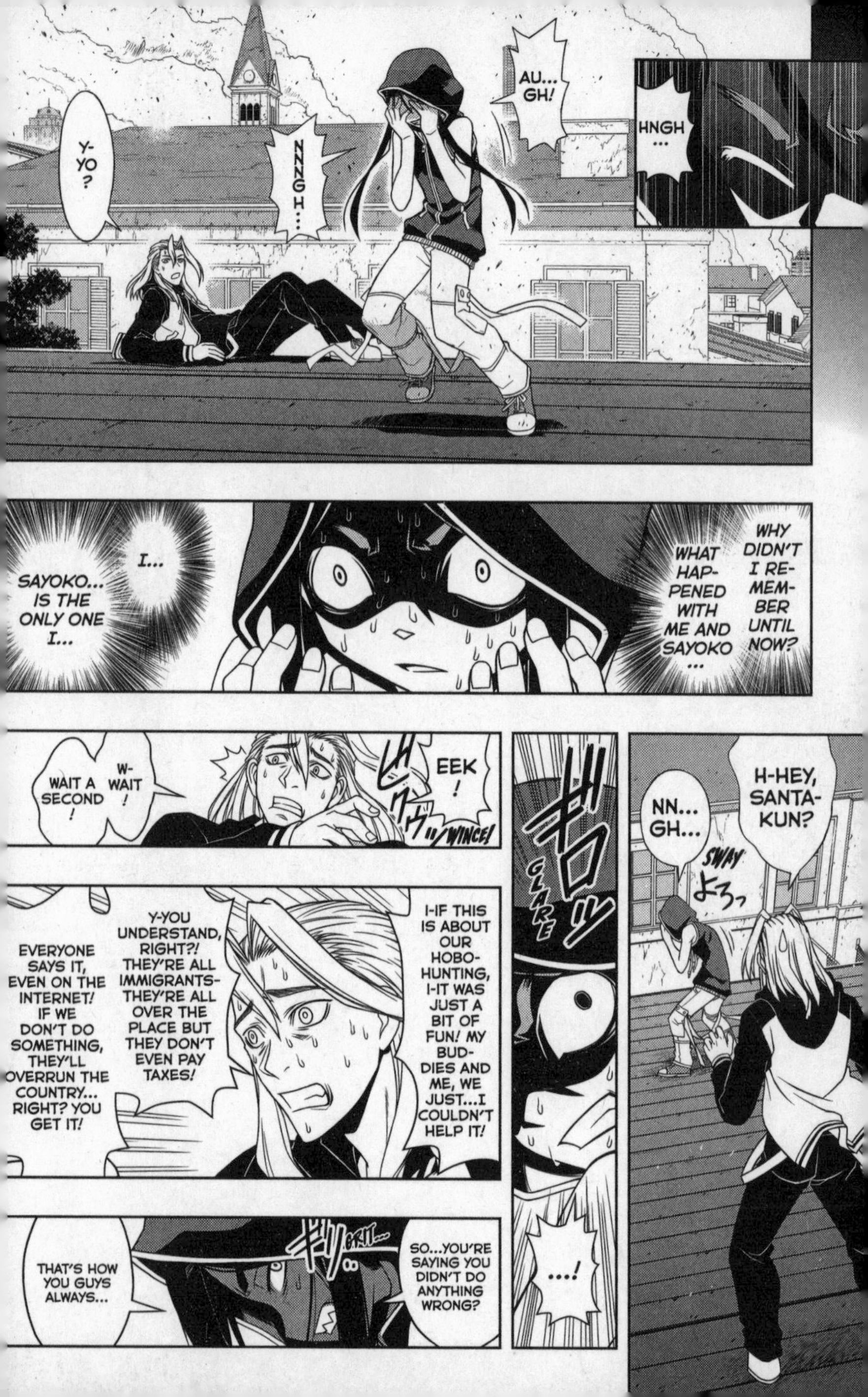
HNGH...
AU...GH!
NNNGH...
Y-YO?
WHY DIDN'T I REMEMBER UNTIL NOW?
WHAT HAPPENED WITH ME AND SAYOKO...
I...
SAYOKO... IS THE ONLY ONE I...
H-HEY, SANTA-KUN?
NN...GH...
SWAY
よろっ
ギロッ
GLARE
...!
EEK!
WINCE!
W-WAIT!
WAIT A SECOND!
I-IF THIS IS ABOUT OUR HOBO-HUNTING, I-IT WAS JUST A BIT OF FUN! MY BUDDIES AND ME, WE JUST...I COULDN'T HELP IT!
Y-YOU UNDERSTAND, RIGHT?! THEY'RE ALL IMMIGRANTS-THEY'RE ALL OVER THE PLACE BUT THEY DON'T EVEN PAY TAXES!
EVERYONE SAYS IT, EVEN ON THE INTERNET! IF WE DON'T DO SOMETHING, THEY'LL OVERRUN THE COUNTRY... RIGHT? YOU GET IT!
SO...YOU'RE SAYING YOU DIDN'T DO ANYTHING WRONG?
GRIT...
THAT'S HOW YOU GUYS ALWAYS...

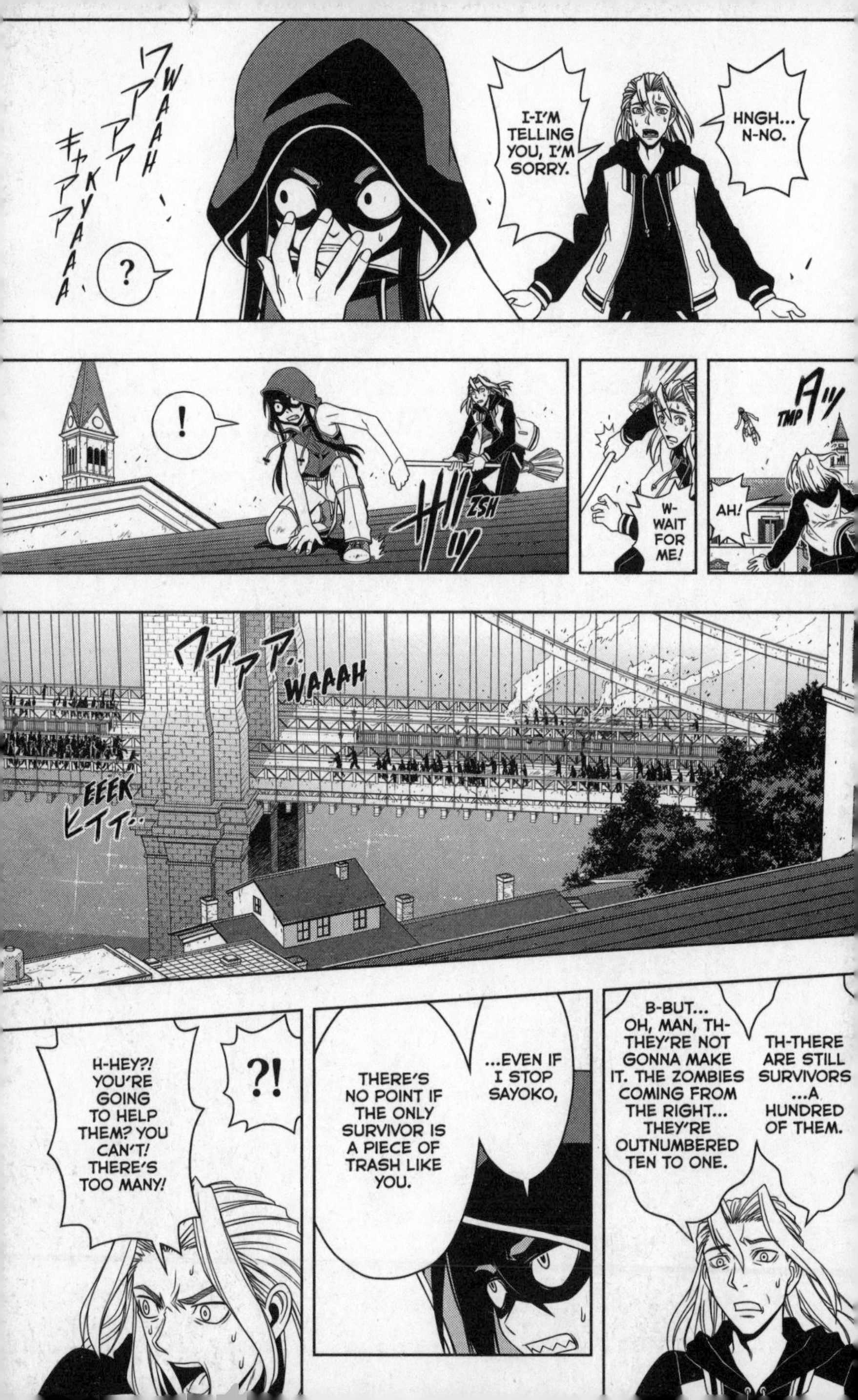
HNGH... N-NO.
I-I'M TELLING YOU, I'M SORRY.
ワアアア WAAAH
キャアア KYAAAA
?
アッ TMP
AH!
W-WAIT FOR ME!
!
ザッ ZSH
ワアア.. WAAAH
EEEK ヒイイ..
TH-THERE ARE STILL SURVIVORS ...A HUNDRED OF THEM.
B-BUT... OH, MAN, TH-THEY'RE NOT GONNA MAKE IT. THE ZOMBIES COMING FROM THE RIGHT... THEY'RE OUTNUMBERED TEN TO ONE.
...EVEN IF I STOP SAYOKO,
THERE'S NO POINT IF THE ONLY SURVIVOR IS A PIECE OF TRASH LIKE YOU.
?!
H-HEY?! YOU'RE GOING TO HELP THEM? YOU CAN'T! THERE'S TOO MANY!

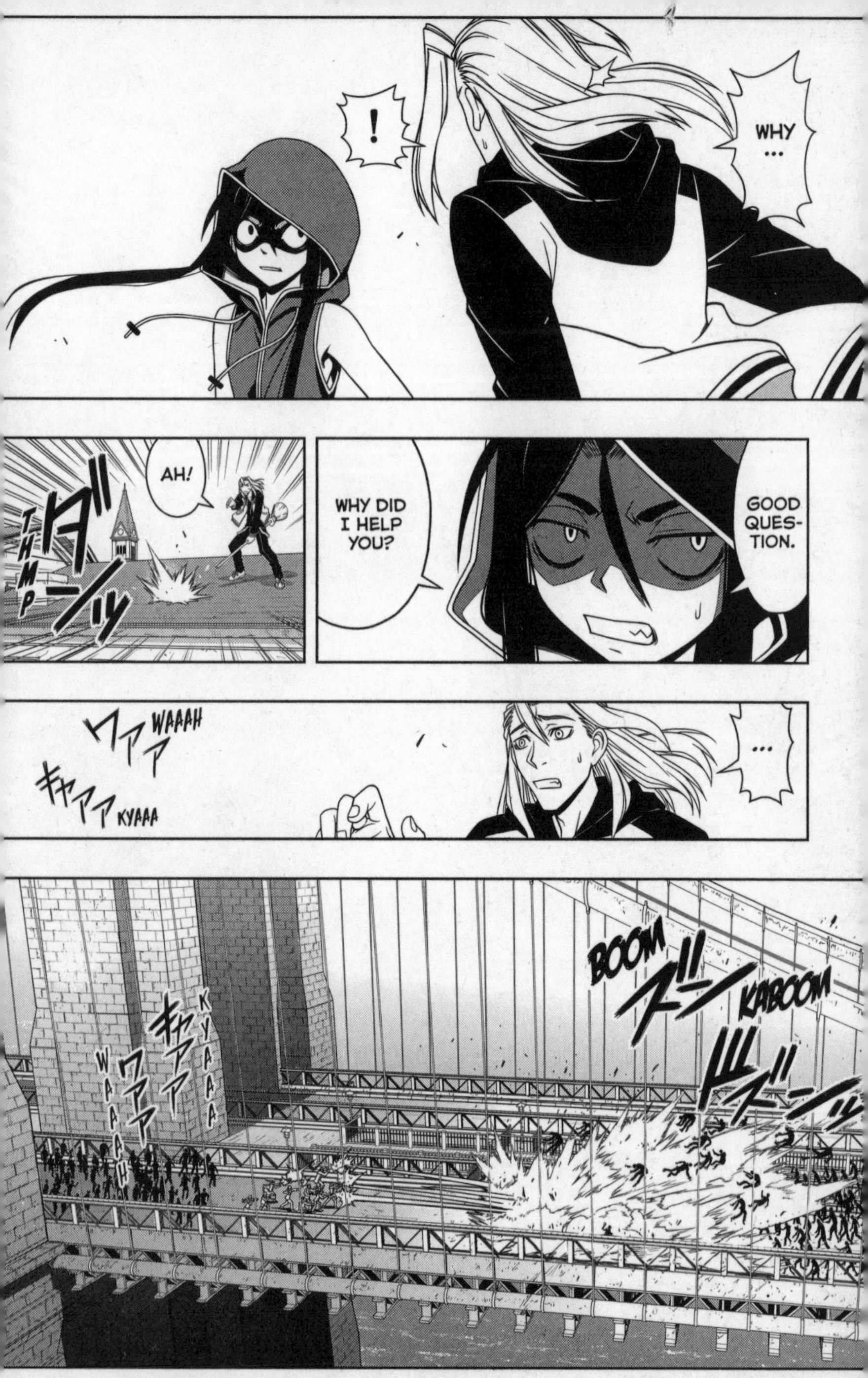

WHY ...
!
GOOD QUES-TION.
WHY DID I HELP YOU?
AH!
THUMP
...
ワァァ WAAAH
キャァァ KYAAA
BOOM
KABOOM
KYAAA
WAAAAH

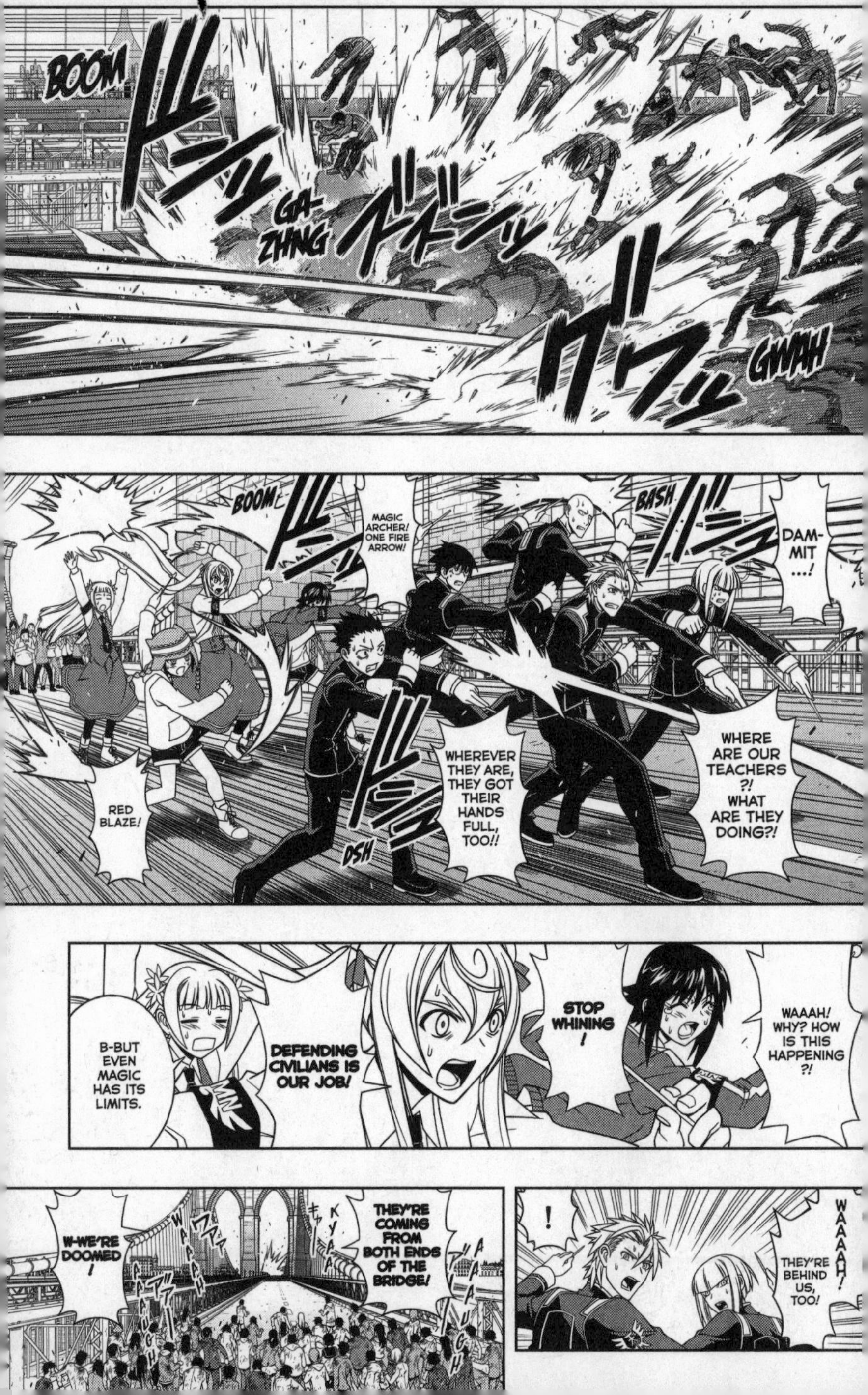
GWAH
GA-ZHNG
BOOM
DAM-MIT ...!
BASH
MAGIC ARCHER! ONE FIRE ARROW!
BOOM
WHERE ARE OUR TEACHERS ?! WHAT ARE THEY DOING?!
WHEREVER THEY ARE, THEY GOT THEIR HANDS FULL, TOO!!
DSH
RED BLAZE!
WAAAH! WHY? HOW IS THIS HAPPENING ?!
STOP WHINING !
DEFENDING CIVILIANS IS OUR JOB!
B-BUT EVEN MAGIC HAS ITS LIMITS.
WAAAAH!
THEY'RE BEHIND US, TOO!
!
AAAAUGH
THEY'RE COMING FROM BOTH ENDS OF THE BRIDGE!
KYAAA
WAAAAH
AAAAUGH
W-WE'RE DOOMED !

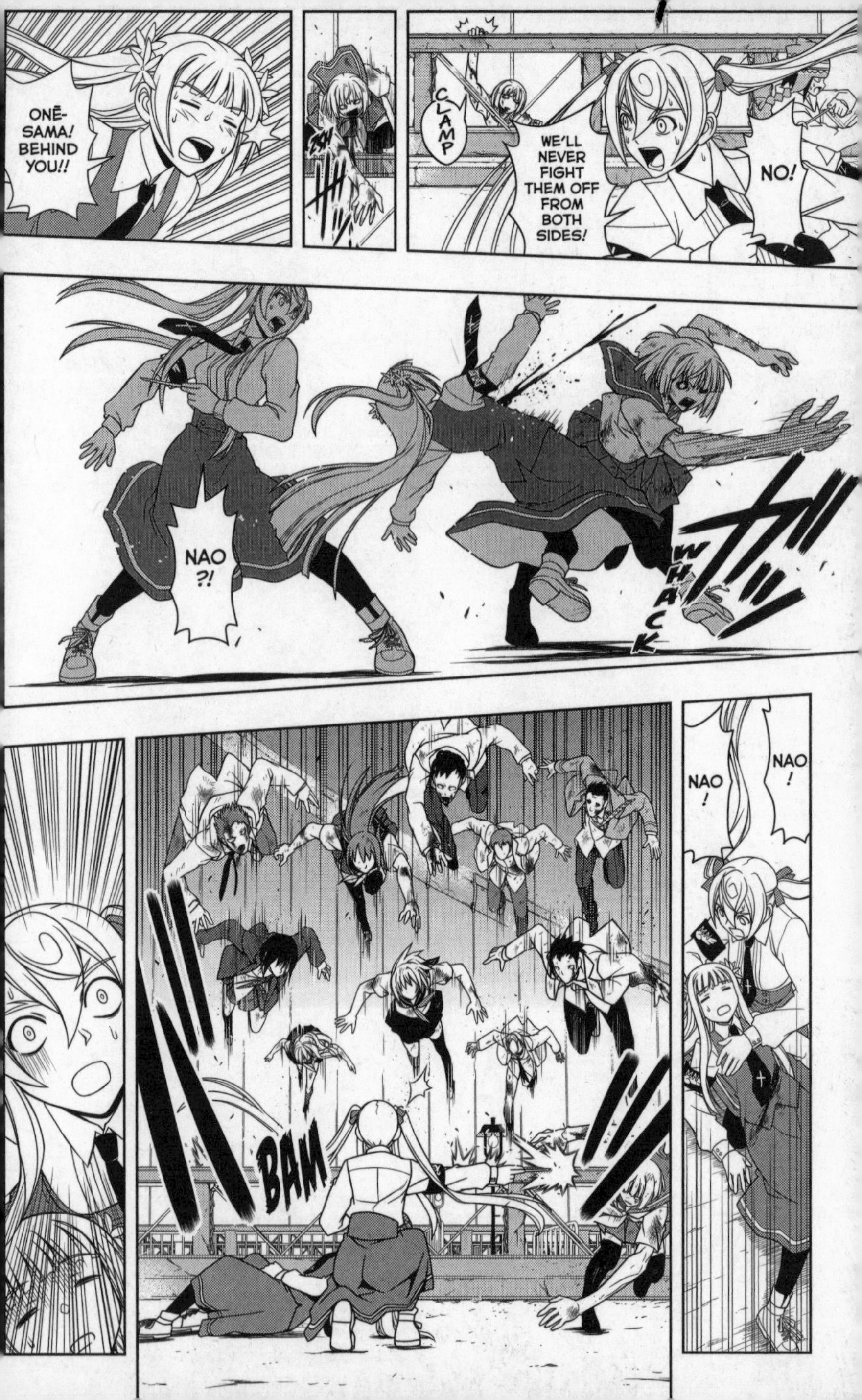
NO!
CLAMP
WE'LL NEVER FIGHT THEM OFF FROM BOTH SIDES!
ZSH
ONĒ-SAMA! BEHIND YOU!!
WHACK
NAO ?!
NAO!
NAO!
BAM

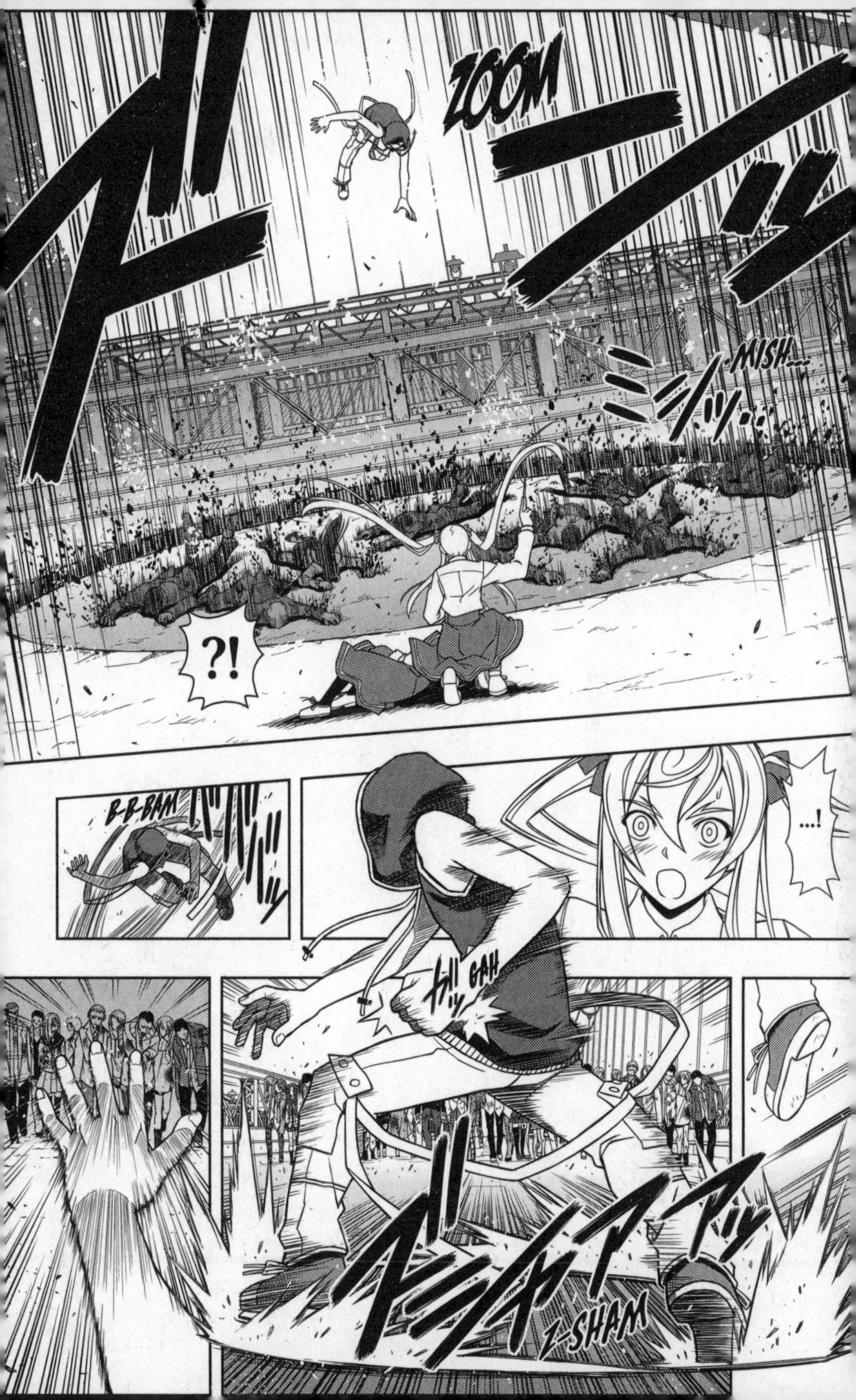
ZOOM
MISH...
?!
...!
B-B-BAM
GAH
Z-SHAM

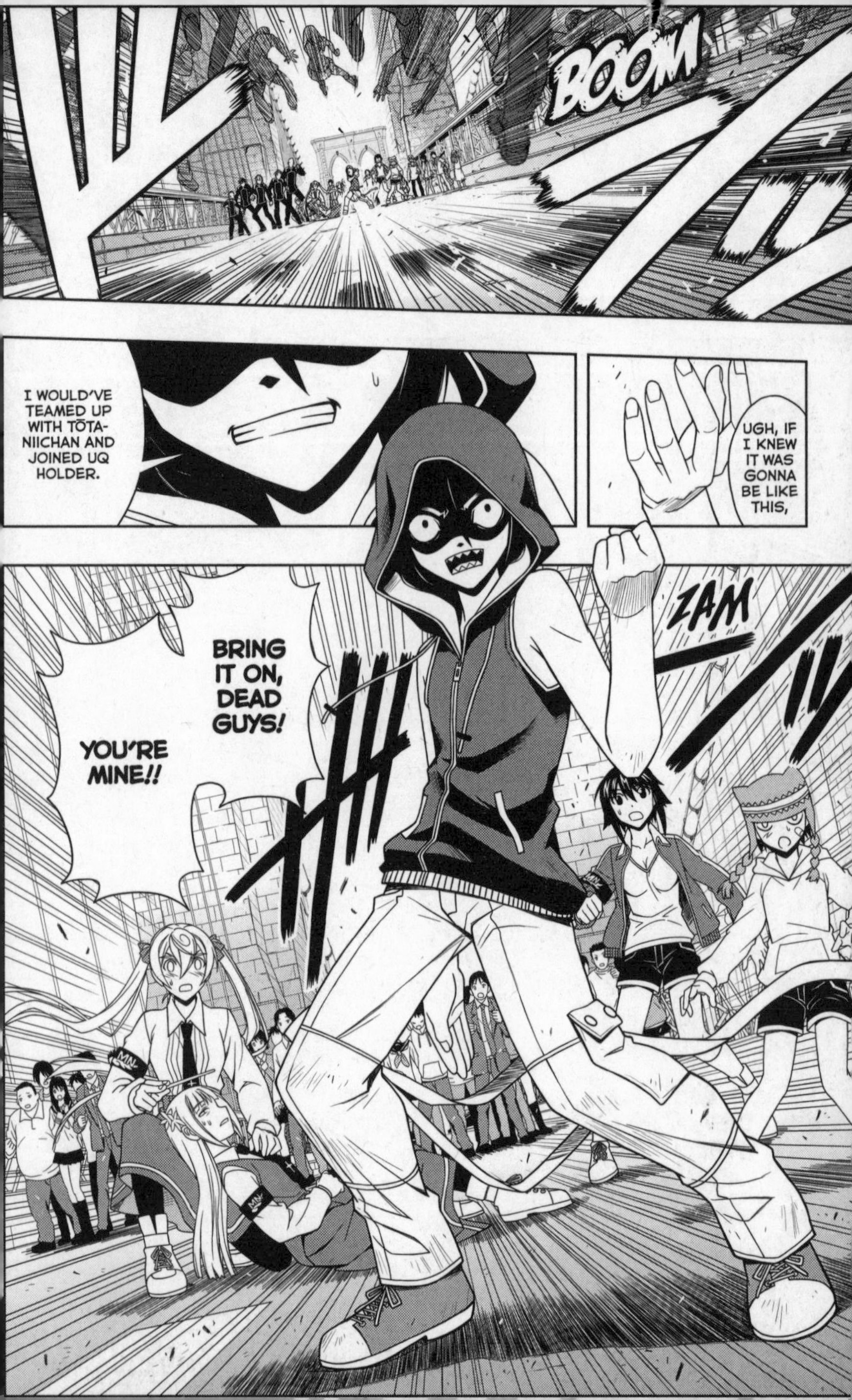
BOOM
UGH, IF I KNEW IT WAS GONNA BE LIKE THIS,
I WOULD'VE TEAMED UP WITH TŌTA-NIICHAN AND JOINED UQ HOLDER.
ZAM
BRING IT ON, DEAD GUYS!
YOU'RE MINE!!

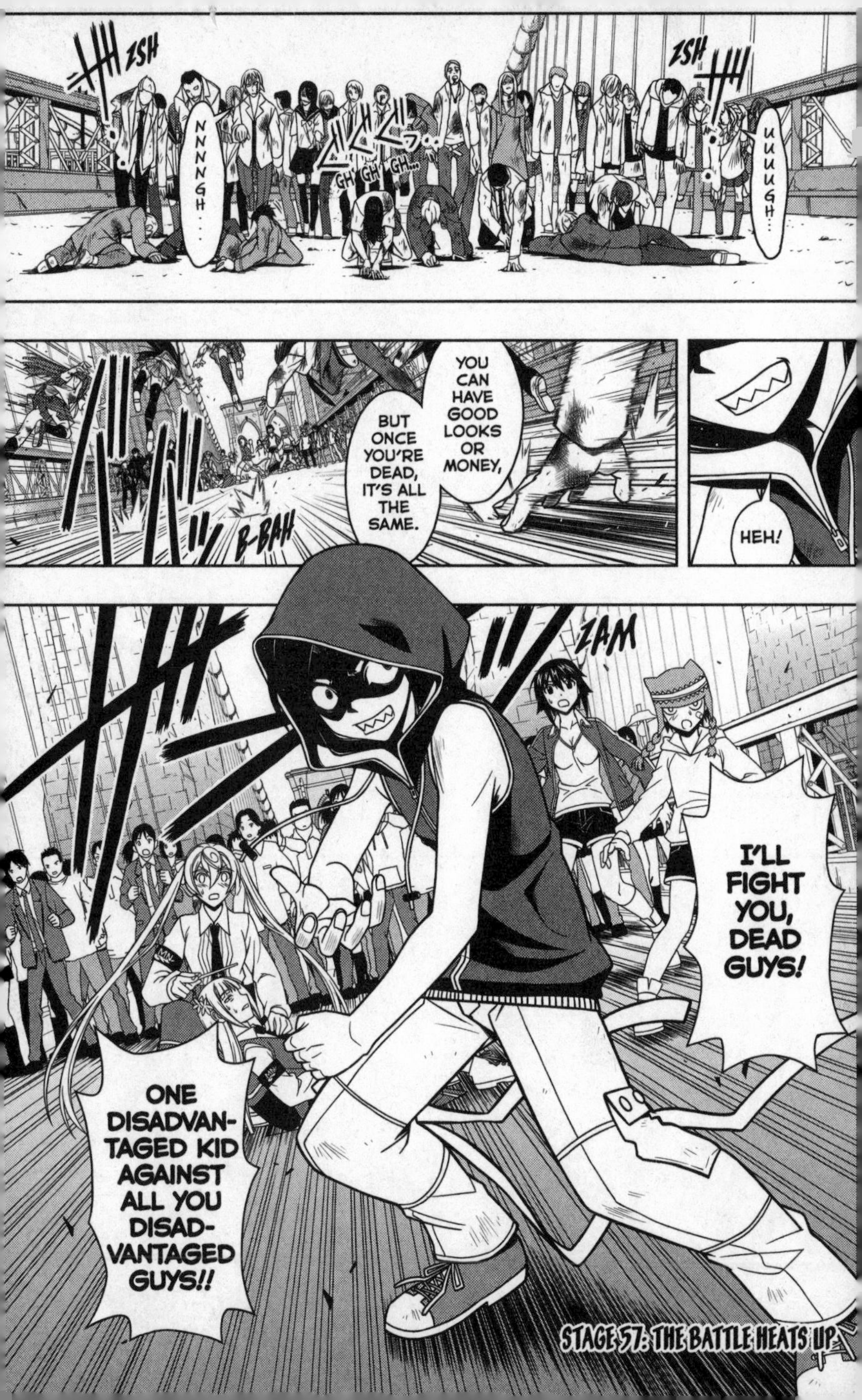
ZSH
UUUUGH...
GH GH GH...
NNNNGH...
ZSH
HEH!
YOU CAN HAVE GOOD LOOKS OR MONEY,
BUT ONCE YOU'RE DEAD, IT'S ALL THE SAME.
B-BAH
ZAM
I'LL FIGHT YOU, DEAD GUYS!
ONE DISADVANTAGED KID AGAINST ALL YOU DISADVANTAGED GUYS!!
STAGE 57: THE BATTLE HEATS UP

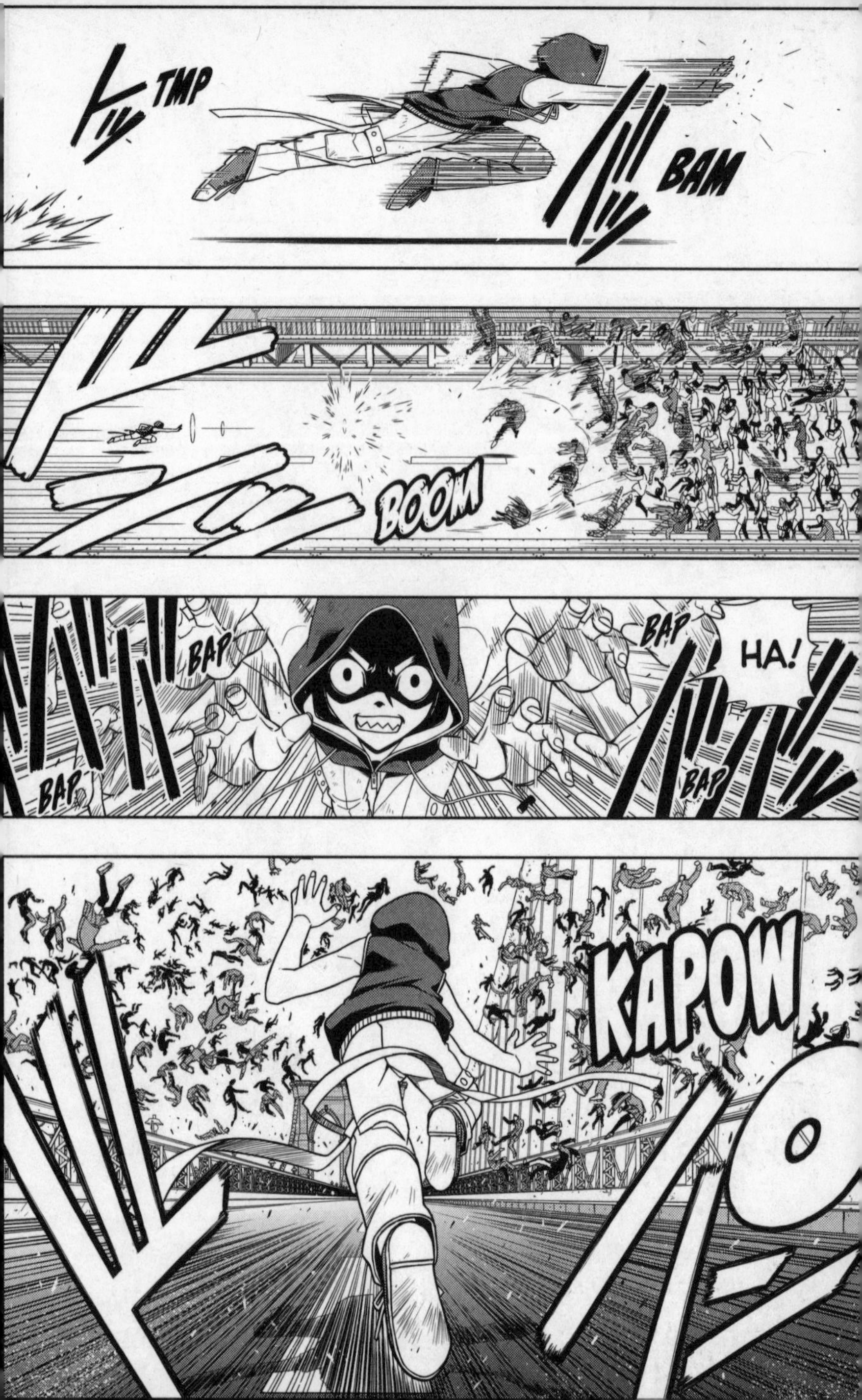
BAM
TMP
BOOM
HA!
BAP
BAP
BAP
BAP
KAPOW

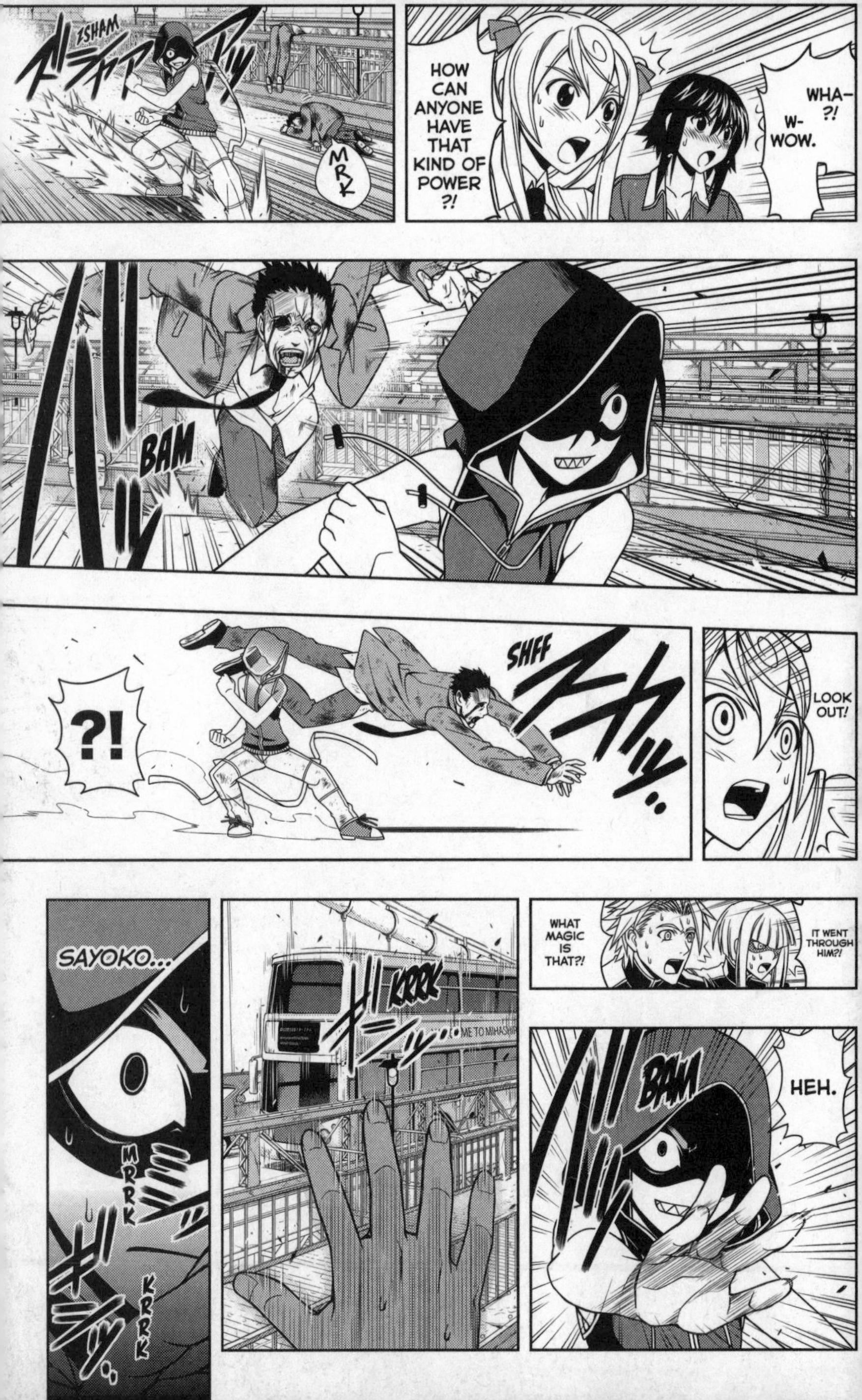
WHA-?!
W- WOW.
HOW CAN ANYONE HAVE THAT KIND OF POWER?!
ISHAM
MRK
BAM
LOOK OUT!
SHFF
?!
IT WENT THROUGH HIM?!
WHAT MAGIC IS THAT?!
HEH.
BAM
KRRK
ME TO MIHASHI
SAYOKO...
MRRK
KRRK

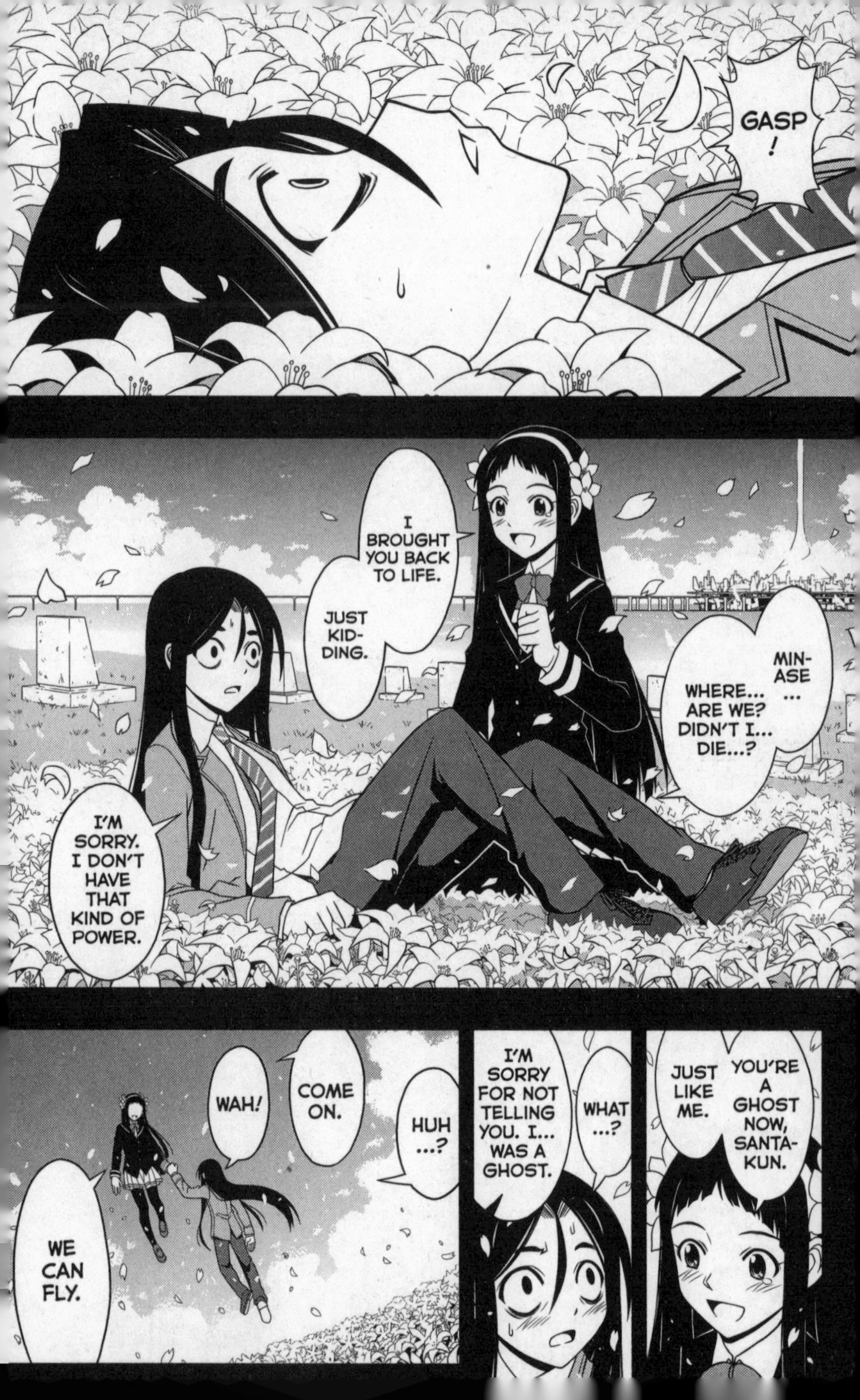
GASP!
MINASE... WHERE... ARE WE? DIDN'T I... DIE...?
I BROUGHT YOU BACK TO LIFE.
JUST KIDDING.
I'M SORRY. I DON'T HAVE THAT KIND OF POWER.
YOU'RE A GHOST NOW, SANTA-KUN.
JUST LIKE ME.
WHAT...?
I'M SORRY FOR NOT TELLING YOU. I... WAS A GHOST.
HUH...?
COME ON.
WAH!
WE CAN FLY.

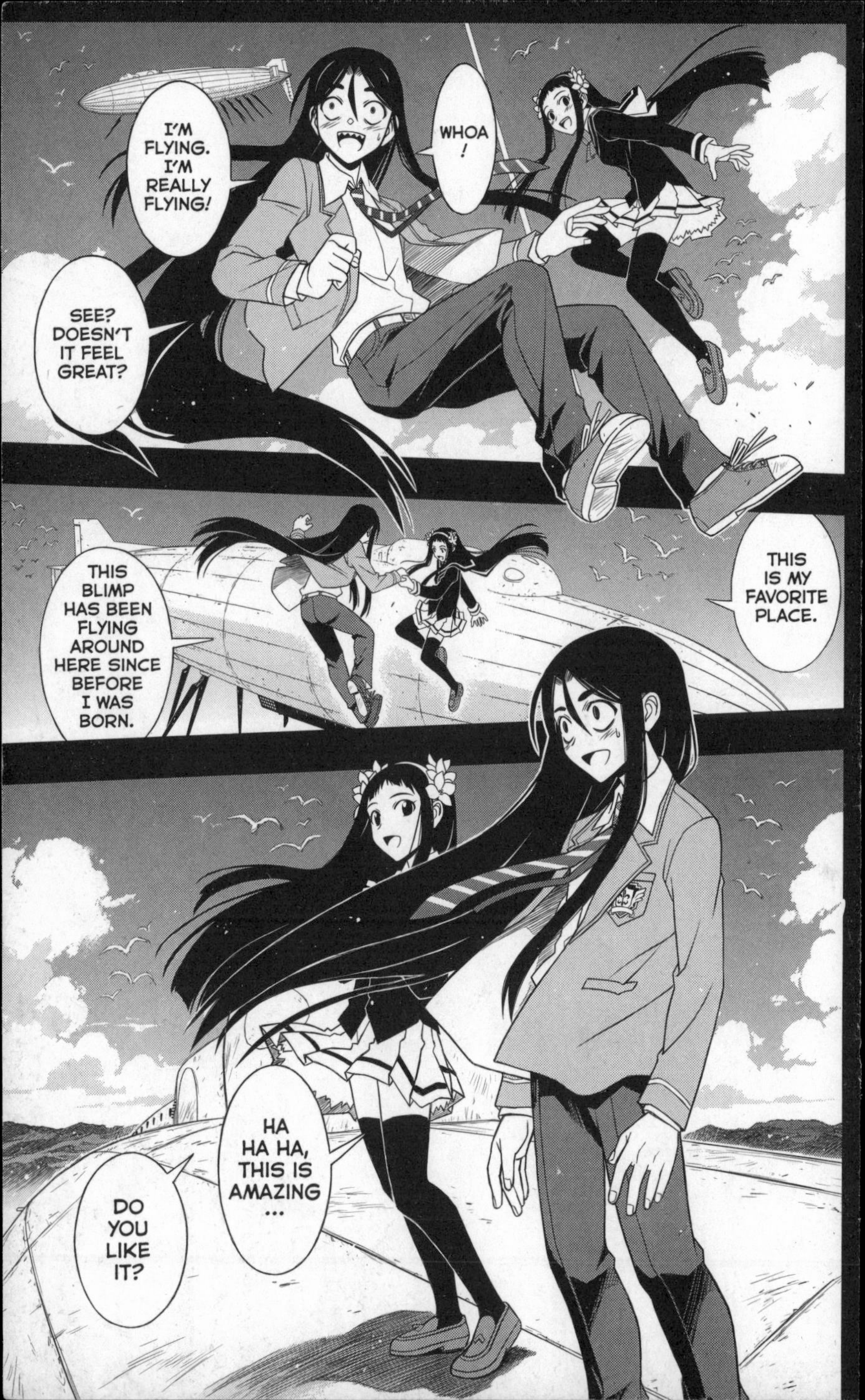
WHOA!
I'M FLYING. I'M REALLY FLYING!
SEE? DOESN'T IT FEEL GREAT?
THIS IS MY FAVORITE PLACE.
THIS BLIMP HAS BEEN FLYING AROUND HERE SINCE BEFORE I WAS BORN.
HA HA HA, THIS IS AMAZING...
DO YOU LIKE IT?

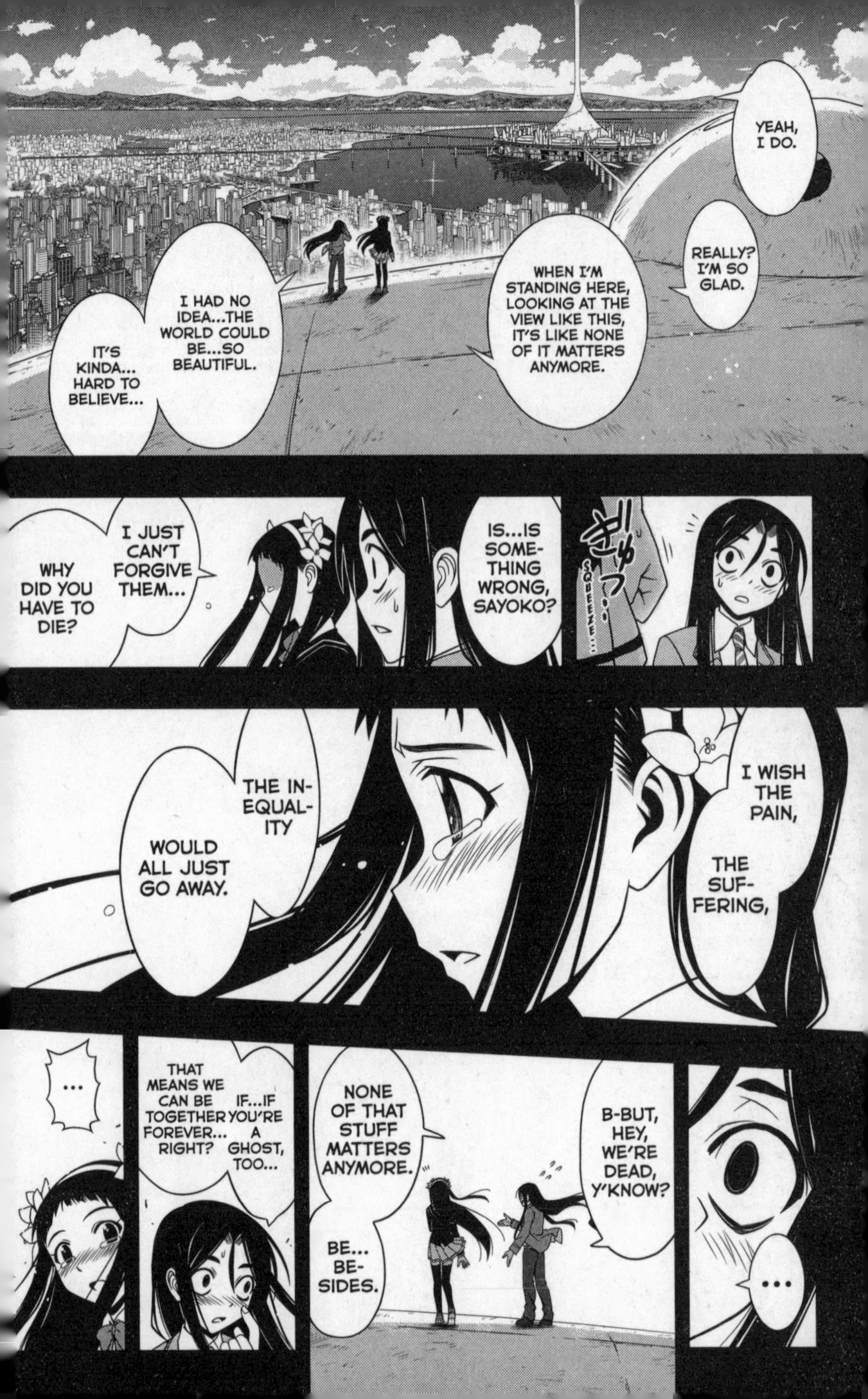
YEAH, I DO.
REALLY? I'M SO GLAD.
WHEN I'M STANDING HERE, LOOKING AT THE VIEW LIKE THIS, IT'S LIKE NONE OF IT MATTERS ANYMORE.
I HAD NO IDEA...THE WORLD COULD BE...SO BEAUTIFUL.
IT'S KINDA... HARD TO BELIEVE...
ぎゅっ
SQUEEZE...
IS...IS SOMETHING WRONG, SAYOKO?
I JUST CAN'T FORGIVE THEM...
WHY DID YOU HAVE TO DIE?
I WISH THE PAIN,
THE SUFFERING,
THE INEQUALITY
WOULD ALL JUST GO AWAY.
...
B-BUT, HEY, WE'RE DEAD, Y'KNOW?
NONE OF THAT STUFF MATTERS ANYMORE.
BE... BESIDES.
IF...IF YOU'RE A GHOST, TOO...
THAT MEANS WE CAN BE TOGETHER FOREVER... RIGHT?
...

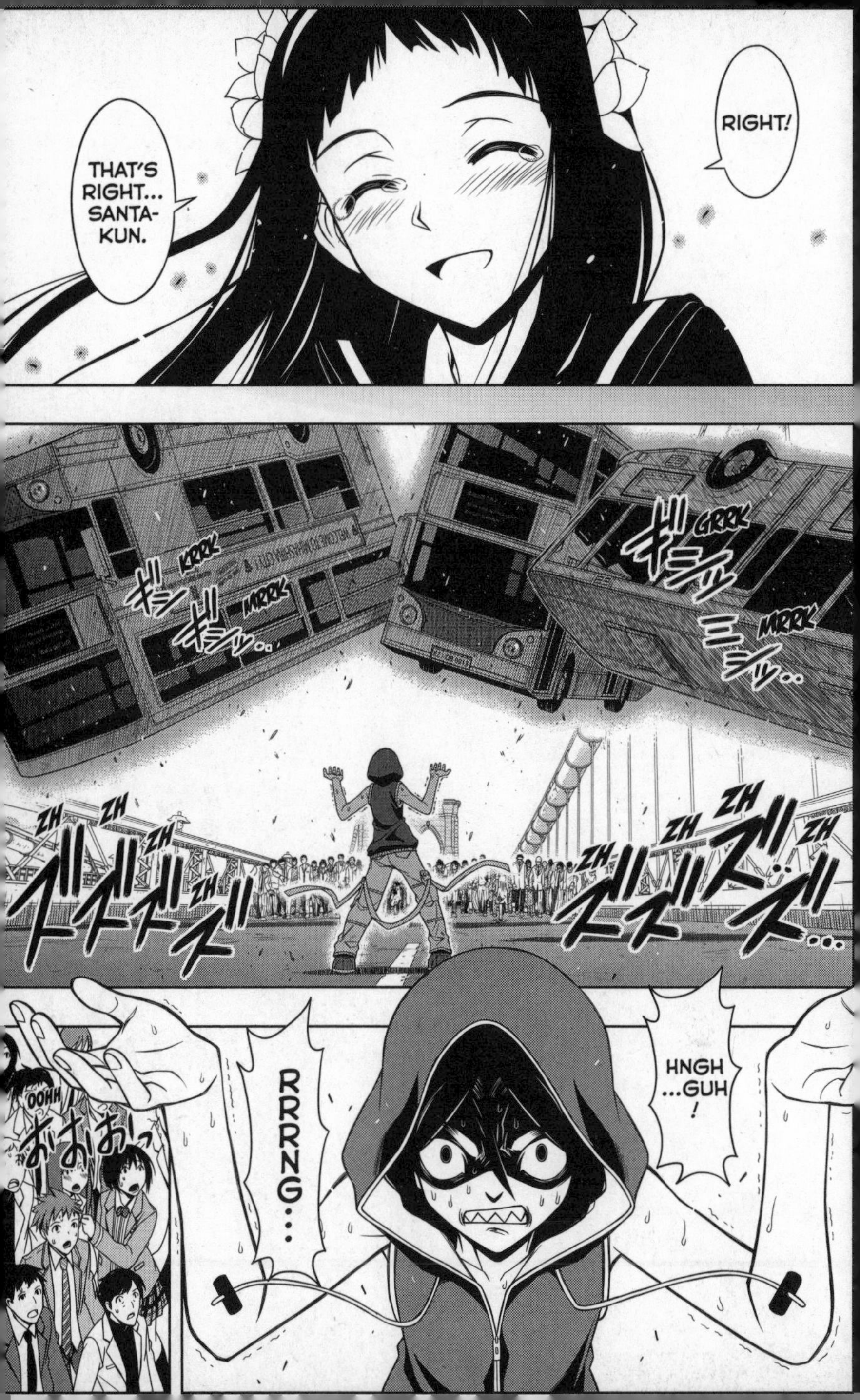
RIGHT!
THAT'S RIGHT... SANTA-KUN.
GRRK
MRRK
KRRK
MRRK
ZH ZH ZH ZH
ZH ZH ZH ZH
HNGH ...GUH!
RRRNG...
OOHH

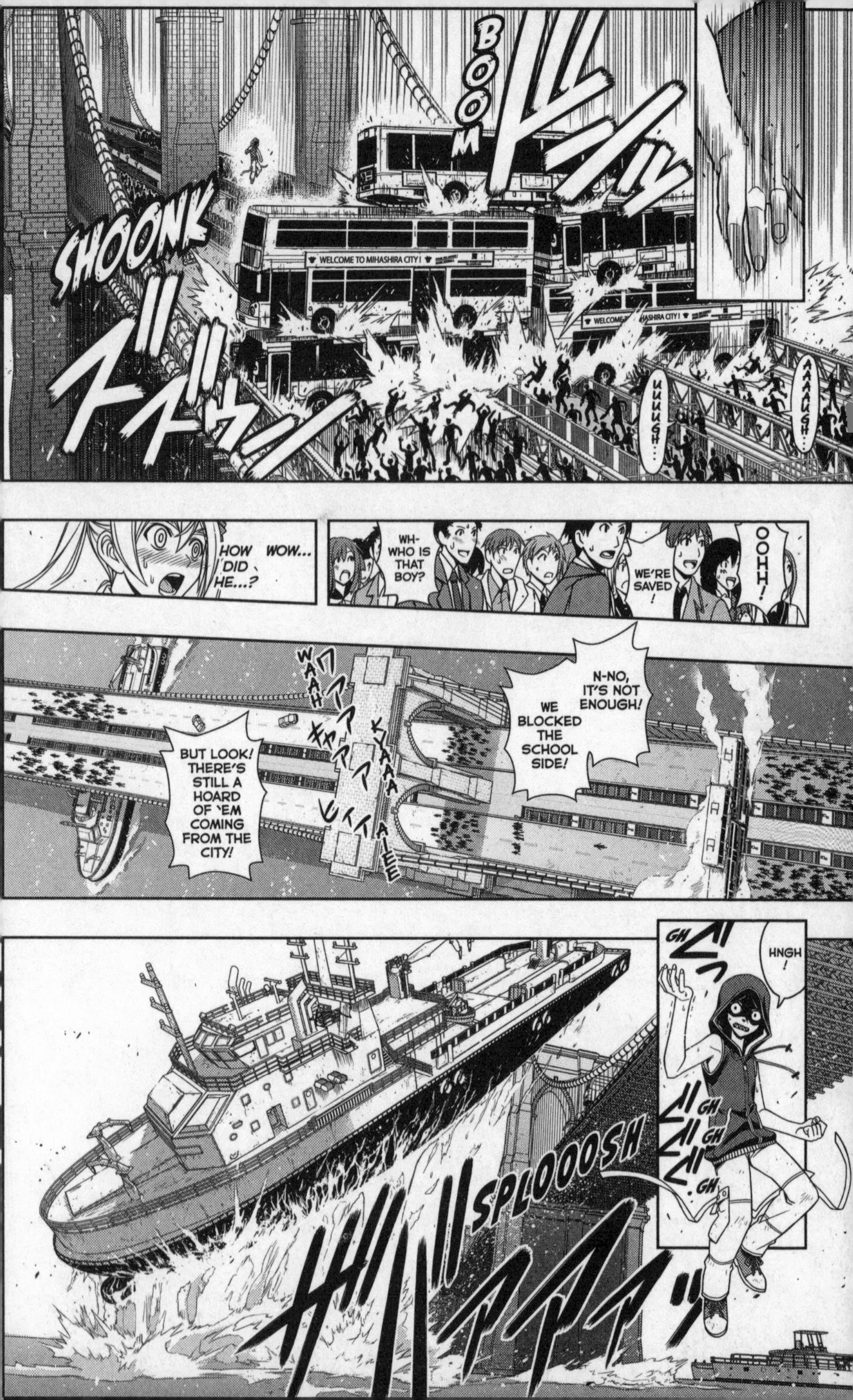
BOOM
AAAAUGH...
UUUUGH...
WELCOME TO MIHASHIRA CITY!
SHOONK
OOHH!
WE'RE SAVED!
WH- WHO IS THAT BOY?
WOW...
HOW DID HE...?
N-NO, IT'S NOT ENOUGH!
WE BLOCKED THE SCHOOL SIDE!
KYAAA AIEE
WAAH
BUT LOOK! THERE'S STILL A HOARD OF 'EM COMING FROM THE CITY!
HNGH!
GH
GH
GH
GH
SPLOOOSH

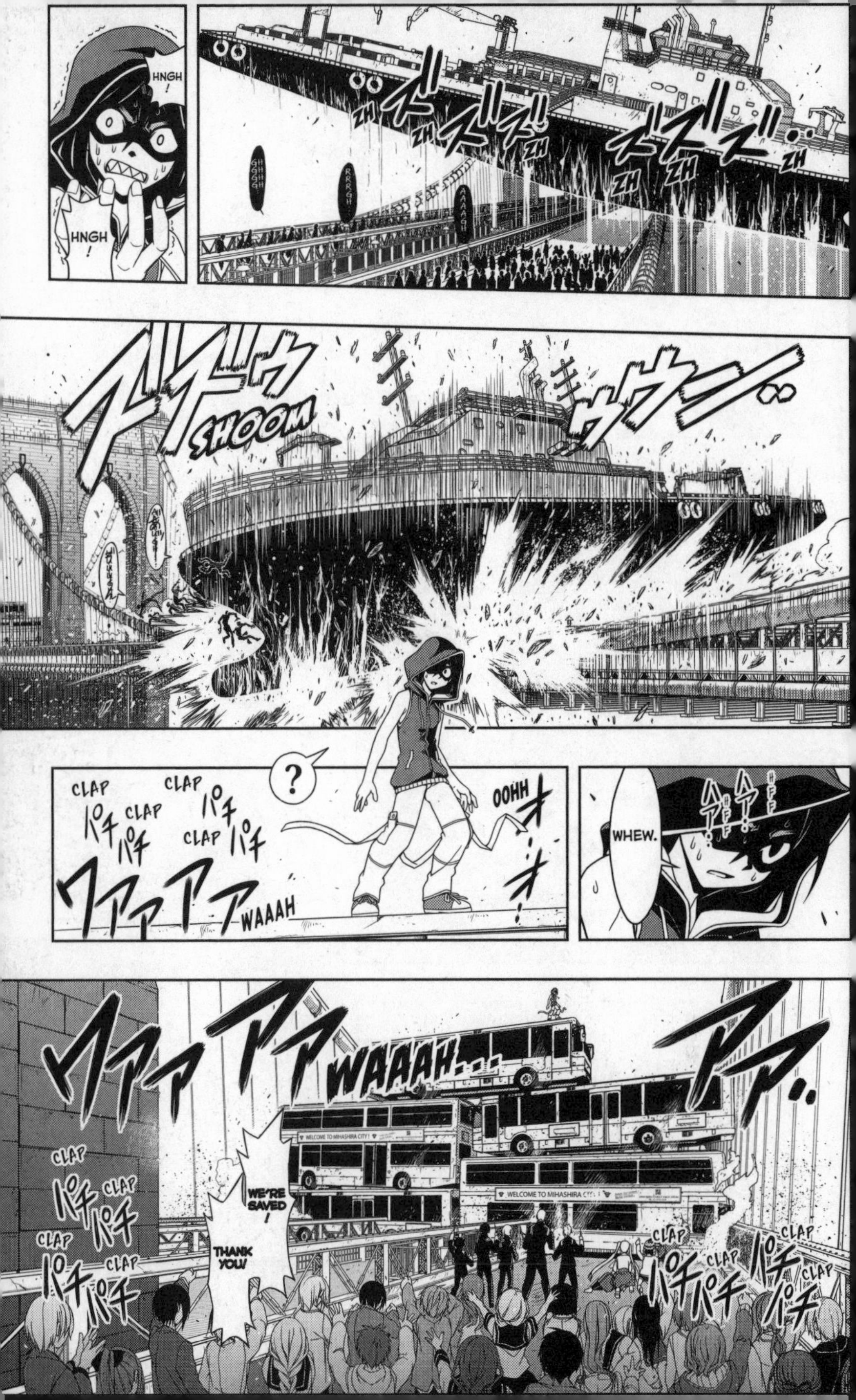
ZH ZH ZH ZH ZH ZH
RRRGH
AAAAGH
HNGH!
HNGH!
SHOOM
WHEW.
OOHH
?
CLAP CLAP CLAP CLAP
WAAAH
WAAAH
WE'RE SAVED!
THANK YOU!
CLAP CLAP CLAP CLAP
CLAP CLAP CLAP CLAP

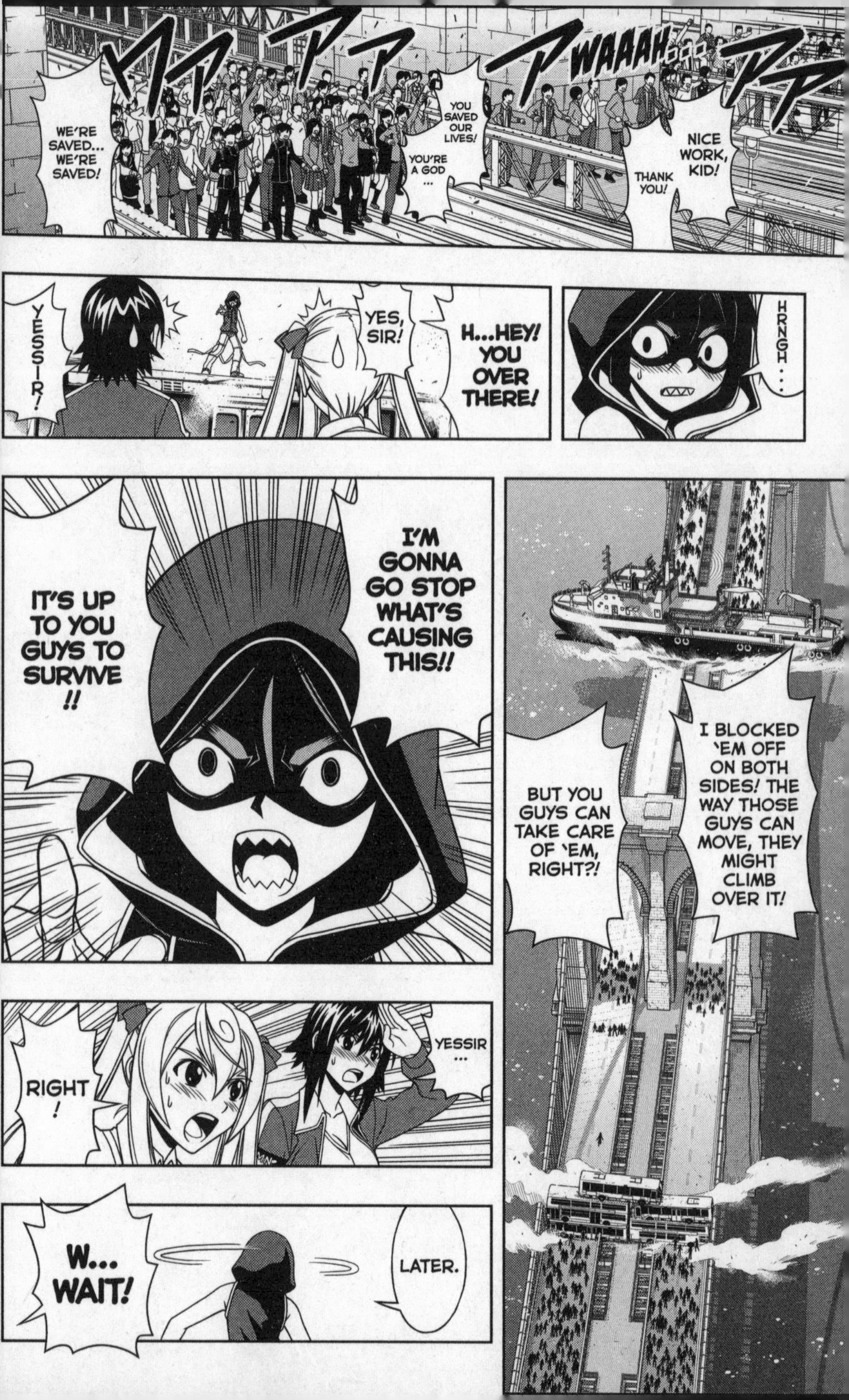
WAAAH...
NICE WORK, KID!
THANK YOU!
YOU SAVED OUR LIVES!
YOU'RE A GOD ...
WE'RE SAVED... WE'RE SAVED!
HRNGH...
H...HEY! YOU OVER THERE!
YES, SIR!
YESSIR!
I BLOCKED 'EM OFF ON BOTH SIDES! THE WAY THOSE GUYS CAN MOVE, THEY MIGHT CLIMB OVER IT!
BUT YOU GUYS CAN TAKE CARE OF 'EM, RIGHT?!
I'M GONNA GO STOP WHAT'S CAUSING THIS!!
IT'S UP TO YOU GUYS TO SURVIVE!!
YESSIR ...
RIGHT!
LATER.
W... WAIT!

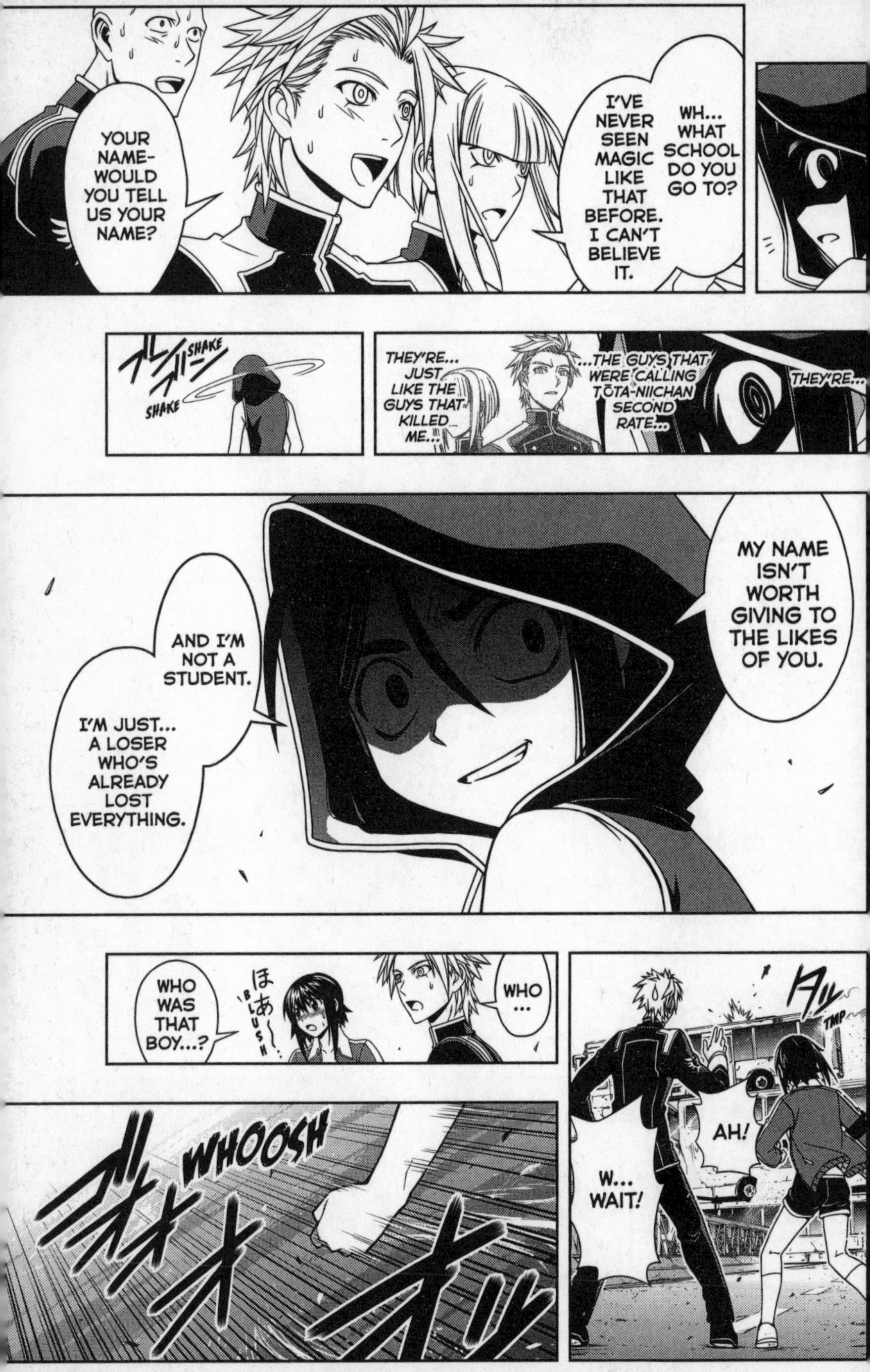
WH... WHAT SCHOOL DO YOU GO TO?
I'VE NEVER SEEN MAGIC LIKE THAT BEFORE. I CAN'T BELIEVE IT.
YOUR NAME- WOULD YOU TELL US YOUR NAME?
THEY'RE...
...THE GUYS THAT WERE CALLING TŌTA-NIICHAN SECOND RATE...
THEY'RE... JUST LIKE THE GUYS THAT KILLED ME...
SHAKE
SHAKE
MY NAME ISN'T WORTH GIVING TO THE LIKES OF YOU.
AND I'M NOT A STUDENT.
I'M JUST... A LOSER WHO'S ALREADY LOST EVERYTHING.
TMP
AH!
W... WAIT!
WHO ...
ほあ〜
BLUSH
WHO WAS THAT BOY...?
WHOOSH

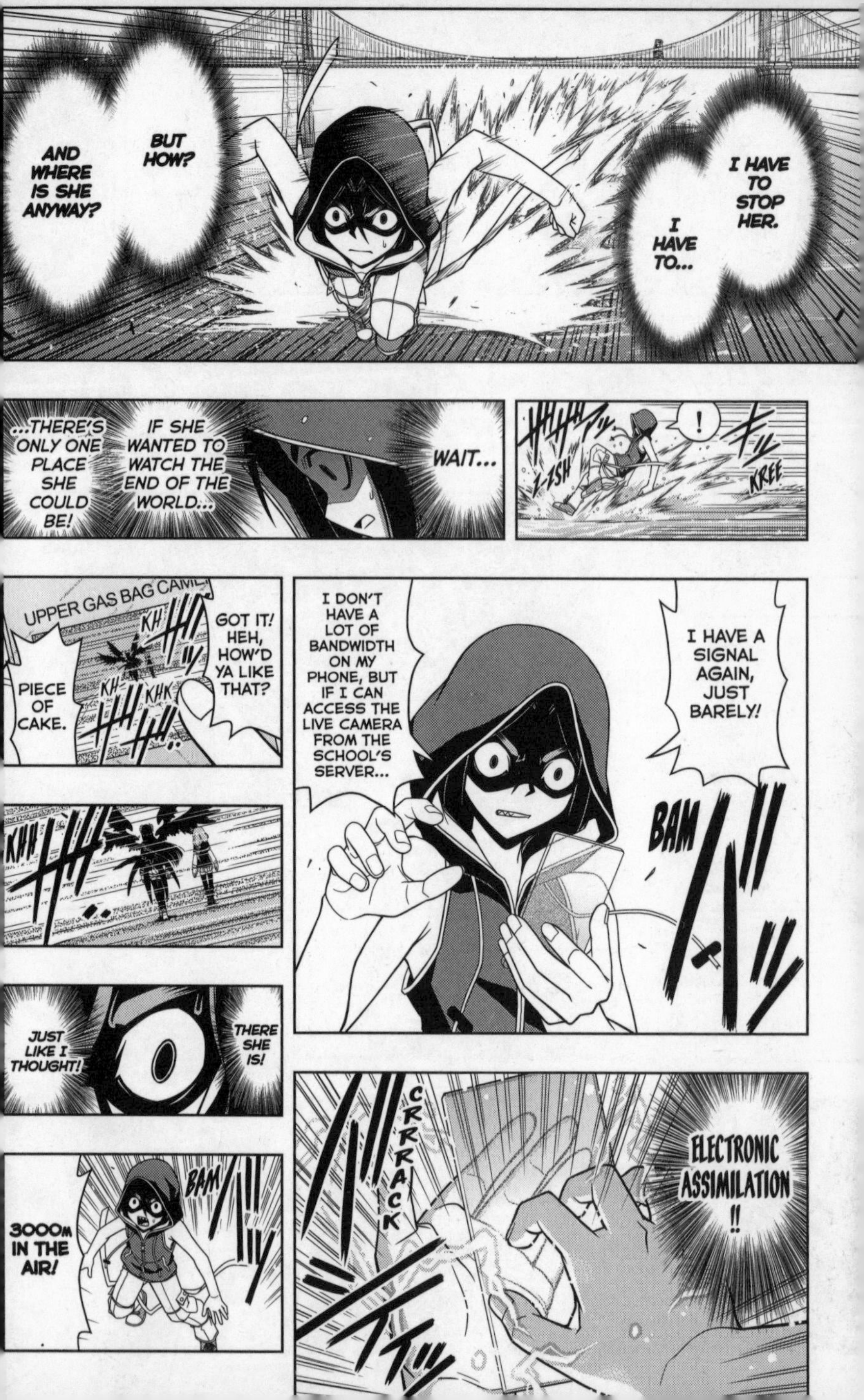
I HAVE TO STOP HER.
I HAVE TO...
BUT HOW?
AND WHERE IS SHE ANYWAY?
!
Z-ISH
KREE
WAIT...
IF SHE WANTED TO WATCH THE END OF THE WORLD...
...THERE'S ONLY ONE PLACE SHE COULD BE!
I HAVE A SIGNAL AGAIN, JUST BARELY!
I DON'T HAVE A LOT OF BANDWIDTH ON MY PHONE, BUT IF I CAN ACCESS THE LIVE CAMERA FROM THE SCHOOL'S SERVER...
BAM
UPPER GAS BAG CAM
GOT IT! HEH, HOW'D YA LIKE THAT?
KH
KHK
PIECE OF CAKE.
THERE SHE IS!
JUST LIKE I THOUGHT!
CRRRACK
ELECTRONIC ASSIMILATION !!
BAM
3000m IN THE AIR!

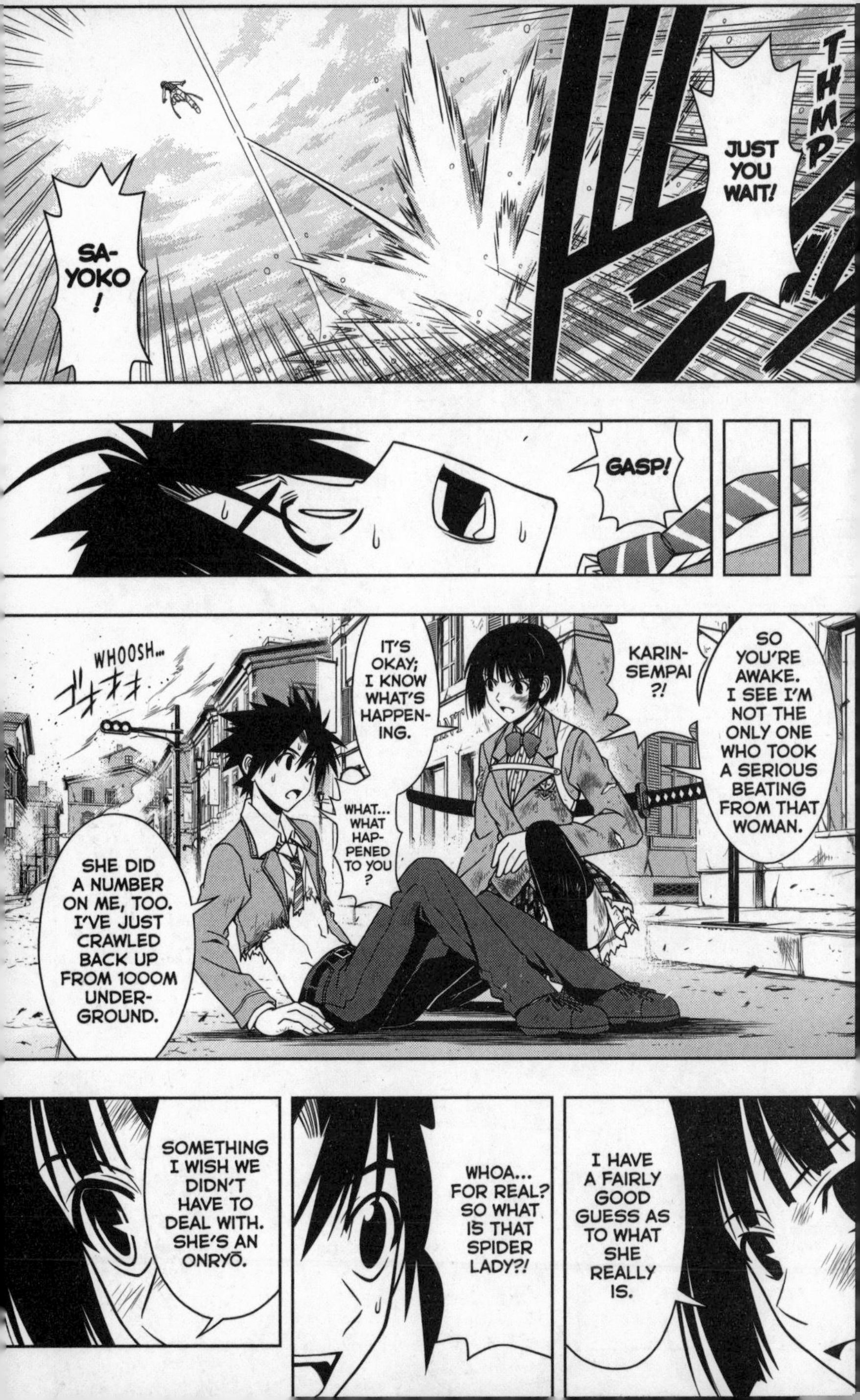
THMP
JUST YOU WAIT!
SA-YOKO!
GASP!
SO YOU'RE AWAKE. I SEE I'M NOT THE ONLY ONE WHO TOOK A SERIOUS BEATING FROM THAT WOMAN.
KARIN-SEMPAI?!
IT'S OKAY; I KNOW WHAT'S HAPPEN-ING.
WHAT... WHAT HAP-PENED TO YOU?
SHE DID A NUMBER ON ME, TOO. I'VE JUST CRAWLED BACK UP FROM 1000M UNDER-GROUND.
WHOOSH...
ゴォォォ
I HAVE A FAIRLY GOOD GUESS AS TO WHAT SHE REALLY IS.
WHOA... FOR REAL? SO WHAT IS THAT SPIDER LADY?!
SOMETHING I WISH WE DIDN'T HAVE TO DEAL WITH. SHE'S AN ONRYŌ.

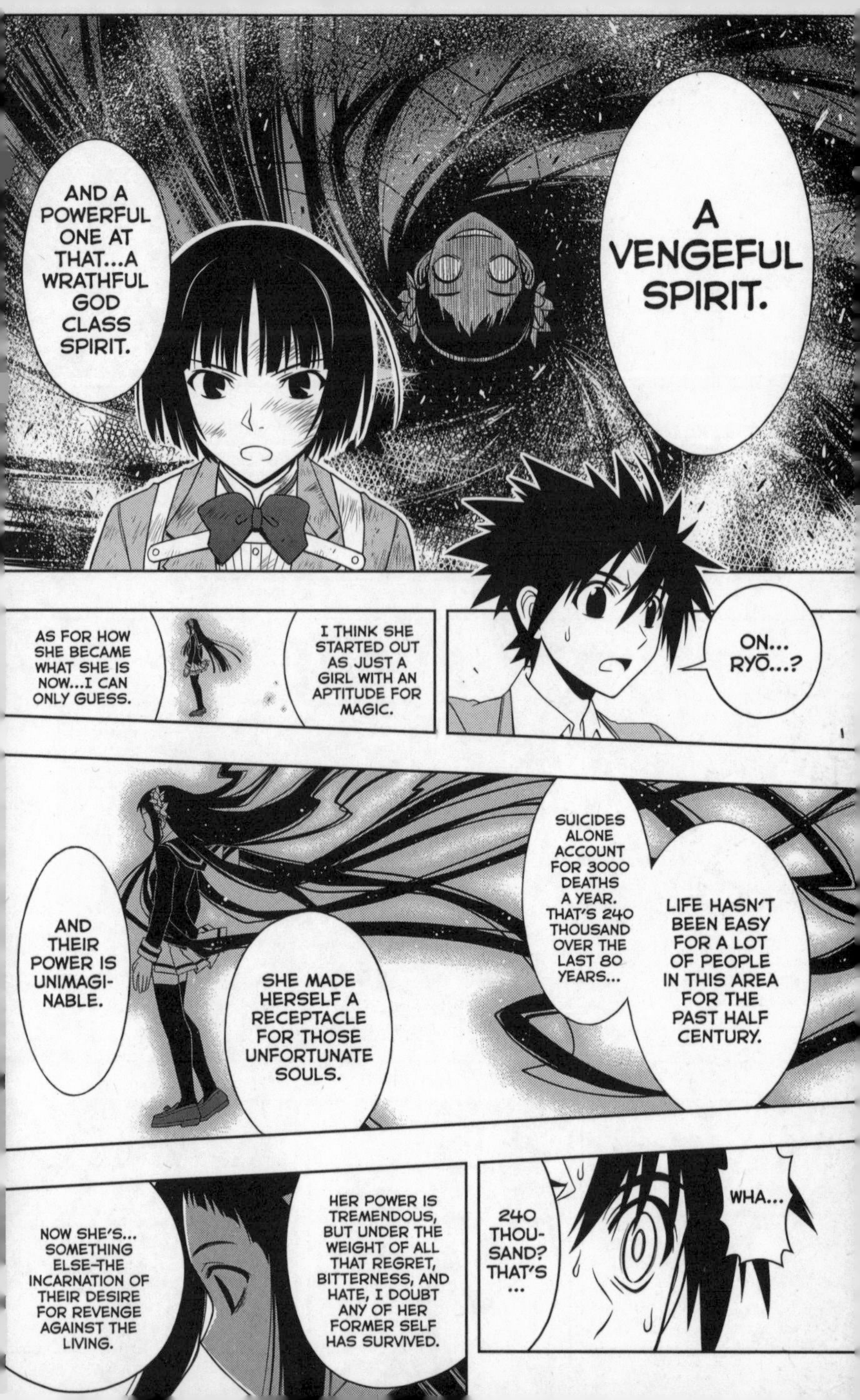
A VENGEFUL SPIRIT.
AND A POWERFUL ONE AT THAT...A WRATHFUL GOD CLASS SPIRIT.
ON... RYŌ...?
I THINK SHE STARTED OUT AS JUST A GIRL WITH AN APTITUDE FOR MAGIC.
AS FOR HOW SHE BECAME WHAT SHE IS NOW...I CAN ONLY GUESS.
LIFE HASN'T BEEN EASY FOR A LOT OF PEOPLE IN THIS AREA FOR THE PAST HALF CENTURY.
SUICIDES ALONE ACCOUNT FOR 3000 DEATHS A YEAR. THAT'S 240 THOUSAND OVER THE LAST 80 YEARS...
SHE MADE HERSELF A RECEPTACLE FOR THOSE UNFORTUNATE SOULS.
AND THEIR POWER IS UNIMAGINABLE.
WHA...
240 THOUSAND? THAT'S ...
HER POWER IS TREMENDOUS, BUT UNDER THE WEIGHT OF ALL THAT REGRET, BITTERNESS, AND HATE, I DOUBT ANY OF HER FORMER SELF HAS SURVIVED.
NOW SHE'S... SOMETHING ELSE—THE INCARNATION OF THEIR DESIRE FOR REVENGE AGAINST THE LIVING.

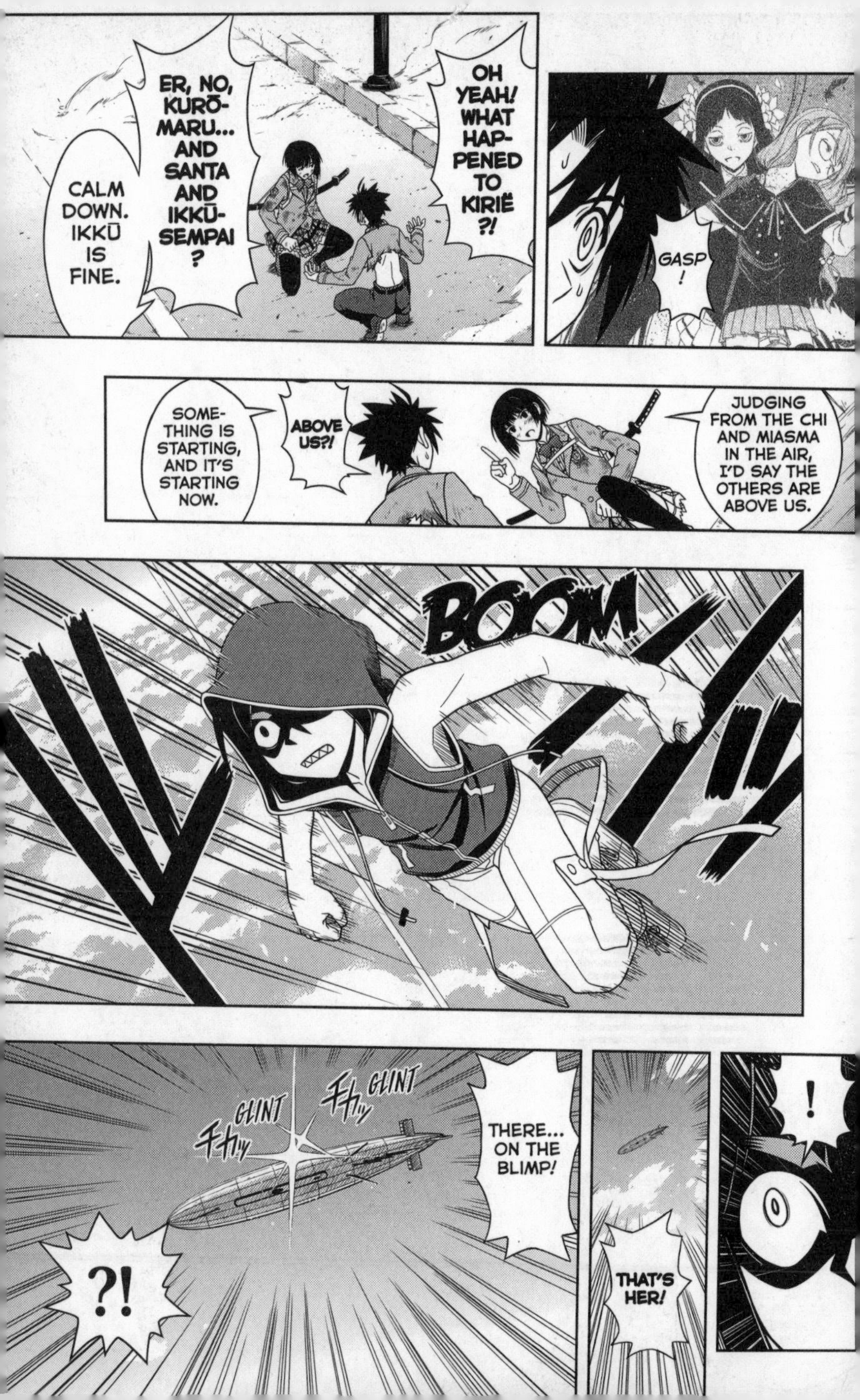
GASP!
OH YEAH! WHAT HAPPENED TO KIRIË?!
ER, NO, KURŌMARU... AND SANTA AND IKKŪ-SEMPAI?
CALM DOWN. IKKŪ IS FINE.
JUDGING FROM THE CHI AND MIASMA IN THE AIR, I'D SAY THE OTHERS ARE ABOVE US.
ABOVE US?!
SOMETHING IS STARTING, AND IT'S STARTING NOW.
BOOM
!
THAT'S HER!
THERE... ON THE BLIMP!
チカッ GLINT
チカッ GLINT
?!

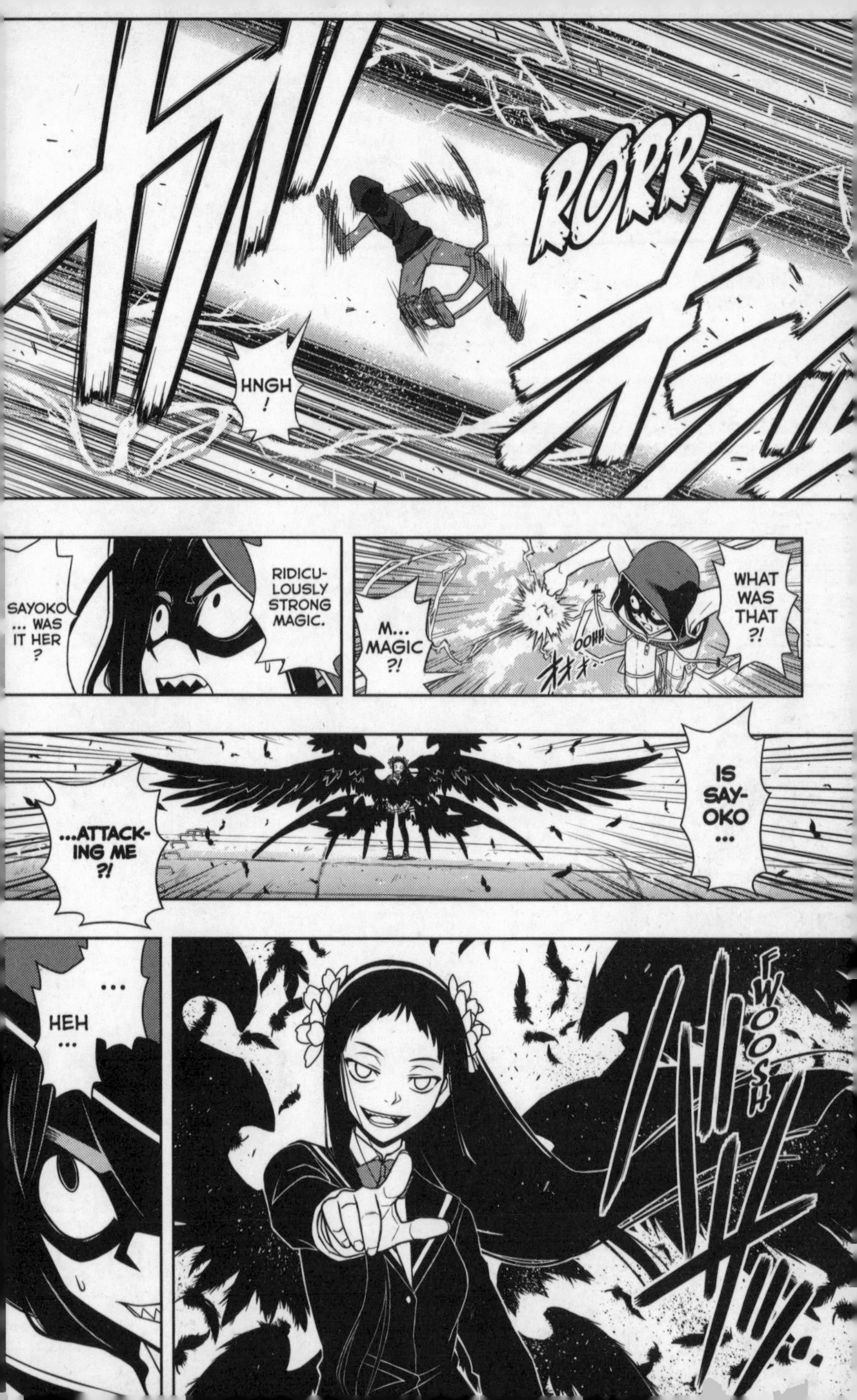
RORR
HNGH!
WHAT WAS THAT?!
M... MAGIC?!
OOHH
オオオ
RIDICU-LOUSLY STRONG MAGIC.
SAYOKO... WAS IT HER?
IS SAY-OKO...
...ATTACK-ING ME?!
FWOOSH
...
HEH...

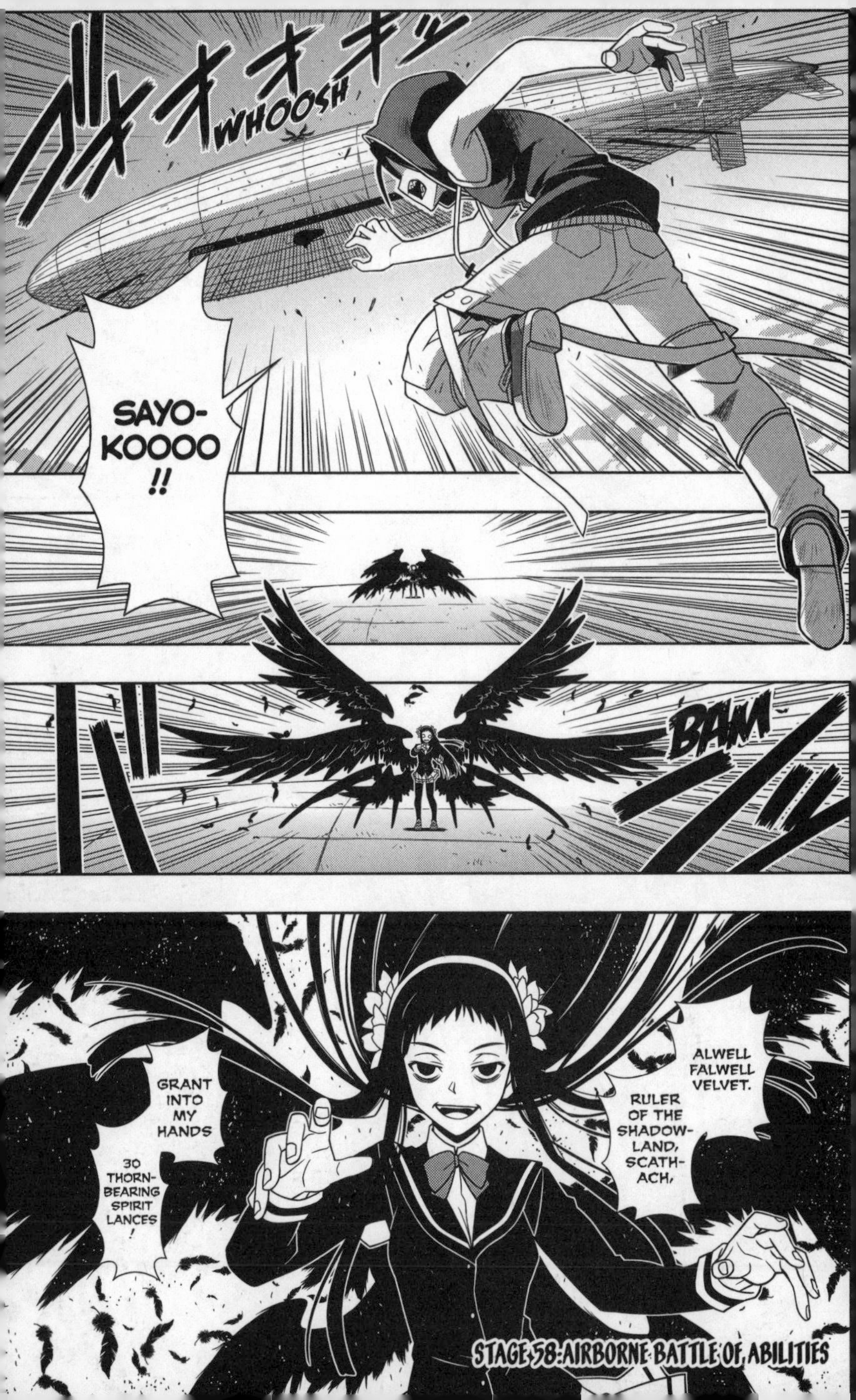
WHOOSH
SAYO-KOOOO!!
BAM
ALWELL FALWELL VELVET.
RULER OF THE SHADOW-LAND, SCATH-ACH,
GRANT INTO MY HANDS
30 THORN-BEARING SPIRIT LANCES!
STAGE 58: AIRBORNE BATTLE OF ABILITIES

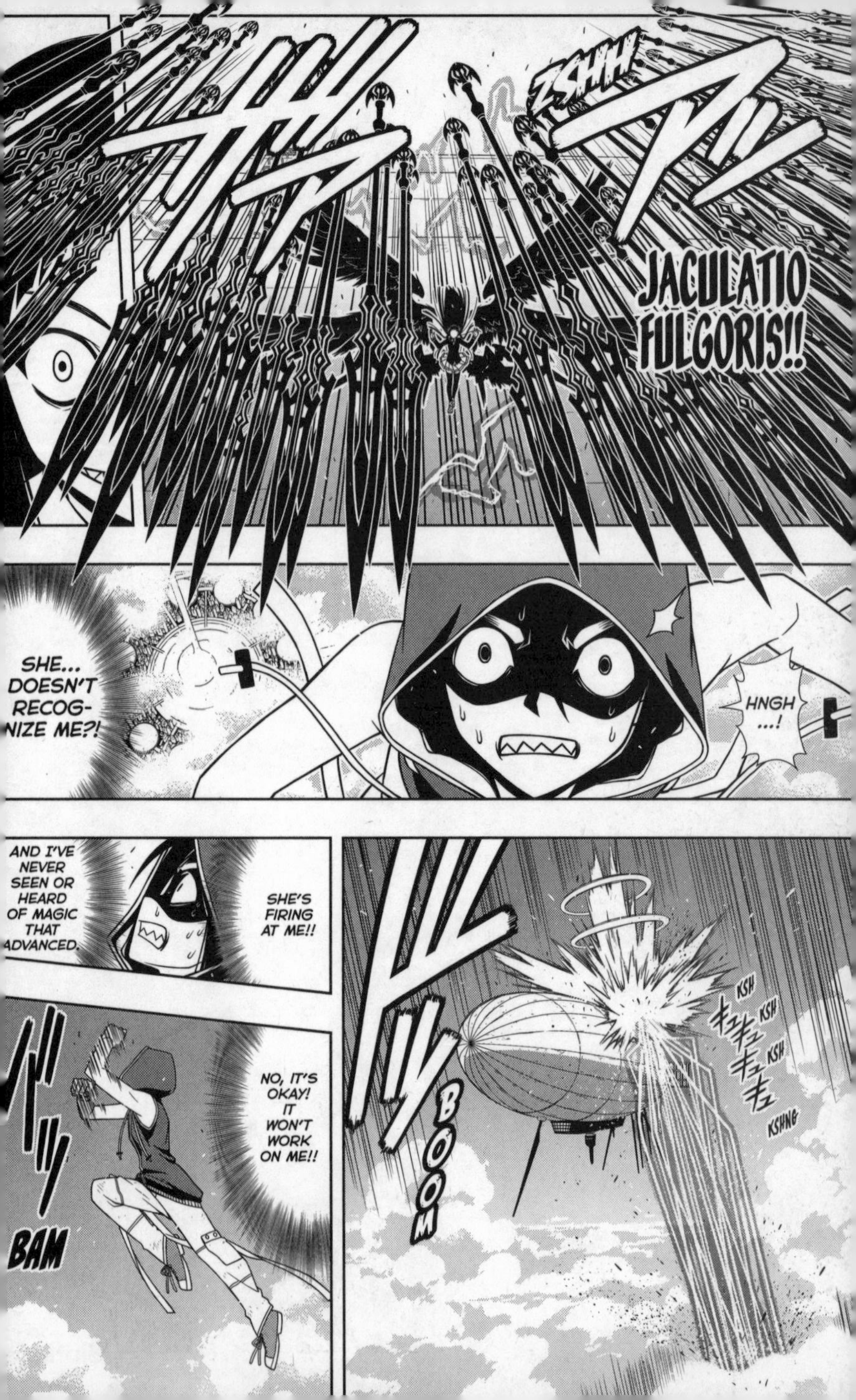
ZSHH
JACULATIO FULGORIS!!
HNGH ...!
SHE... DOESN'T RECOG-NIZE ME?!
BOOM
KSH
KSH
KSH
KSHNG
SHE'S FIRING AT ME!!
AND I'VE NEVER SEEN OR HEARD OF MAGIC THAT ADVANCED.
NO, IT'S OKAY! IT WON'T WORK ON ME!!
BAM

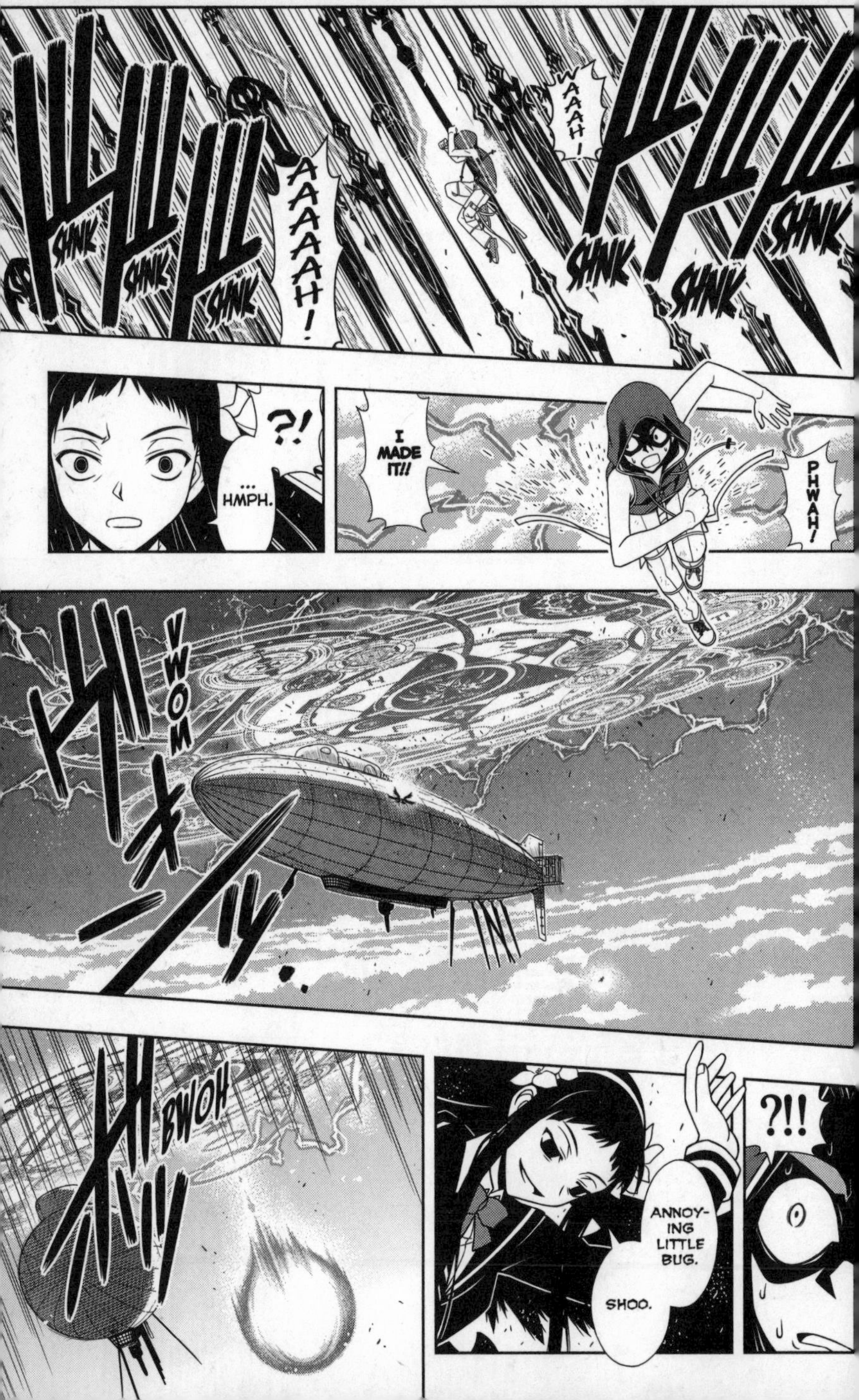
WAAAAH!
SHNK
SHNK
SHNK
AAAAAAH!
SHNK
SHNK
SHNK
PHWAH!
I MADE IT!!
?!
...HMPH.
VWOM
?!!
ANNOY-ING LITTLE BUG.
SHOO.
BWOH

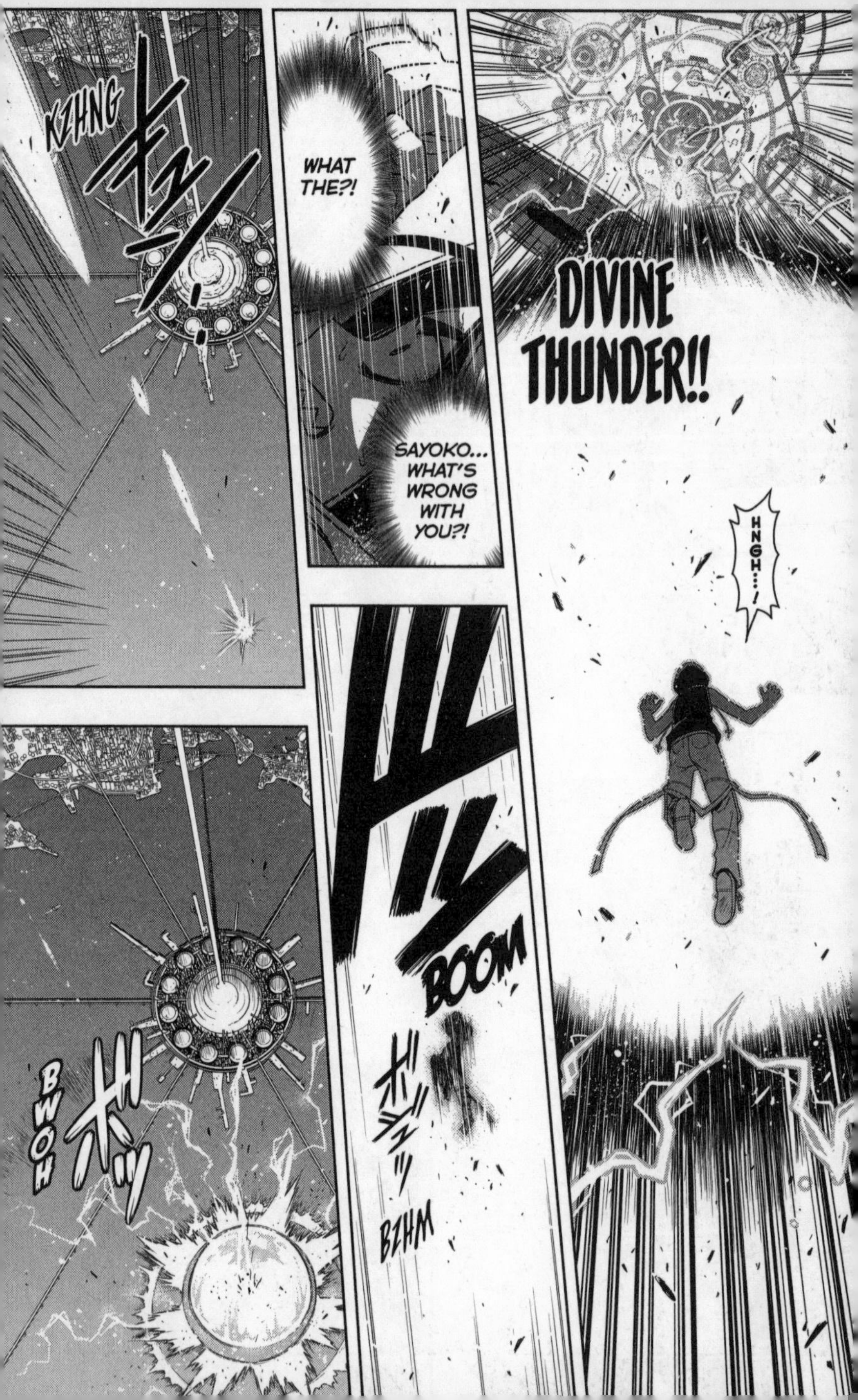
DIVINE THUNDER!!
HNGH...!
WHAT THE?!
SAYOKO... WHAT'S WRONG WITH YOU?!
KZHNG
BOOM
BZHM
BWOH

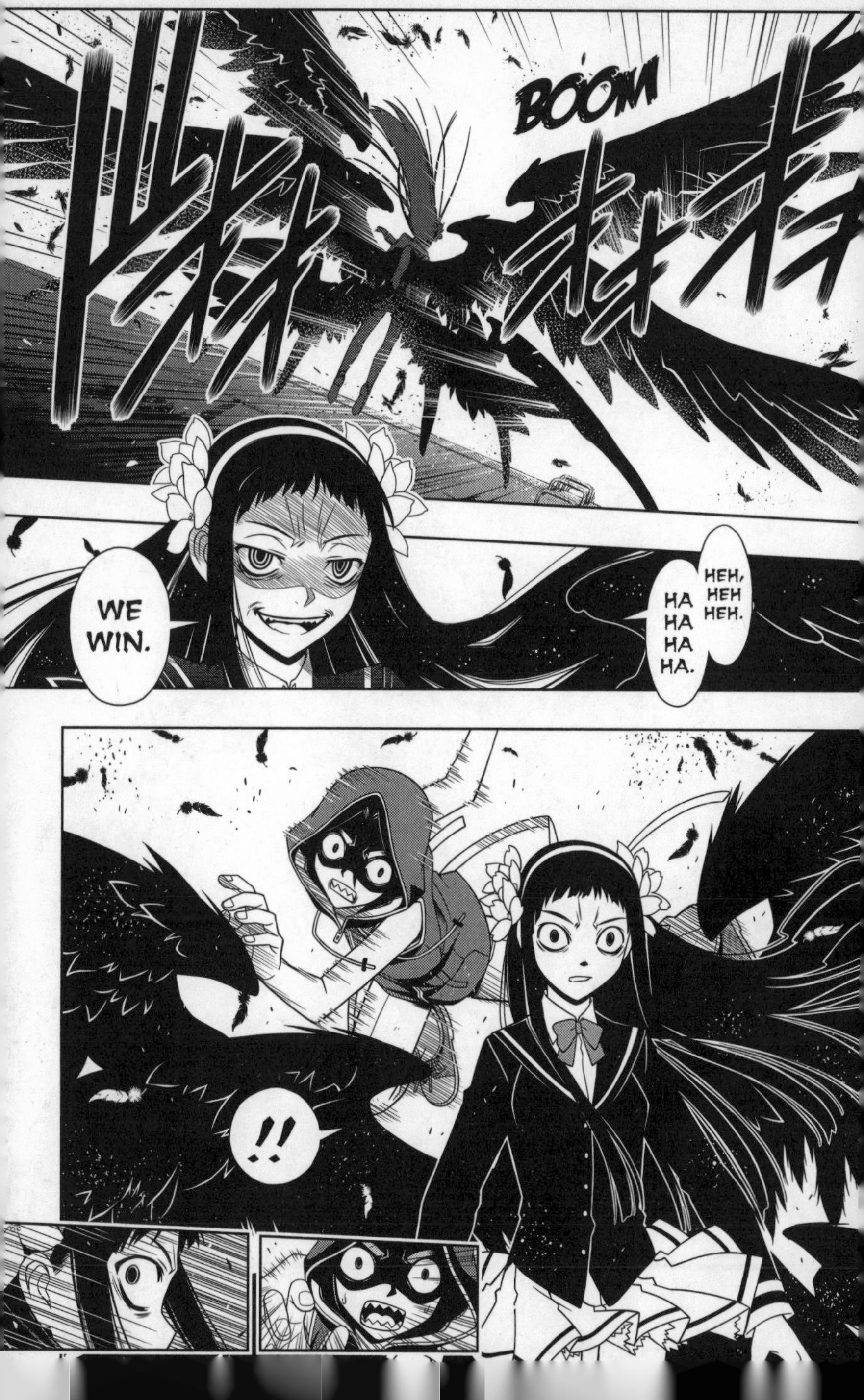
BOOM
HEH, HEH HEH. HA HA HA HA.
WE WIN.
!!

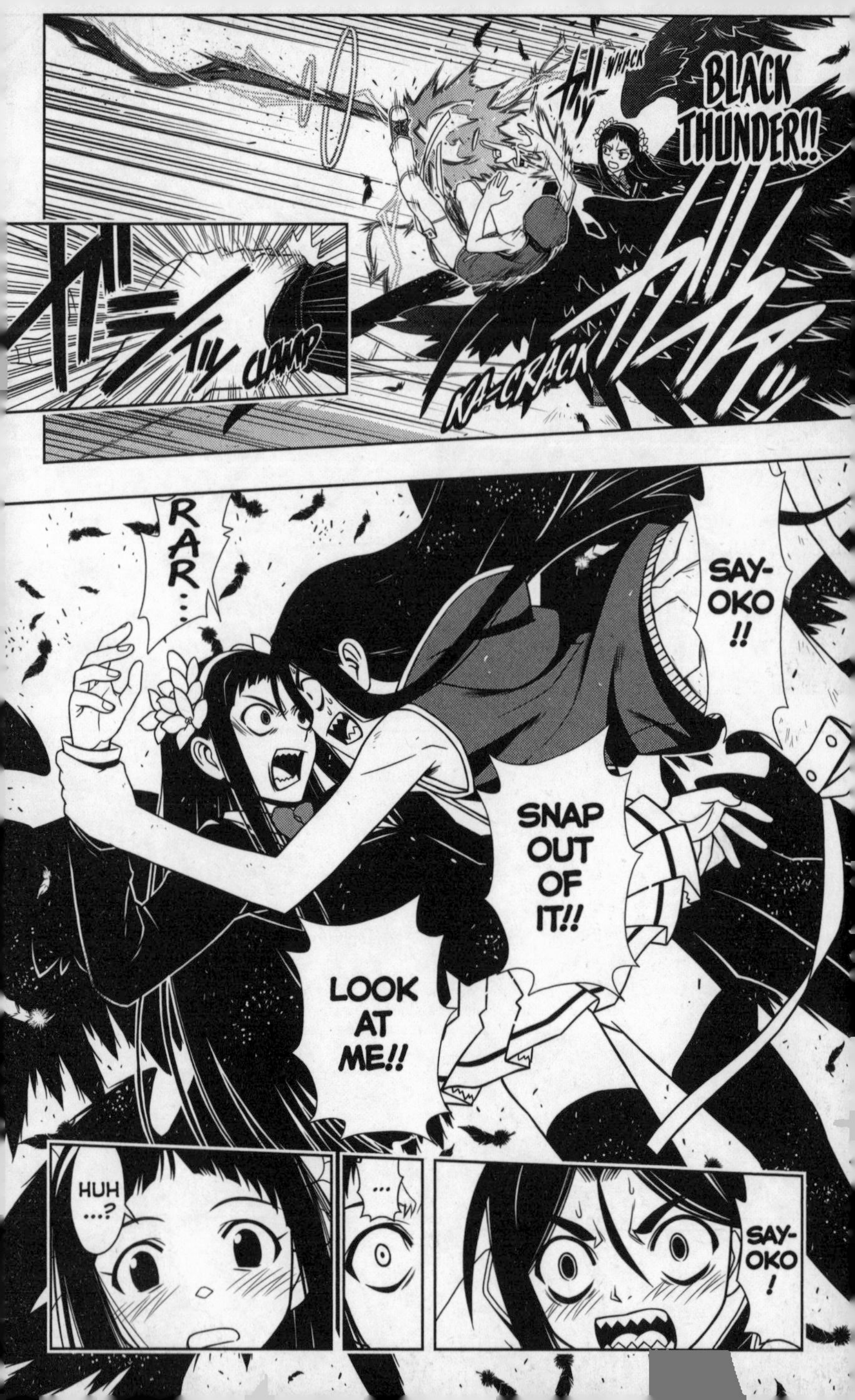
BLACK THUNDER!!
WHACK
KA-CRACK
CLAMP
SAY-OKO!!
RAR...
SNAP OUT OF IT!!
LOOK AT ME!!
SAY-OKO!
...
HUH...?

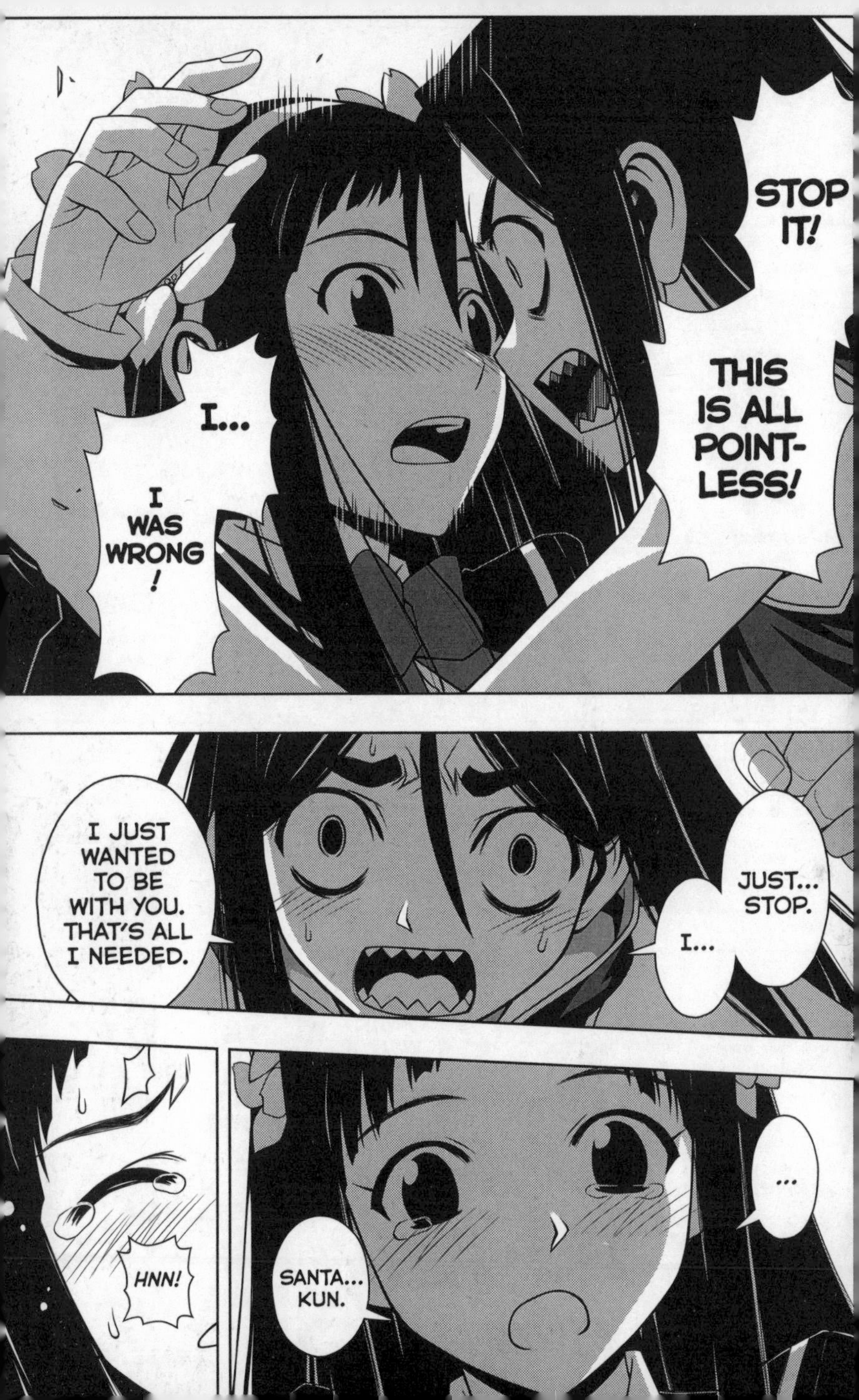
STOP IT!
THIS IS ALL POINT-LESS!
I...
I WAS WRONG!
JUST... STOP.
I...
I JUST WANTED TO BE WITH YOU. THAT'S ALL I NEEDED.
...
SANTA... KUN.
HNN!

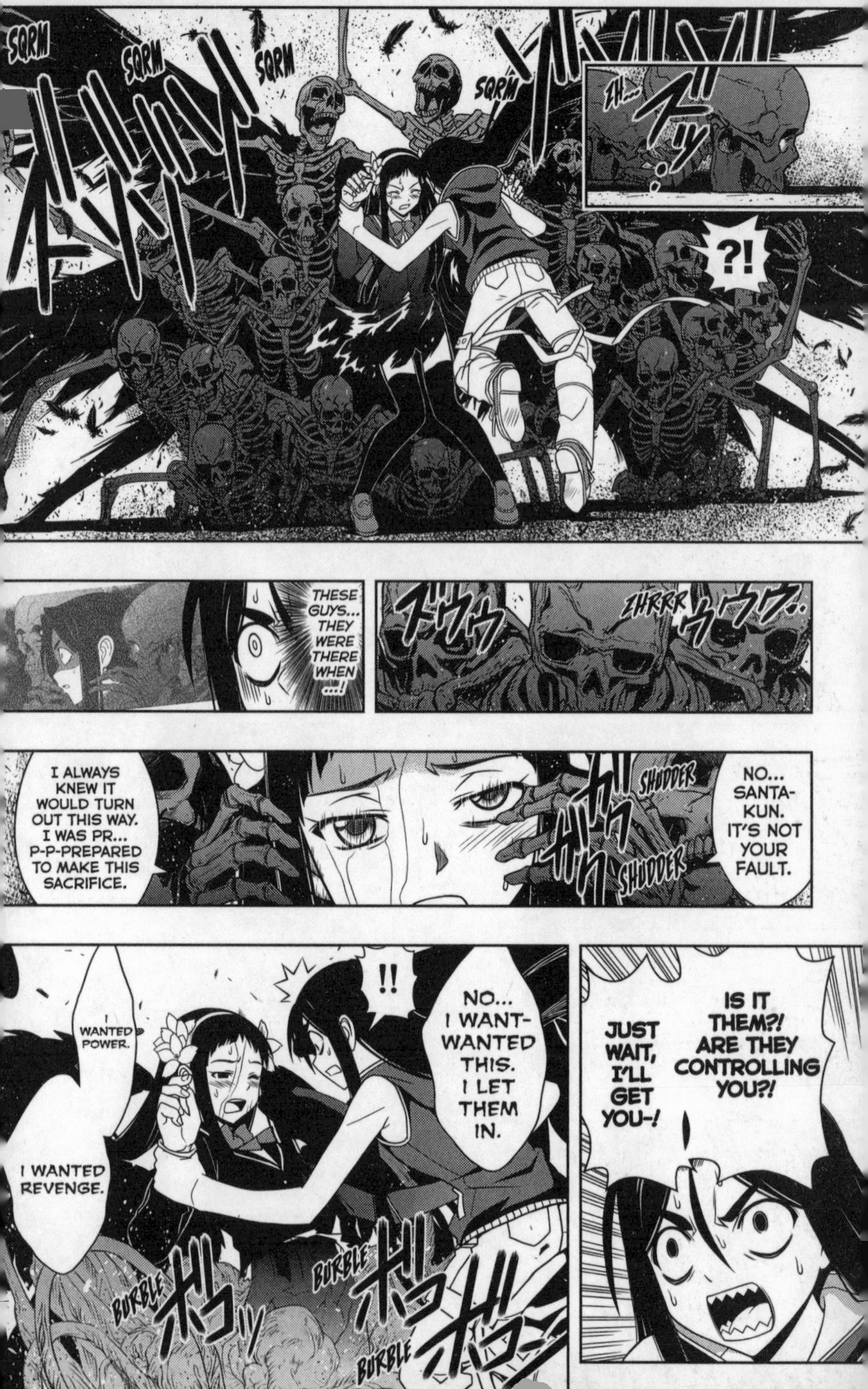
ZH...
SQRM
SQRM
SQRM
SQRM
?!
ZHRRR
THESE GUYS... THEY WERE THERE WHEN ...!
NO... SANTA-KUN. IT'S NOT YOUR FAULT.
SHUDDER
SHUDDER
I ALWAYS KNEW IT WOULD TURN OUT THIS WAY. I WAS PR... P-P-PREPARED TO MAKE THIS SACRIFICE.
IS IT THEM?! ARE THEY CONTROLLING YOU?!
JUST WAIT, I'LL GET YOU-!
!!
NO... I WANT-WANTED THIS. I LET THEM IN.
I WANTED POWER.
I WANTED REVENGE.
BURBLE
BURBLE
BURBLE

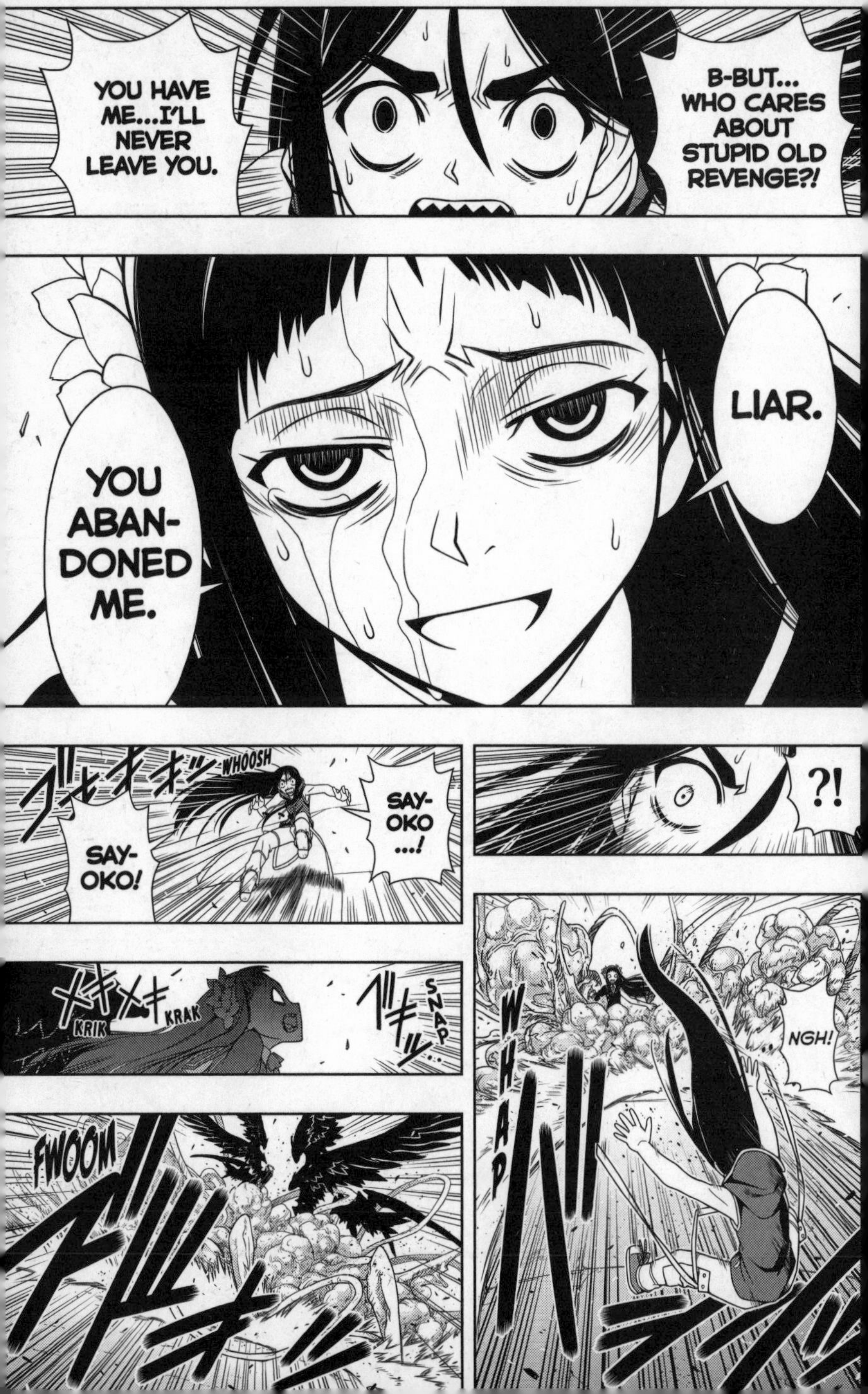
B-BUT... WHO CARES ABOUT STUPID OLD REVENGE?!
YOU HAVE ME...I'LL NEVER LEAVE YOU.
LIAR.
YOU ABAN-DONED ME.
?!
SAY-OKO...!
WHOOSH
SAY-OKO!
NGH!
WHAP
SNAP
KRAK
KRIK
FWOOM

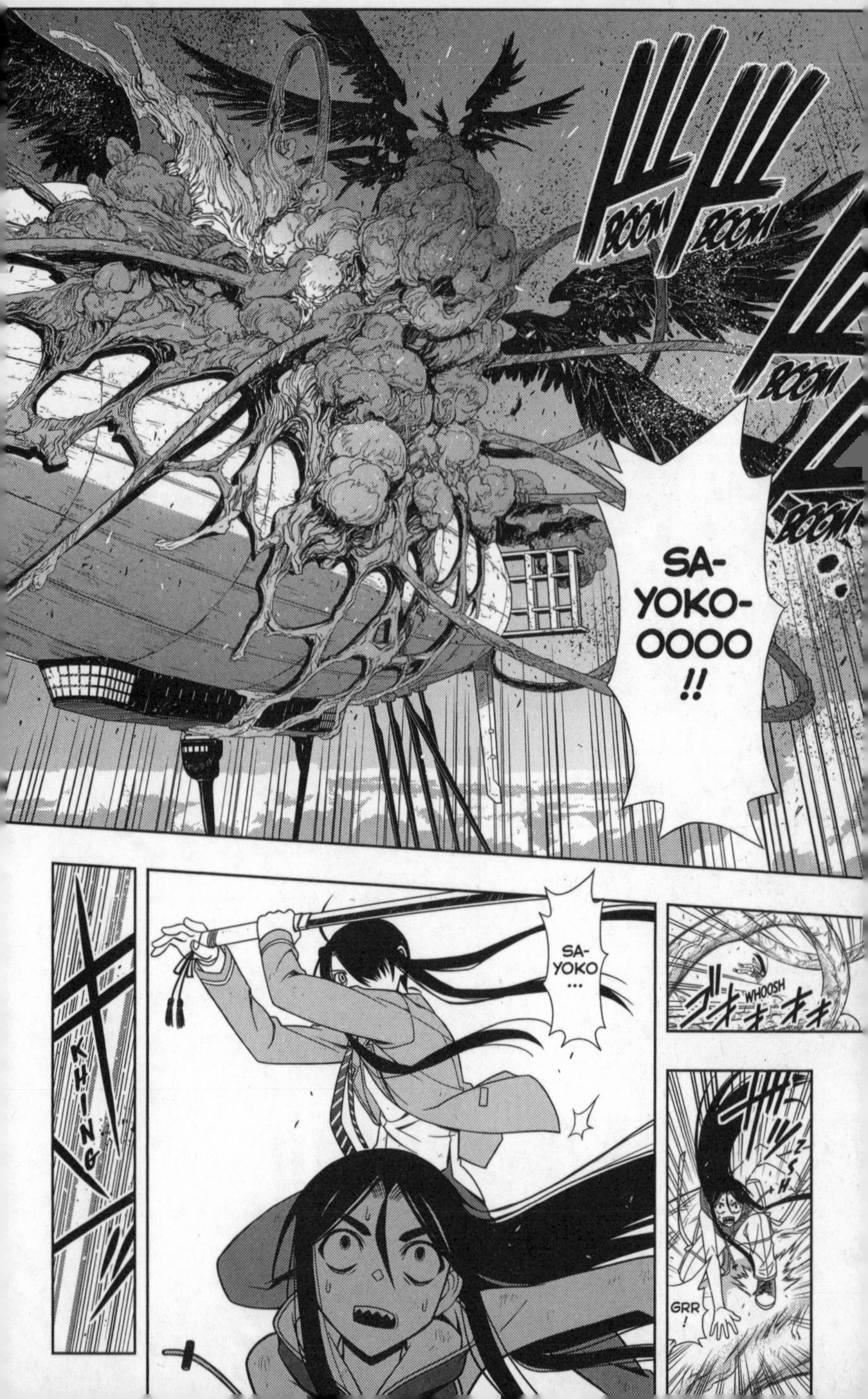
BOOM
BOOM
BOOM
BOOM
SA-YOKO-OOOO!!
WHOOSH
Z-SH
GRR!
SA-YOKO...
KHING

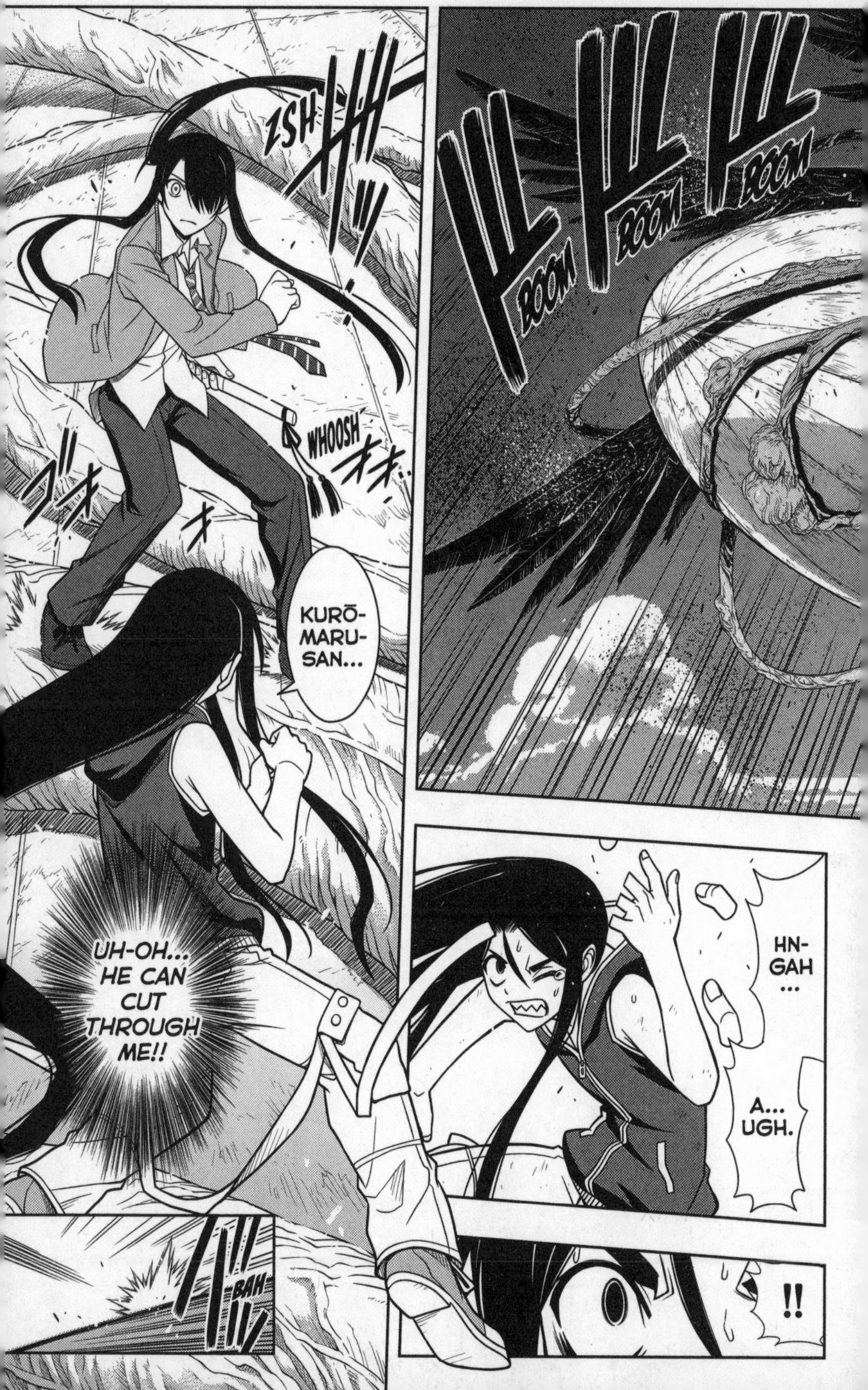

BOOM
BOOM
BOOM
ZSH
WHOOSH
KURŌ-MARU-SAN...
HN-GAH...
A... UGH.
UH-OH... HE CAN CUT THROUGH ME!!
!!
BAH

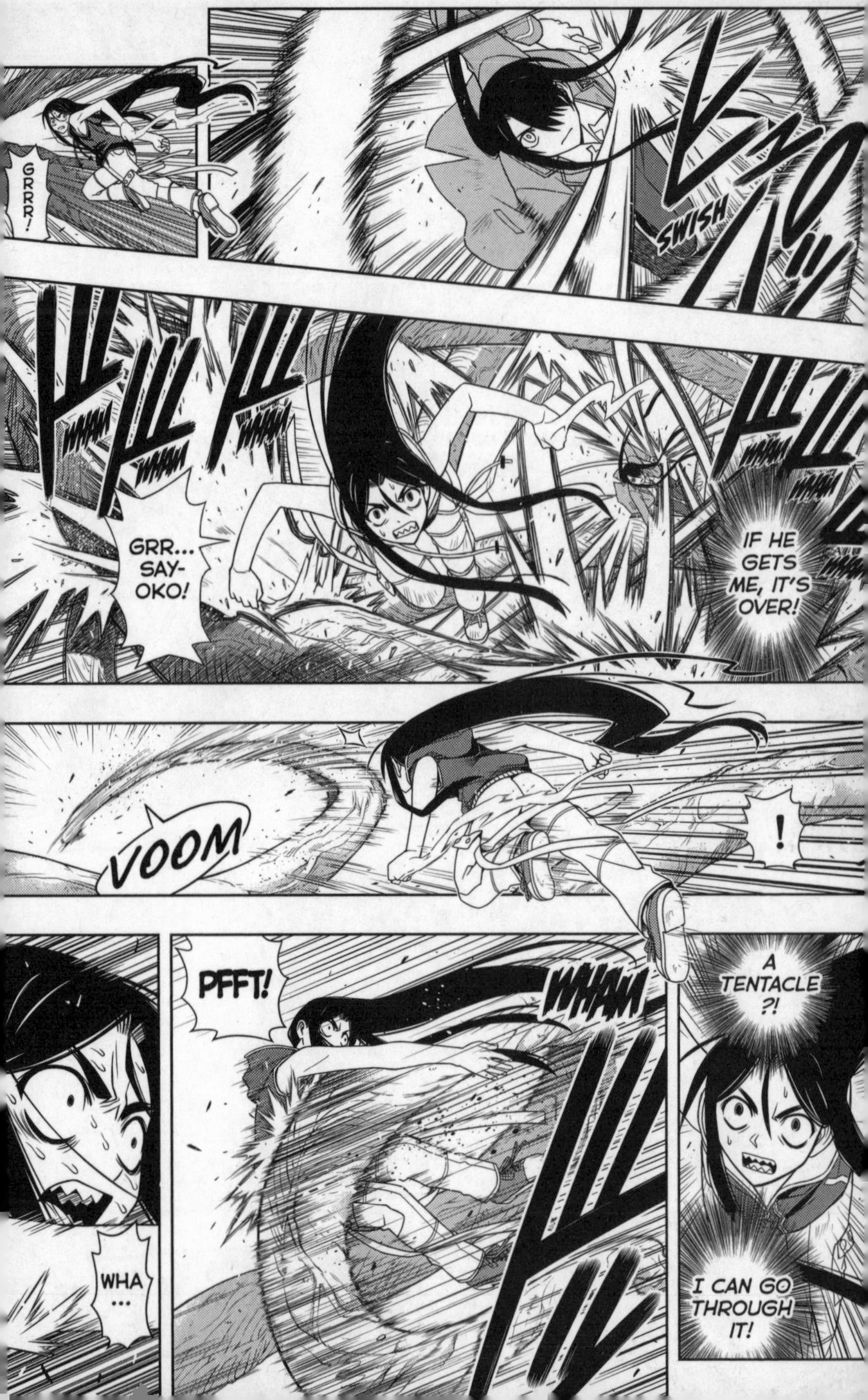
SWISH
GRRR!
IF HE GETS ME, IT'S OVER!
GRR... SAY-OKO!
!
VOOM
A TENTACLE?!
I CAN GO THROUGH IT!
WHAM
PFFT!
WHA...

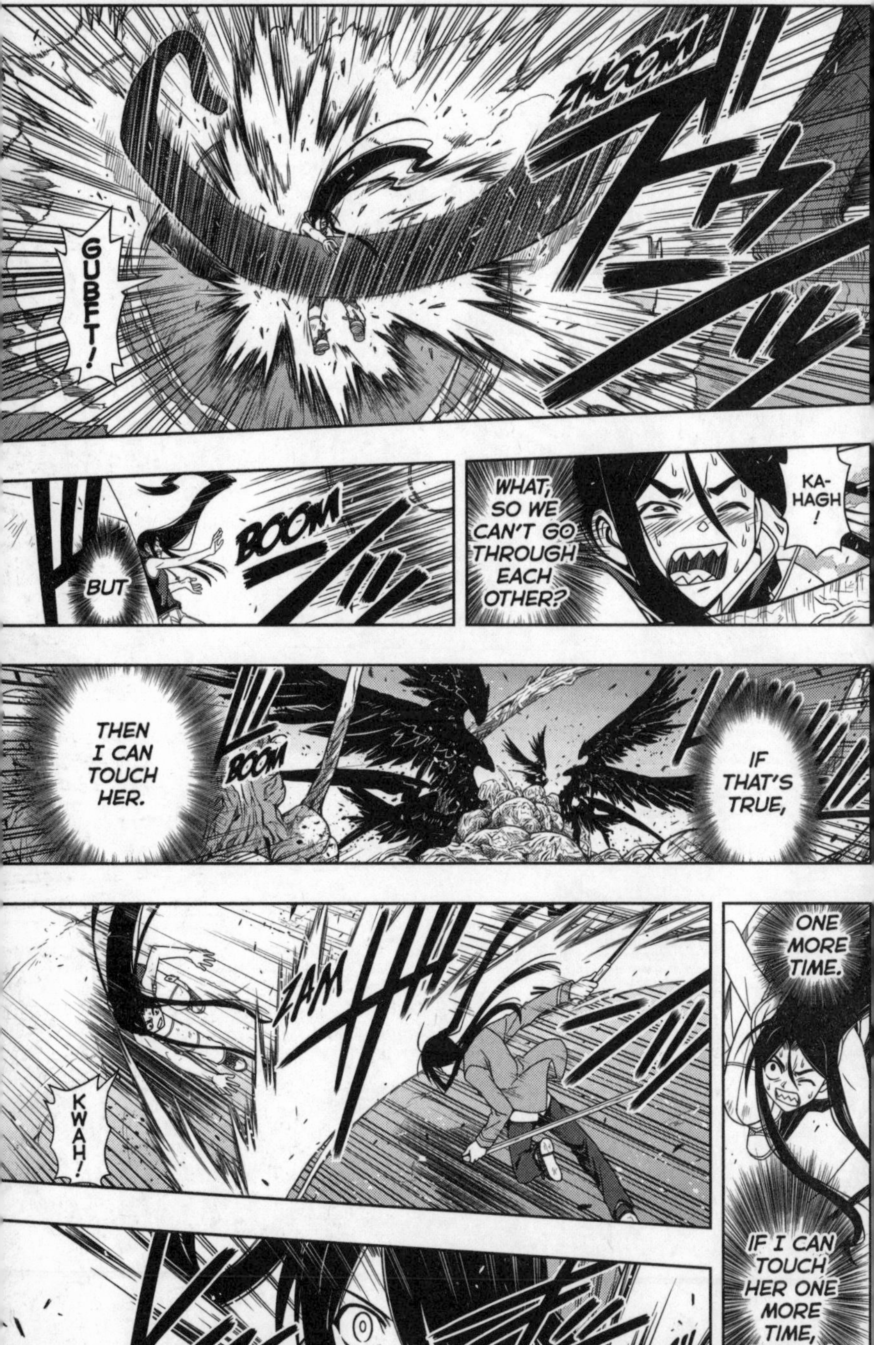
ZHOOM
GUBFT!
KA-HAGH!
WHAT, SO WE CAN'T GO THROUGH EACH OTHER?
BOOM
BUT
IF THAT'S TRUE,
BOOM
THEN I CAN TOUCH HER.
ONE MORE TIME.
IF I CAN TOUCH HER ONE MORE TIME, THEN...!
ZAM
KWAH!
SWOOSH

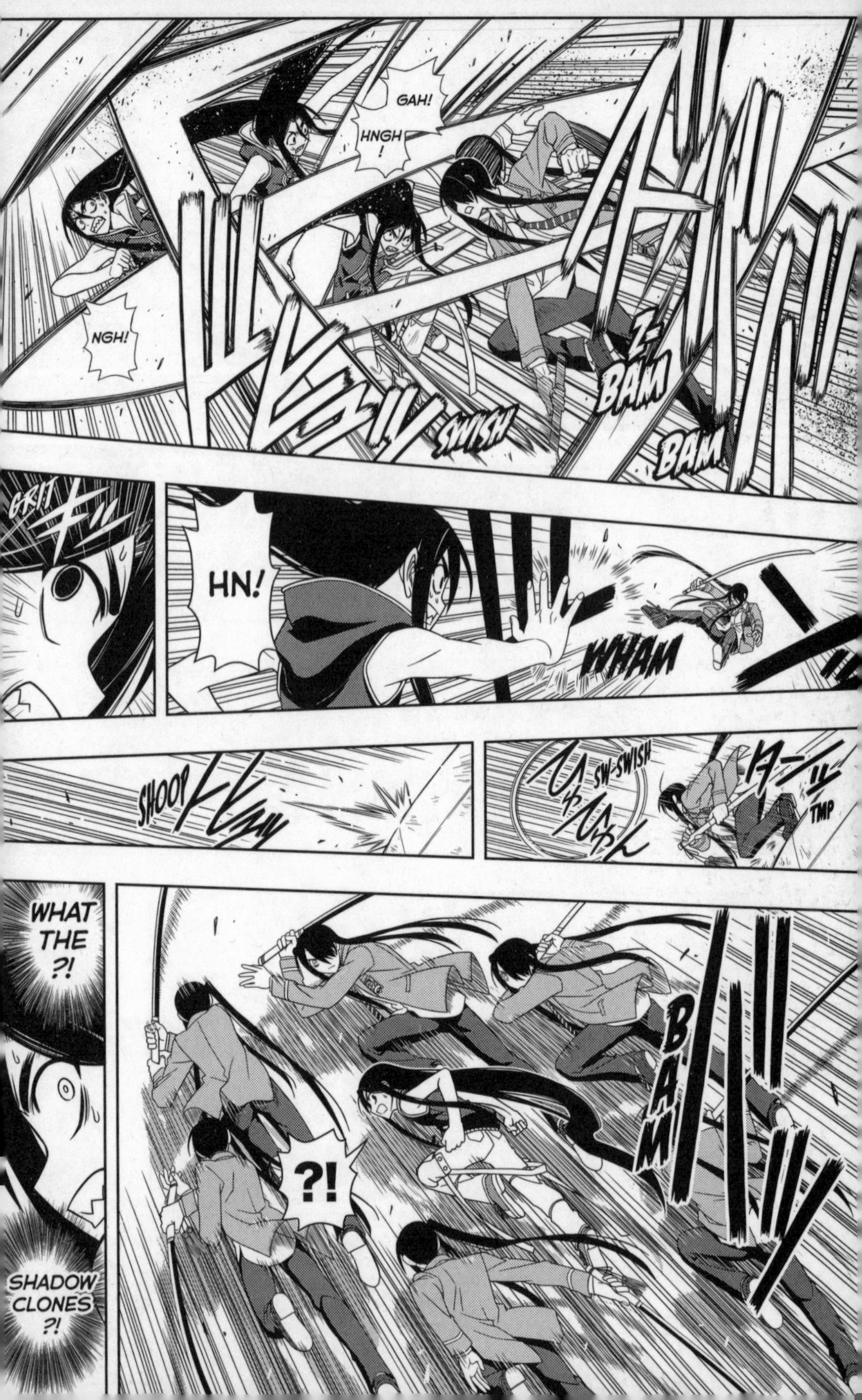
GAH!
HNGH!
Z-BAM
BAM
SWISH
NGH!
HN!
WHAM
GRIT
SW-SWISH
TMP
SHOOP
BAM
?!
WHAT THE ?!
SHADOW CLONES ?!

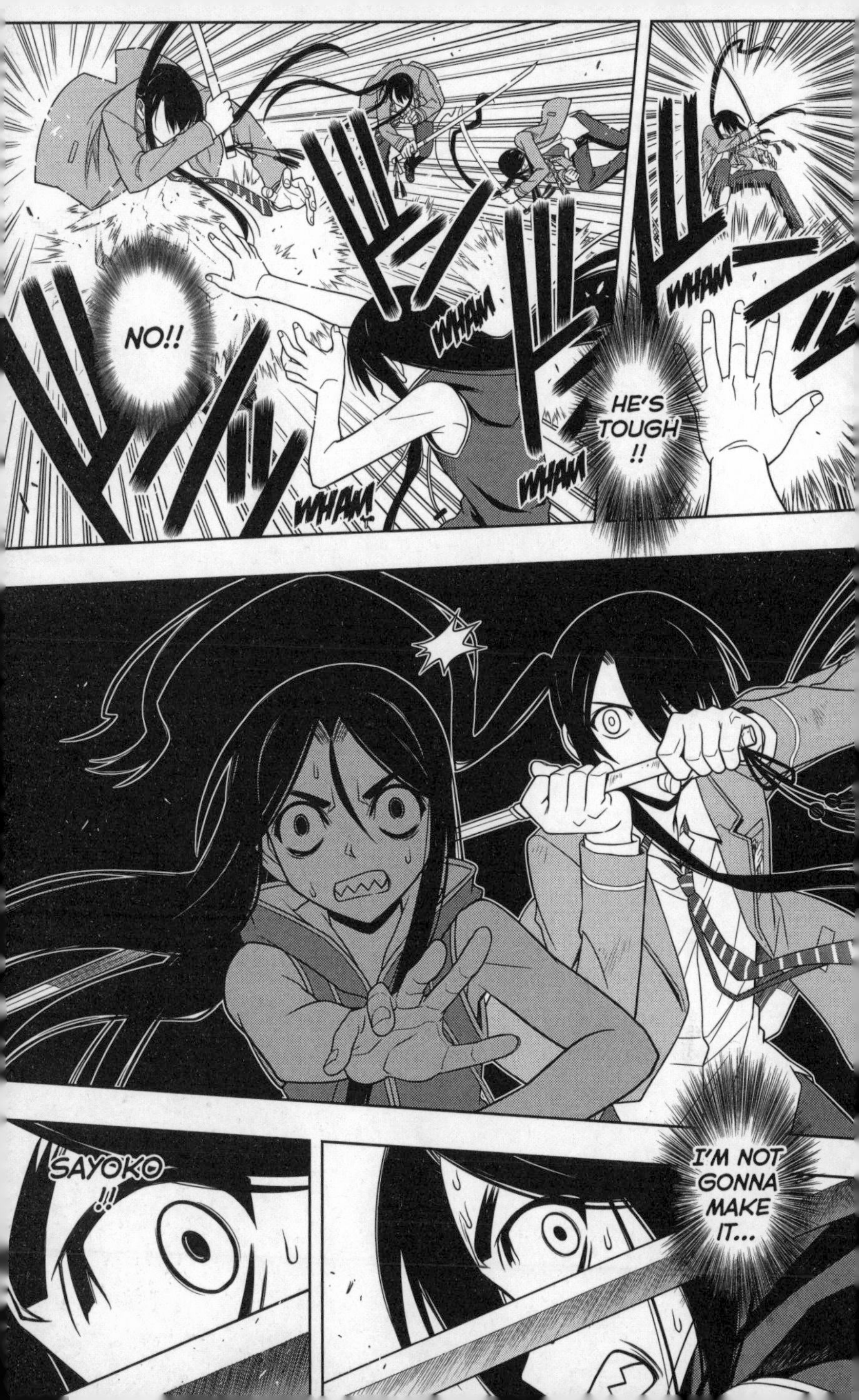
WHAM
HE'S TOUGH !!
WHAM
WHAM
NO!!
WHAM!
I'M NOT GONNA MAKE IT...
SAYOKO !!

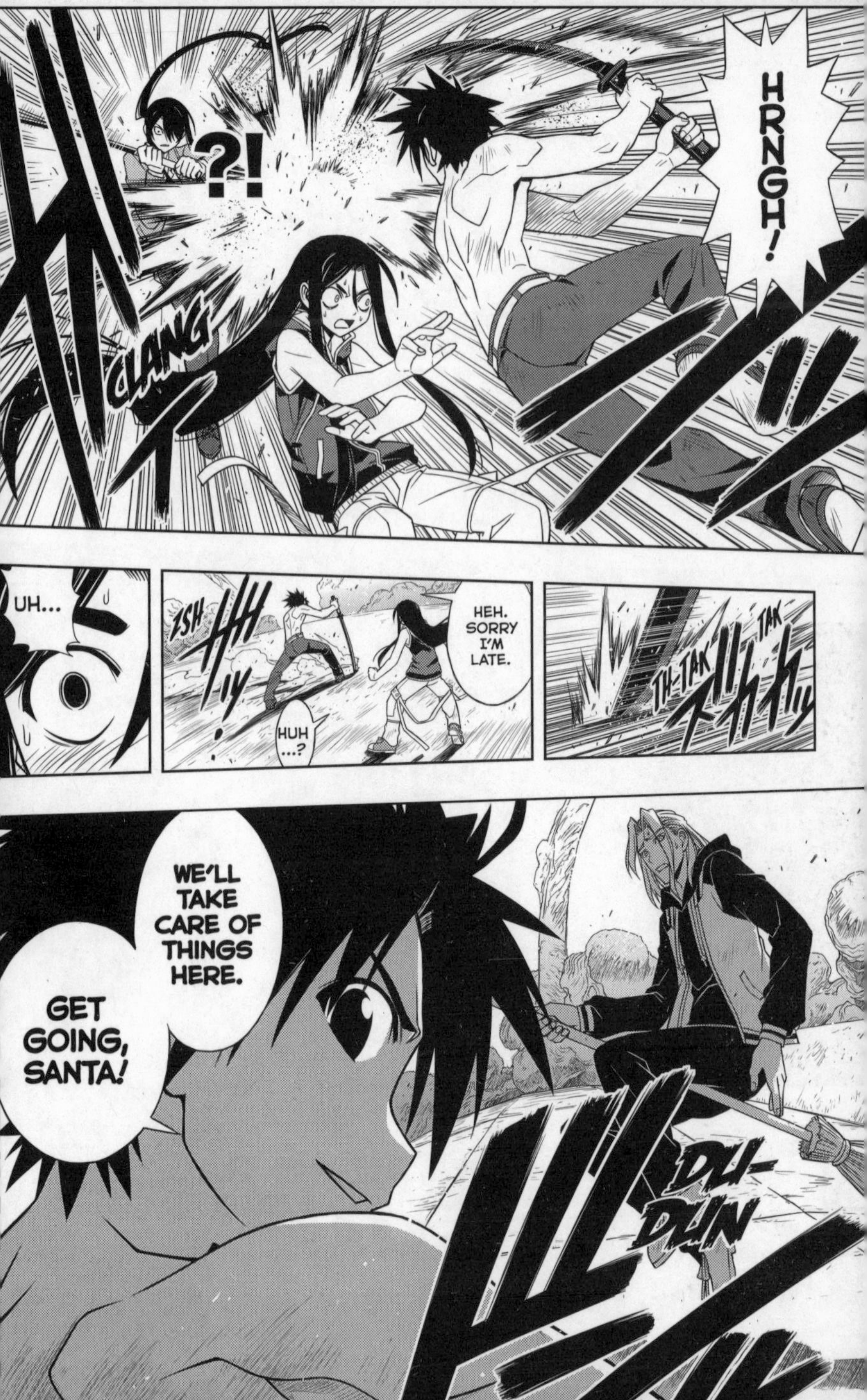
HRNGH!
?!
CLANG
TH-TAK
TAK
HEH. SORRY I'M LATE.
ISH
HUH ...?
UH...
WE'LL TAKE CARE OF THINGS HERE.
GET GOING, SANTA!
DU-DUN

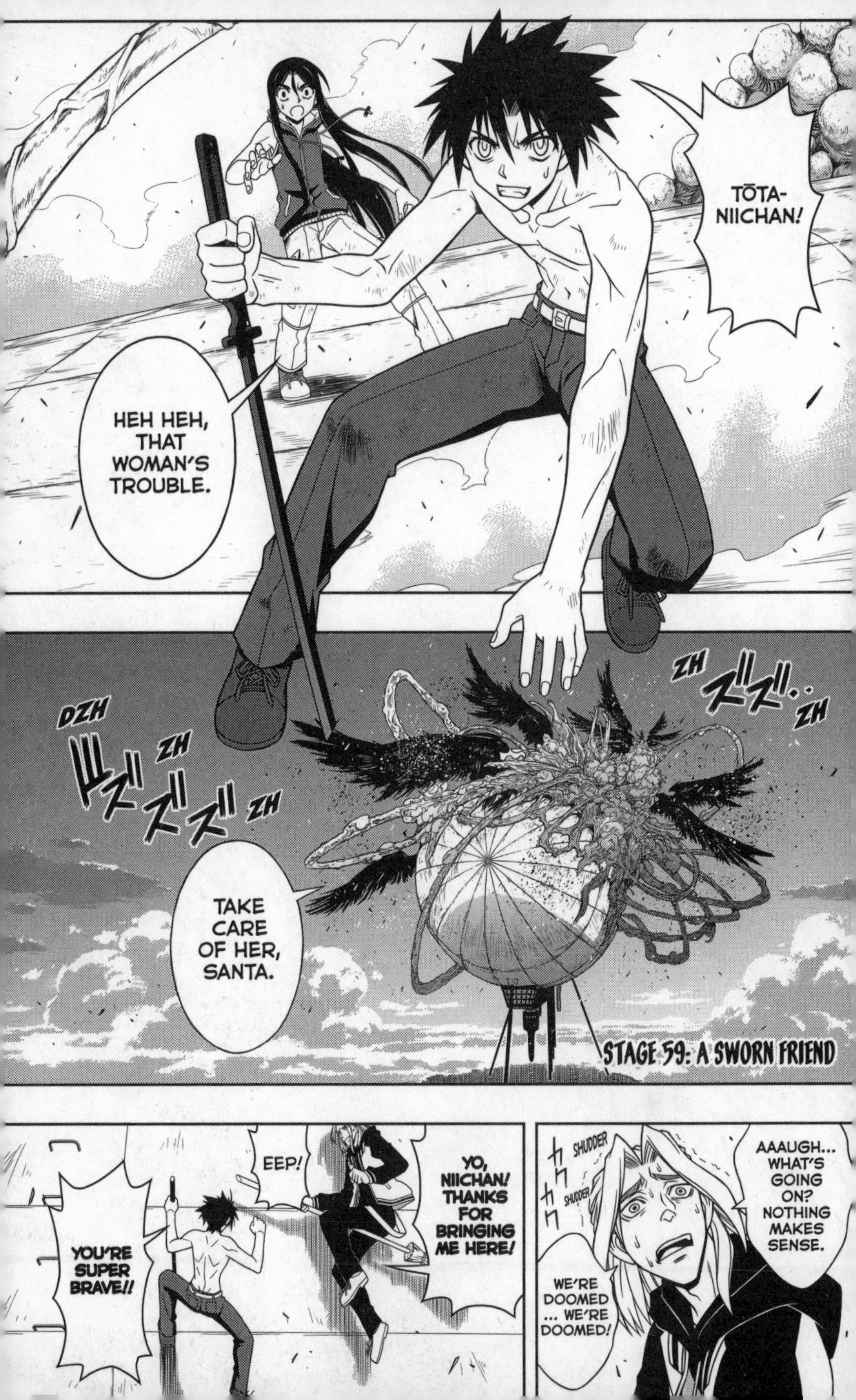
TŌTA-NIICHAN!
HEH HEH, THAT WOMAN'S TROUBLE.
ZH ZH
DZH ZH ZH
TAKE CARE OF HER, SANTA.
STAGE 59: A SWORN FRIEND
AAAUGH... WHAT'S GOING ON? NOTHING MAKES SENSE.
SHUDDER SHUDDER
WE'RE DOOMED ... WE'RE DOOMED!
YO, NIICHAN! THANKS FOR BRINGING ME HERE!
EEP!
YOU'RE SUPER BRAVE!!

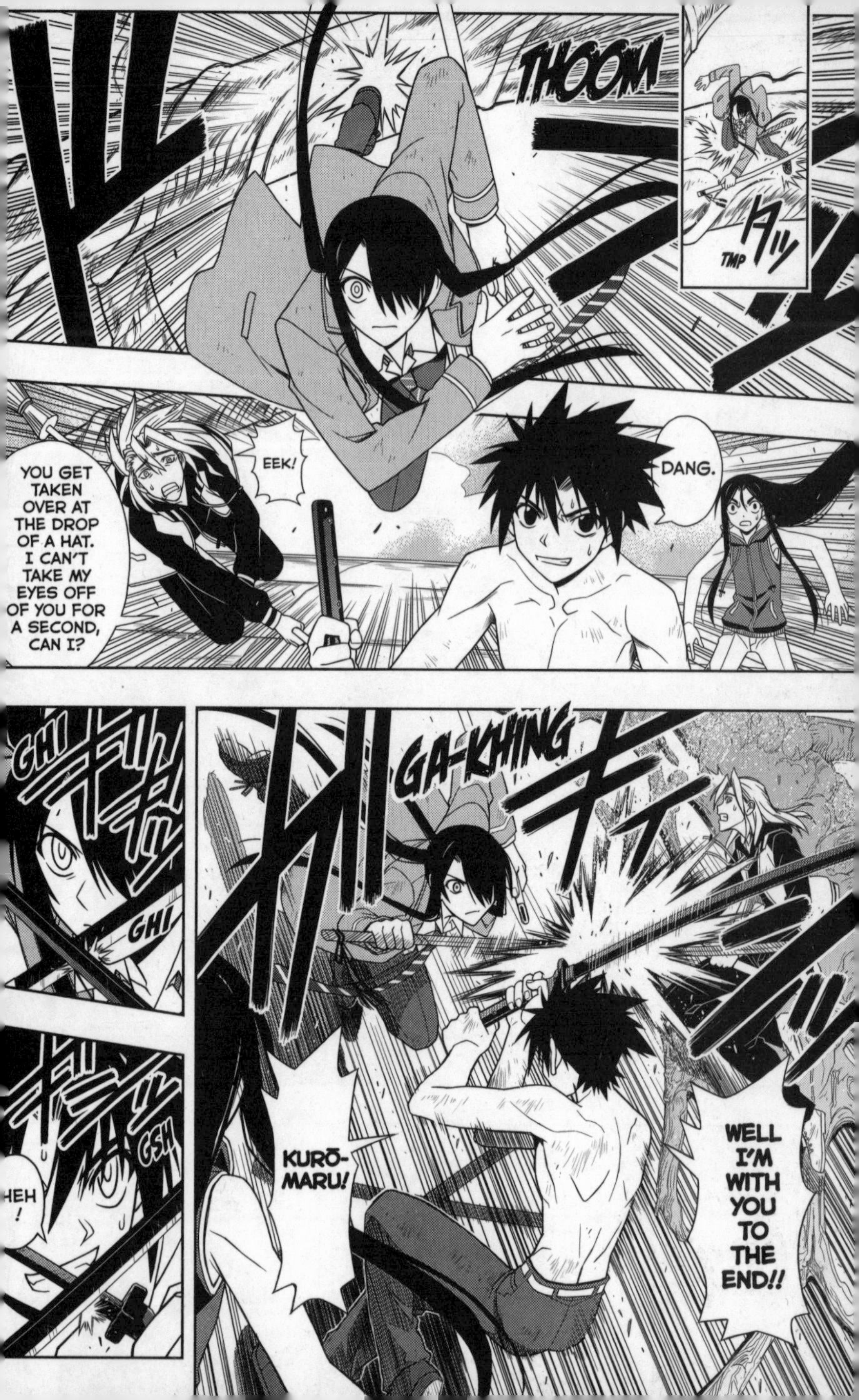
TMP
THOOM
DANG.
EEK!
YOU GET TAKEN OVER AT THE DROP OF A HAT. I CAN'T TAKE MY EYES OFF OF YOU FOR A SECOND, CAN I?
GA-KHING
WELL I'M WITH YOU TO THE END!!
KURŌ-MARU!
GHI
GHI
GSH
HEH!

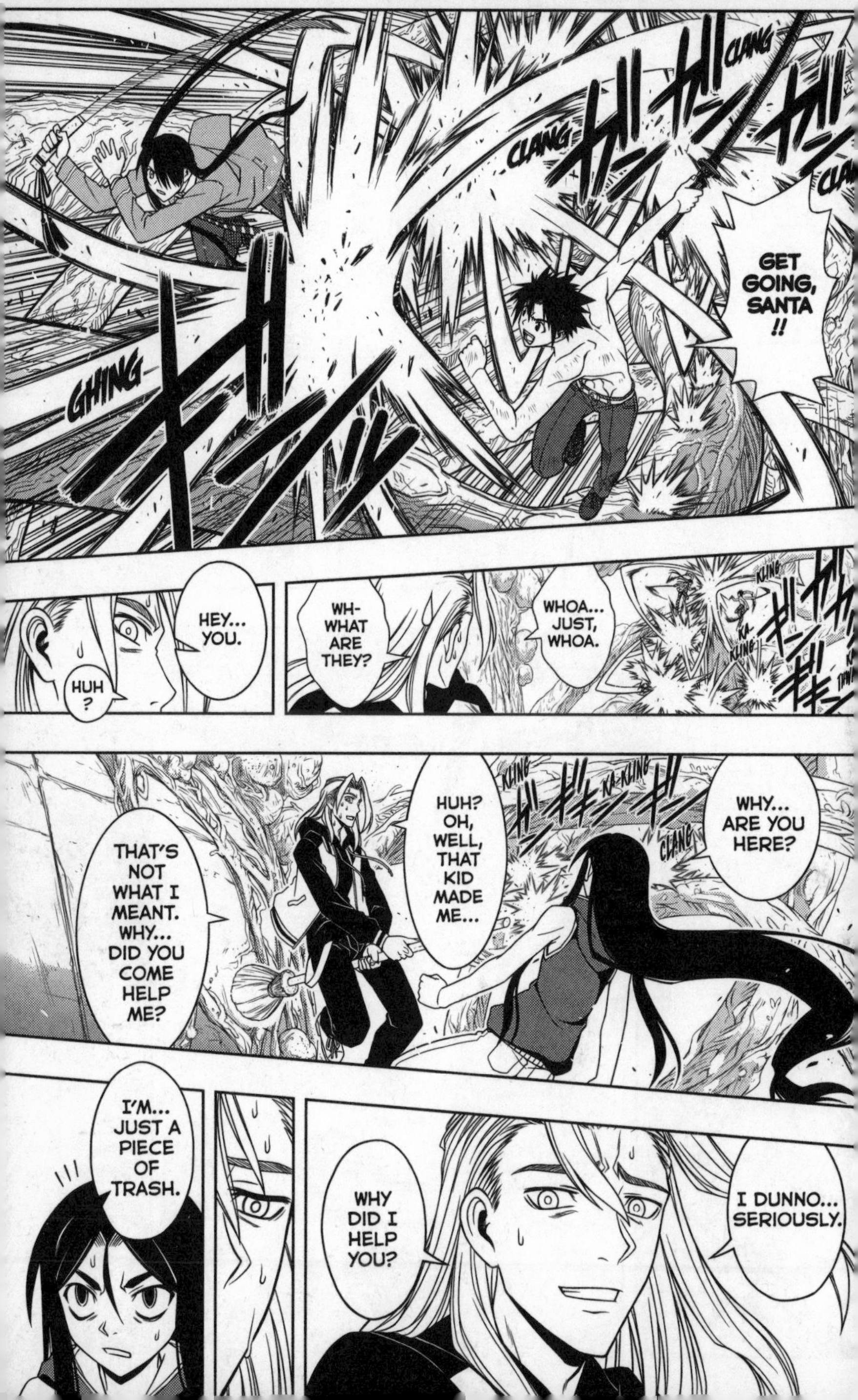
CLANG
GET GOING, SANTA!!
CLANG
CLANG
GHING
KLING
KA-KLING
WHOA... JUST, WHOA.
WH- WHAT ARE THEY?
HEY... YOU.
HUH?
WHY... ARE YOU HERE?
KLING
KA-KLING
CLANG
HUH? OH, WELL, THAT KID MADE ME...
THAT'S NOT WHAT I MEANT. WHY... DID YOU COME HELP ME?
I DUNNO... SERIOUSLY.
WHY DID I HELP YOU?
I'M... JUST A PIECE OF TRASH.

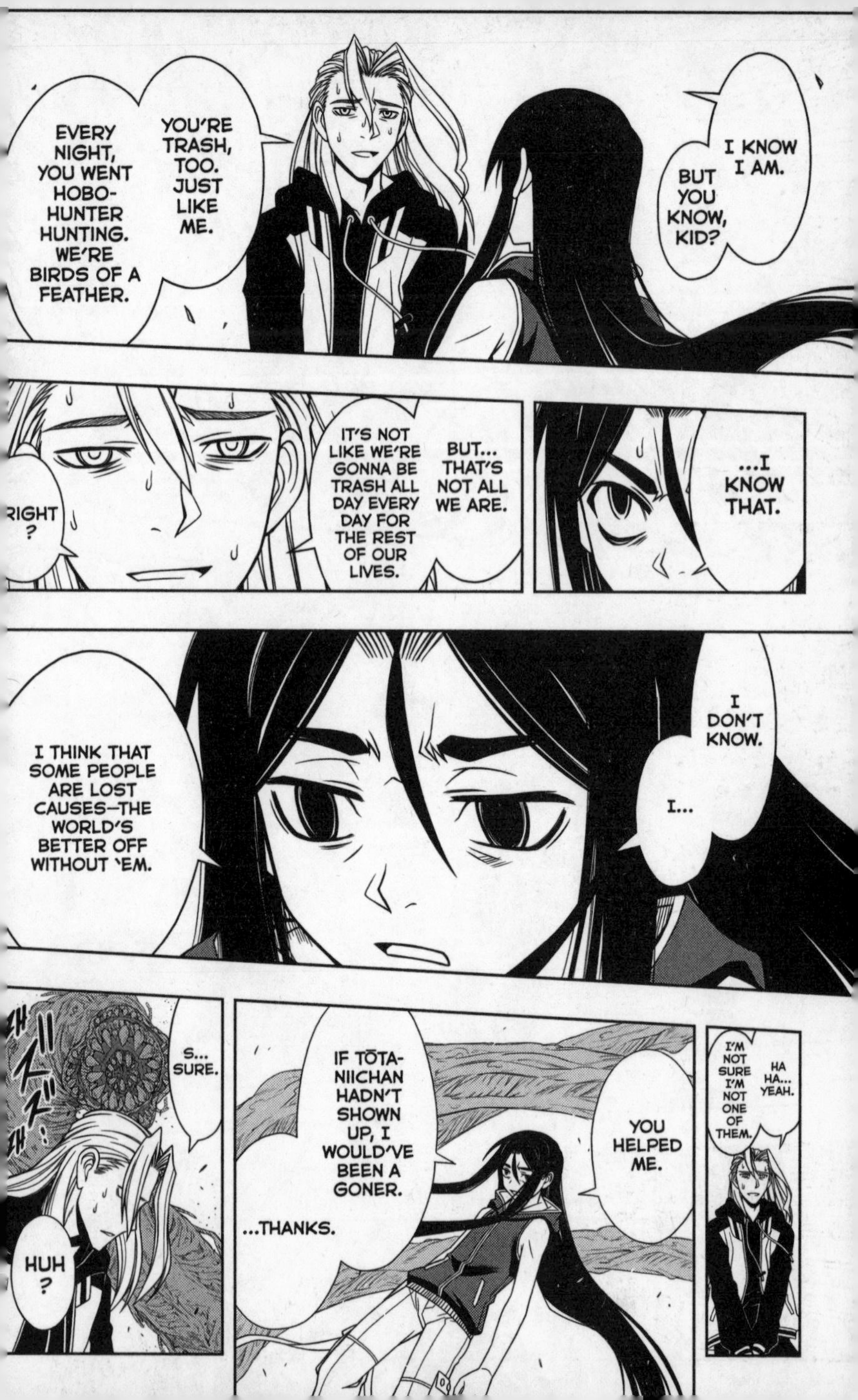
I KNOW I AM.
BUT YOU KNOW, KID?
YOU'RE TRASH, TOO. JUST LIKE ME.
EVERY NIGHT, YOU WENT HOBO-HUNTER HUNTING. WE'RE BIRDS OF A FEATHER.
...I KNOW THAT.
BUT... THAT'S NOT ALL WE ARE.
IT'S NOT LIKE WE'RE GONNA BE TRASH ALL DAY EVERY DAY FOR THE REST OF OUR LIVES.
RIGHT?
I DON'T KNOW.
I...
I THINK THAT SOME PEOPLE ARE LOST CAUSES—THE WORLD'S BETTER OFF WITHOUT 'EM.
HA HA... YEAH.
I'M NOT SURE I'M NOT ONE OF THEM.
YOU HELPED ME.
IF TŌTA-NIICHAN HADN'T SHOWN UP, I WOULD'VE BEEN A GONER.
...THANKS.
S... SURE.
HUH?
ZH

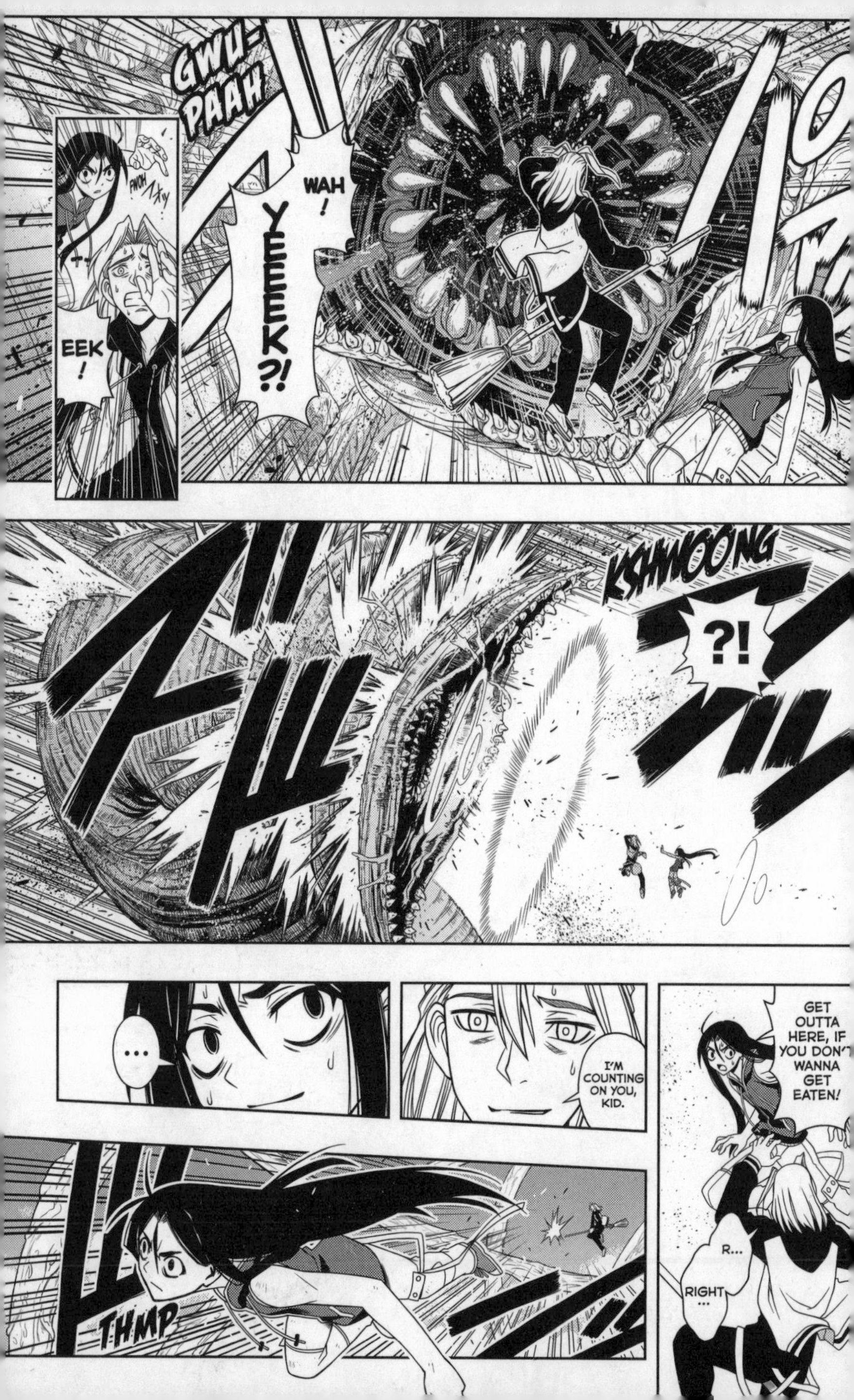
GWU-PAAH
WAH! YEEEEK?!
PWOH
EEK!
KSHWOONG
?!
GET OUTTA HERE, IF YOU DON'T WANNA GET EATEN!
R... RIGHT...
I'M COUNTING ON YOU, KID.
...
THMP

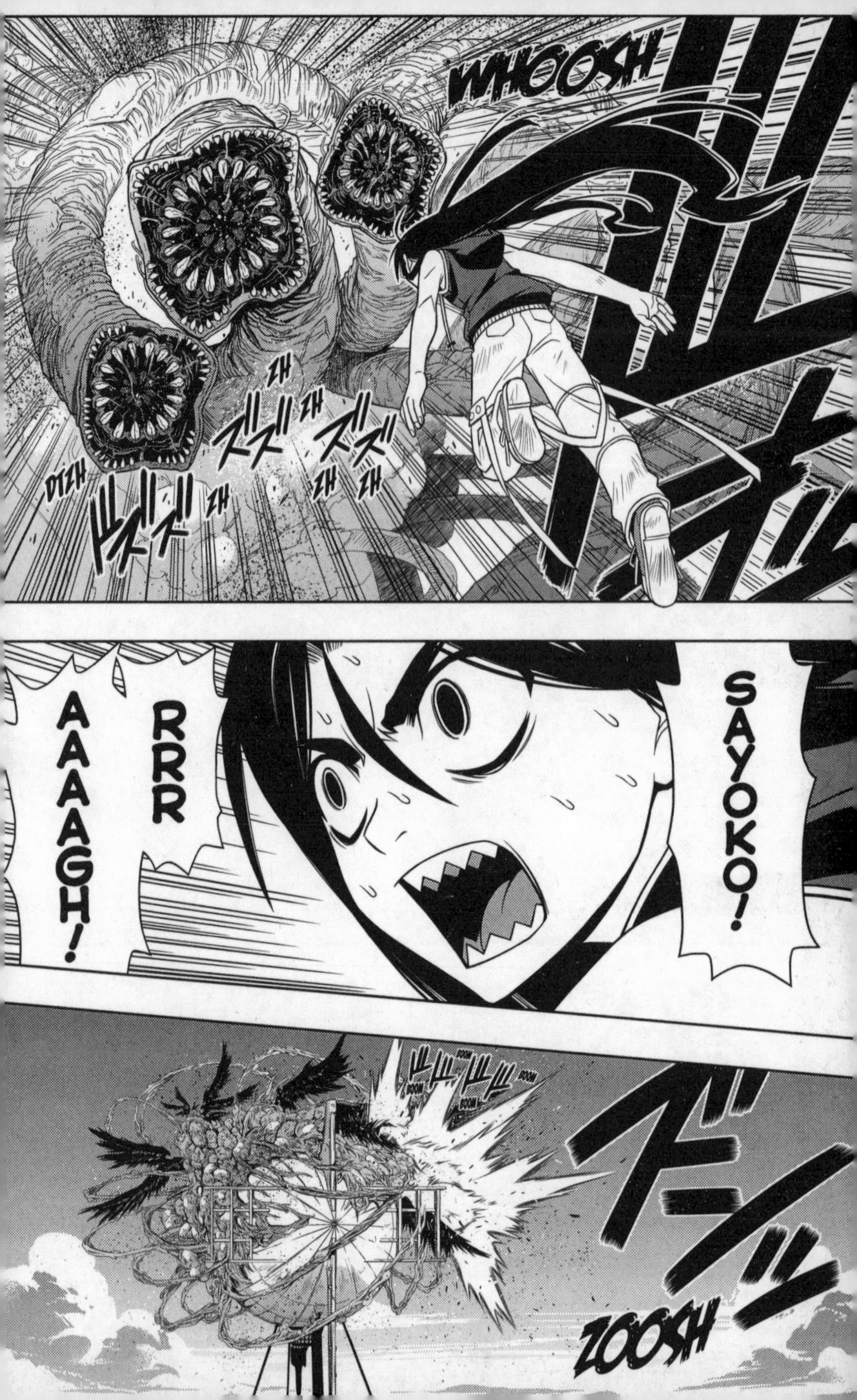
WHOOSH
ZH
ZH
ZH
ZH
ZH
ZH
DTZH
SAYOKO!
RRR AAAAGH!
BOOM
BOOM
BOOM
BOOM
ZOOSH

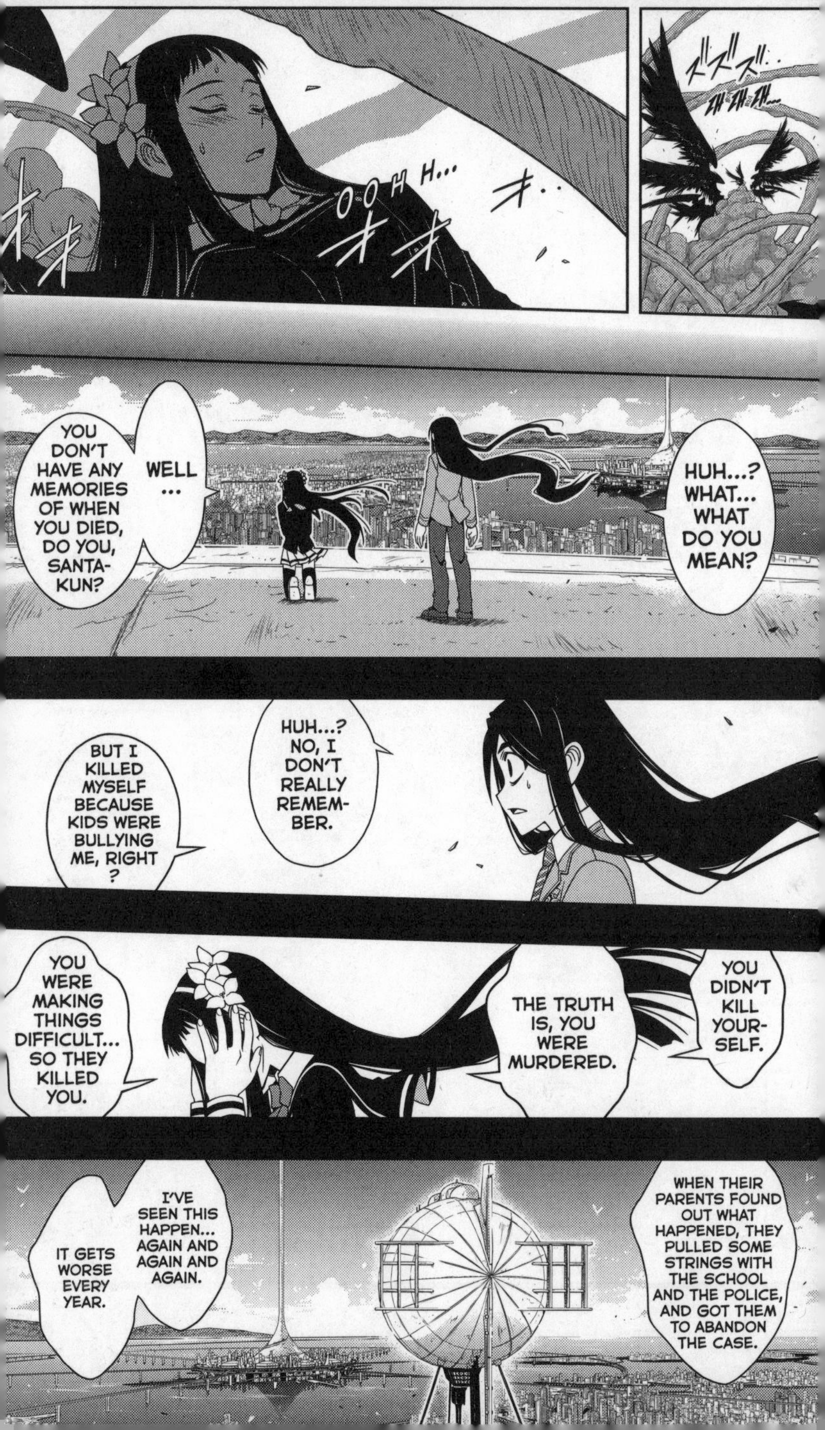
ズズズ...
ZH ZH ZH...
OOHH...
オオオオ...
HUH...? WHAT... WHAT DO YOU MEAN?
WELL ...
YOU DON'T HAVE ANY MEMORIES OF WHEN YOU DIED, DO YOU, SANTA-KUN?
HUH...? NO, I DON'T REALLY REMEMBER.
BUT I KILLED MYSELF BECAUSE KIDS WERE BULLYING ME, RIGHT ?
YOU DIDN'T KILL YOURSELF.
THE TRUTH IS, YOU WERE MURDERED.
YOU WERE MAKING THINGS DIFFICULT... SO THEY KILLED YOU.
WHEN THEIR PARENTS FOUND OUT WHAT HAPPENED, THEY PULLED SOME STRINGS WITH THE SCHOOL AND THE POLICE, AND GOT THEM TO ABANDON THE CASE.
I'VE SEEN THIS HAPPEN... AGAIN AND AGAIN AND AGAIN.
IT GETS WORSE EVERY YEAR.

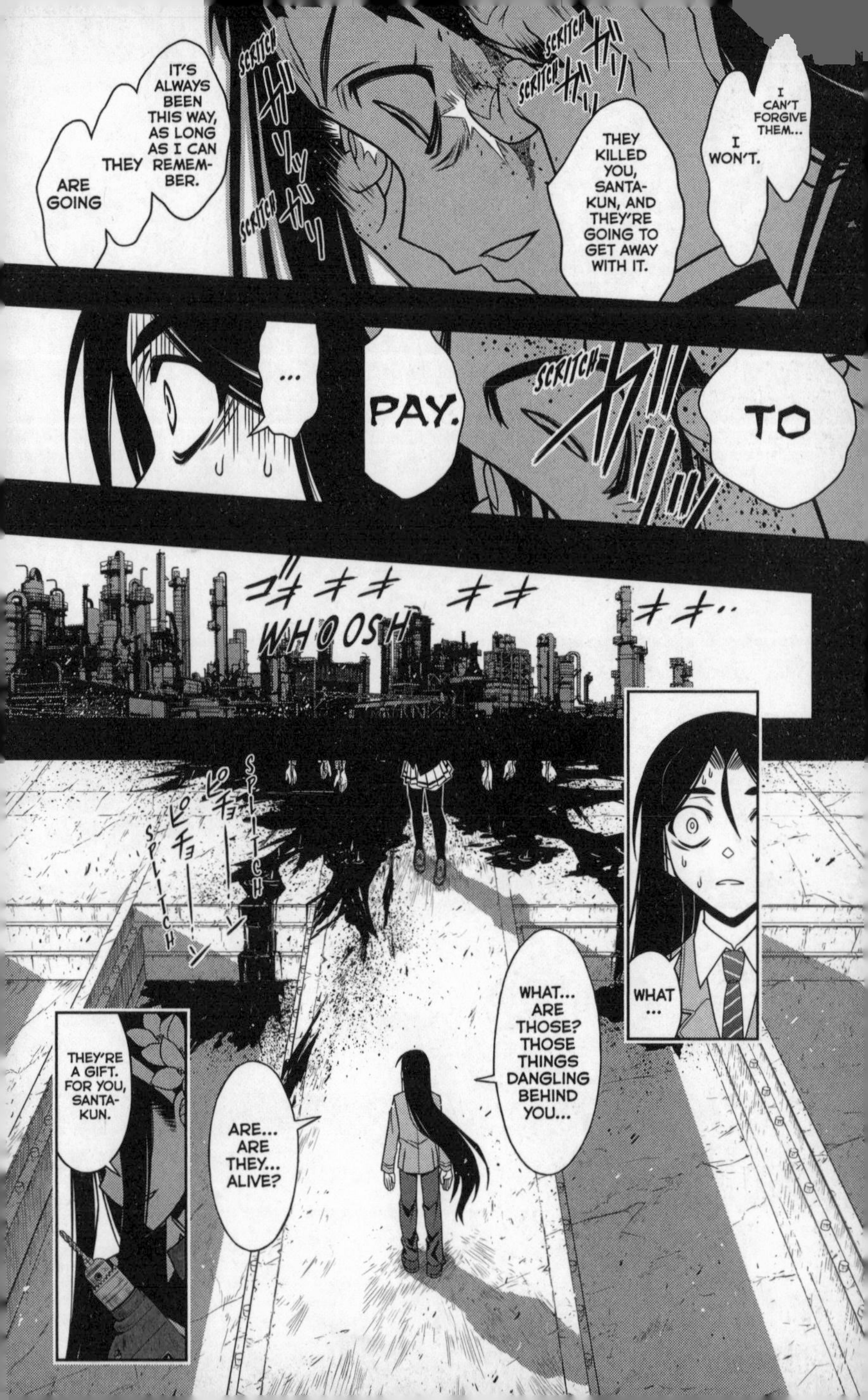
I CAN'T FORGIVE THEM...
I WON'T.
SCRITCH
SCRITCH
THEY KILLED YOU, SANTA-KUN, AND THEY'RE GOING TO GET AWAY WITH IT.
SCRITCH
SCRITCH
IT'S ALWAYS BEEN THIS WAY, AS LONG AS I CAN REMEMBER.
THEY ARE GOING
TO
SCRITCH
PAY.
...
WHOOSH
SPLITCH
SPLITCH
WHAT ...
WHAT... ARE THOSE? THOSE THINGS DANGLING BEHIND YOU...
ARE... ARE THEY... ALIVE?
THEY'RE A GIFT. FOR YOU, SANTA-KUN.

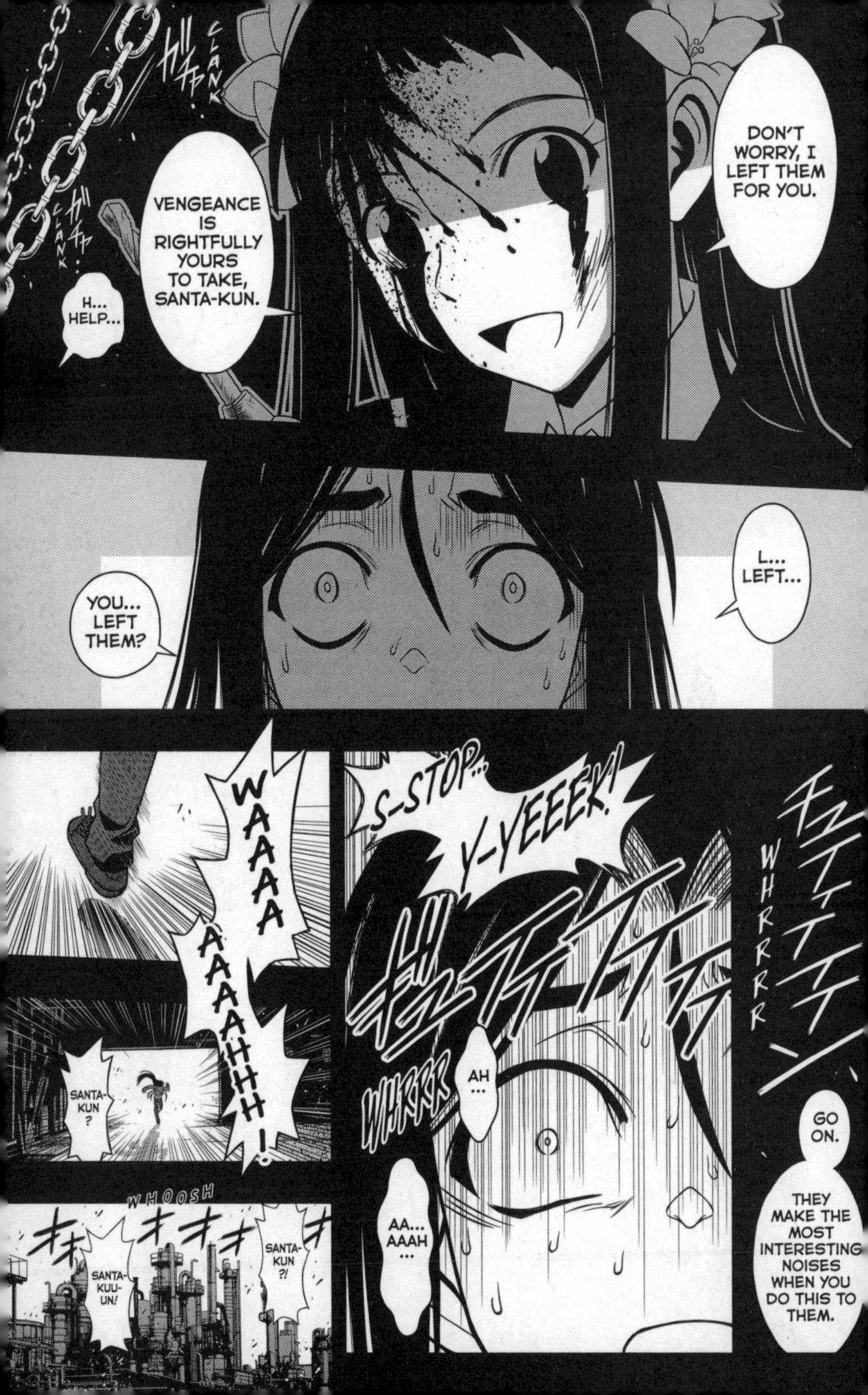
DON'T WORRY, I LEFT THEM FOR YOU.
VENGEANCE IS RIGHTFULLY YOURS TO TAKE, SANTA-KUN.
CLANK
CLANK
H... HELP...
L... LEFT...
YOU... LEFT THEM?
WHRRRR
S-STOP...
Y-YEEEK!
AH...
WHRRR
GO ON.
THEY MAKE THE MOST INTERESTING NOISES WHEN YOU DO THIS TO THEM.
AA... AAAH...
WAAAAAAAAAHHHH!
SANTA-KUN?
WHOOSH
SANTA-KUN?!
SANTA-KUU-UN!

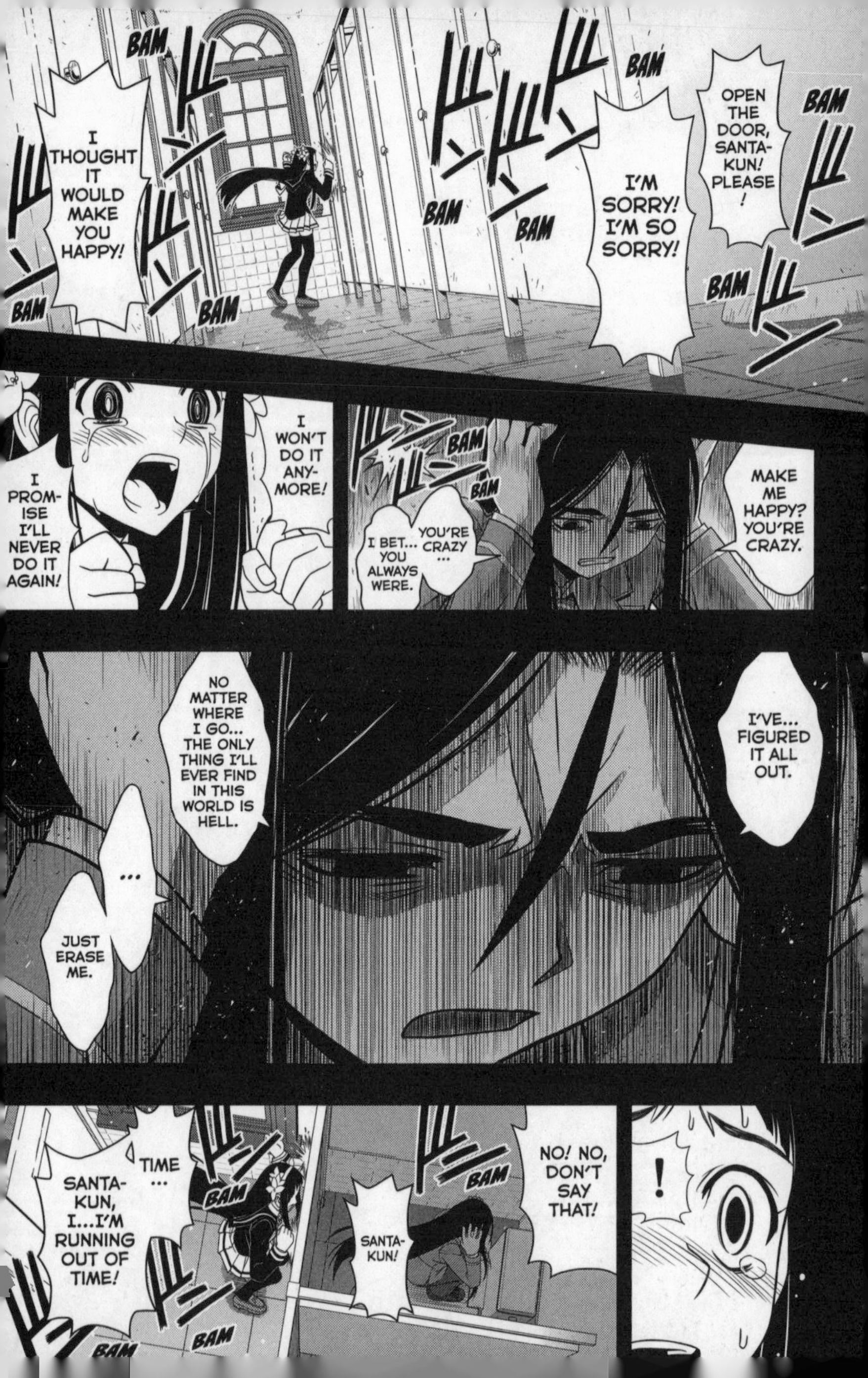
BAM
OPEN THE DOOR, SANTA-KUN! PLEASE!
BAM
BAM
I'M SORRY! I'M SO SORRY!
BAM
BAM
BAM
I THOUGHT IT WOULD MAKE YOU HAPPY!
BAM
BAM
MAKE ME HAPPY? YOU'RE CRAZY.
BAM
BAM
YOU'RE CRAZY...
I BET... YOU ALWAYS WERE.
I WON'T DO IT ANYMORE!
I PROMISE I'LL NEVER DO IT AGAIN!
I'VE... FIGURED IT ALL OUT.
NO MATTER WHERE I GO... THE ONLY THING I'LL EVER FIND IN THIS WORLD IS HELL.
...
JUST ERASE ME.
!
NO! NO, DON'T SAY THAT!
BAM
SANTA-KUN!
TIME...
SANTA-KUN, I...I'M RUNNING OUT OF TIME!
BAM
BAM
BAM

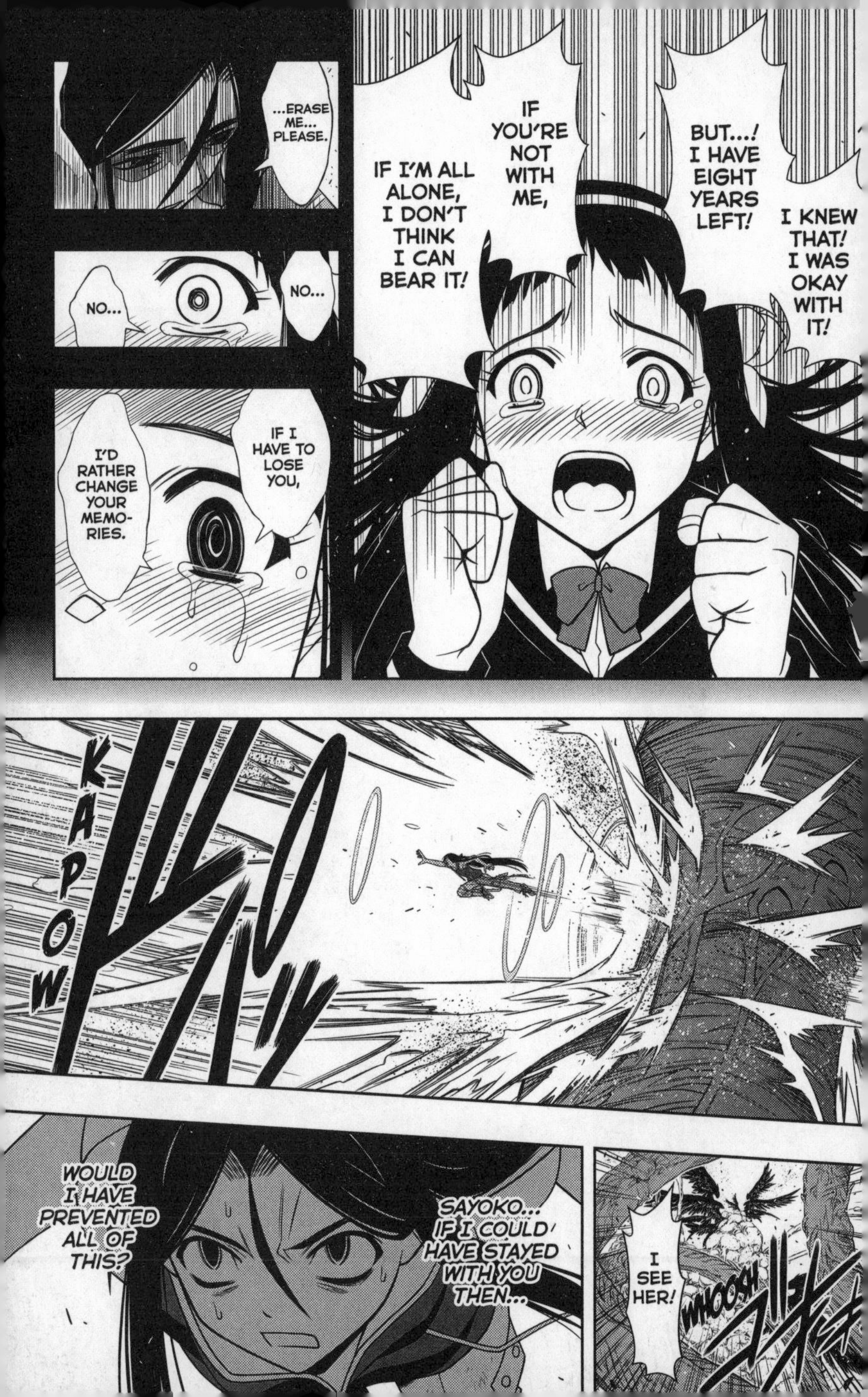
I KNEW THAT! I WAS OKAY WITH IT!
BUT...! I HAVE EIGHT YEARS LEFT!
IF YOU'RE NOT WITH ME,
IF I'M ALL ALONE, I DON'T THINK I CAN BEAR IT!
...ERASE ME... PLEASE.
NO...
NO...
IF I HAVE TO LOSE YOU,
I'D RATHER CHANGE YOUR MEMORIES.
KAPOW
WHOOSH
I SEE HER!
SAYOKO... IF I COULD HAVE STAYED WITH YOU THEN...
WOULD I HAVE PREVENTED ALL OF THIS?

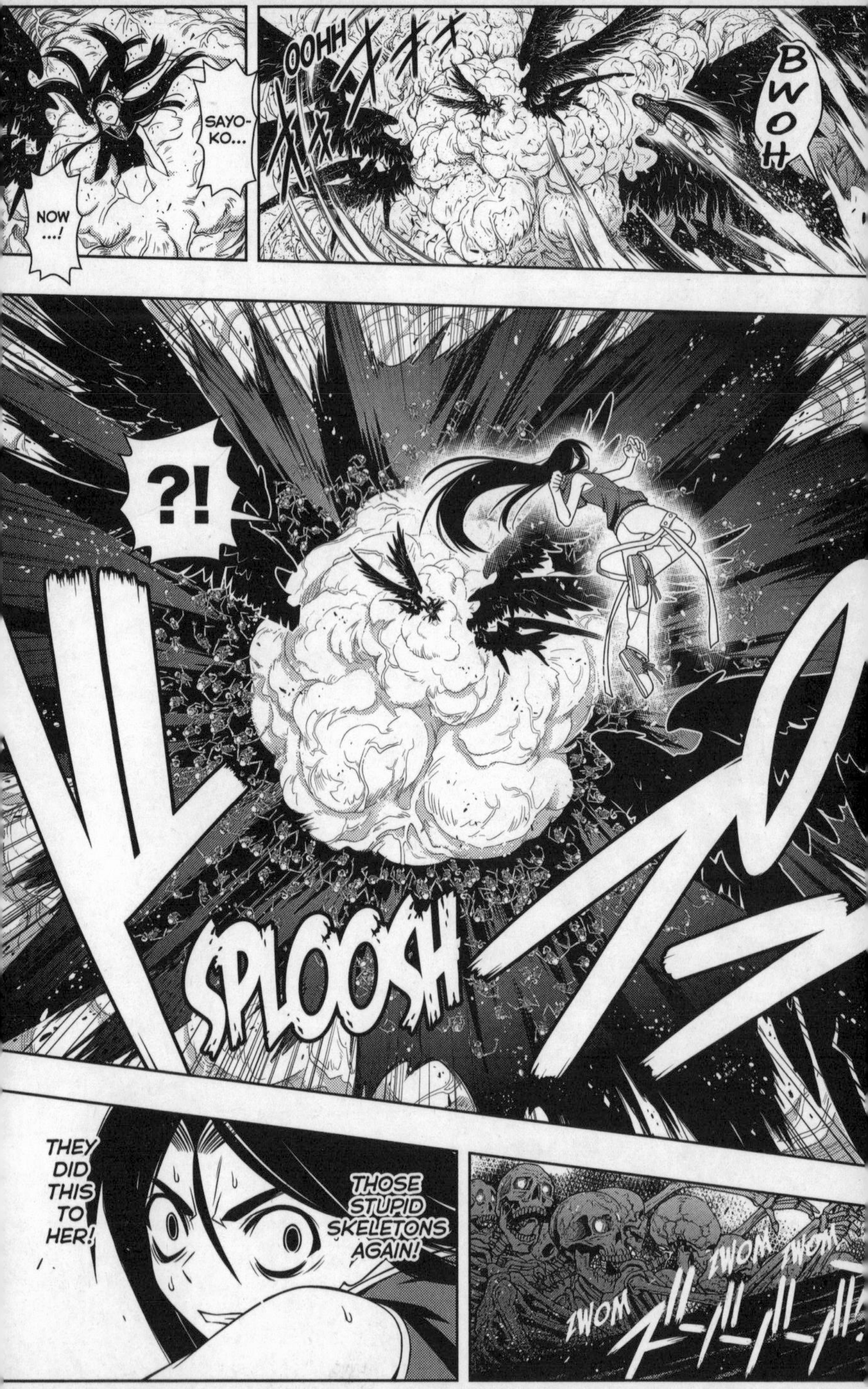
BWOH
OOHH
SAYO-KO...
NOW ...!
?!
SPLOOSH
ZWOM
ZWOM
ZWOM
THOSE STUPID SKELETONS AGAIN!
THEY DID THIS TO HER!

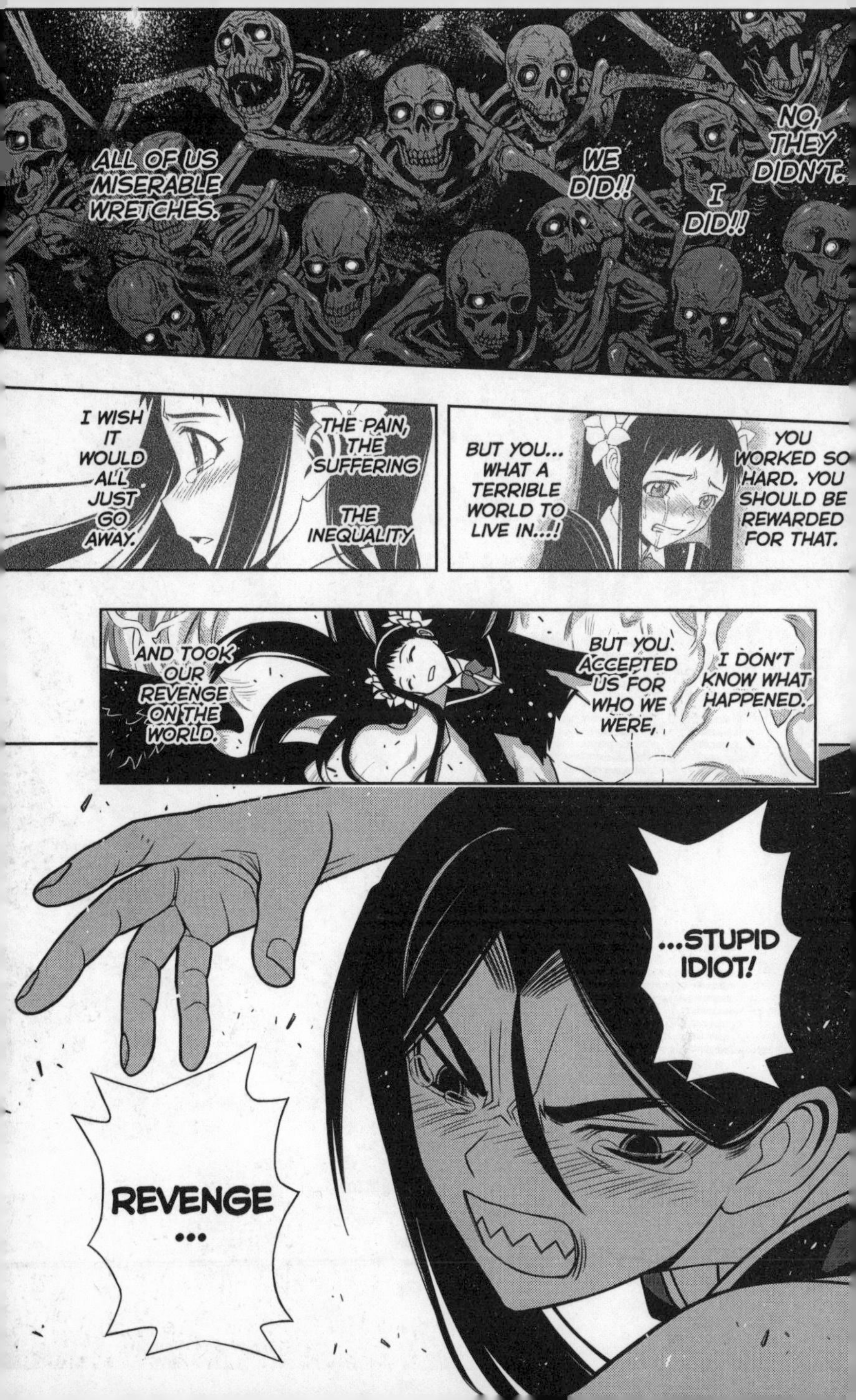
NO, THEY DIDN'T.
I DID!!
WE DID!!
ALL OF US MISERABLE WRETCHES.
YOU WORKED SO HARD. YOU SHOULD BE REWARDED FOR THAT.
BUT YOU... WHAT A TERRIBLE WORLD TO LIVE IN...!
THE PAIN, THE SUFFERING
THE INEQUALITY
I WISH IT WOULD ALL JUST GO AWAY.
I DON'T KNOW WHAT HAPPENED.
BUT YOU ACCEPTED US FOR WHO WE WERE,
AND TOOK OUR REVENGE ON THE WORLD.
...STUPID IDIOT!
REVENGE
...

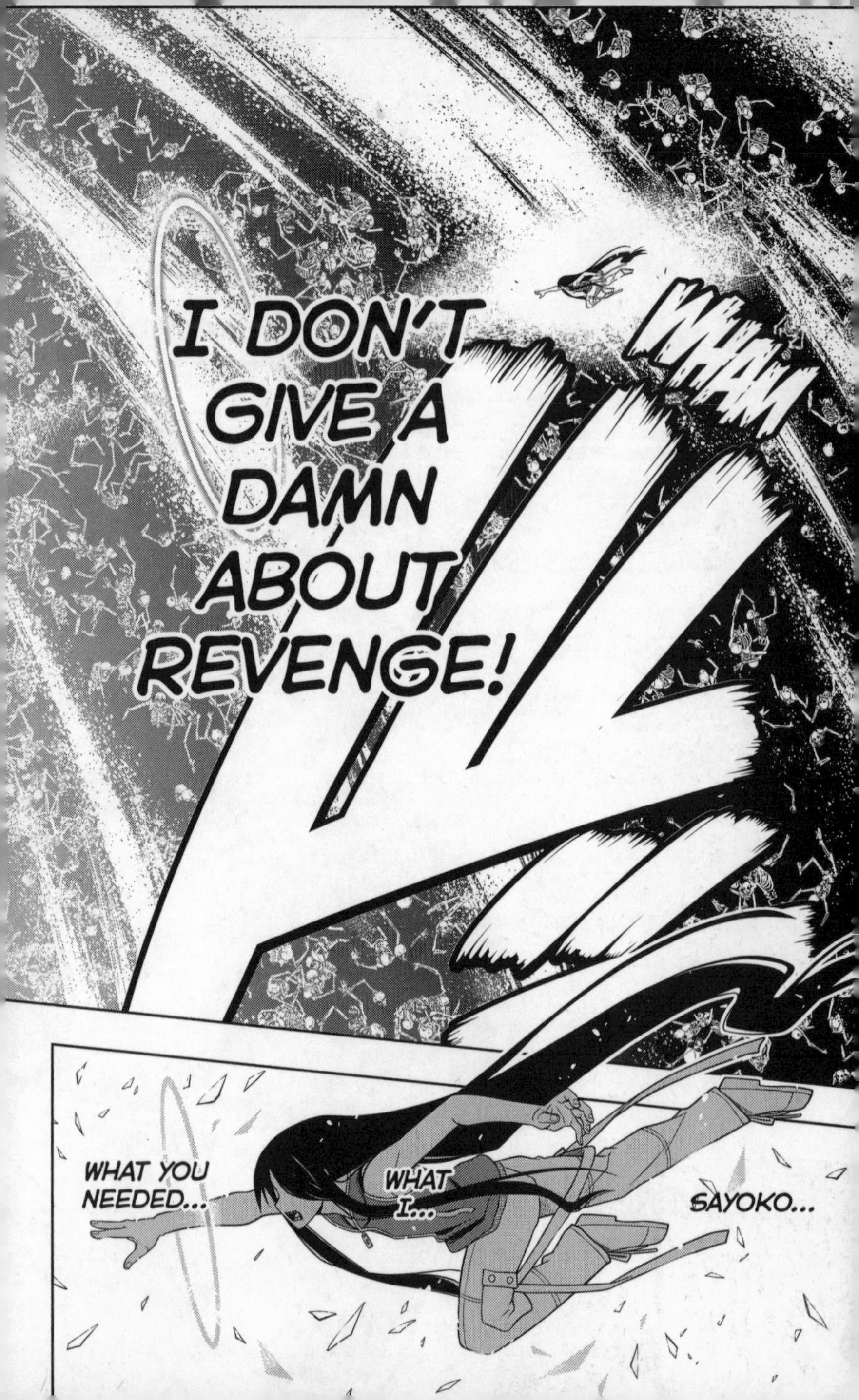
WHAM
I DON'T GIVE A DAMN ABOUT REVENGE!
SAYOKO...
WHAT I...
WHAT YOU NEEDED...

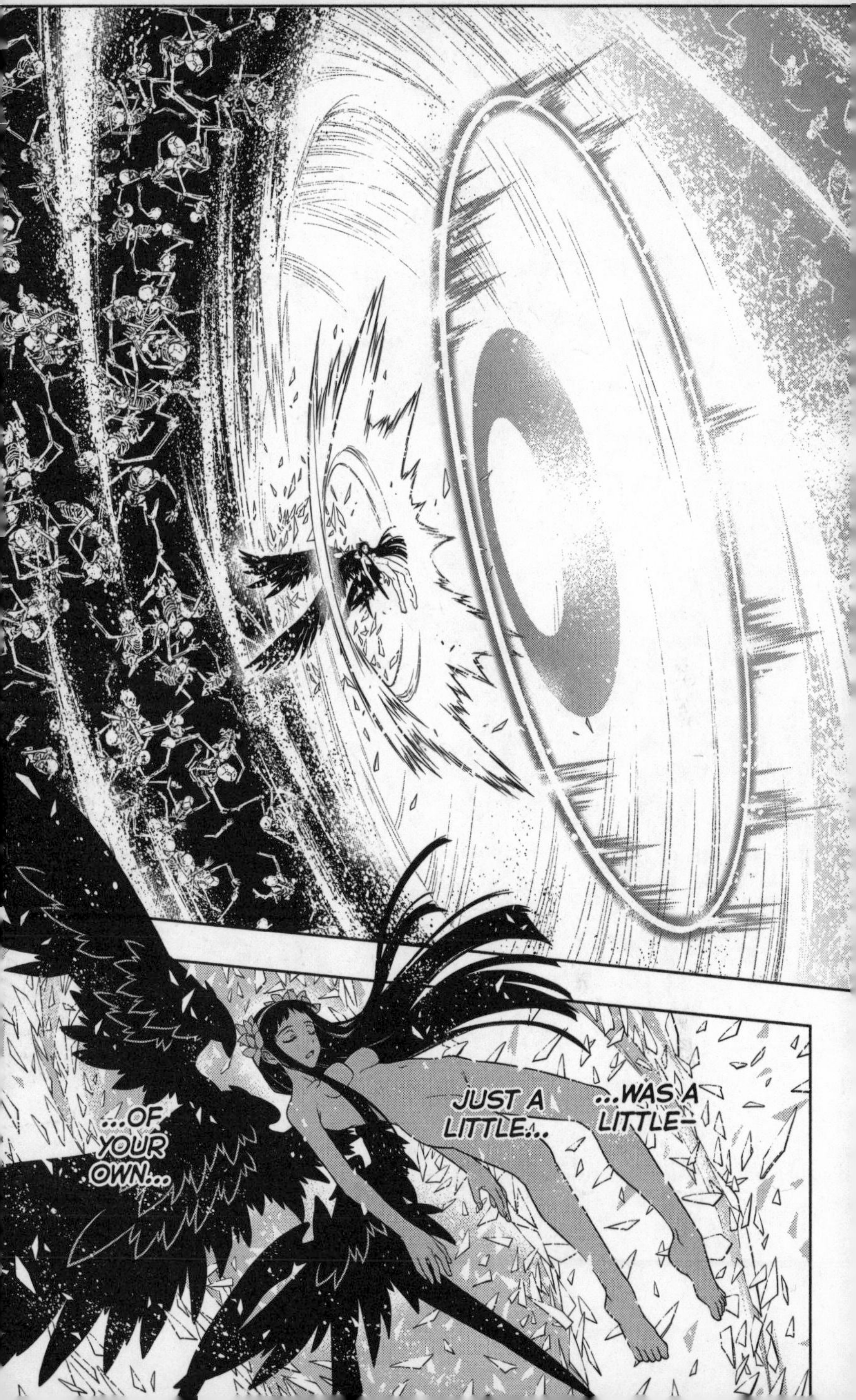
...WAS A LITTLE-
JUST A LITTLE...
...OF YOUR OWN...

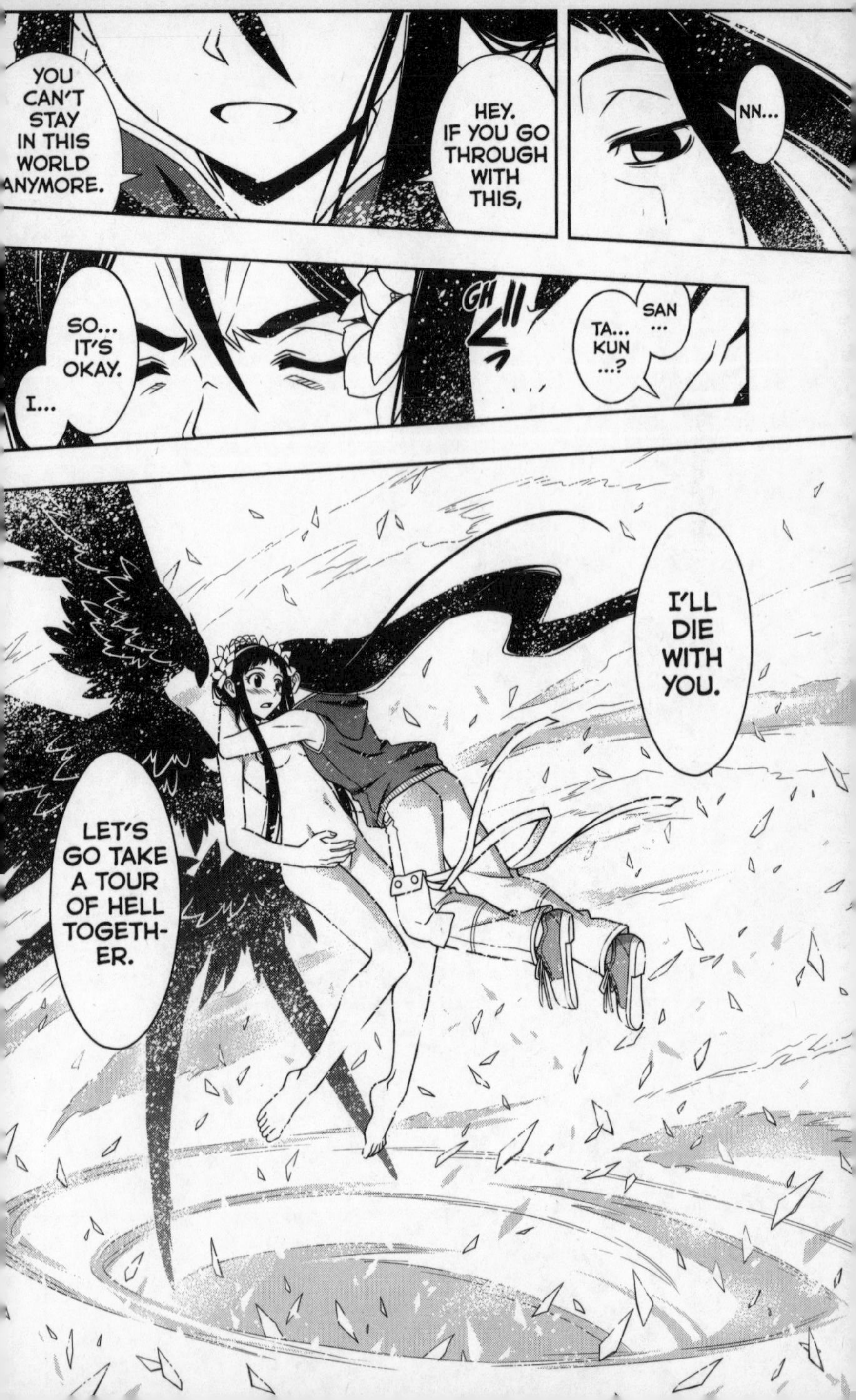
NN...
HEY. IF YOU GO THROUGH WITH THIS,
YOU CAN'T STAY IN THIS WORLD ANYMORE.
SAN ... TA... KUN ...?
GH
SO... IT'S OKAY.
I...
I'LL DIE WITH YOU.
LET'S GO TAKE A TOUR OF HELL TOGETH-ER.

UQ HOLDER!

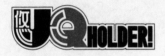

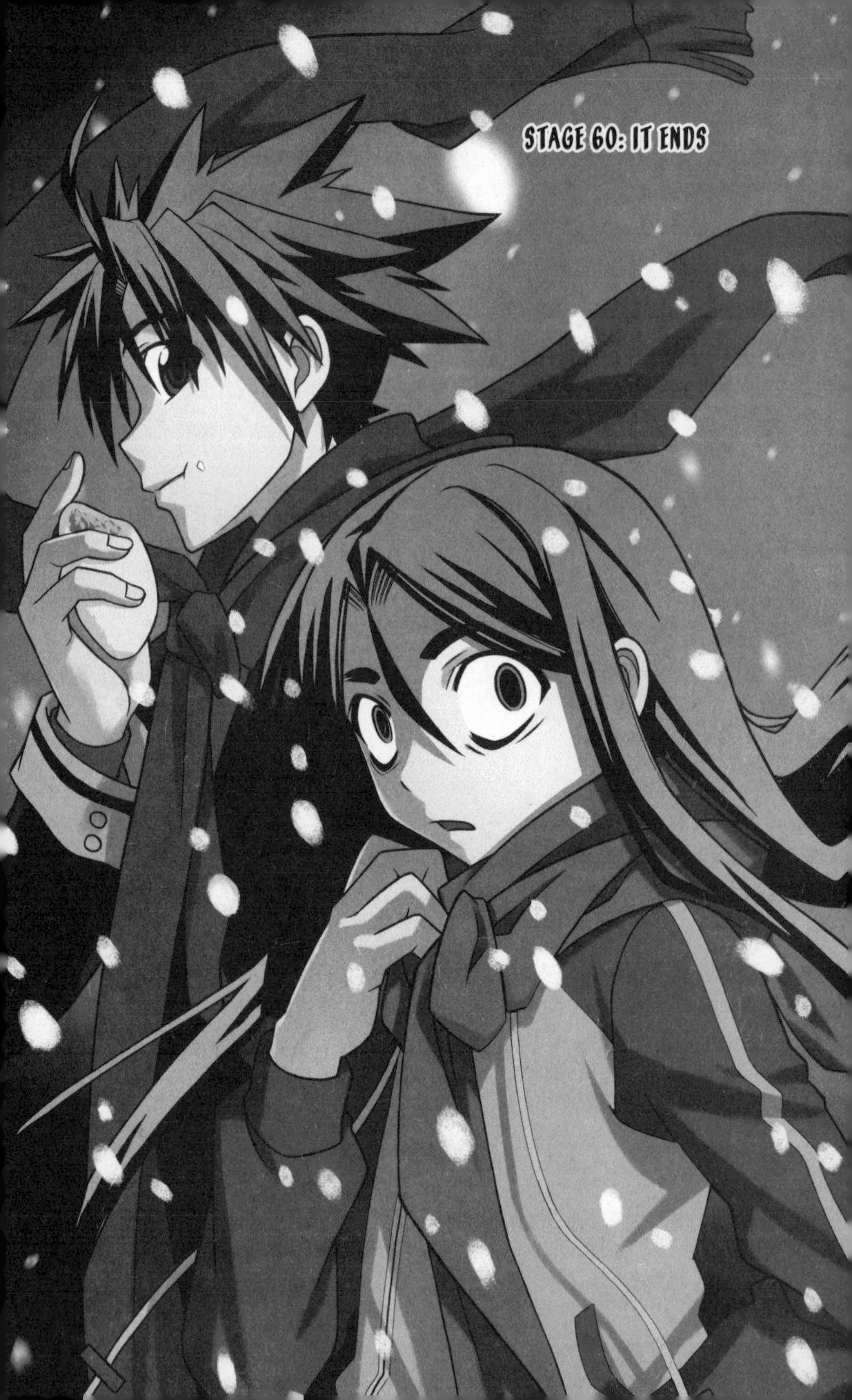
STAGE 60: IT ENDS

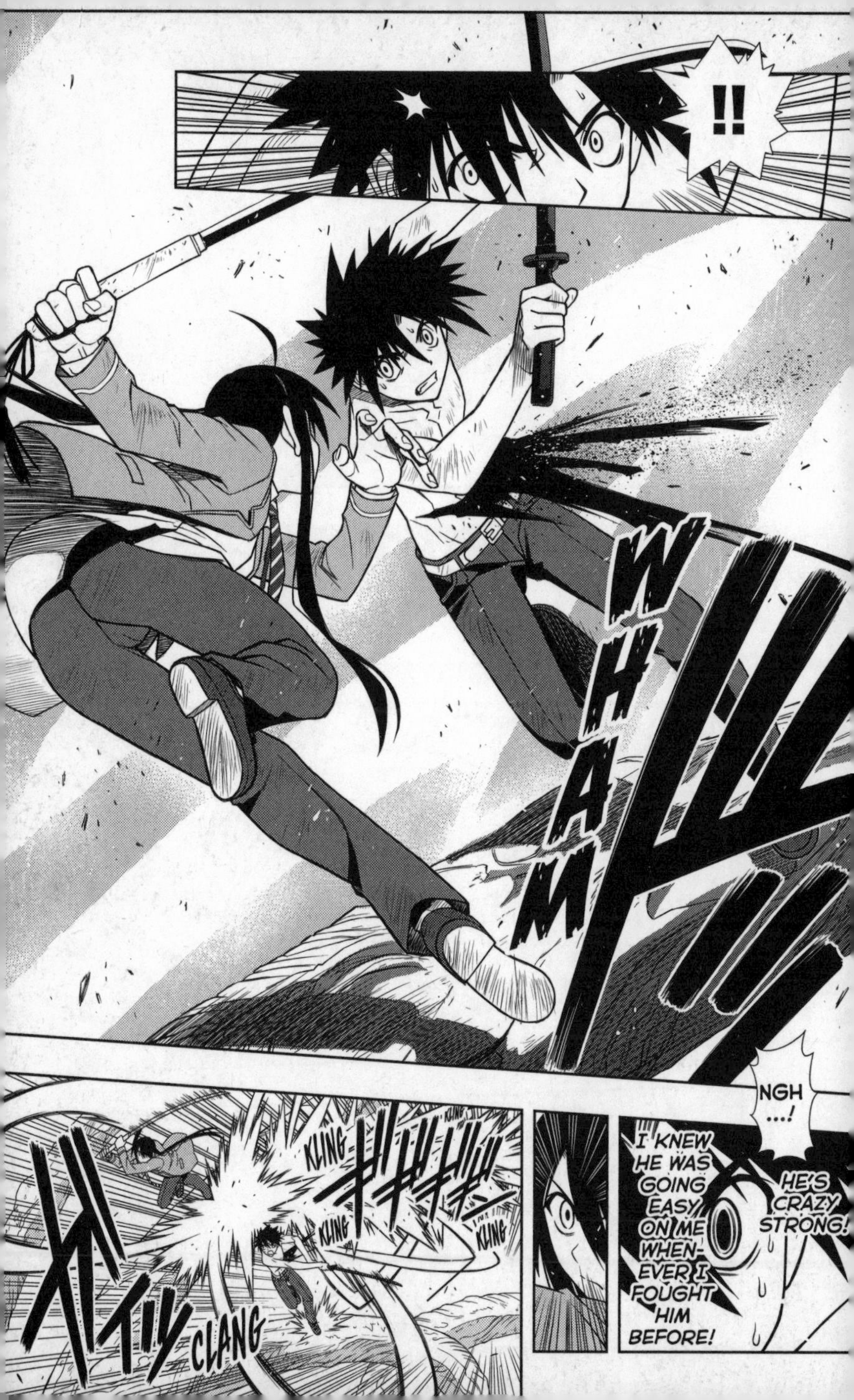
!!
WHAM
NGH ...!
HE'S CRAZY STRONG!
I KNEW HE WAS GOING EASY ON ME WHENEVER I FOUGHT HIM BEFORE!
KLING
KLING
KLING
KLING
CLANG

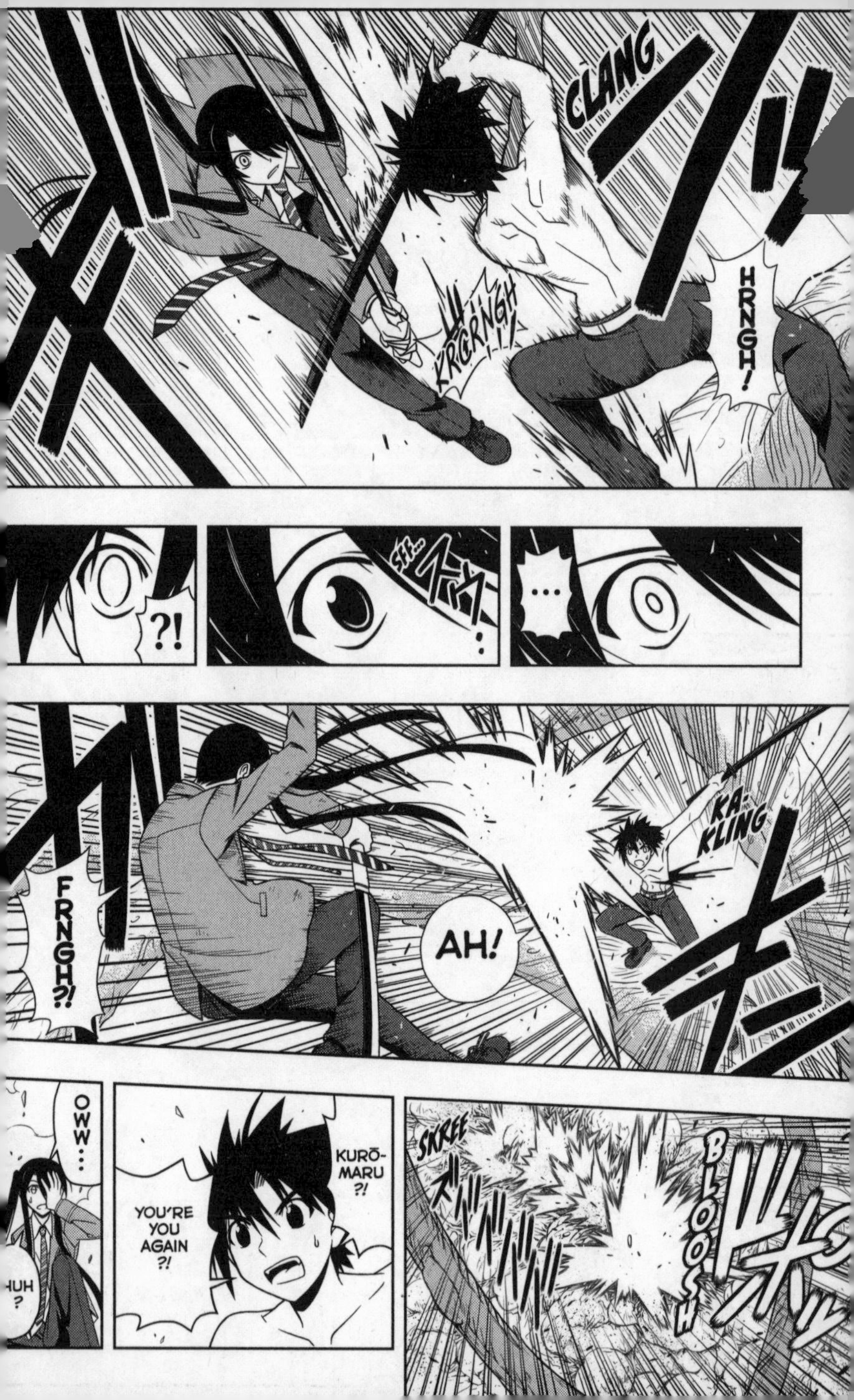
CLANG
HRNGH!
KRGRNGH!
...
SFF...
?!
KA-KLING
AH!
FRNGH?!
SKREE
BLOOOSH
KURŌ-MARU?!
YOU'RE YOU AGAIN?!
OWW...
HUH?

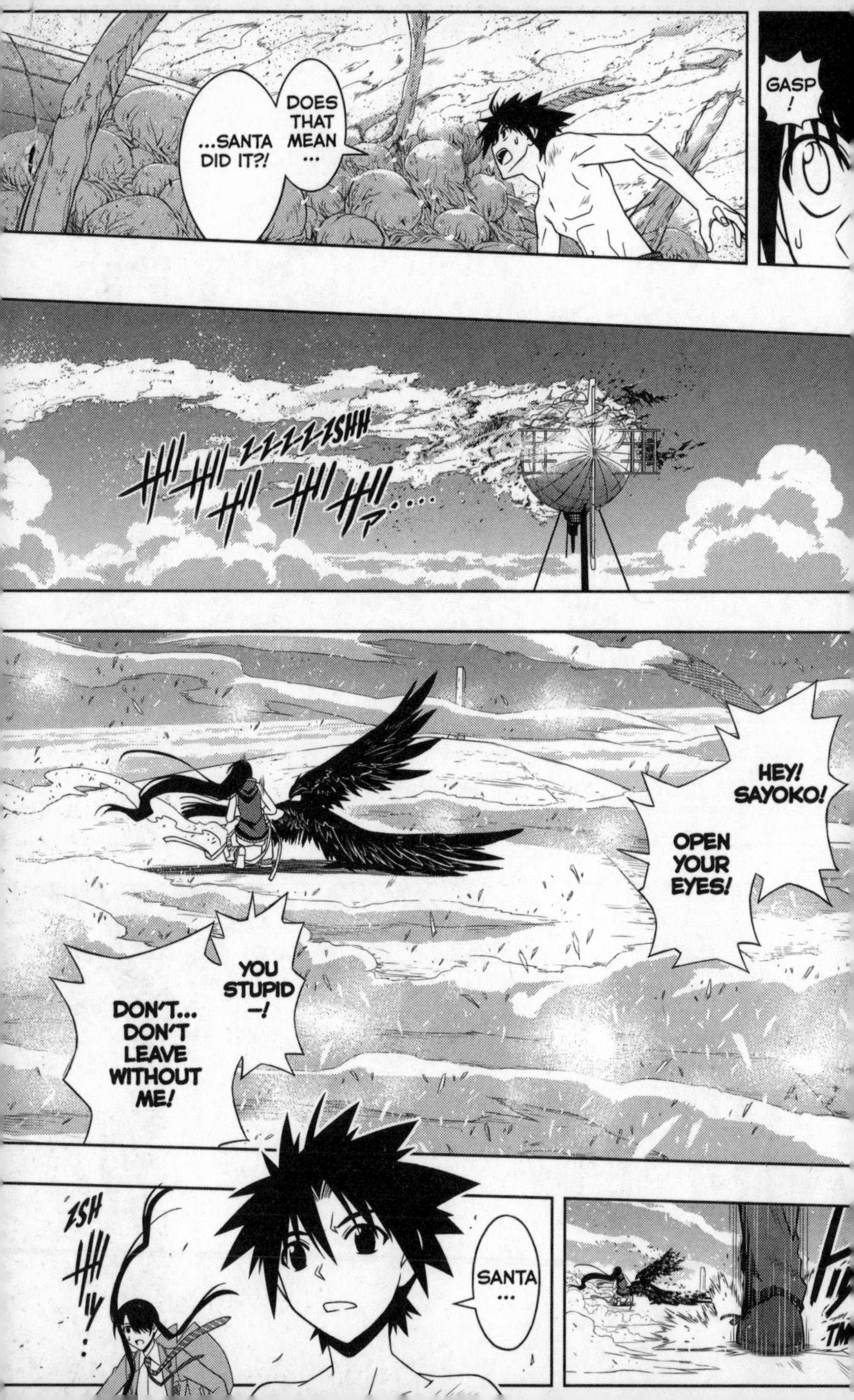
GASP!
DOES THAT MEAN...
...SANTA DID IT?!
Z-Z-Z-Z-Z-ZSHH
HEY! SAYOKO!
OPEN YOUR EYES!
YOU STUPID—!
DON'T... DON'T LEAVE WITHOUT ME!
SANTA...
ZSH

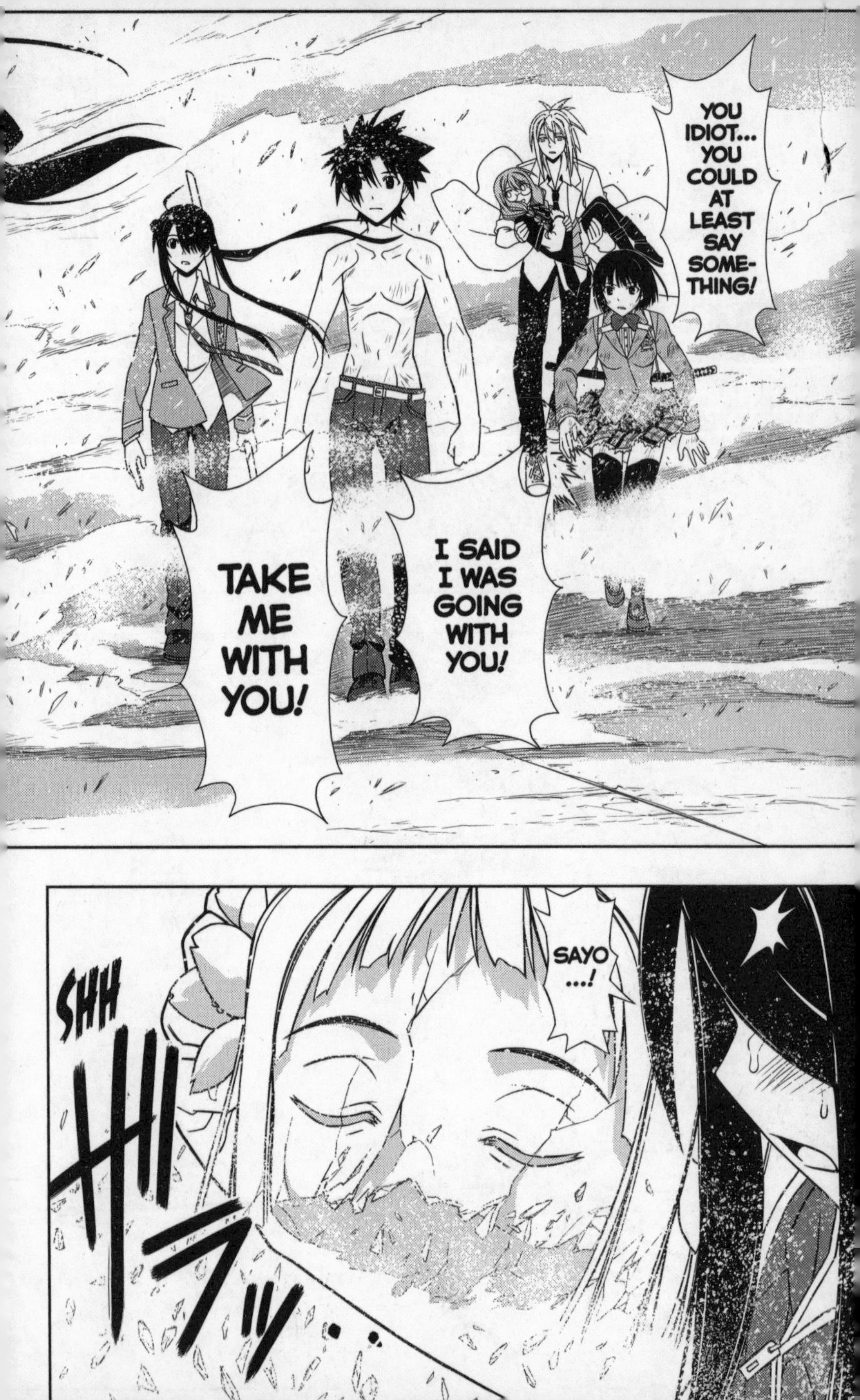
YOU IDIOT... YOU COULD AT LEAST SAY SOME-THING!
I SAID I WAS GOING WITH YOU!
TAKE ME WITH YOU!
SAYO ...!
SHH

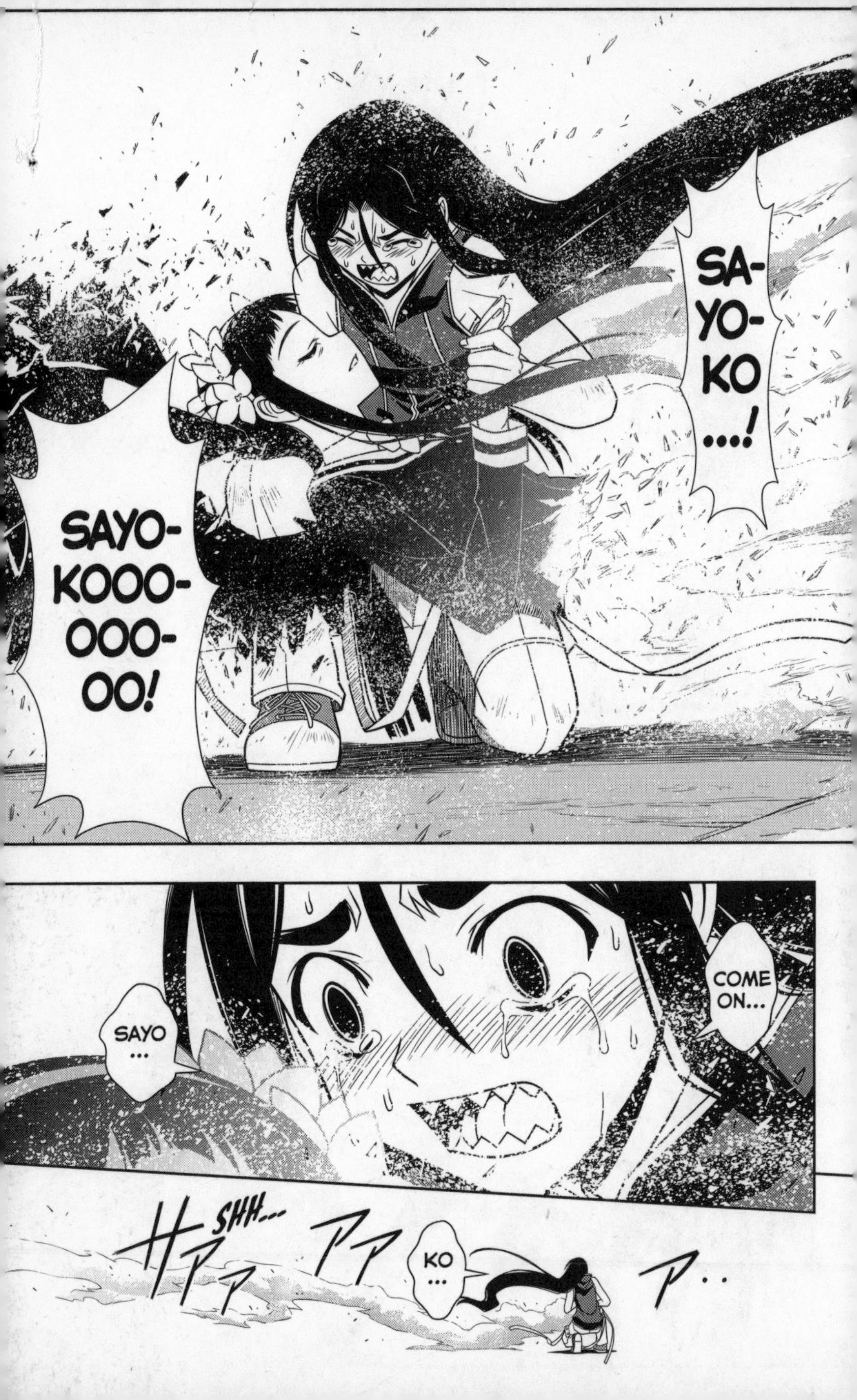
SA-YO-KO...!
SAYO-KOOO-OOO-OO!
COME ON...
SAYO ...
SHH...
KO ...

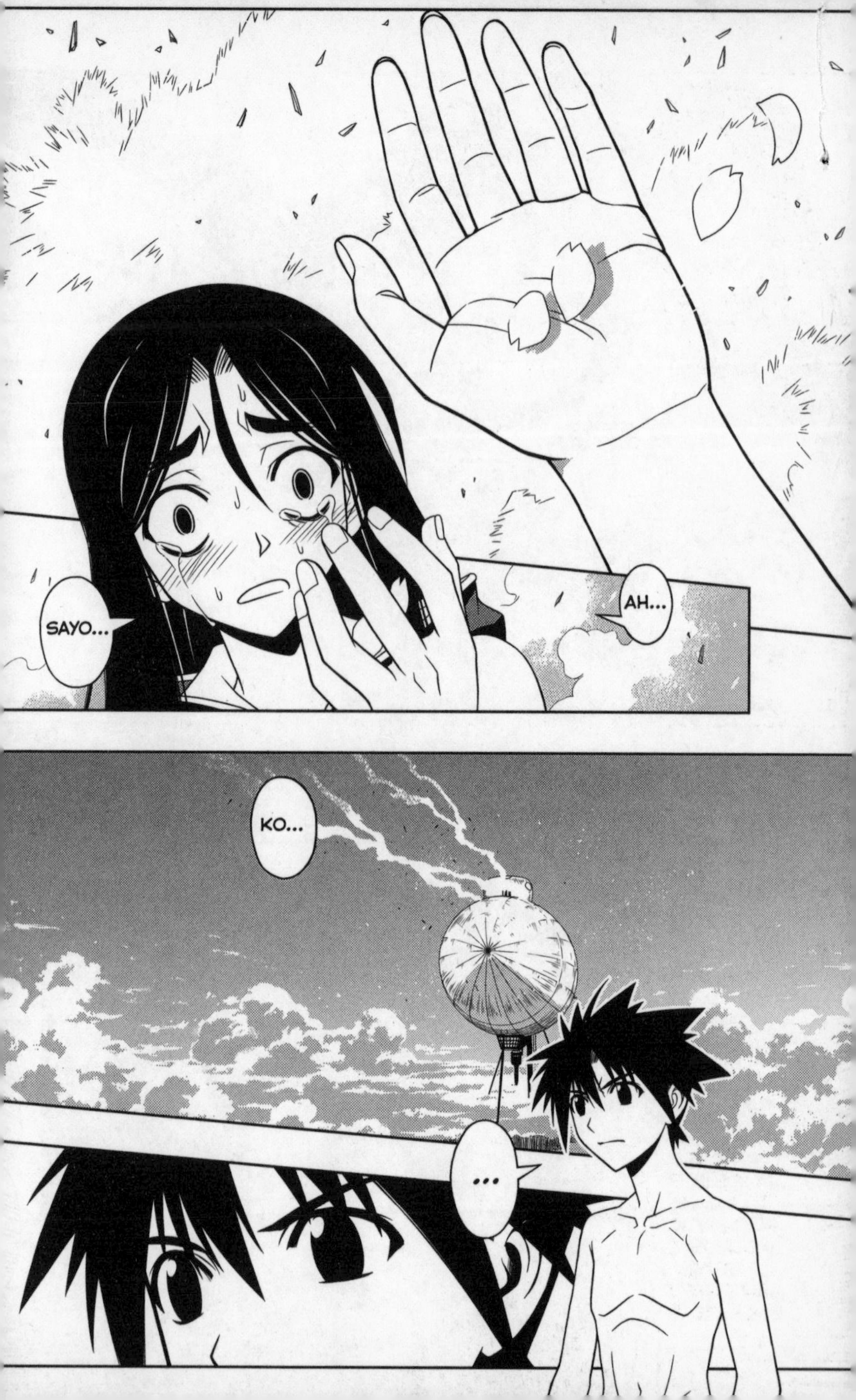
AH...
SAYO...
KO...
...

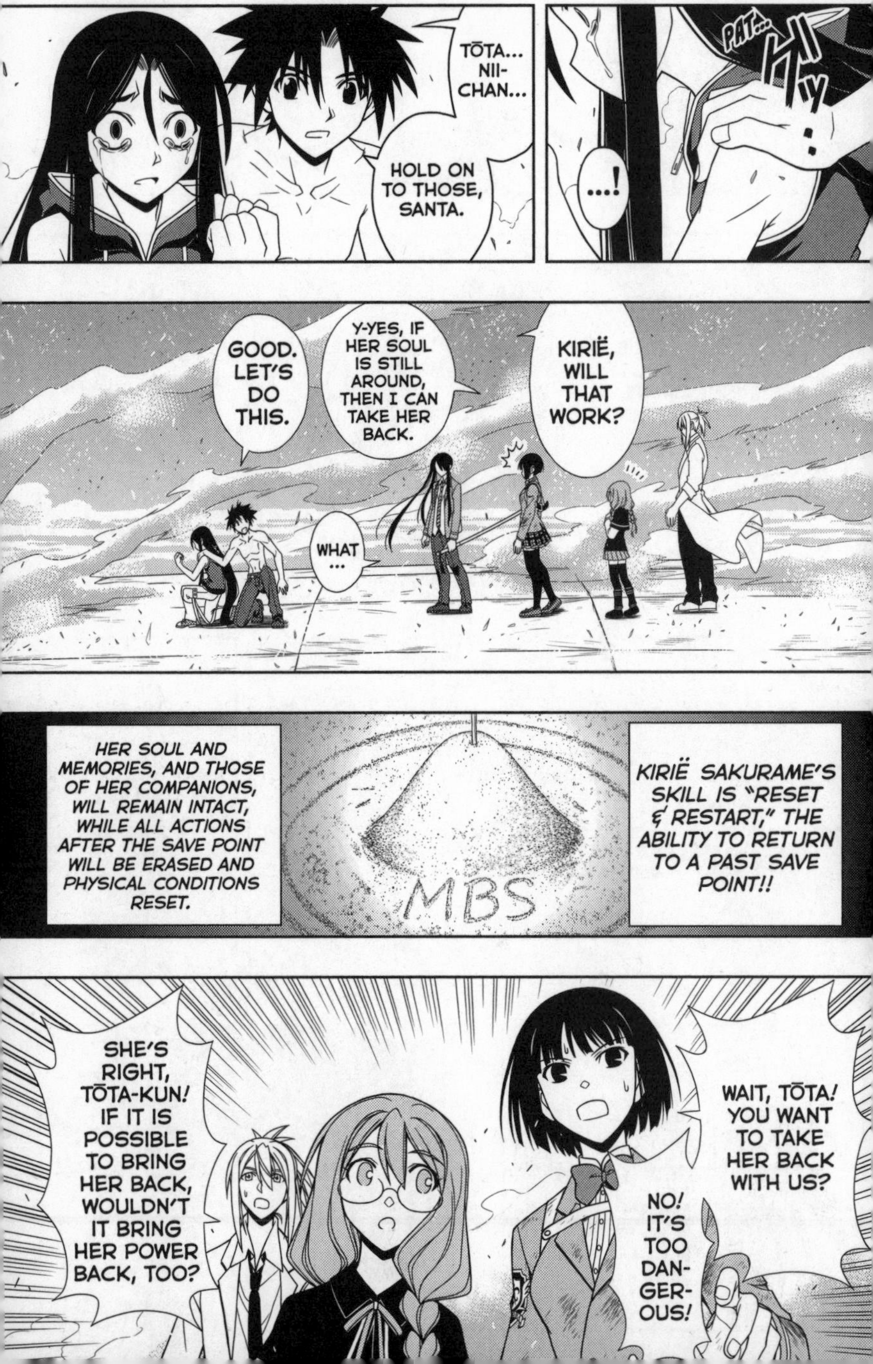
PAT...
...!
TŌTA... NII-CHAN...
HOLD ON TO THOSE, SANTA.
KIRIË, WILL THAT WORK?
Y-YES, IF HER SOUL IS STILL AROUND, THEN I CAN TAKE HER BACK.
GOOD. LET'S DO THIS.
WHAT ...
KIRIË SAKURAME'S SKILL IS "RESET & RESTART," THE ABILITY TO RETURN TO A PAST SAVE POINT!!
MBS
HER SOUL AND MEMORIES, AND THOSE OF HER COMPANIONS, WILL REMAIN INTACT, WHILE ALL ACTIONS AFTER THE SAVE POINT WILL BE ERASED AND PHYSICAL CONDITIONS RESET.
WAIT, TŌTA! YOU WANT TO TAKE HER BACK WITH US?
NO! IT'S TOO DAN-GER-OUS!
SHE'S RIGHT, TŌTA-KUN! IF IT IS POSSIBLE TO BRING HER BACK, WOULDN'T IT BRING HER POWER BACK, TOO?

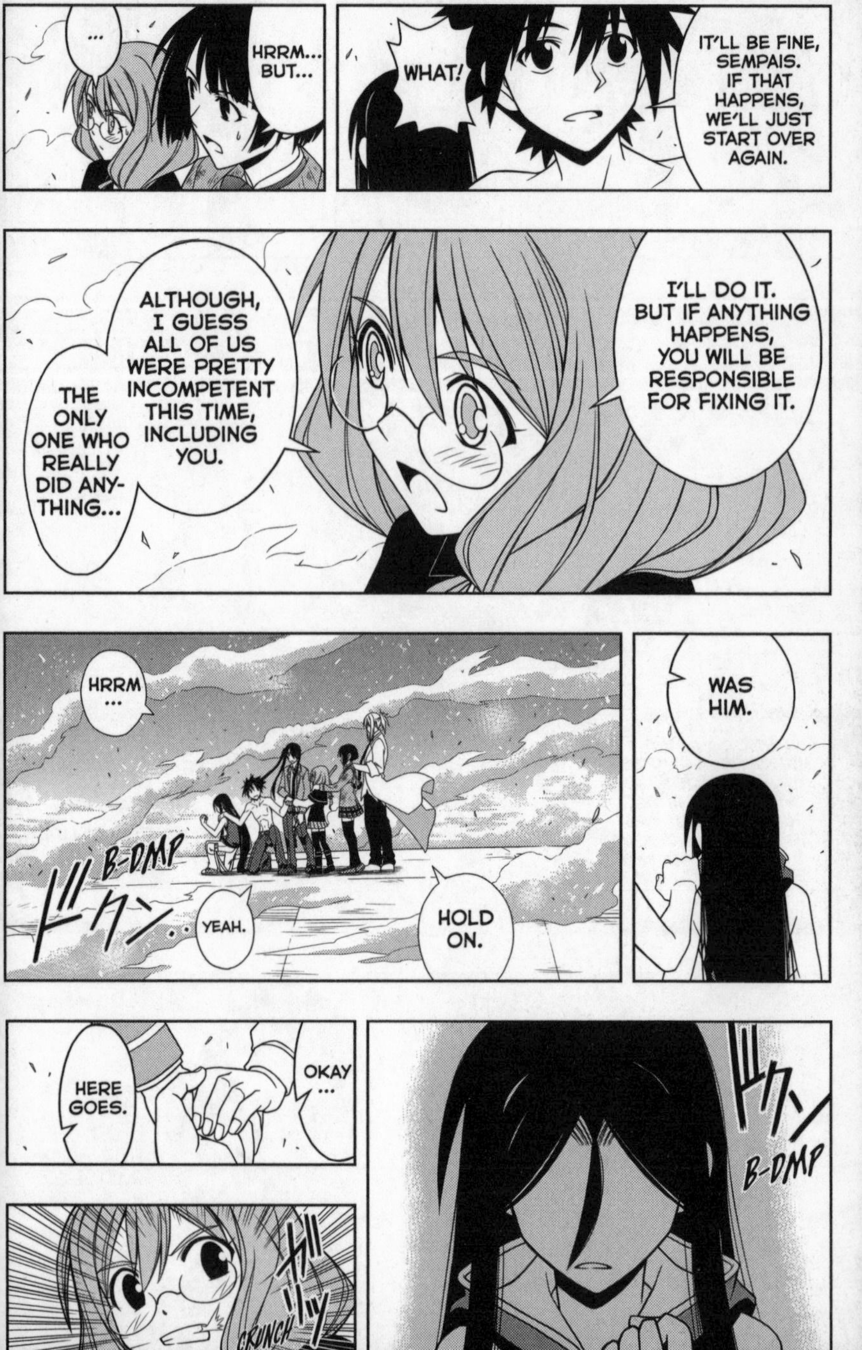
IT'LL BE FINE, SEMPAIS. IF THAT HAPPENS, WE'LL JUST START OVER AGAIN.
WHAT!
HRRM... BUT...
...
I'LL DO IT. BUT IF ANYTHING HAPPENS, YOU WILL BE RESPONSIBLE FOR FIXING IT.
ALTHOUGH, I GUESS ALL OF US WERE PRETTY INCOMPETENT THIS TIME, INCLUDING YOU.
THE ONLY ONE WHO REALLY DID ANY-THING...
WAS HIM.
HRRM ...
HOLD ON.
YEAH.
ドクン
B-DMP
ドクン
B-DMP
OKAY ...
HERE GOES.
ガリッ
CRUNCH

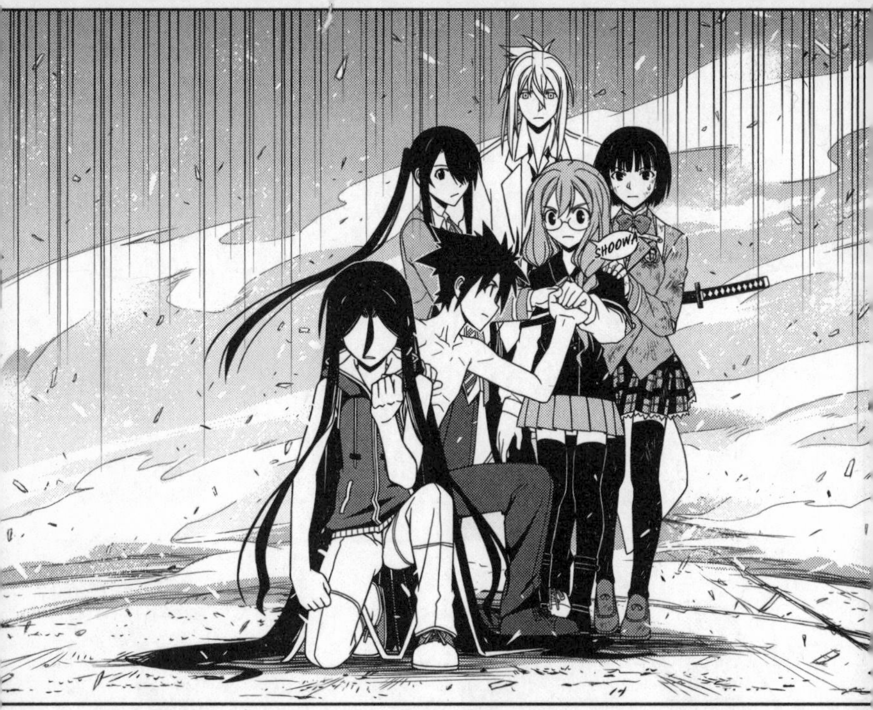
SHOOWA

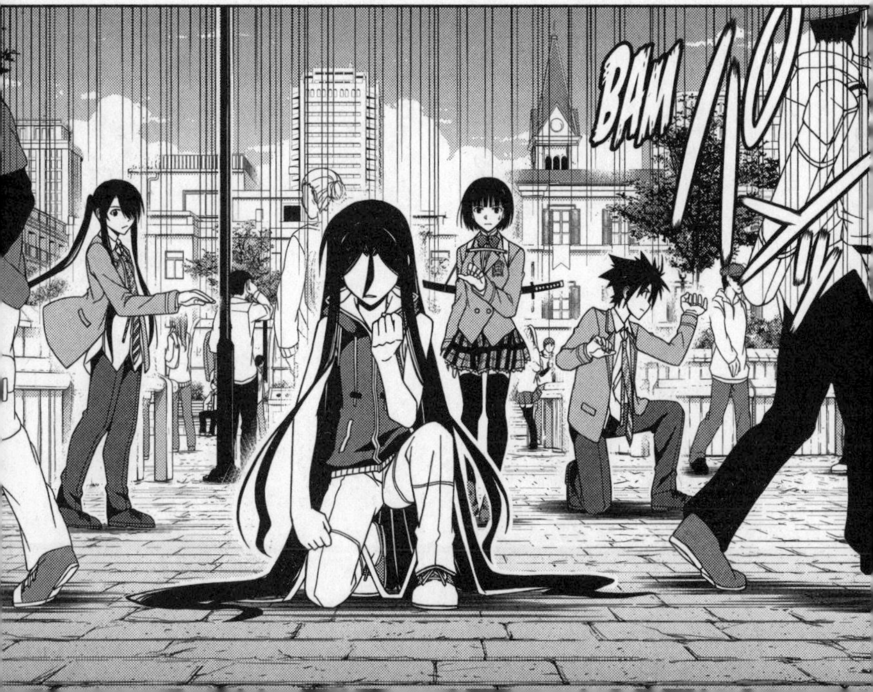
BAM

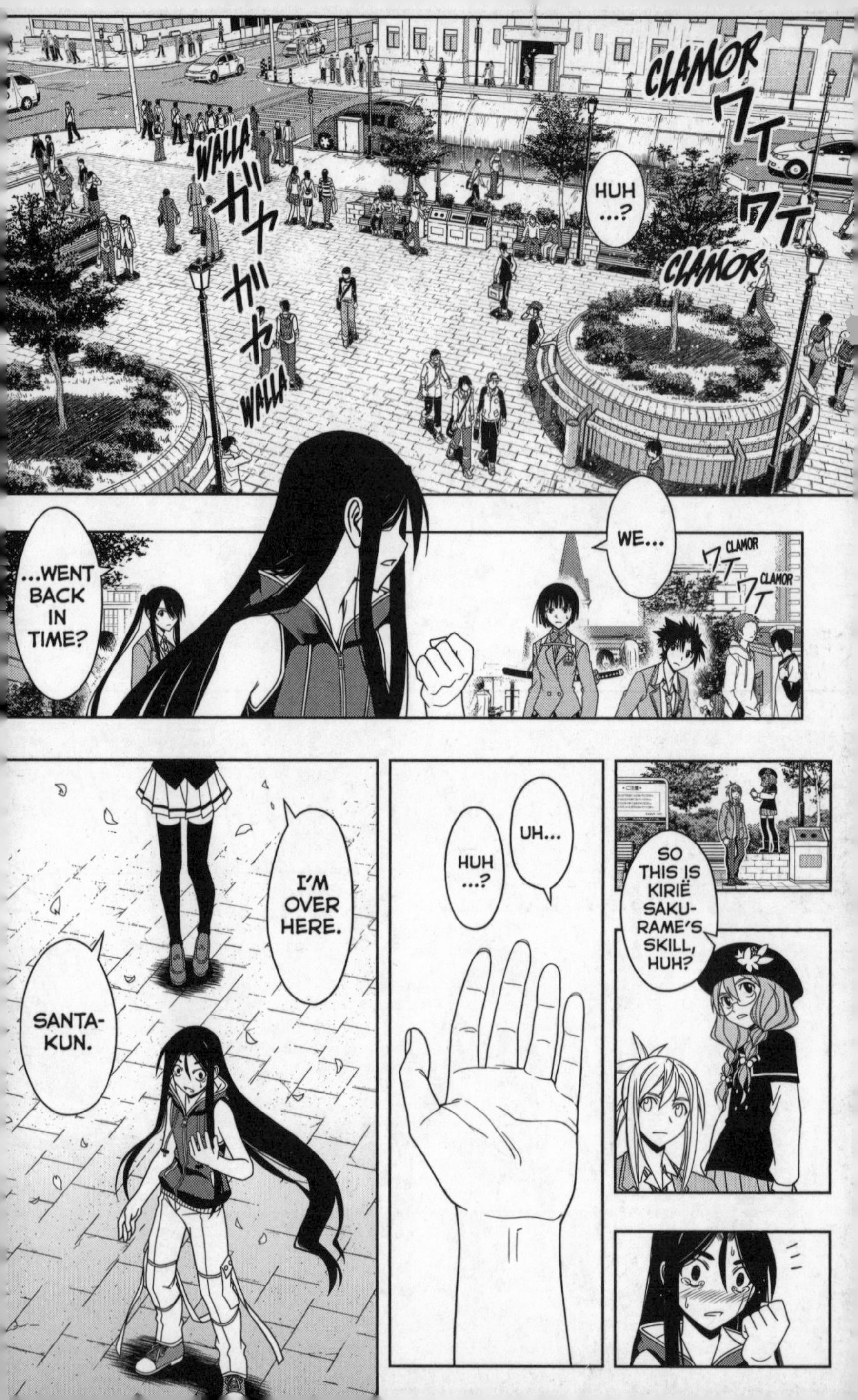
CLAMOR
ワイワイ
HUH ...?
CLAMOR
WALLA
ガヤガヤ
WALLA
WE...
CLAMOR
CLAMOR
...WENT BACK IN TIME?
SO THIS IS KIRIË SAKU-RAME'S SKILL, HUH?
UH...
HUH ...?
I'M OVER HERE.
SANTA-KUN.

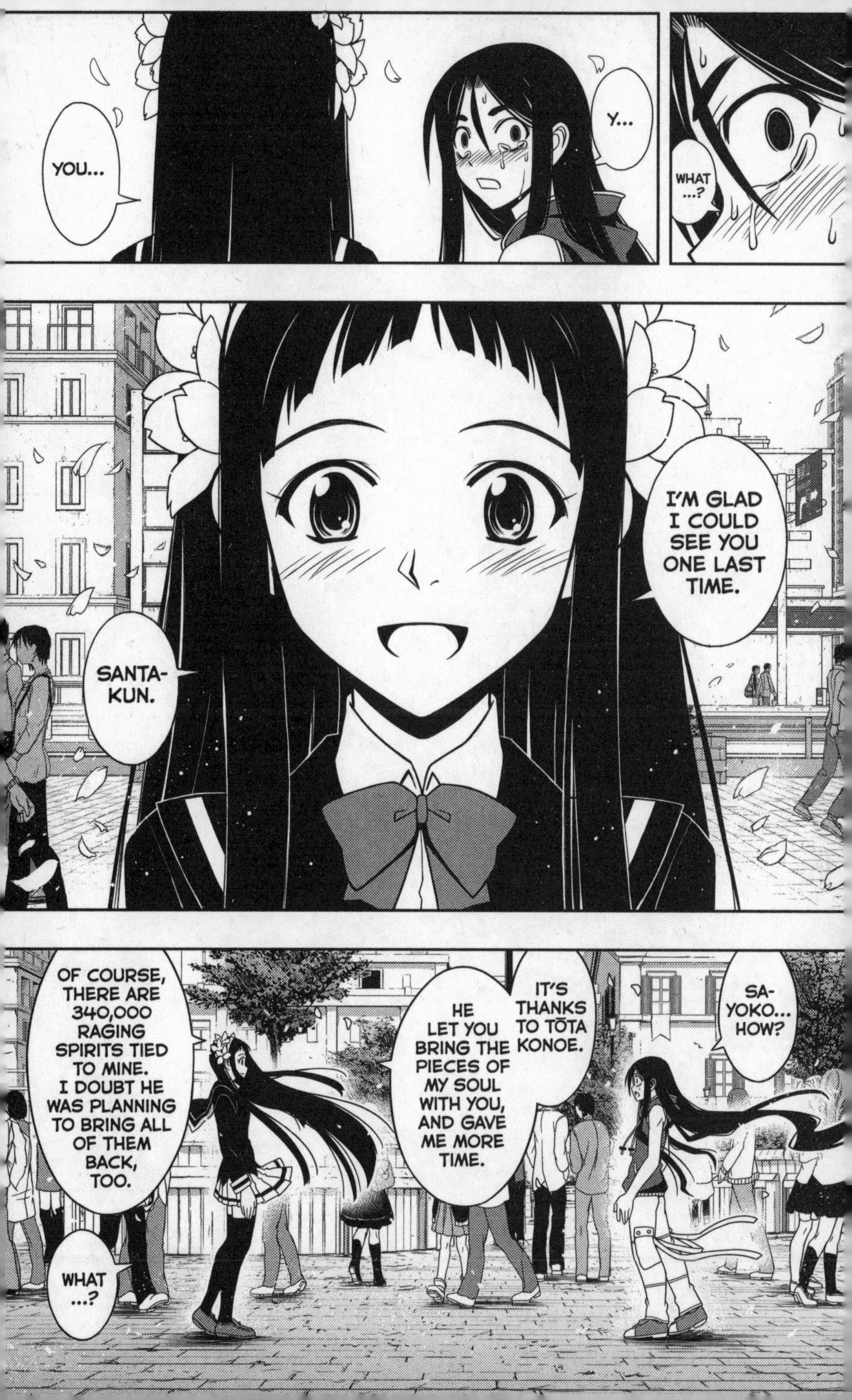
WHAT ...?
Y...
YOU...
I'M GLAD I COULD SEE YOU ONE LAST TIME.
SANTA-KUN.
SA-YOKO... HOW?
IT'S THANKS TO TŌTA KONOE.
HE LET YOU BRING THE PIECES OF MY SOUL WITH YOU, AND GAVE ME MORE TIME.
OF COURSE, THERE ARE 340,000 RAGING SPIRITS TIED TO MINE. I DOUBT HE WAS PLANNING TO BRING ALL OF THEM BACK, TOO.
WHAT ...?

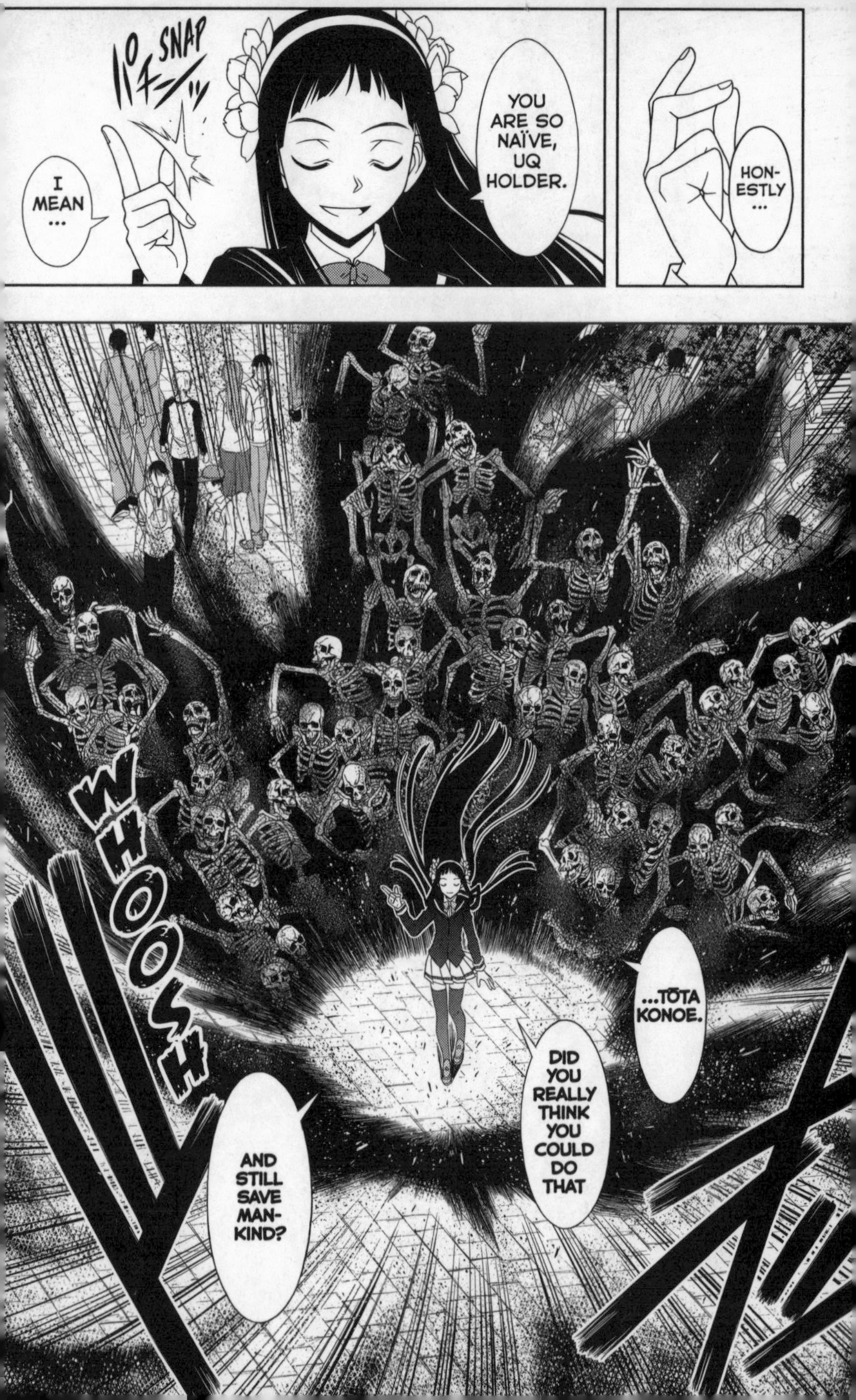
HON-ESTLY...
YOU ARE SO NAÏVE, UQ HOLDER.
SNAP
I MEAN...
...TŌTA KONOE.
DID YOU REALLY THINK YOU COULD DO THAT
AND STILL SAVE MAN-KIND?
WHOOSH

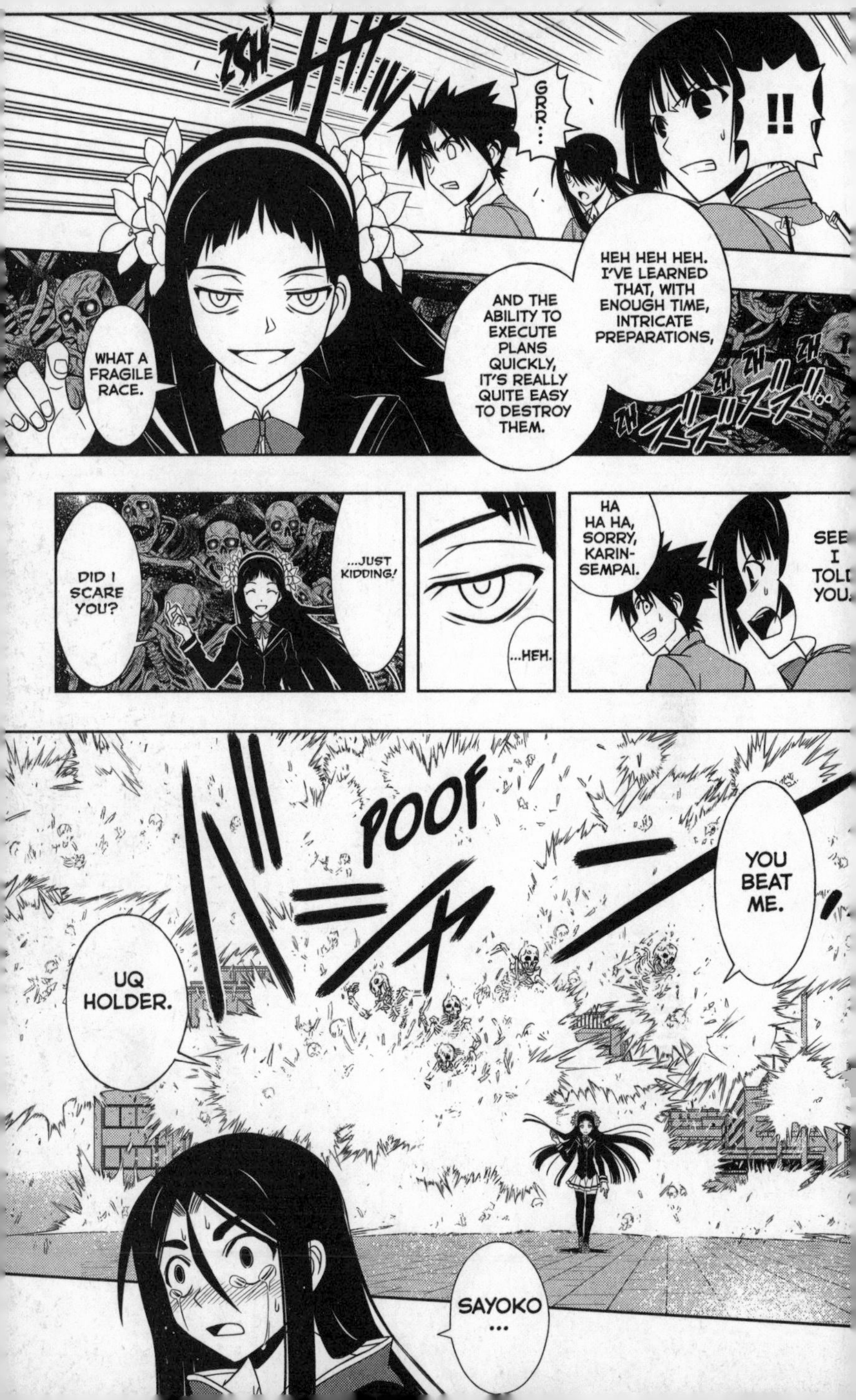
!!
GRR...
ZSH
HEH HEH HEH. I'VE LEARNED THAT, WITH ENOUGH TIME, INTRICATE PREPARATIONS,
AND THE ABILITY TO EXECUTE PLANS QUICKLY, IT'S REALLY QUITE EASY TO DESTROY THEM.
ZH ZH ZH ZH
WHAT A FRAGILE RACE.
SEE I TOLD YOU.
HA HA HA, SORRY, KARIN-SEMPAI.
...HEH.
...JUST KIDDING!
DID I SCARE YOU?
YOU BEAT ME.
POOF
UQ HOLDER.
SAYOKO ...

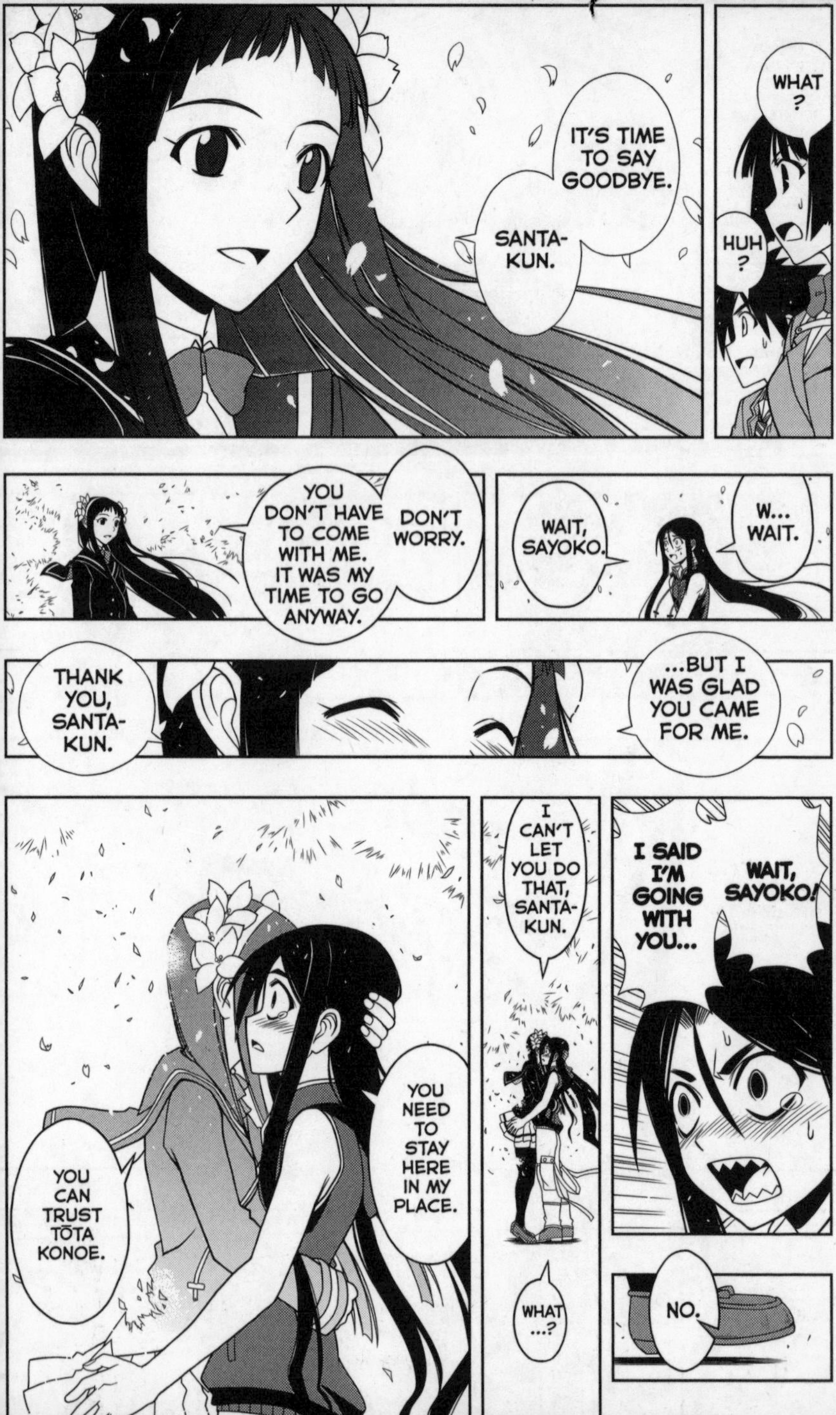
WHAT?
HUH?
IT'S TIME TO SAY GOODBYE.
SANTA-KUN.
W... WAIT.
WAIT, SAYOKO.
DON'T WORRY.
YOU DON'T HAVE TO COME WITH ME. IT WAS MY TIME TO GO ANYWAY.
...BUT I WAS GLAD YOU CAME FOR ME.
THANK YOU, SANTA-KUN.
WAIT, SAYOKO!
I SAID I'M GOING WITH YOU...
NO.
I CAN'T LET YOU DO THAT, SANTA-KUN.
WHAT...?
YOU NEED TO STAY HERE IN MY PLACE.
YOU CAN TRUST TŌTA KONOE.

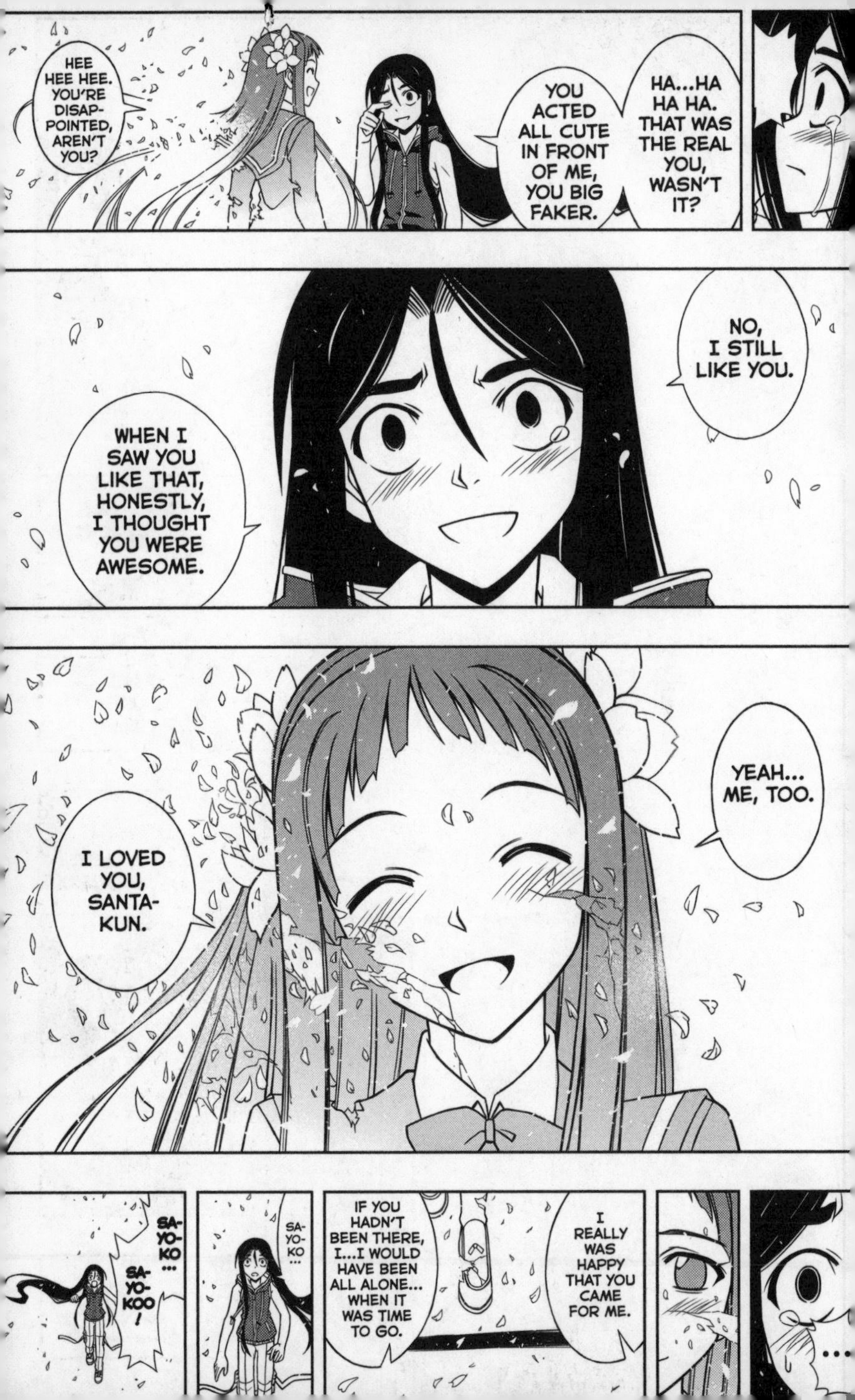
HA...HA HA HA. THAT WAS THE REAL YOU, WASN'T IT?
YOU ACTED ALL CUTE IN FRONT OF ME, YOU BIG FAKER.
HEE HEE HEE. YOU'RE DISAP-POINTED, AREN'T YOU?
NO, I STILL LIKE YOU.
WHEN I SAW YOU LIKE THAT, HONESTLY, I THOUGHT YOU WERE AWESOME.
YEAH... ME, TOO.
I LOVED YOU, SANTA-KUN.
...
I REALLY WAS HAPPY THAT YOU CAME FOR ME.
IF YOU HADN'T BEEN THERE, I...I WOULD HAVE BEEN ALL ALONE... WHEN IT WAS TIME TO GO.
SA-YO-KO ...
SA-YO-KO ...
SA-YO-KOO!

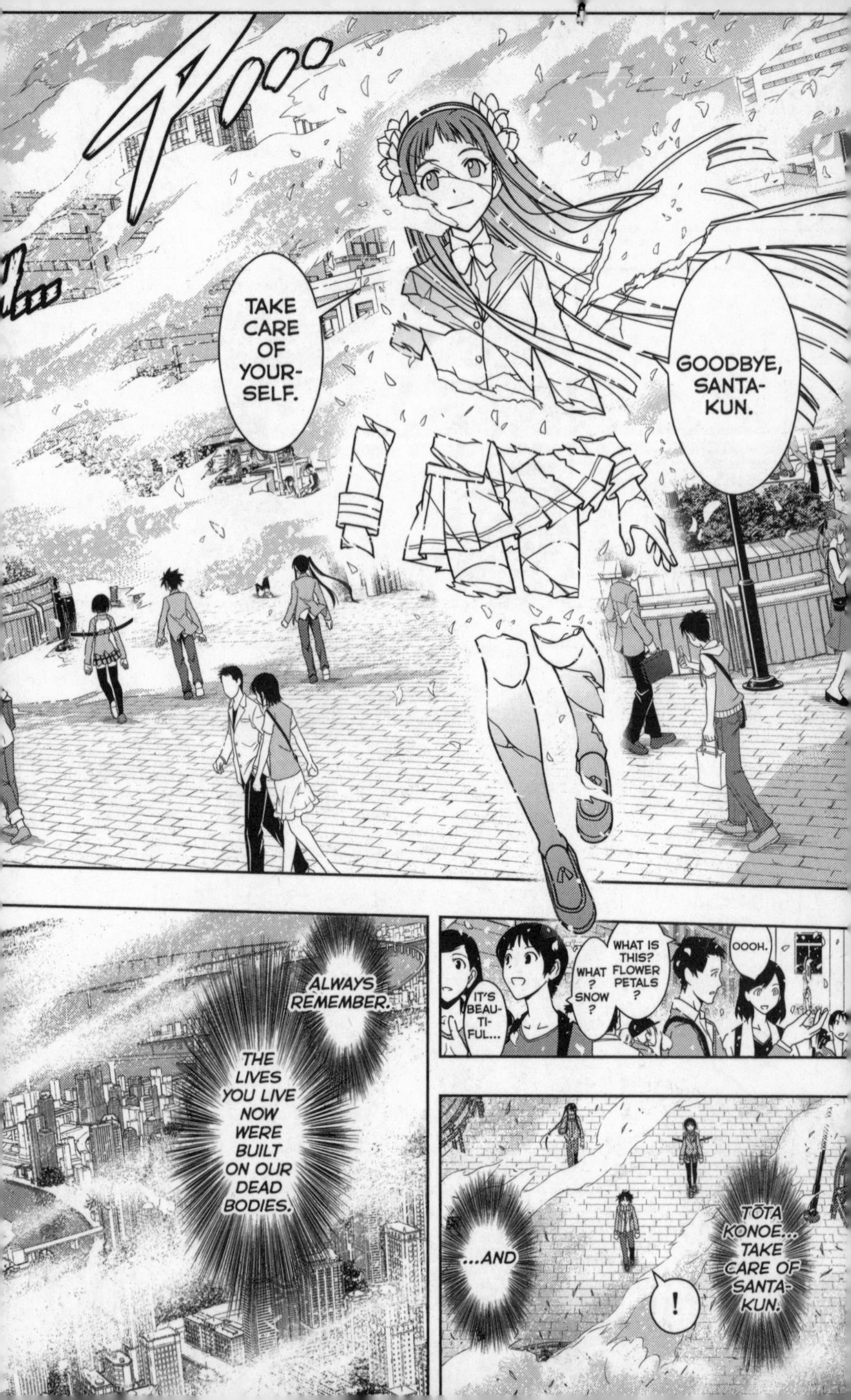
GOODBYE, SANTA-KUN.
TAKE CARE OF YOURSELF.
OOOH.
WHAT IS THIS? FLOWER PETALS?
WHAT? SNOW?
IT'S BEAUTIFUL...
TŌTA KONOE... TAKE CARE OF SANTA-KUN.
!
...AND
ALWAYS REMEMBER.
THE LIVES YOU LIVE NOW WERE BUILT ON OUR DEAD BODIES.

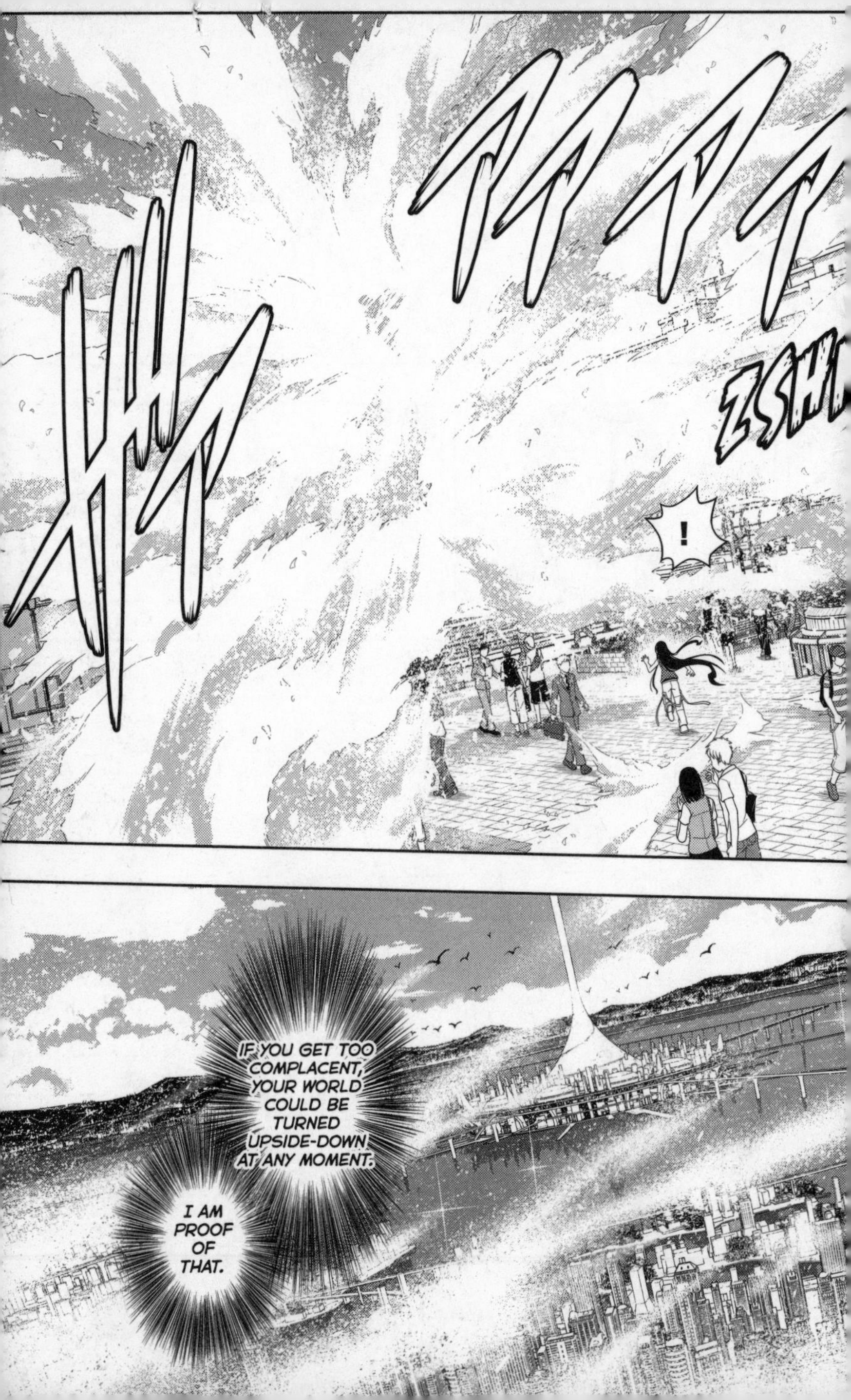
ZSH
!
IF YOU GET TOO COMPLACENT, YOUR WORLD COULD BE TURNED UPSIDE-DOWN AT ANY MOMENT.
I AM PROOF OF THAT.

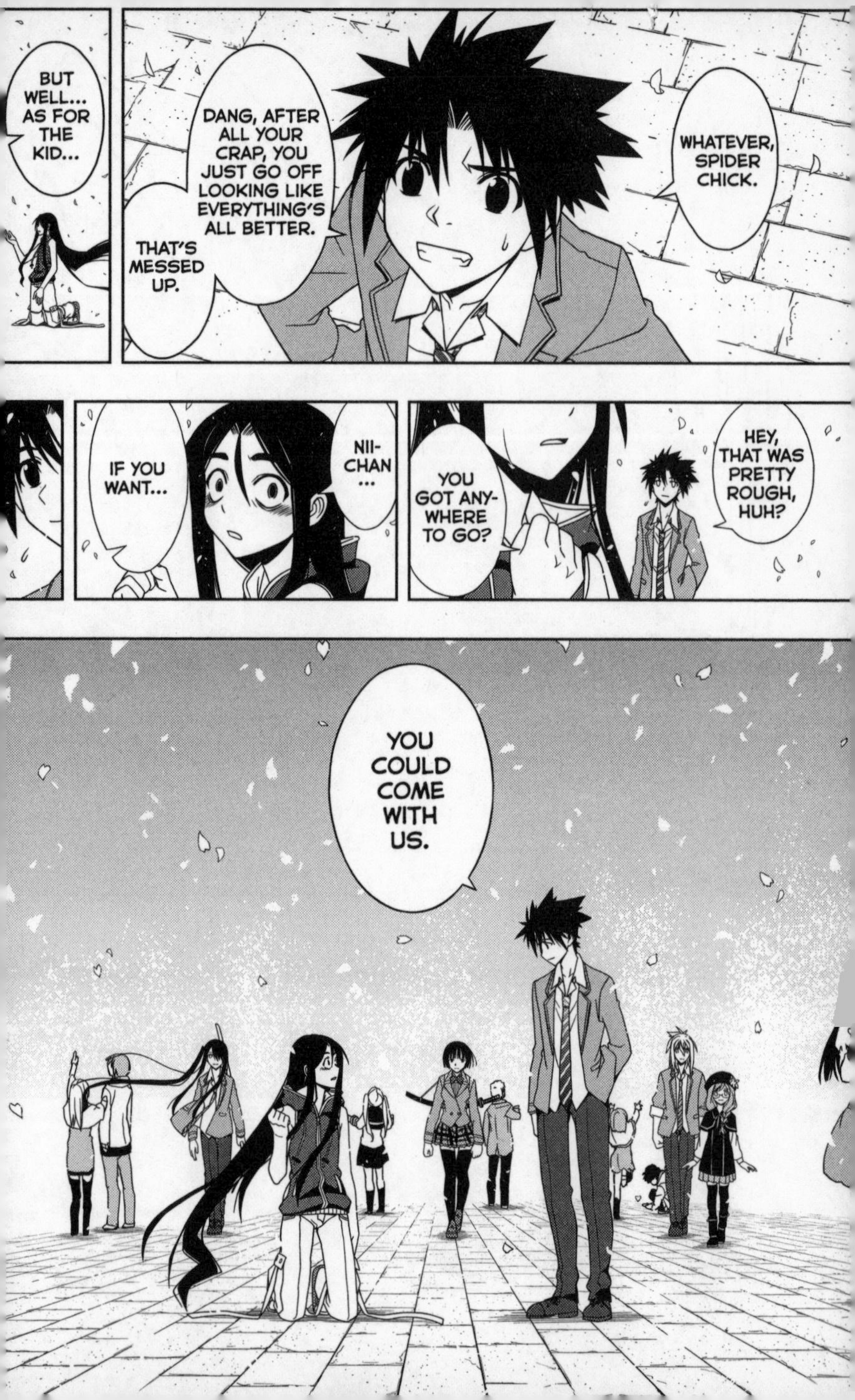
WHATEVER, SPIDER CHICK.
DANG, AFTER ALL YOUR CRAP, YOU JUST GO OFF LOOKING LIKE EVERYTHING'S ALL BETTER.
THAT'S MESSED UP.
BUT WELL... AS FOR THE KID...
HEY, THAT WAS PRETTY ROUGH, HUH?
YOU GOT ANY-WHERE TO GO?
NII-CHAN...
IF YOU WANT...
YOU COULD COME WITH US.

UQ HOLDER!

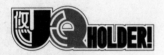

UQ HOLDER!

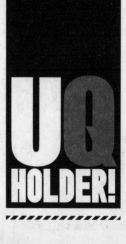

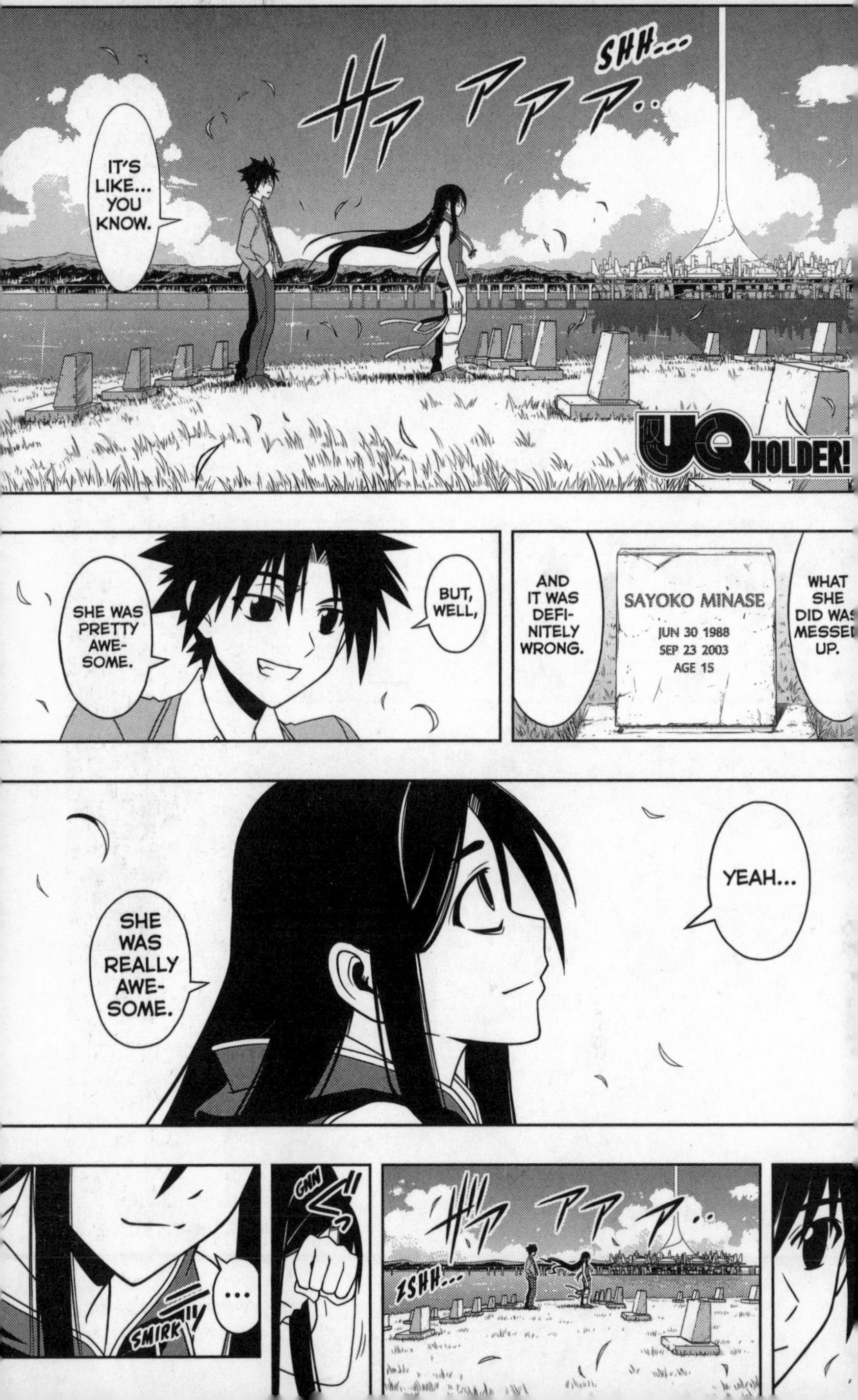
SHH...
IT'S LIKE... YOU KNOW.
UQ HOLDER!
WHAT SHE DID WAS MESSED UP.
AND IT WAS DEFI-NITELY WRONG.
SAYOKO MINASE
JUN 30 1988
SEP 23 2003
AGE 15
BUT, WELL,
SHE WAS PRETTY AWE-SOME.
YEAH...
SHE WAS REALLY AWE-SOME.
ZSHH...
GNN
...
SMIRK

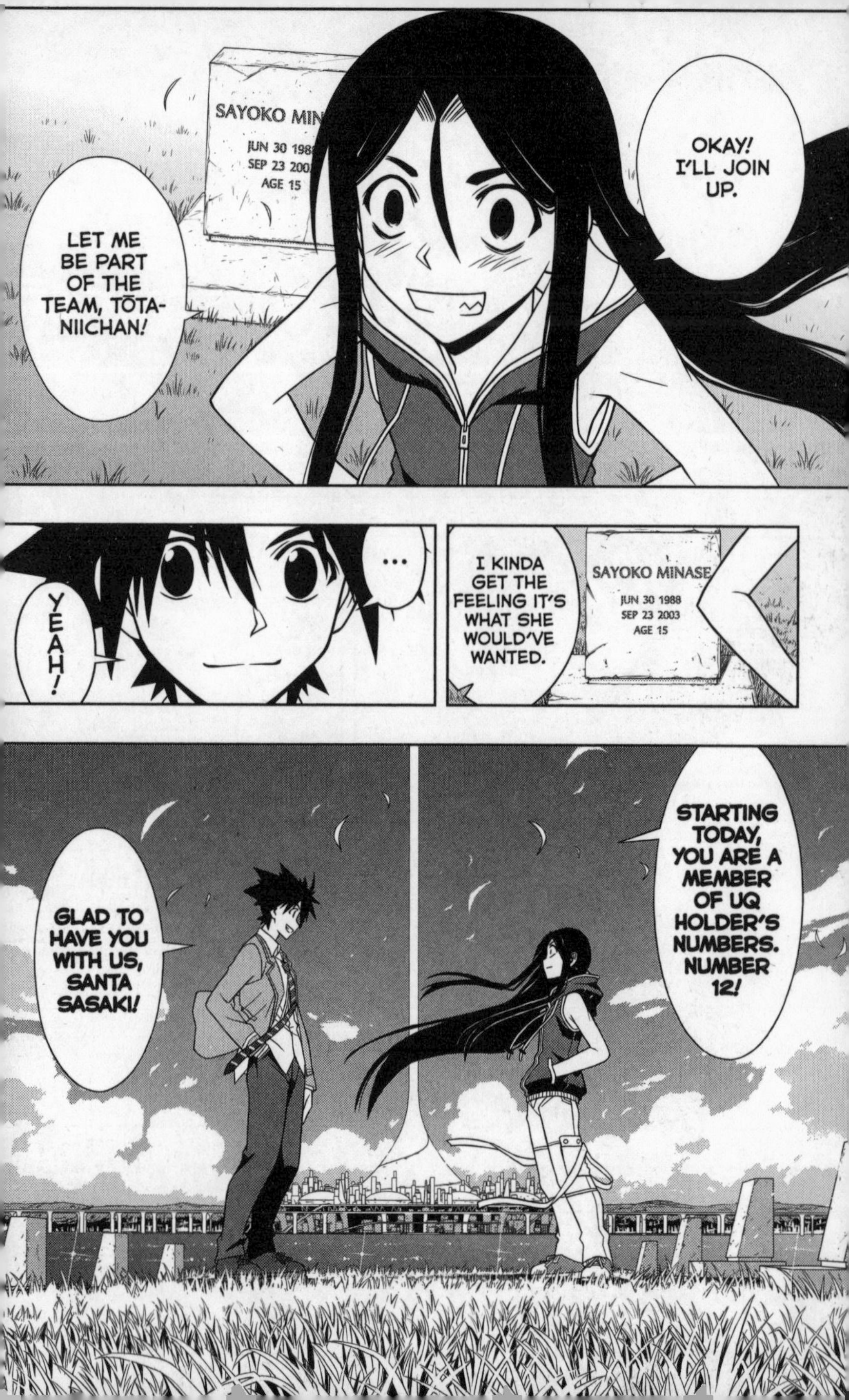
OKAY! I'LL JOIN UP.
LET ME BE PART OF THE TEAM, TŌTA-NIICHAN!
I KINDA GET THE FEELING IT'S WHAT SHE WOULD'VE WANTED.
SAYOKO MINASE
JUN 30 1988
SEP 23 2003
AGE 15
...
YEAH!
STARTING TODAY, YOU ARE A MEMBER OF UQ HOLDER'S NUMBERS. NUMBER 12!
GLAD TO HAVE YOU WITH US, SANTA SASAKI!

CHAPTER 61: KURŌMARU'S WOE'S

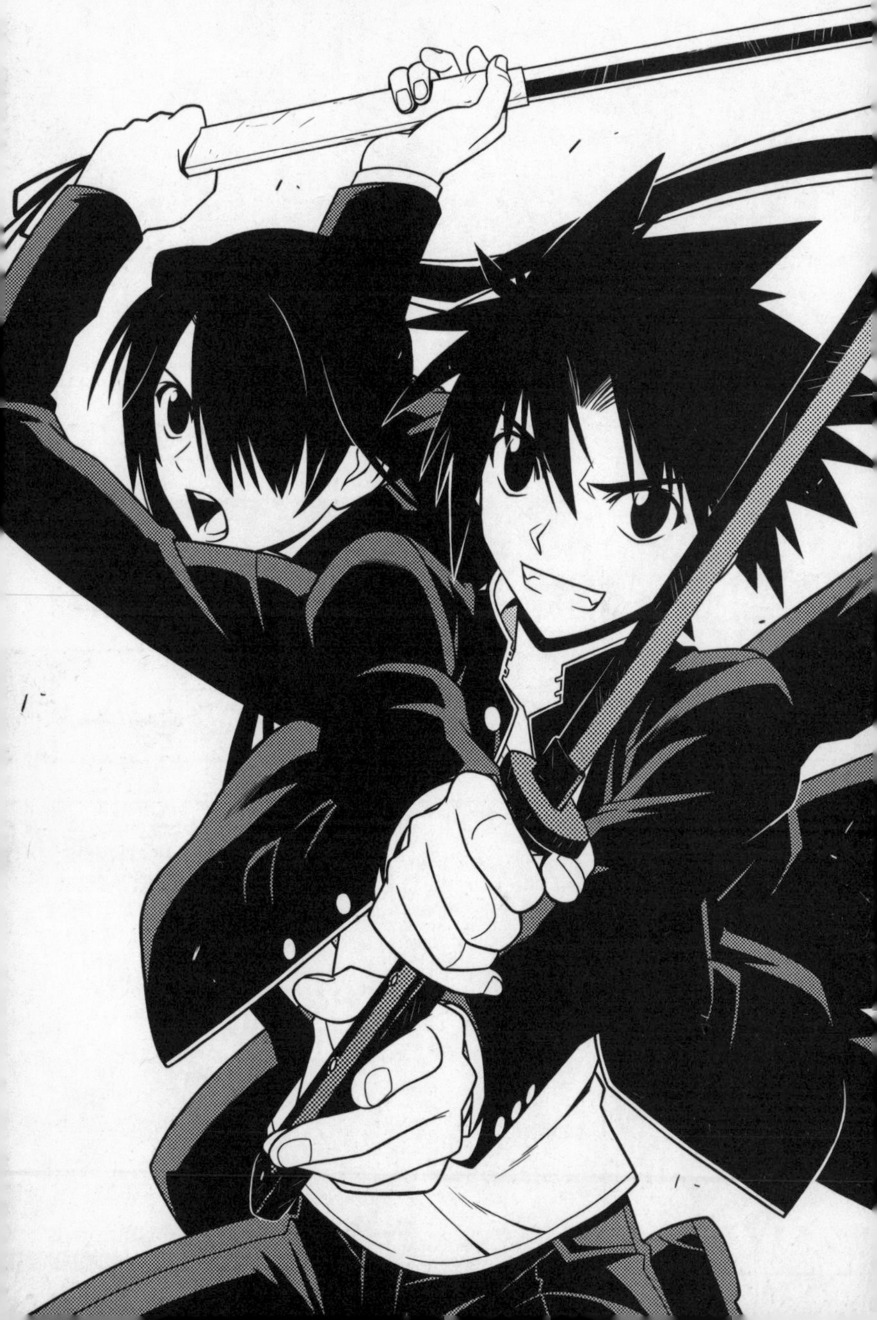

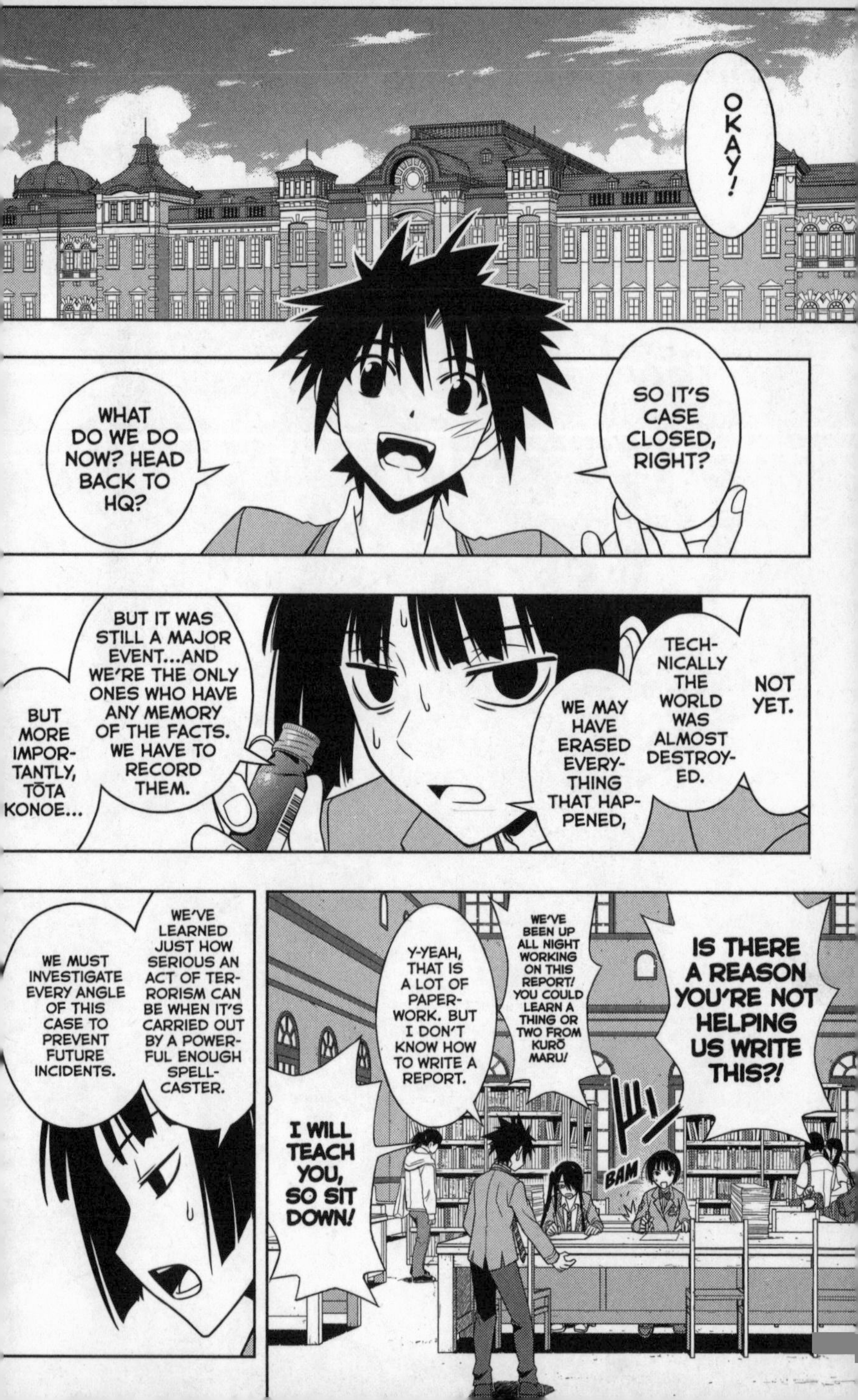

OKAY!
SO IT'S CASE CLOSED, RIGHT?
WHAT DO WE DO NOW? HEAD BACK TO HQ?
NOT YET.
TECHNICALLY THE WORLD WAS ALMOST DESTROYED.
WE MAY HAVE ERASED EVERYTHING THAT HAPPENED,
BUT IT WAS STILL A MAJOR EVENT...AND WE'RE THE ONLY ONES WHO HAVE ANY MEMORY OF THE FACTS. WE HAVE TO RECORD THEM.
BUT MORE IMPORTANTLY, TŌTA KONOE...
IS THERE A REASON YOU'RE NOT HELPING US WRITE THIS?!
BAM
WE'VE BEEN UP ALL NIGHT WORKING ON THIS REPORT! YOU COULD LEARN A THING OR TWO FROM KURŌ MARU!
Y-YEAH, THAT IS A LOT OF PAPERWORK. BUT I DON'T KNOW HOW TO WRITE A REPORT.
I WILL TEACH YOU, SO SIT DOWN!
WE'VE LEARNED JUST HOW SERIOUS AN ACT OF TERRORISM CAN BE WHEN IT'S CARRIED OUT BY A POWERFUL ENOUGH SPELLCASTER.
WE MUST INVESTIGATE EVERY ANGLE OF THIS CASE TO PREVENT FUTURE INCIDENTS.

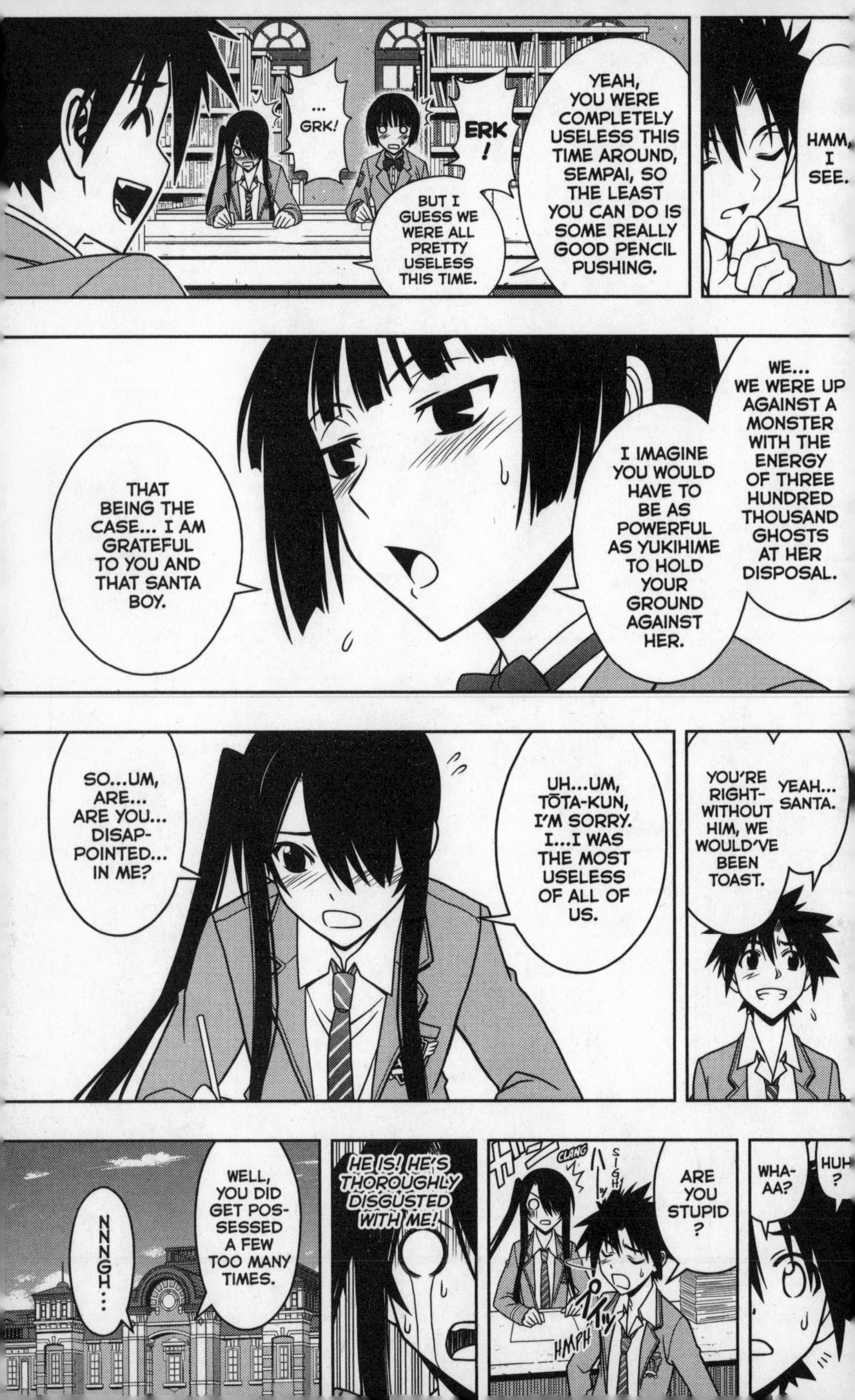
HMM, I SEE.
YEAH, YOU WERE COMPLETELY USELESS THIS TIME AROUND, SEMPAI, SO THE LEAST YOU CAN DO IS SOME REALLY GOOD PENCIL PUSHING.
ERK!
... GRK!
BUT I GUESS WE WERE ALL PRETTY USELESS THIS TIME.
WE... WE WERE UP AGAINST A MONSTER WITH THE ENERGY OF THREE HUNDRED THOUSAND GHOSTS AT HER DISPOSAL.
I IMAGINE YOU WOULD HAVE TO BE AS POWERFUL AS YUKIHIME TO HOLD YOUR GROUND AGAINST HER.
THAT BEING THE CASE... I AM GRATEFUL TO YOU AND THAT SANTA BOY.
YEAH... SANTA.
YOU'RE RIGHT- WITHOUT HIM, WE WOULD'VE BEEN TOAST.
UH...UM, TŌTA-KUN, I'M SORRY. I...I WAS THE MOST USELESS OF ALL OF US.
SO...UM, ARE... ARE YOU... DISAP-POINTED... IN ME?
HUH?
WHA-AA?
ARE YOU STUPID?
CLANG
SIGH
HMPH
HE IS! HE'S THOROUGHLY DISGUSTED WITH ME!
WELL, YOU DID GET POS-SESSED A FEW TOO MANY TIMES.
NNNGH...

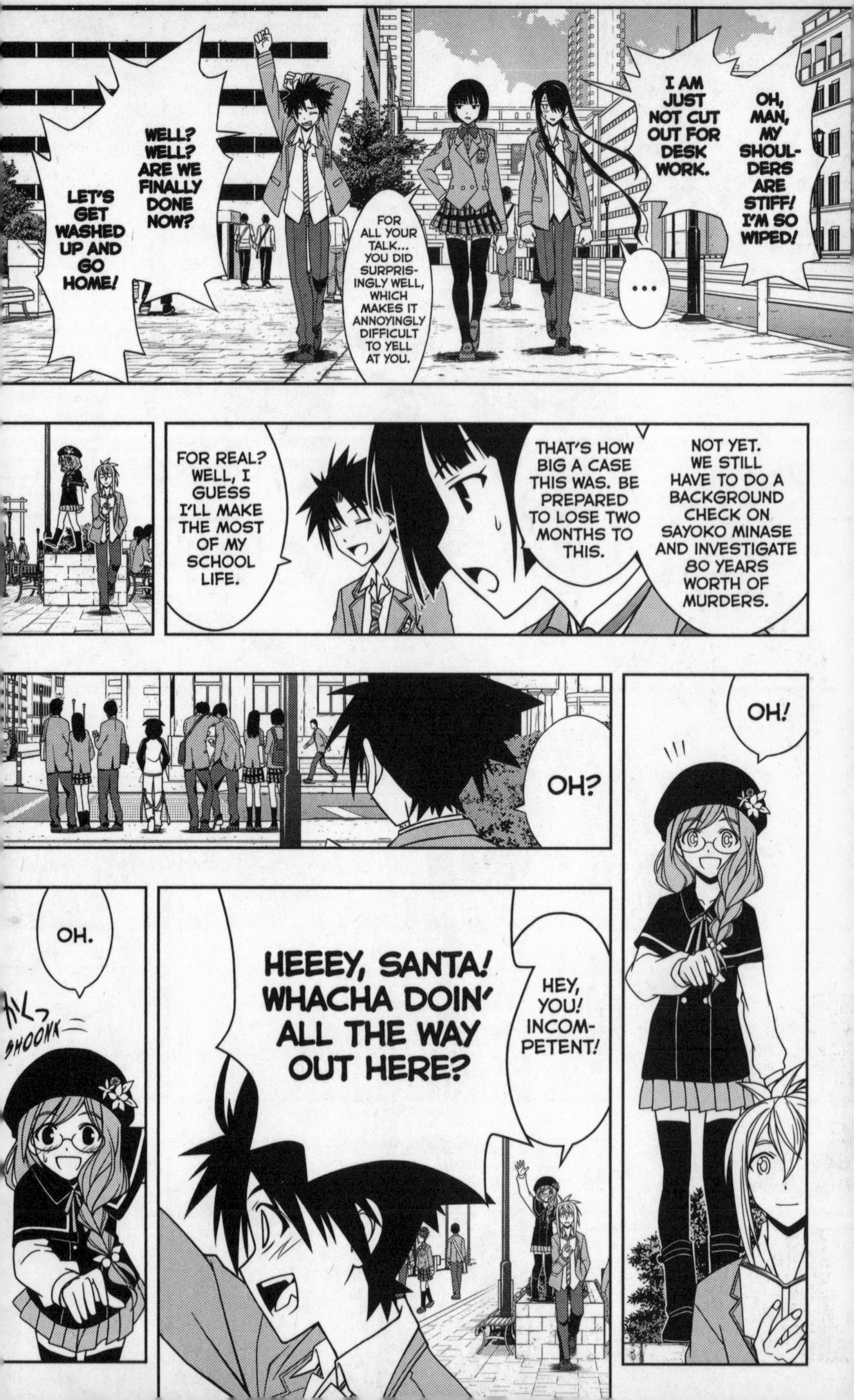
OH, MAN, MY SHOULDERS ARE STIFF! I'M SO WIPED!
I AM JUST NOT CUT OUT FOR DESK WORK.
...
FOR ALL YOUR TALK... YOU DID SURPRISINGLY WELL, WHICH MAKES IT ANNOYINGLY DIFFICULT TO YELL AT YOU.
WELL? WELL? ARE WE FINALLY DONE NOW?
LET'S GET WASHED UP AND GO HOME!
NOT YET. WE STILL HAVE TO DO A BACKGROUND CHECK ON SAYOKO MINASE AND INVESTIGATE 80 YEARS WORTH OF MURDERS.
THAT'S HOW BIG A CASE THIS WAS. BE PREPARED TO LOSE TWO MONTHS TO THIS.
FOR REAL? WELL, I GUESS I'LL MAKE THE MOST OF MY SCHOOL LIFE.
OH!
OH?
HEY, YOU! INCOMPETENT!
HEEEY, SANTA! WHACHA DOIN' ALL THE WAY OUT HERE?
OH.
SHOONK

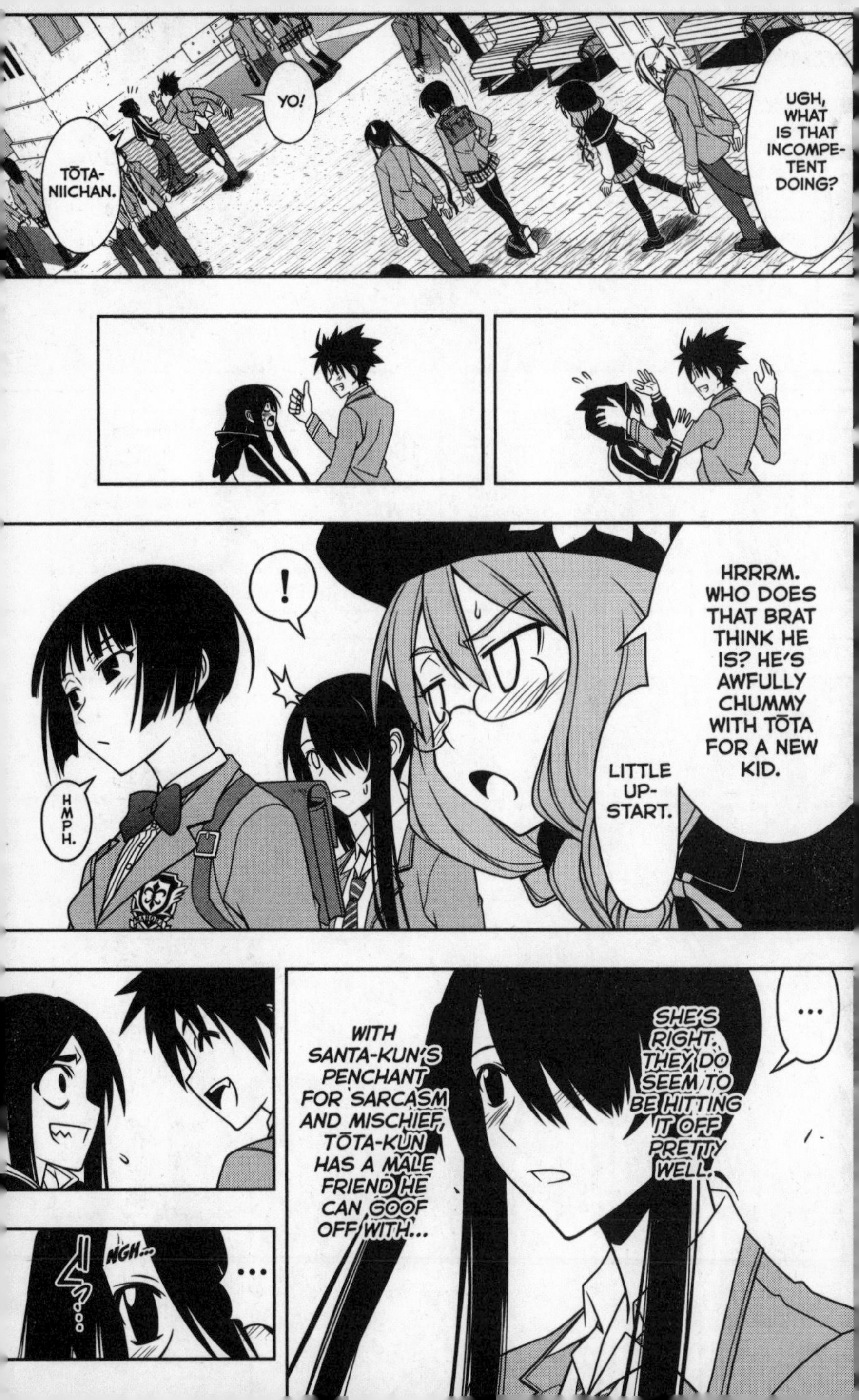
UGH, WHAT IS THAT INCOMPETENT DOING?
YO!
TŌTA-NIICHAN.
HRRRM. WHO DOES THAT BRAT THINK HE IS? HE'S AWFULLY CHUMMY WITH TŌTA FOR A NEW KID.
LITTLE UP-START.
!
HMPH.
...
SHE'S RIGHT. THEY DO SEEM TO BE HITTING IT OFF PRETTY WELL.
WITH SANTA-KUN'S PENCHANT FOR SARCASM AND MISCHIEF, TŌTA-KUN HAS A MALE FRIEND HE CAN GOOF OFF WITH...
NGH...
...

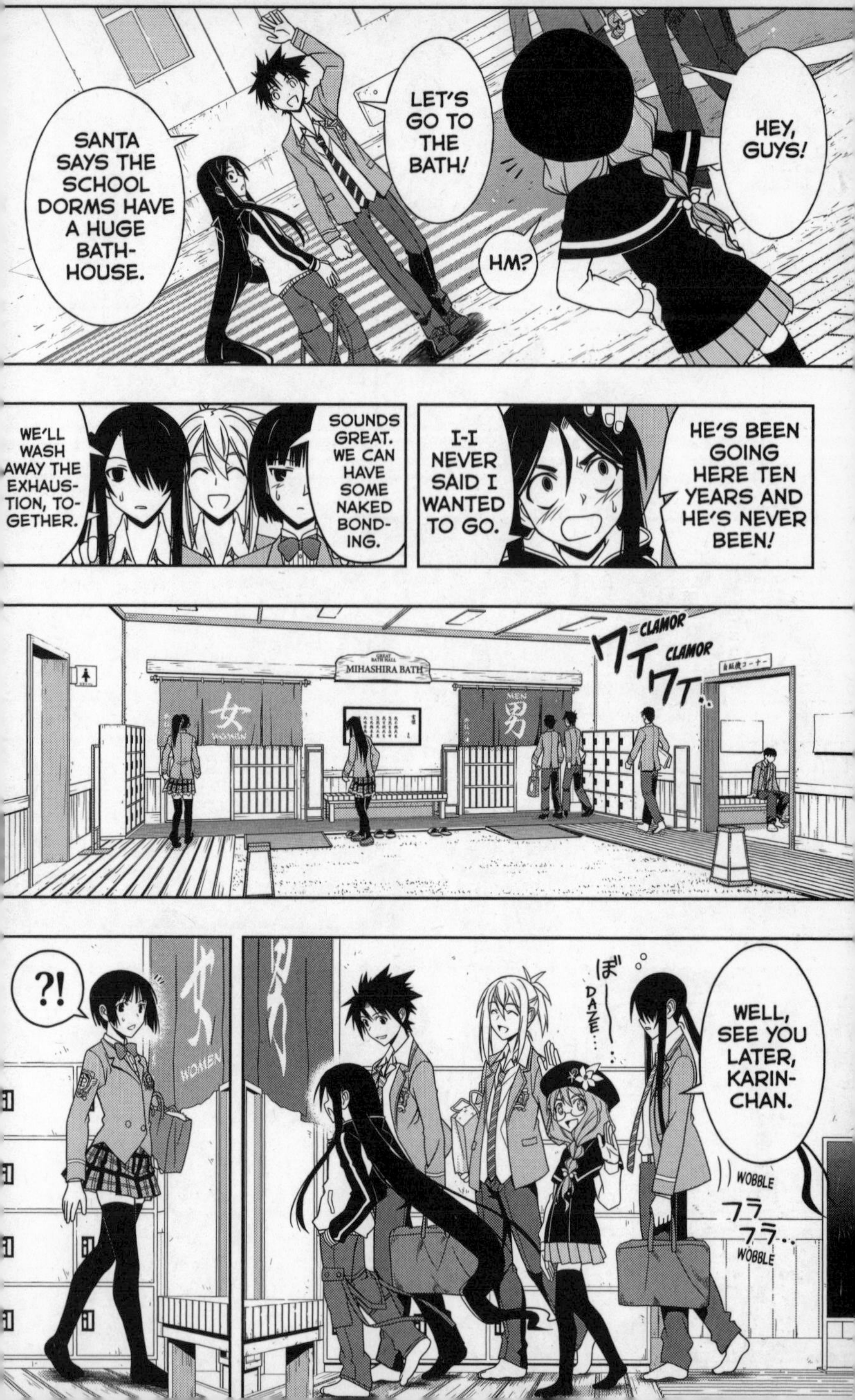
HEY, GUYS!
HM?
LET'S GO TO THE BATH!
SANTA SAYS THE SCHOOL DORMS HAVE A HUGE BATHHOUSE.
HE'S BEEN GOING HERE TEN YEARS AND HE'S NEVER BEEN!
I-I NEVER SAID I WANTED TO GO.
SOUNDS GREAT. WE CAN HAVE SOME NAKED BONDING.
WE'LL WASH AWAY THE EXHAUSTION, TOGETHER.
ワイ CLAMOR
ワイ CLAMOR
GREAT BATH HALL
MIHASHIRA BATH
男 MEN
女 WOMEN
WELL, SEE YOU LATER, KARIN-CHAN.
フラ WOBBLE
フラ… WOBBLE
ぼー DAZE…
?!
女 WOMEN

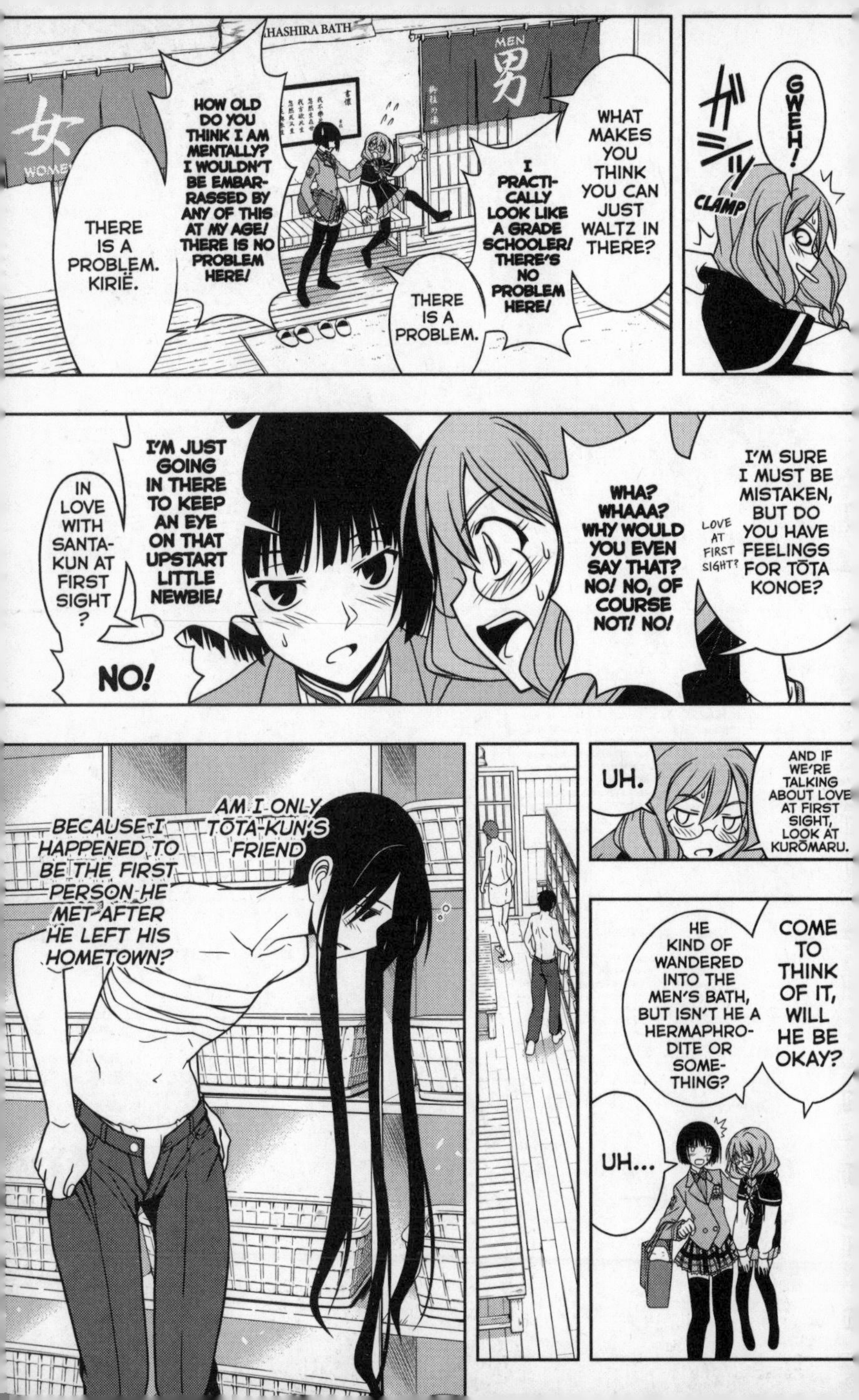

GWEH!
ガシッ
CLAMP
HASHIRA BATH
MEN
男
女
WHAT MAKES YOU THINK YOU CAN JUST WALTZ IN THERE?
I PRACTICALLY LOOK LIKE A GRADE SCHOOLER! THERE'S NO PROBLEM HERE!
THERE IS A PROBLEM.
HOW OLD DO YOU THINK I AM MENTALLY? I WOULDN'T BE EMBARRASSED BY ANY OF THIS AT MY AGE! THERE IS NO PROBLEM HERE!
THERE IS A PROBLEM. KIRIË.
I'M SURE I MUST BE MISTAKEN, BUT DO YOU HAVE FEELINGS FOR TŌTA KONOE?
LOVE AT FIRST SIGHT?
WHA? WHAAA? WHY WOULD YOU EVEN SAY THAT? NO! NO, OF COURSE NOT! NO!
I'M JUST GOING IN THERE TO KEEP AN EYE ON THAT UPSTART LITTLE NEWBIE!
IN LOVE WITH SANTA-KUN AT FIRST SIGHT?
NO!
AND IF WE'RE TALKING ABOUT LOVE AT FIRST SIGHT, LOOK AT KUROMARU.
UH.
COME TO THINK OF IT, WILL HE BE OKAY?
HE KIND OF WANDERED INTO THE MEN'S BATH, BUT ISN'T HE A HERMAPHRODITE OR SOMETHING?
UH...
AM I ONLY TŌTA-KUN'S FRIEND
BECAUSE I HAPPENED TO BE THE FIRST PERSON HE MET AFTER HE LEFT HIS HOMETOWN?

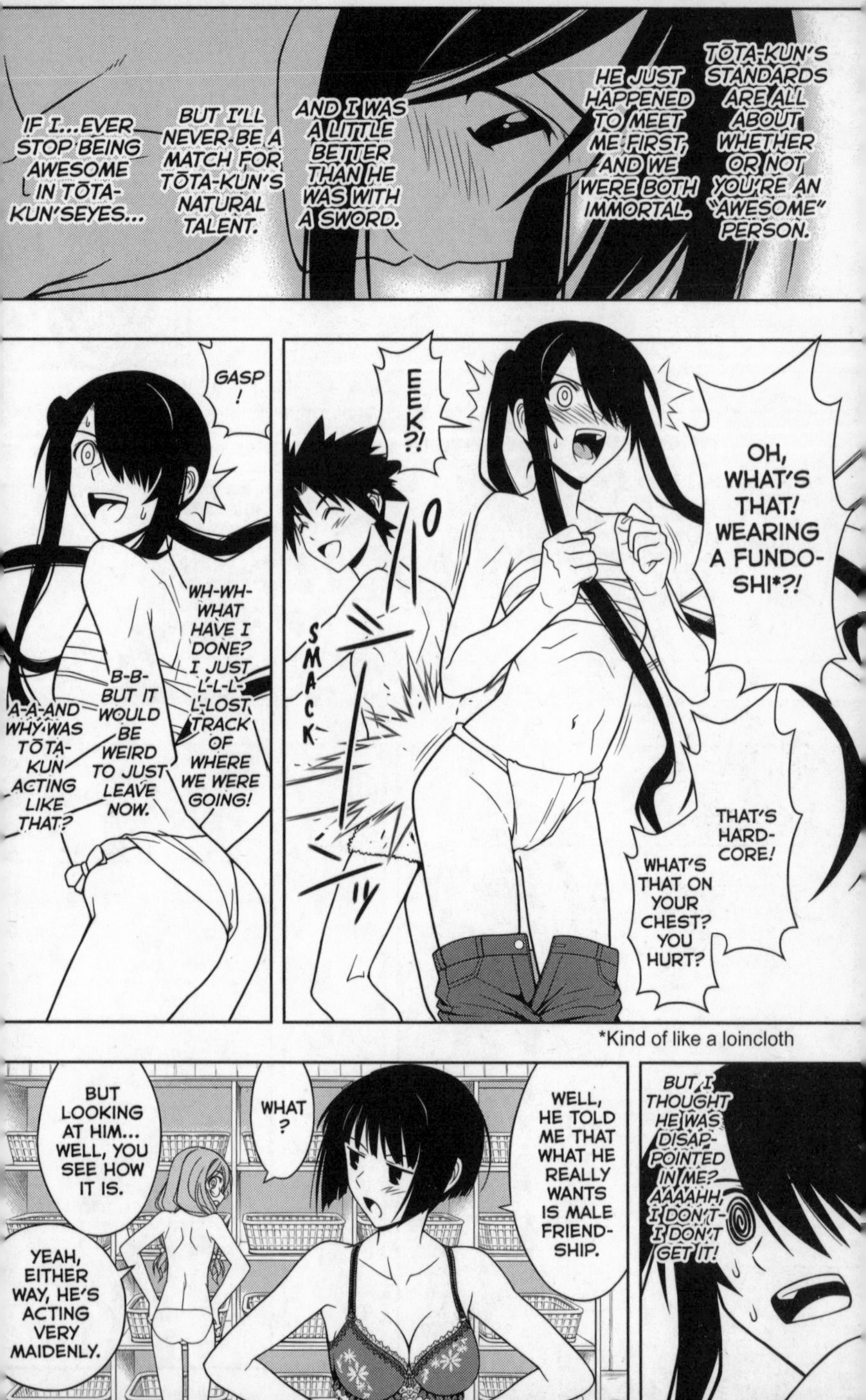
TŌTA-KUN'S STANDARDS ARE ALL ABOUT WHETHER OR NOT YOU'RE AN "AWESOME" PERSON.
HE JUST HAPPENED TO MEET ME FIRST, AND WE WERE BOTH IMMORTAL.
AND I WAS A LITTLE BETTER THAN HE WAS WITH A SWORD.
BUT I'LL NEVER BE A MATCH FOR TŌTA-KUN'S NATURAL TALENT.
IF I...EVER STOP BEING AWESOME IN TŌTA-KUN'SEYES...
OH, WHAT'S THAT! WEARING A FUNDO-SHI*?!
EEK?!
SMACK
THAT'S HARD-CORE!
WHAT'S THAT ON YOUR CHEST? YOU HURT?
GASP!
WH-WH-WHAT HAVE I DONE? I JUST L-L-L-L-LOST TRACK OF WHERE WE WERE GOING!
B-B-BUT IT WOULD BE WEIRD TO JUST LEAVE NOW.
A-A-AND WHY WAS TŌTA-KUN ACTING LIKE THAT?
BUT I THOUGHT HE WAS DISAP-POINTED IN ME? AAAAHH, I DON'T- I DON'T GET IT!
WELL, HE TOLD ME THAT WHAT HE REALLY WANTS IS MALE FRIEND-SHIP.
WHAT?
BUT LOOKING AT HIM... WELL, YOU SEE HOW IT IS.
YEAH, EITHER WAY, HE'S ACTING VERY MAIDENLY.
*Kind of like a loincloth

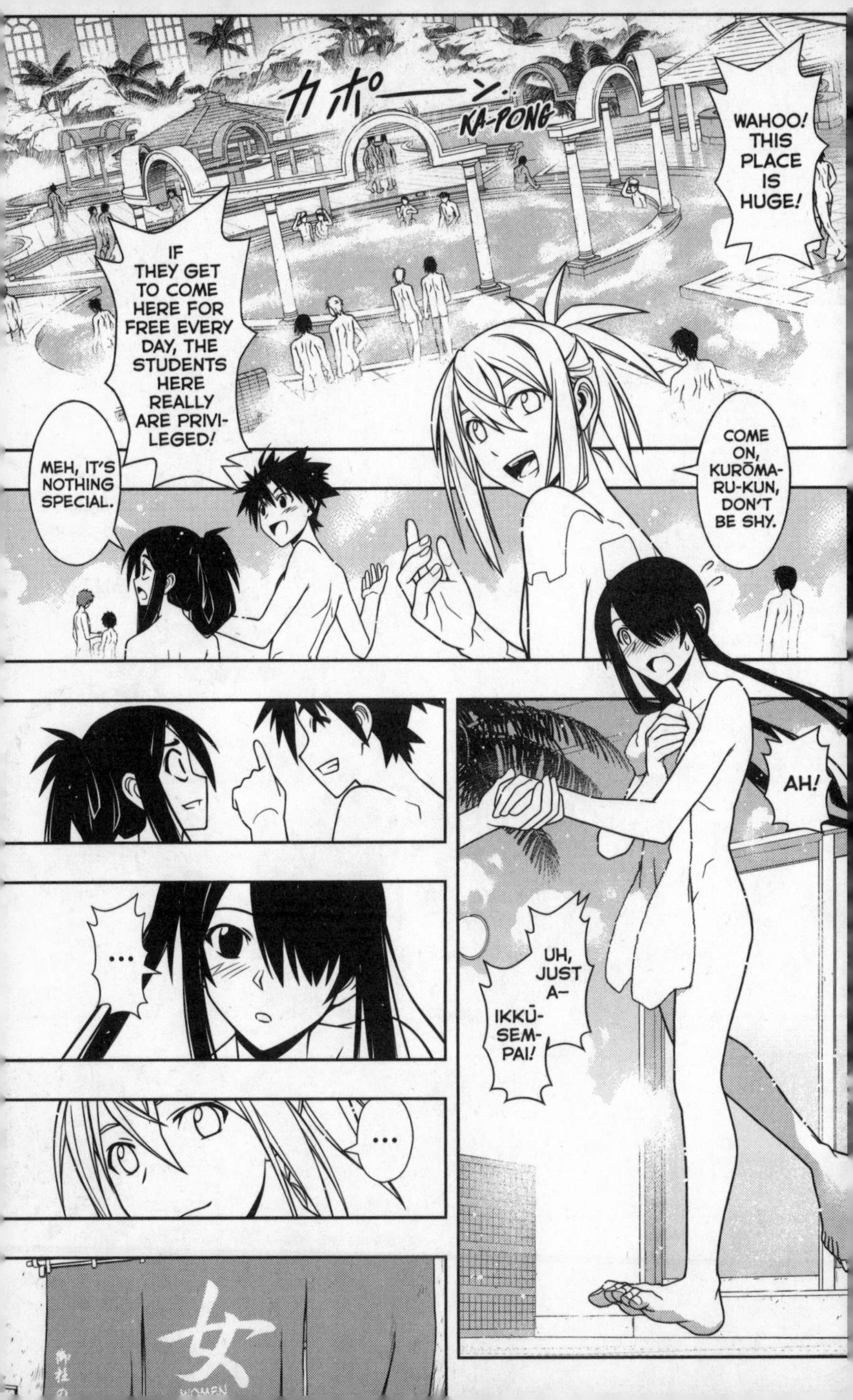
カポーン
KA-PONG
WAHOO! THIS PLACE IS HUGE!
IF THEY GET TO COME HERE FOR FREE EVERY DAY, THE STUDENTS HERE REALLY ARE PRIVILEGED!
COME ON, KURŌMARU-KUN, DON'T BE SHY.
MEH, IT'S NOTHING SPECIAL.
AH!
UH, JUST A— IKKŪ-SEMPAI!
...
...
女
WOMEN

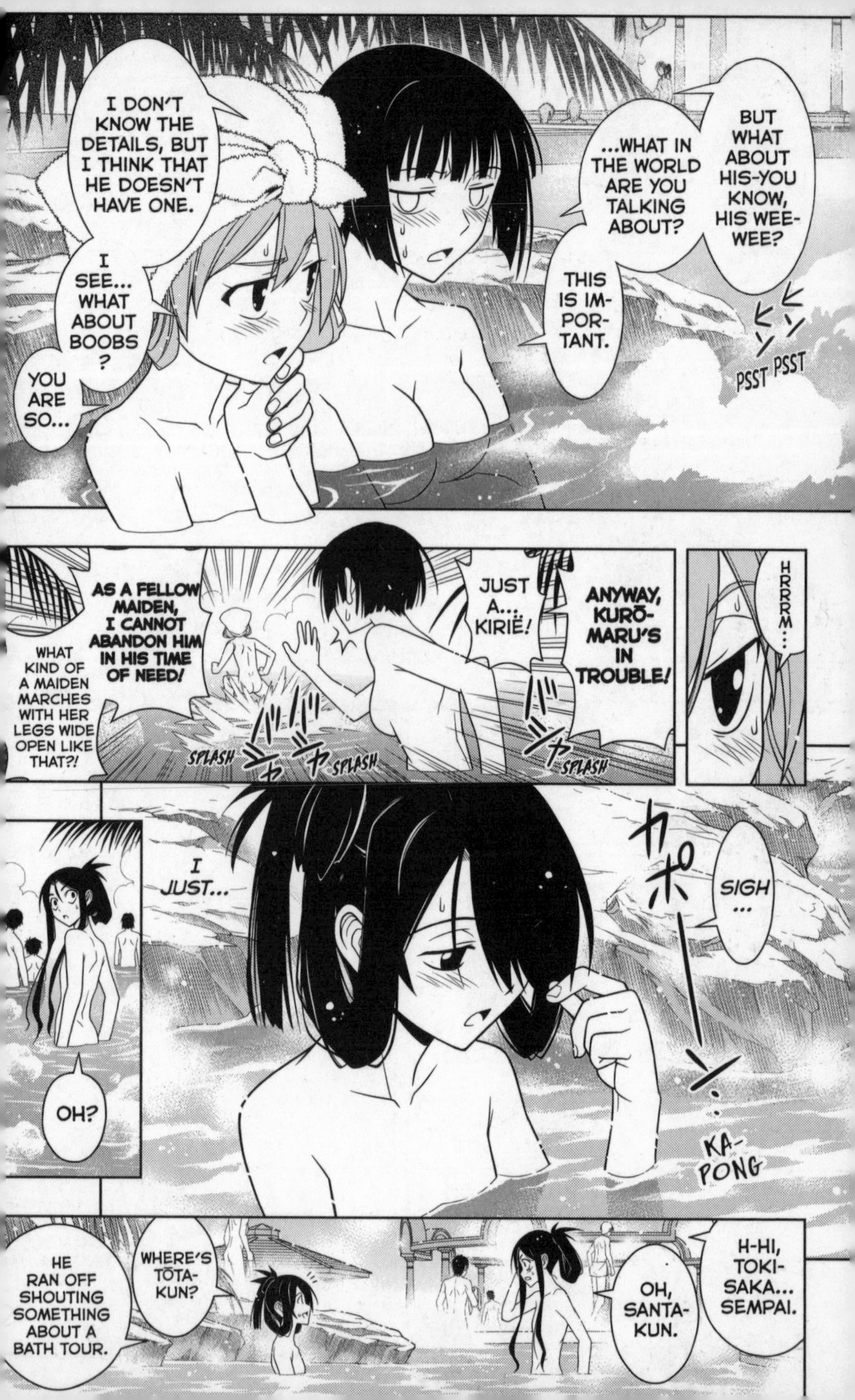
BUT WHAT ABOUT HIS-YOU KNOW, HIS WEE-WEE?
PSST PSST
...WHAT IN THE WORLD ARE YOU TALKING ABOUT?
THIS IS IM-POR-TANT.
I DON'T KNOW THE DETAILS, BUT I THINK THAT HE DOESN'T HAVE ONE.
I SEE... WHAT ABOUT BOOBS?
YOU ARE SO...
HRRRM...
ANYWAY, KURŌMARU'S IN TROUBLE!
JUST A... KIRIË!
SPLASH
AS A FELLOW MAIDEN, I CANNOT ABANDON HIM IN HIS TIME OF NEED!
SPLASH
WHAT KIND OF A MAIDEN MARCHES WITH HER LEGS WIDE OPEN LIKE THAT?!
SPLASH
SIGH...
KA-PONG
I JUST...
OH?
H-HI, TOKI-SAKA... SEMPAI.
OH, SANTA-KUN.
WHERE'S TŌTA-KUN?
HE RAN OFF SHOUTING SOMETHING ABOUT A BATH TOUR.

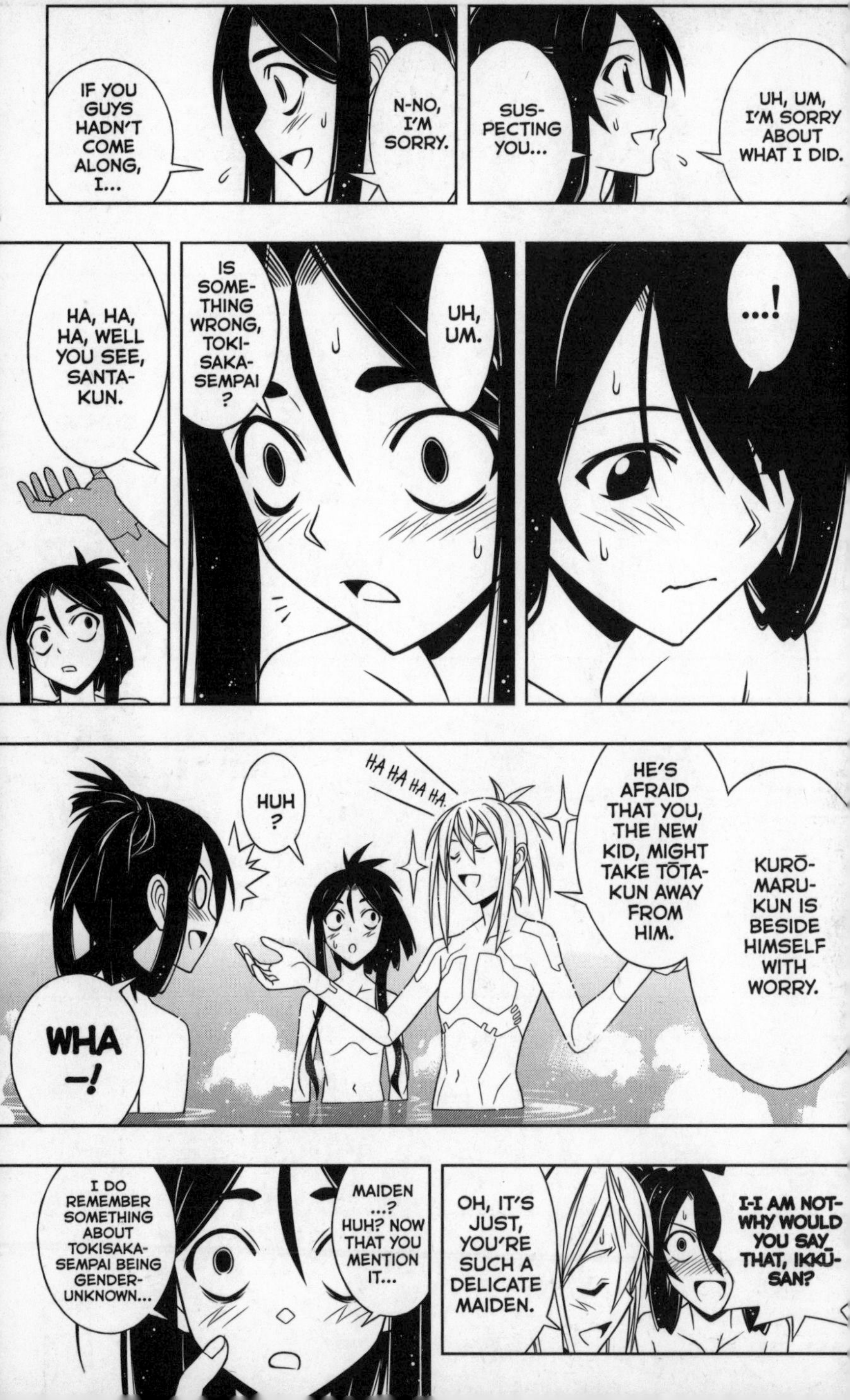
UH, UM, I'M SORRY ABOUT WHAT I DID.
SUS-PECTING YOU...
N-NO, I'M SORRY.
IF YOU GUYS HADN'T COME ALONG, I...
...!
UH, UM.
IS SOME-THING WRONG, TOKI-SAKA-SEMPAI?
HA, HA, HA, WELL YOU SEE, SANTA-KUN.
KURŌ-MARU-KUN IS BESIDE HIMSELF WITH WORRY.
HE'S AFRAID THAT YOU, THE NEW KID, MIGHT TAKE TŌTA-KUN AWAY FROM HIM.
HA HA HA HA.
HUH?
WHA-!
OH, IT'S JUST, YOU'RE SUCH A DELICATE MAIDEN.
I-I AM NOT- WHY WOULD YOU SAY THAT, IKKŪ-SAN?
MAIDEN...? HUH? NOW THAT YOU MENTION IT...
I DO REMEMBER SOMETHING ABOUT TOKISAKA-SEMPAI BEING GENDER-UNKNOWN...

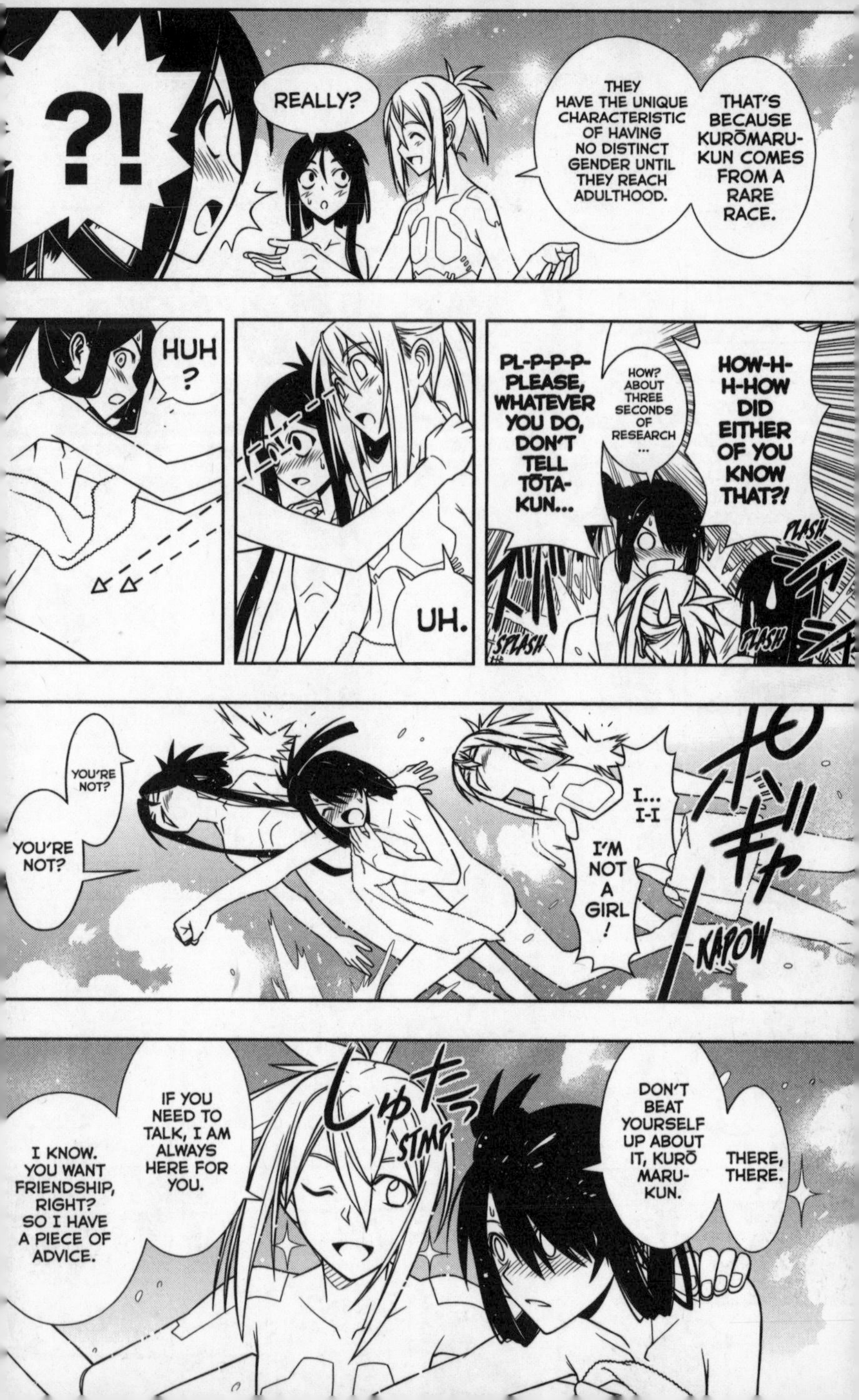
THAT'S BECAUSE KURŌMARU-KUN COMES FROM A RARE RACE.
THEY HAVE THE UNIQUE CHARACTERISTIC OF HAVING NO DISTINCT GENDER UNTIL THEY REACH ADULTHOOD.
REALLY?
?!
HOW-H-H-HOW DID EITHER OF YOU KNOW THAT?!
HOW? ABOUT THREE SECONDS OF RESEARCH ...
PL-P-P-P-PLEASE, WHATEVER YOU DO, DON'T TELL TŌTA-KUN...
PLASH
PLASH
SPLASH
UH.
HUH?
KAPOW
I... I-I
I'M NOT A GIRL!
YOU'RE NOT?
YOU'RE NOT?
THERE, THERE.
DON'T BEAT YOURSELF UP ABOUT IT, KURŌ MARU-KUN.
STMP
IF YOU NEED TO TALK, I AM ALWAYS HERE FOR YOU.
I KNOW. YOU WANT FRIENDSHIP, RIGHT? SO I HAVE A PIECE OF ADVICE.

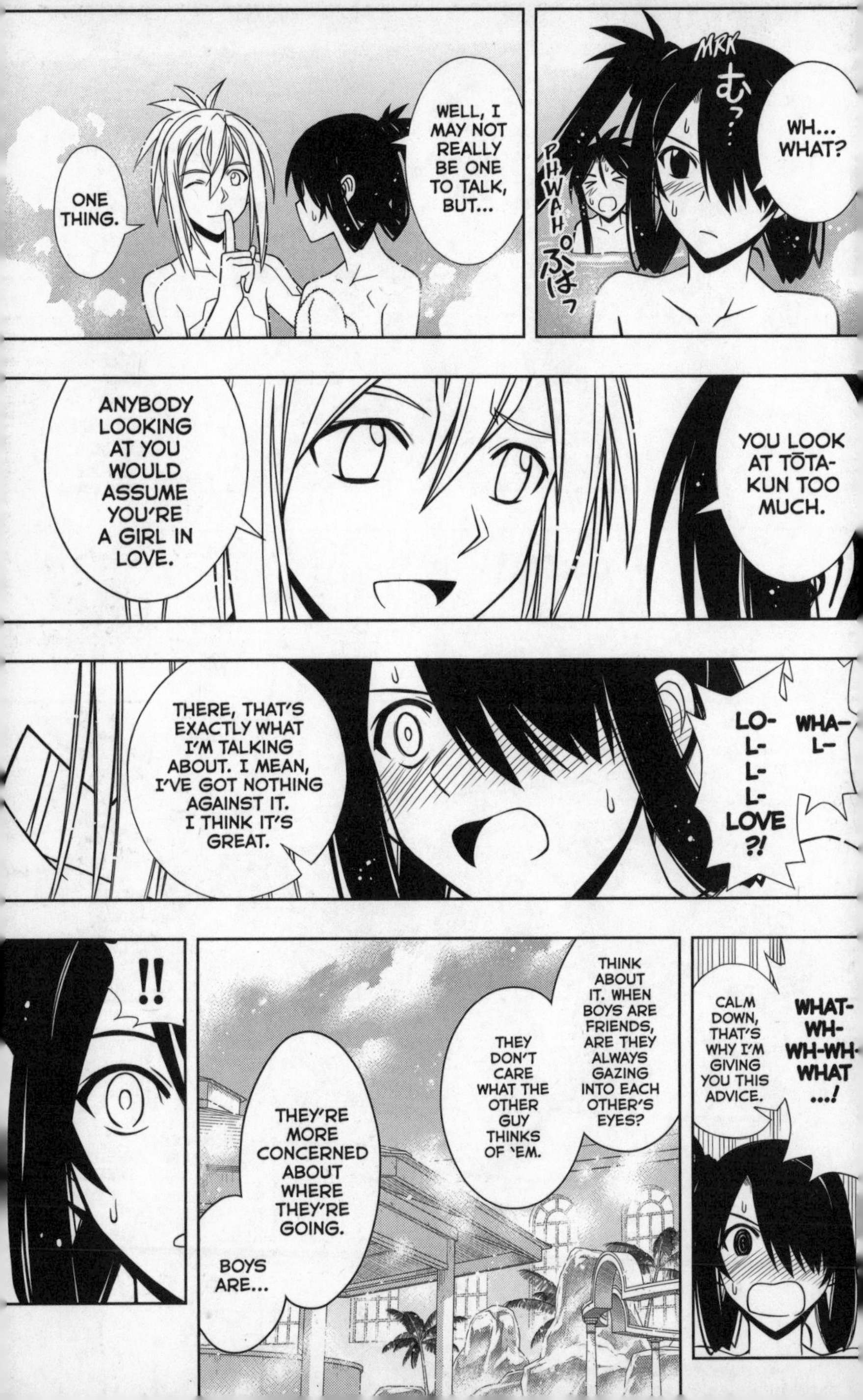
MRK
むっ
WH... WHAT?
PHWAH
ぷはっ
WELL, I MAY NOT REALLY BE ONE TO TALK, BUT...
ONE THING.
YOU LOOK AT TŌTA-KUN TOO MUCH.
ANYBODY LOOKING AT YOU WOULD ASSUME YOU'RE A GIRL IN LOVE.
WHA- L-
LO- L- L- L- LOVE ?!
THERE, THAT'S EXACTLY WHAT I'M TALKING ABOUT. I MEAN, I'VE GOT NOTHING AGAINST IT. I THINK IT'S GREAT.
WHAT-WH-WH-WH-WHAT ...!
CALM DOWN, THAT'S WHY I'M GIVING YOU THIS ADVICE.
THINK ABOUT IT. WHEN BOYS ARE FRIENDS, ARE THEY ALWAYS GAZING INTO EACH OTHER'S EYES?
THEY DON'T CARE WHAT THE OTHER GUY THINKS OF 'EM.
THEY'RE MORE CONCERNED ABOUT WHERE THEY'RE GOING.
BOYS ARE...
!!

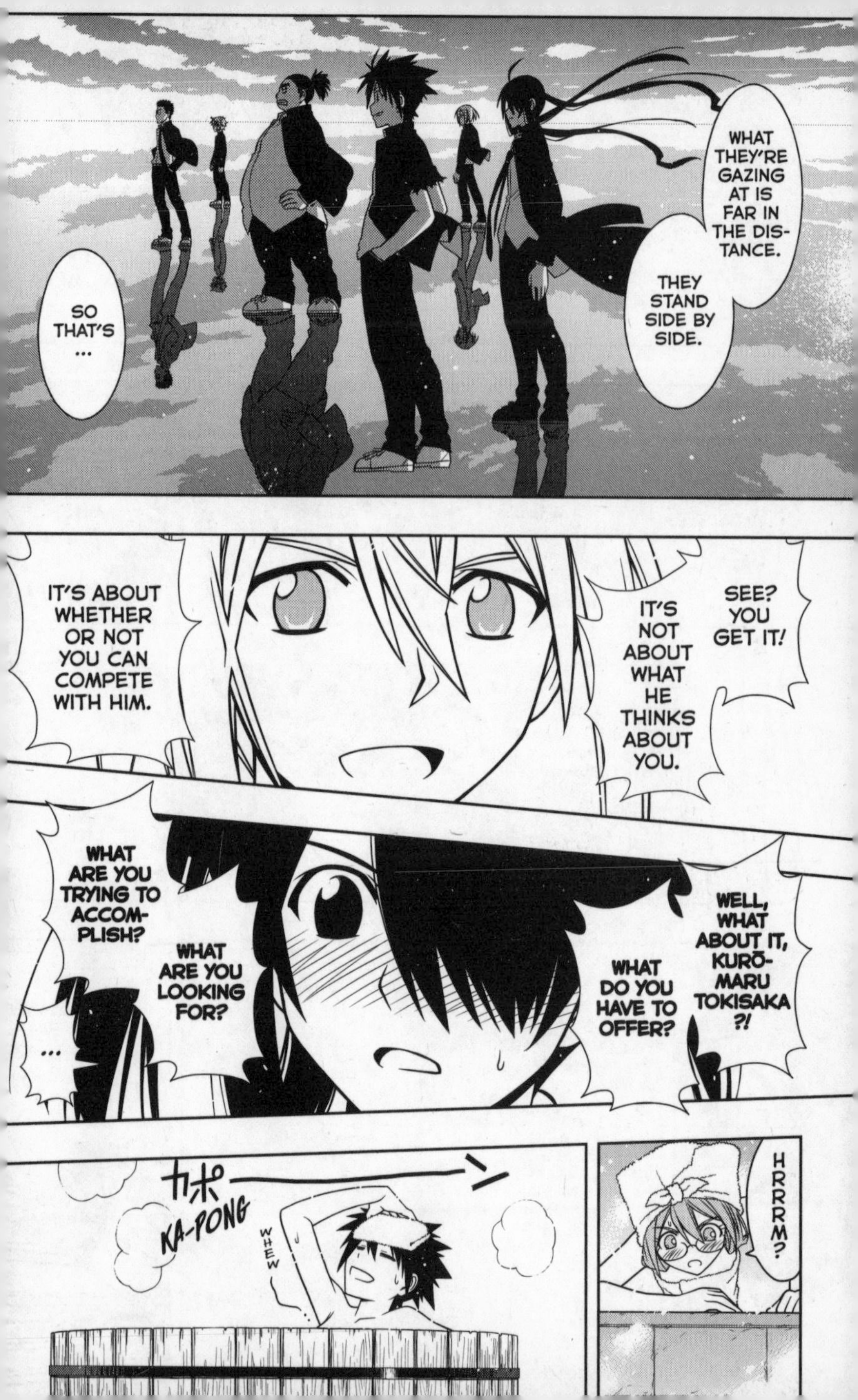
WHAT THEY'RE GAZING AT IS FAR IN THE DISTANCE.
THEY STAND SIDE BY SIDE.
SO THAT'S ...
SEE? YOU GET IT!
IT'S NOT ABOUT WHAT HE THINKS ABOUT YOU.
IT'S ABOUT WHETHER OR NOT YOU CAN COMPETE WITH HIM.
WELL, WHAT ABOUT IT, KURŌMARU TOKISAKA?!
WHAT DO YOU HAVE TO OFFER?
WHAT ARE YOU LOOKING FOR?
WHAT ARE YOU TRYING TO ACCOMPLISH?
...
HRRRM?
カポ——ン
KA-PONG
WHEW

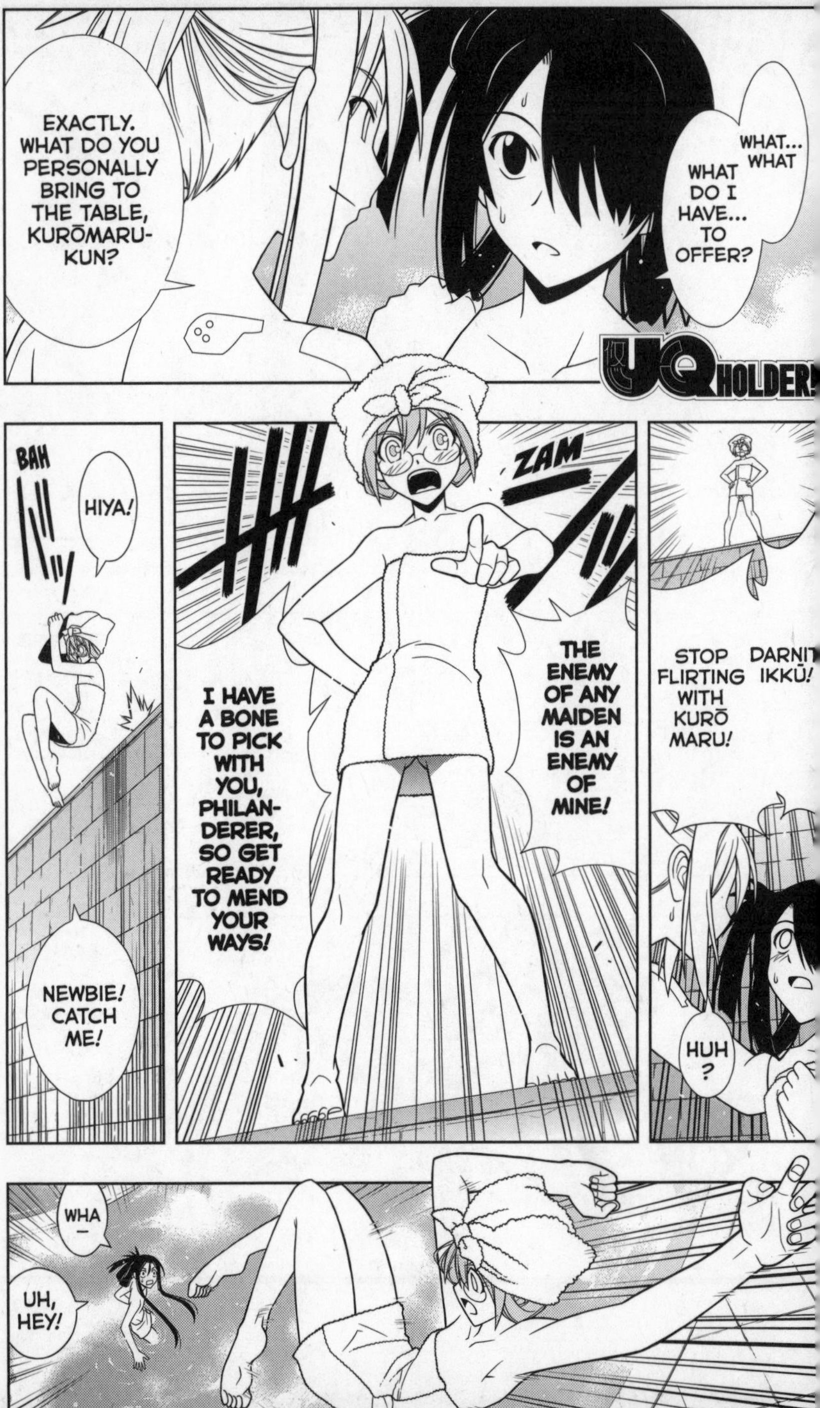
WHAT... WHAT WHAT DO I HAVE... TO OFFER?
EXACTLY. WHAT DO YOU PERSONALLY BRING TO THE TABLE, KURŌMARU-KUN?
UQ HOLDER!
DARNIT IKKŪ!
STOP FLIRTING WITH KURŌ MARU!
HUH?
ZAM
THE ENEMY OF ANY MAIDEN IS AN ENEMY OF MINE!
I HAVE A BONE TO PICK WITH YOU, PHILANDERER, SO GET READY TO MEND YOUR WAYS!
BAH
HIYA!
NEWBIE! CATCH ME!
WHA—
UH, HEY!

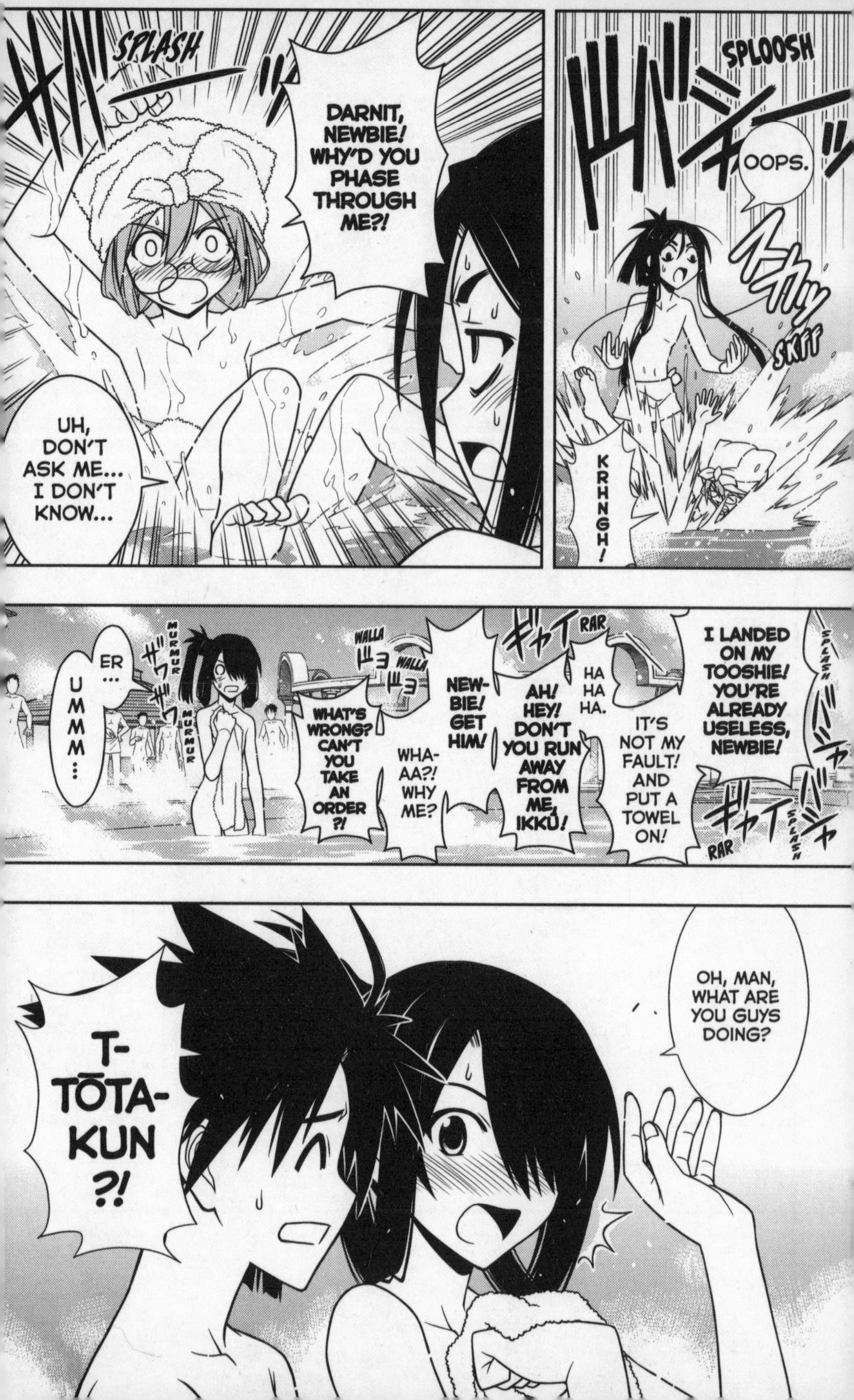
SPLOOSH
OOPS.
SKFF
KRHNGH!
SPLASH
DARNIT, NEWBIE! WHY'D YOU PHASE THROUGH ME?!
UH, DON'T ASK ME... I DON'T KNOW...
SPLASH
RAR
I LANDED ON MY TOOSHIE! YOU'RE ALREADY USELESS, NEWBIE!
SPLASH
RAR
IT'S NOT MY FAULT! AND PUT A TOWEL ON!
HA HA HA.
AH! HEY! DON'T YOU RUN AWAY FROM ME, IKKŪ!
RAR
NEWBIE! GET HIM!
WHA-AA?! WHY ME?
WALLA
WALLA
WHAT'S WRONG? CAN'T YOU TAKE AN ORDER?!
MURMUR
MURMUR
ER... UMMM...
OH, MAN, WHAT ARE YOU GUYS DOING?
T-TŌTA-KUN?!

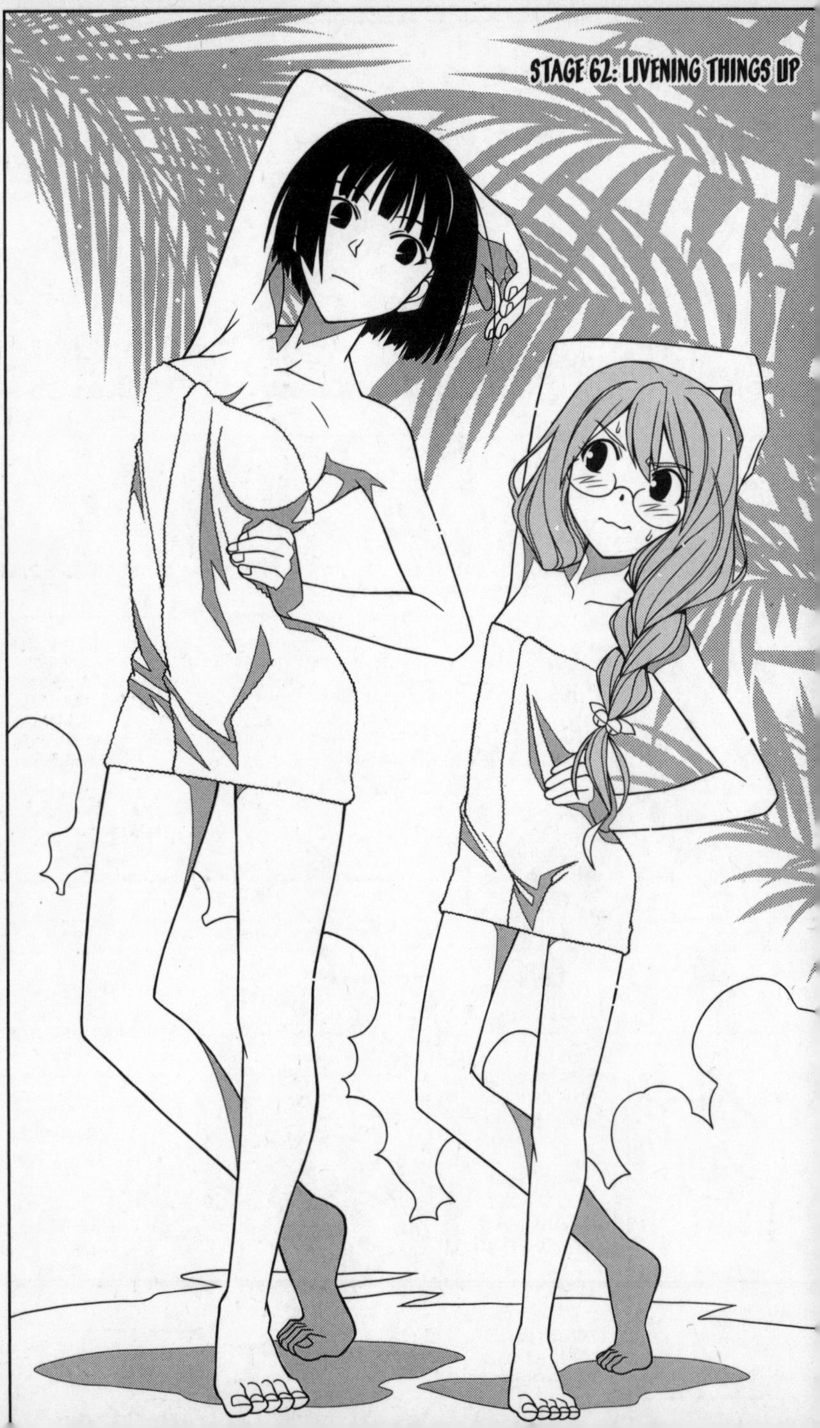
STAGE 62: LIVENING THINGS UP

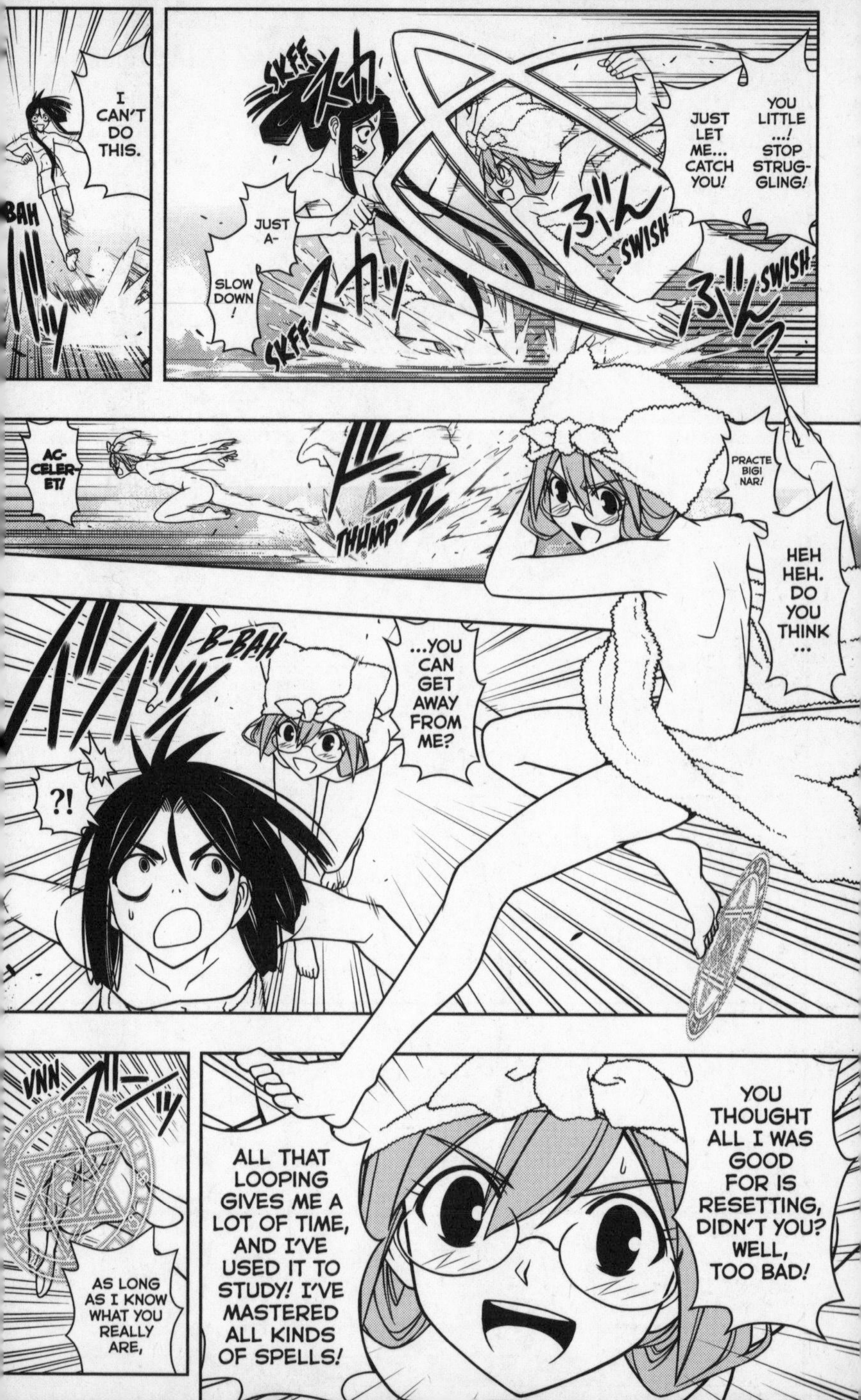
YOU LITTLE ...! STOP STRUG-GLING!
JUST LET ME... CATCH YOU!
SKFF
JUST A-
SLOW DOWN!
ぶん
SWISH
SWISH
SKFF
I CAN'T DO THIS.
BAH
PRACTE BIGI NAR!
THUMP
AC-CELER-ET!
HEH HEH. DO YOU THINK...
...YOU CAN GET AWAY FROM ME?
B-BAH
?!
YOU THOUGHT ALL I WAS GOOD FOR IS RESETTING, DIDN'T YOU? WELL, TOO BAD!
ALL THAT LOOPING GIVES ME A LOT OF TIME, AND I'VE USED IT TO STUDY! I'VE MASTERED ALL KINDS OF SPELLS!
VNN
AS LONG AS I KNOW WHAT YOU REALLY ARE,

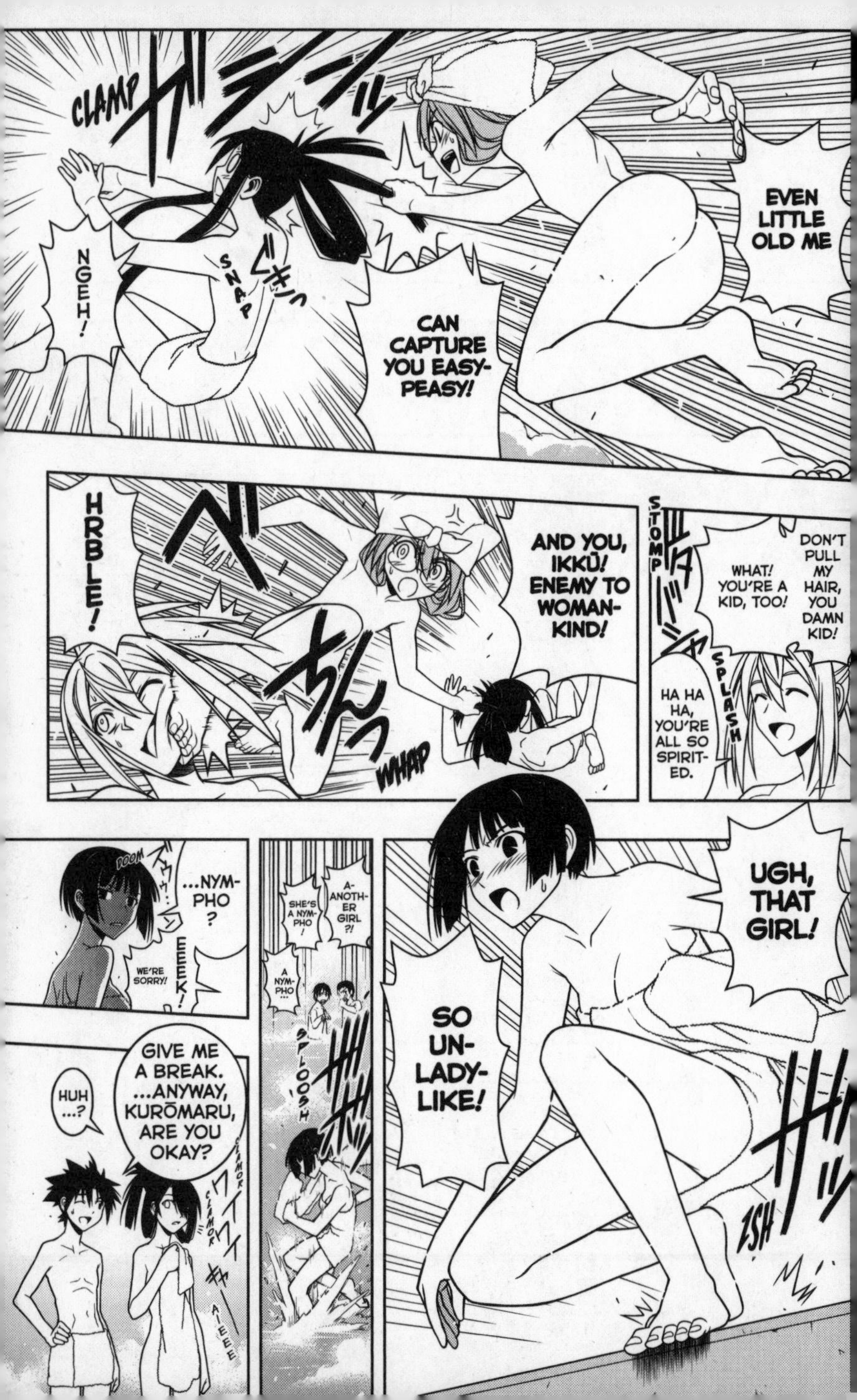
EVEN LITTLE OLD ME
CAN CAPTURE YOU EASY-PEASY!
CLAMP
NGEH!
SNAP
DON'T PULL MY HAIR, YOU DAMN KID!
WHAT! YOU'RE A KID, TOO!
STOMP
SPLASH
HA HA HA, YOU'RE ALL SO SPIRIT-ED.
AND YOU, IKKŪ! ENEMY TO WOMAN-KIND!
HRBLE!
WHAP
UGH, THAT GIRL!
SO UN-LADY-LIKE!
ISH
A-ANOTH-ER GIRL?!
SHE'S A NYM-PHO!
A NYM-PHO...
SPLOOSH
...NYM-PHO?
DOOM
EEEEK!
WE'RE SORRY!
GIVE ME A BREAK. ...ANYWAY, KURŌMARU, ARE YOU OKAY?
HUH...?
CLAMOR
CLAMOR
AIEEE

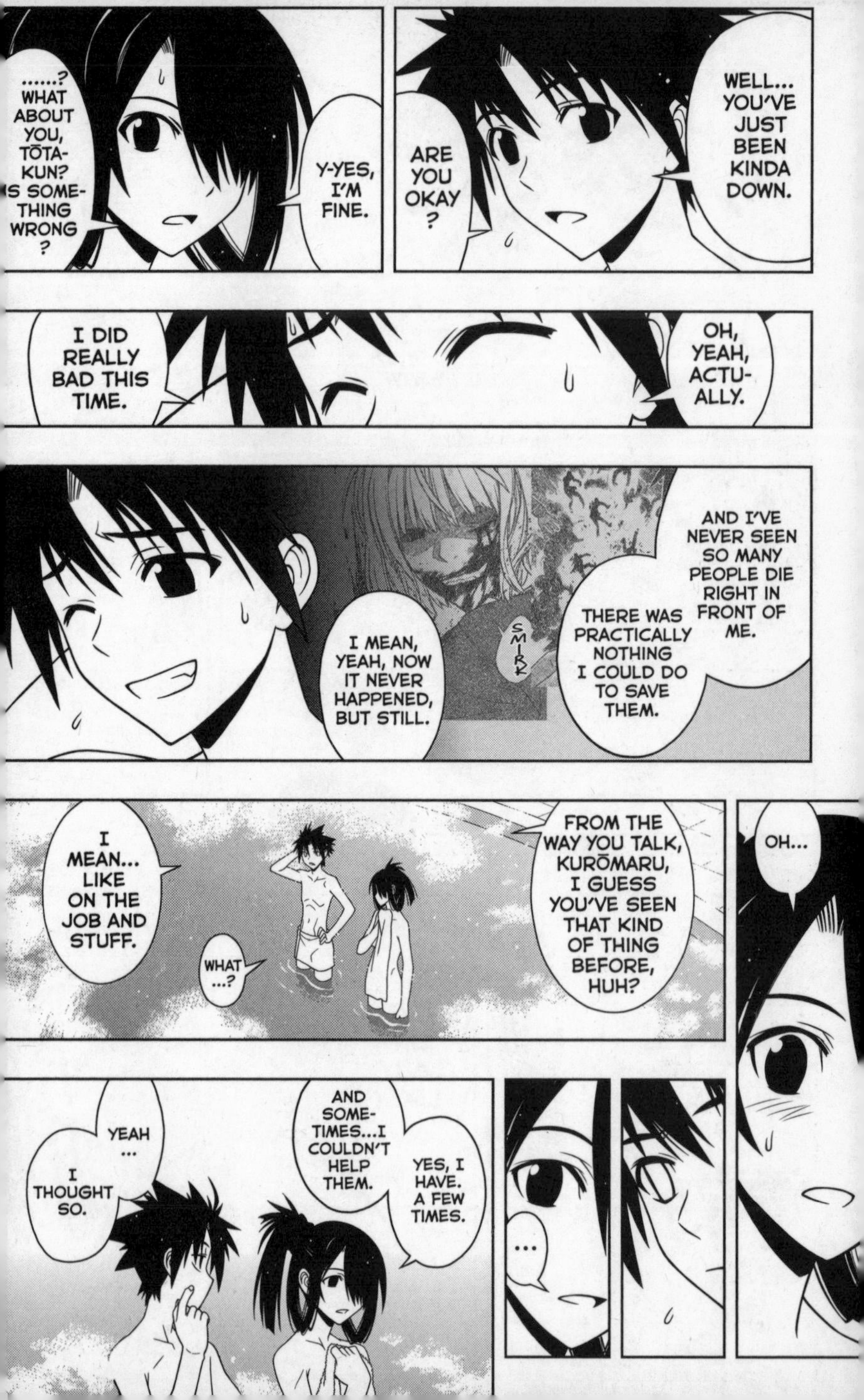
WELL... YOU'VE JUST BEEN KINDA DOWN.
ARE YOU OKAY?
Y-YES, I'M FINE.
......? WHAT ABOUT YOU, TŌTA-KUN? IS SOMETHING WRONG?
OH, YEAH, ACTUALLY.
I DID REALLY BAD THIS TIME.
AND I'VE NEVER SEEN SO MANY PEOPLE DIE RIGHT IN FRONT OF ME.
THERE WAS PRACTICALLY NOTHING I COULD DO TO SAVE THEM.
SMIRK
I MEAN, YEAH, NOW IT NEVER HAPPENED, BUT STILL.
OH...
FROM THE WAY YOU TALK, KURŌMARU, I GUESS YOU'VE SEEN THAT KIND OF THING BEFORE, HUH?
WHAT...?
I MEAN... LIKE ON THE JOB AND STUFF.
...
YES, I HAVE. A FEW TIMES.
AND SOMETIMES...I COULDN'T HELP THEM.
YEAH... I THOUGHT SO.

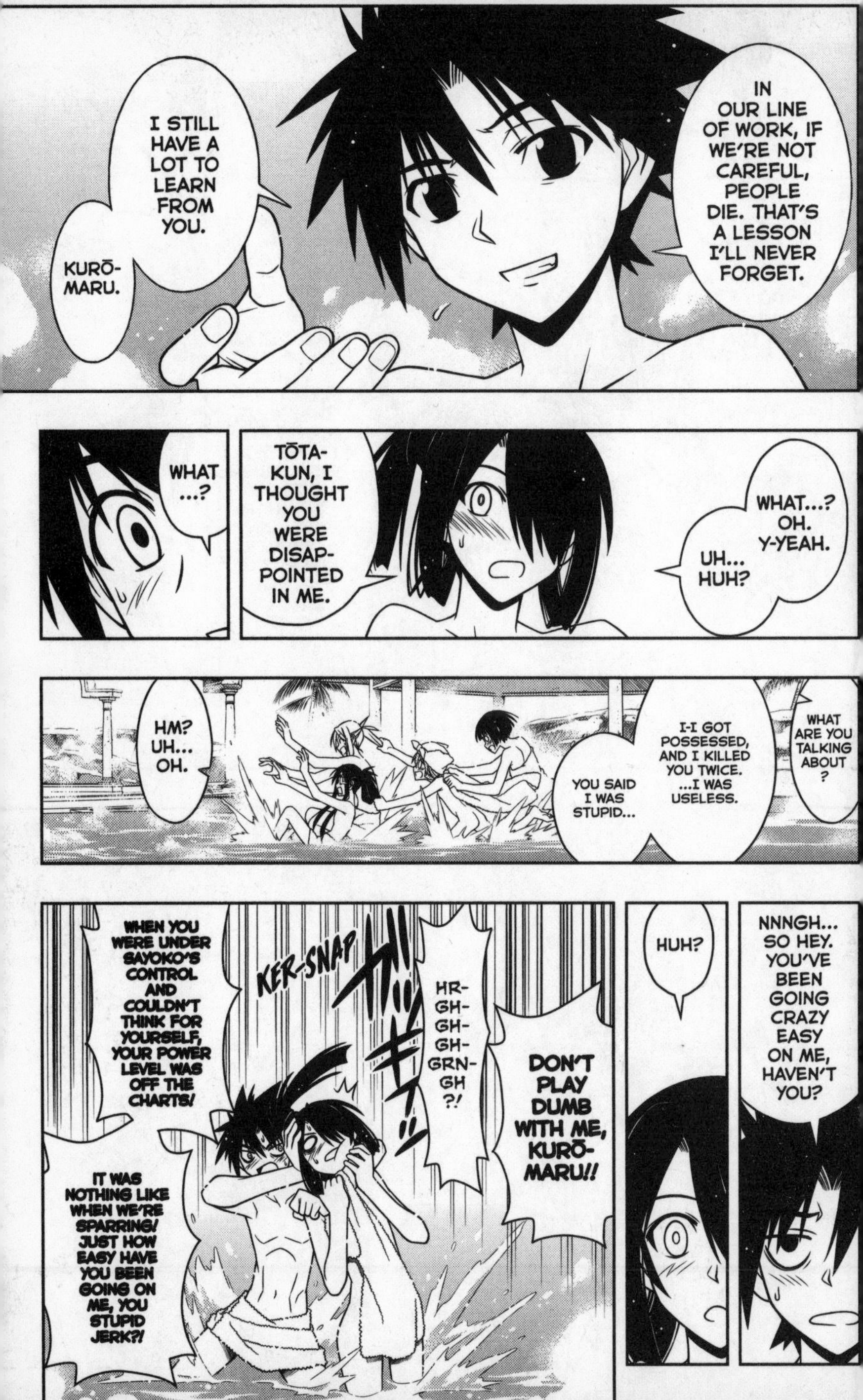
IN OUR LINE OF WORK, IF WE'RE NOT CAREFUL, PEOPLE DIE. THAT'S A LESSON I'LL NEVER FORGET.
I STILL HAVE A LOT TO LEARN FROM YOU.
KURŌ-MARU.
WHAT...? OH. Y-YEAH.
UH... HUH?
TŌTA-KUN, I THOUGHT YOU WERE DISAPPOINTED IN ME.
WHAT ...?
WHAT ARE YOU TALKING ABOUT?
I-I GOT POSSESSED, AND I KILLED YOU TWICE. ...I WAS USELESS.
YOU SAID I WAS STUPID...
HM? UH... OH.
NNNGH... SO HEY. YOU'VE BEEN GOING CRAZY EASY ON ME, HAVEN'T YOU?
HUH?
DON'T PLAY DUMB WITH ME, KURŌ-MARU!!
HR-GH-GH-GH-GRN-GH?!
KER-SNAP
WHEN YOU WERE UNDER SAYOKO'S CONTROL AND COULDN'T THINK FOR YOURSELF, YOUR POWER LEVEL WAS OFF THE CHARTS!
IT WAS NOTHING LIKE WHEN WE'RE SPARRING! JUST HOW EASY HAVE YOU BEEN GOING ON ME, YOU STUPID JERK?!

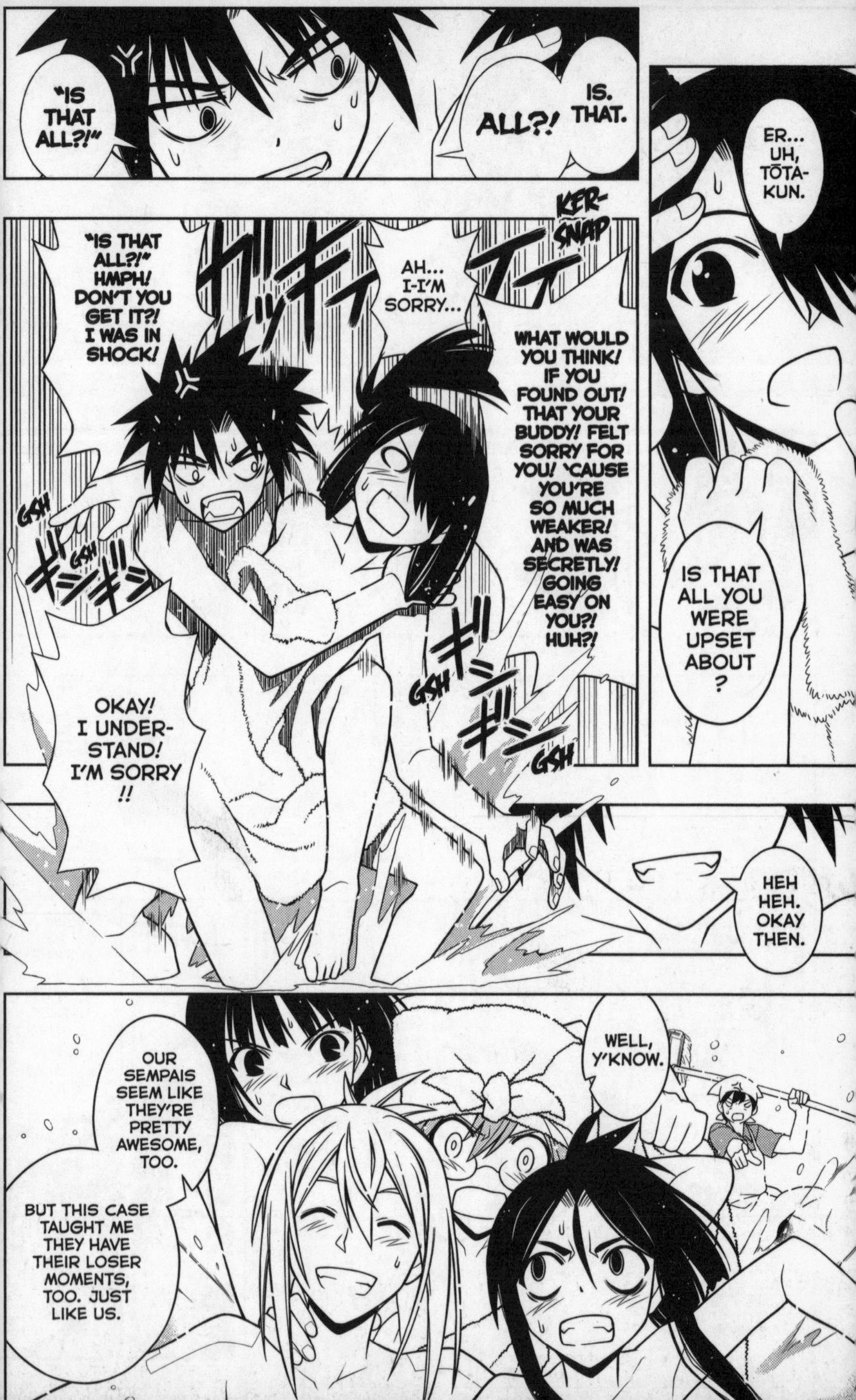
ER... UH, TŌTA-KUN.
IS THAT ALL YOU WERE UPSET ABOUT?
IS. THAT. ALL?!
"IS THAT ALL?!"
KER-SNAP
AH... I-I'M SORRY...
"IS THAT ALL?!" HMPH! DON'T YOU GET IT?! I WAS IN SHOCK!
WHAT WOULD YOU THINK! IF YOU FOUND OUT! THAT YOUR BUDDY! FELT SORRY FOR YOU! 'CAUSE YOU'RE SO MUCH WEAKER! AND WAS SECRETLY! GOING EASY ON YOU?! HUH?!
GSH GSH
GSH GSH
OKAY! I UNDERSTAND! I'M SORRY !!
HEH HEH. OKAY THEN.
WELL, Y'KNOW.
OUR SEMPAIS SEEM LIKE THEY'RE PRETTY AWESOME, TOO.
BUT THIS CASE TAUGHT ME THEY HAVE THEIR LOSER MOMENTS, TOO. JUST LIKE US.

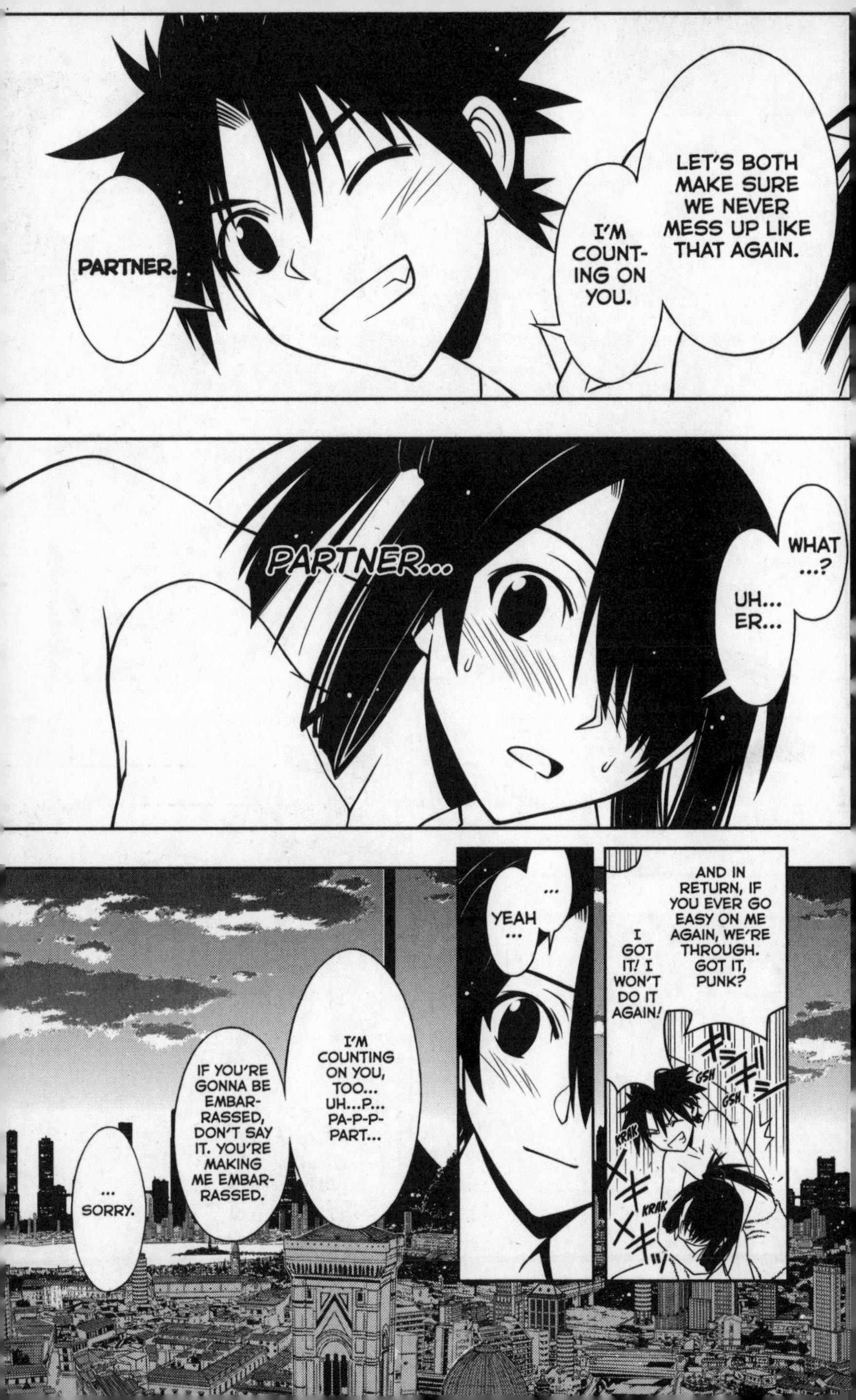
LET'S BOTH MAKE SURE WE NEVER MESS UP LIKE THAT AGAIN.
I'M COUNTING ON YOU.
PARTNER...
WHAT ...?
UH... ER...
PARTNER...
AND IN RETURN, IF YOU EVER GO EASY ON ME AGAIN, WE'RE THROUGH. GOT IT, PUNK?
I GOT IT! I WON'T DO IT AGAIN!
GSH
GSH
KRAK
KRAK
...
YEAH ...
I'M COUNTING ON YOU, TOO... UH...P... PA-P-P-PART...
IF YOU'RE GONNA BE EMBARRASSED, DON'T SAY IT. YOU'RE MAKING ME EMBARRASSED.
... SORRY.

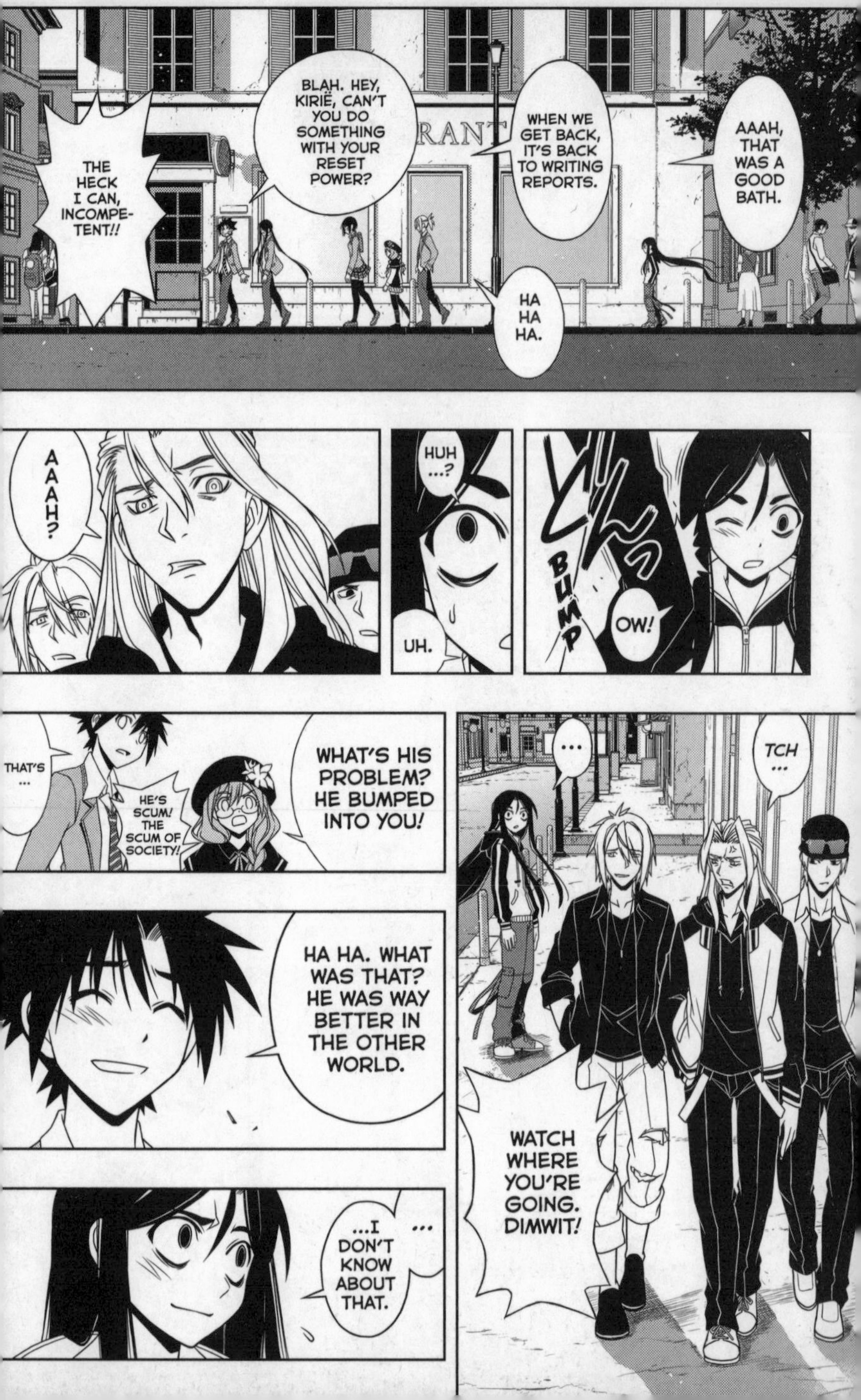
AAAH, THAT WAS A GOOD BATH.
WHEN WE GET BACK, IT'S BACK TO WRITING REPORTS.
HA HA HA.
BLAH. HEY, KIRIË, CAN'T YOU DO SOMETHING WITH YOUR RESET POWER?
THE HECK I CAN, INCOMPETENT!!
BUMP
OW!
HUH ...?
UH.
AAAH?
TCH ...
...
WATCH WHERE YOU'RE GOING. DIMWIT!
WHAT'S HIS PROBLEM? HE BUMPED INTO YOU!
HE'S SCUM! THE SCUM OF SOCIETY!
THAT'S ...
HA HA. WHAT WAS THAT? HE WAS WAY BETTER IN THE OTHER WORLD.
...
...I DON'T KNOW ABOUT THAT.

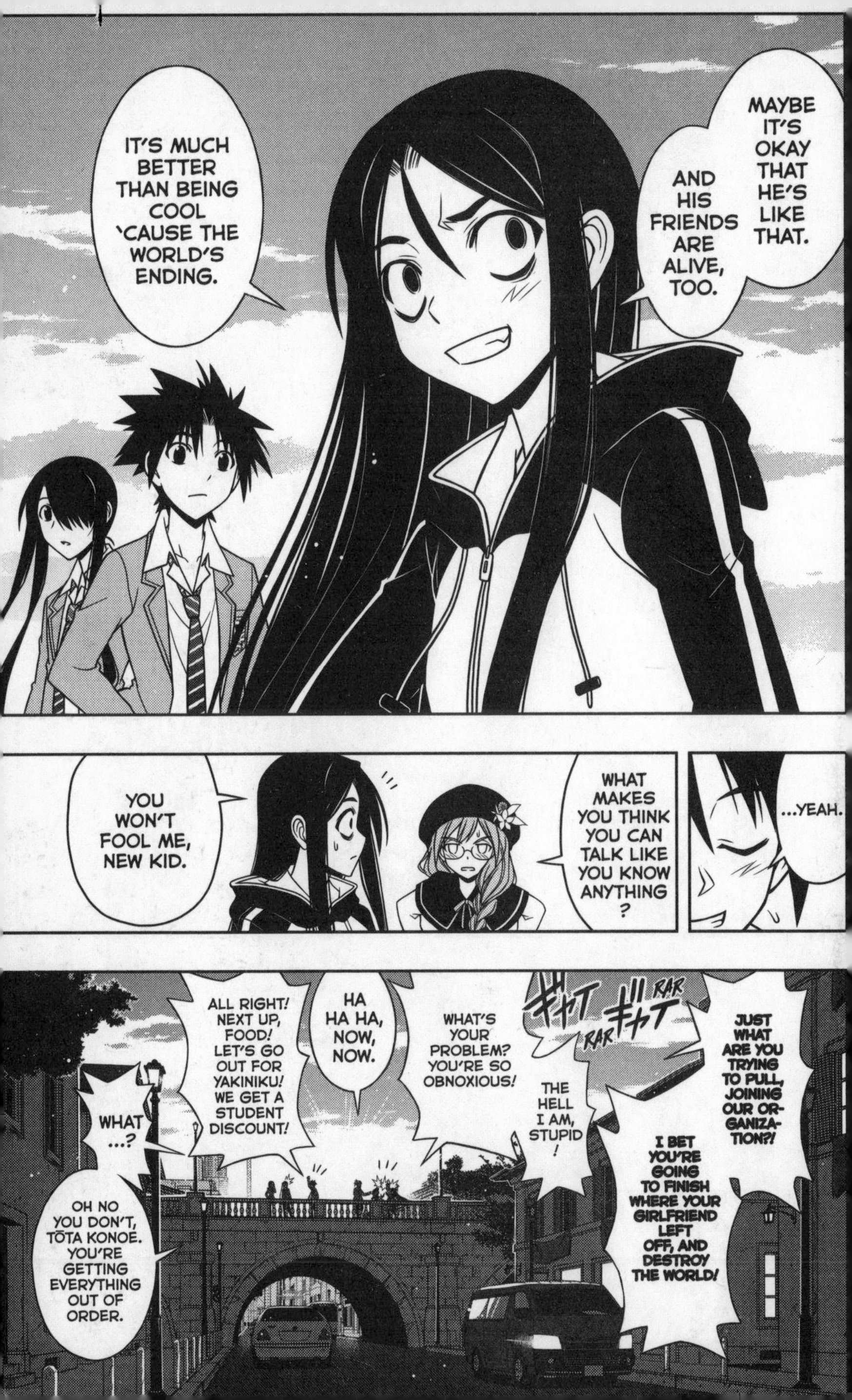
MAYBE IT'S OKAY THAT HE'S LIKE THAT.
AND HIS FRIENDS ARE ALIVE, TOO.
IT'S MUCH BETTER THAN BEING COOL 'CAUSE THE WORLD'S ENDING.
...YEAH.
WHAT MAKES YOU THINK YOU CAN TALK LIKE YOU KNOW ANYTHING?
YOU WON'T FOOL ME, NEW KID.
JUST WHAT ARE YOU TRYING TO PULL, JOINING OUR ORGANIZATION?!
I BET YOU'RE GOING TO FINISH WHERE YOUR GIRLFRIEND LEFT OFF, AND DESTROY THE WORLD!
RAR RAR RAR
THE HELL I AM, STUPID!
WHAT'S YOUR PROBLEM? YOU'RE SO OBNOXIOUS!
HA HA HA, NOW, NOW.
ALL RIGHT! NEXT UP, FOOD! LET'S GO OUT FOR YAKINIKU! WE GET A STUDENT DISCOUNT!
WHAT...?
OH NO YOU DON'T, TŌTA KONOE. YOU'RE GETTING EVERYTHING OUT OF ORDER.

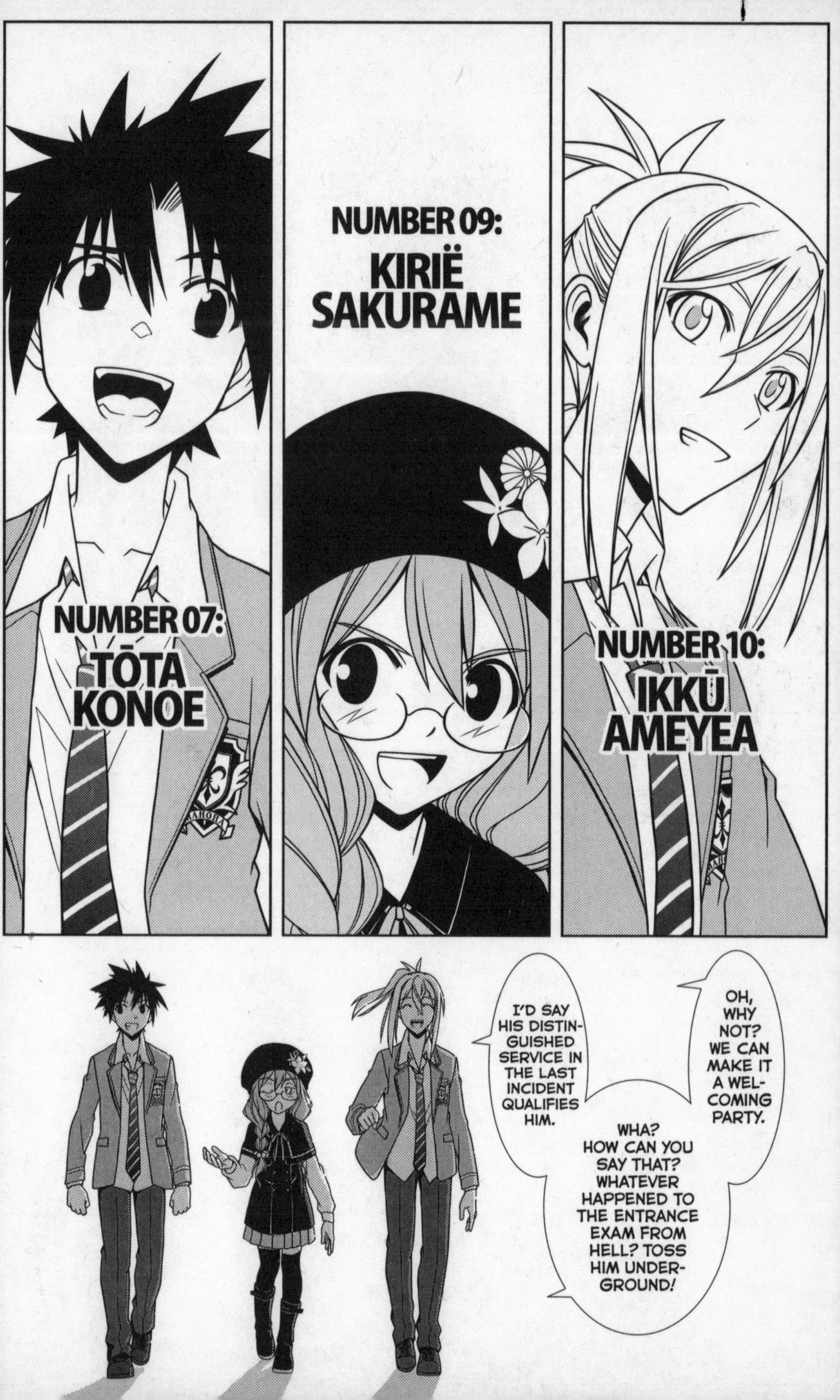
NUMBER 10:
IKKŪ AMEYEA
NUMBER 09:
KIRIË SAKURAME
NUMBER 07:
TŌTA KONOE
MAHORA
OH, WHY NOT? WE CAN MAKE IT A WEL-COMING PARTY.
I'D SAY HIS DISTIN-GUISHED SERVICE IN THE LAST INCIDENT QUALIFIES HIM.
WHA? HOW CAN YOU SAY THAT? WHATEVER HAPPENED TO THE ENTRANCE EXAM FROM HELL? TOSS HIM UNDER-GROUND!

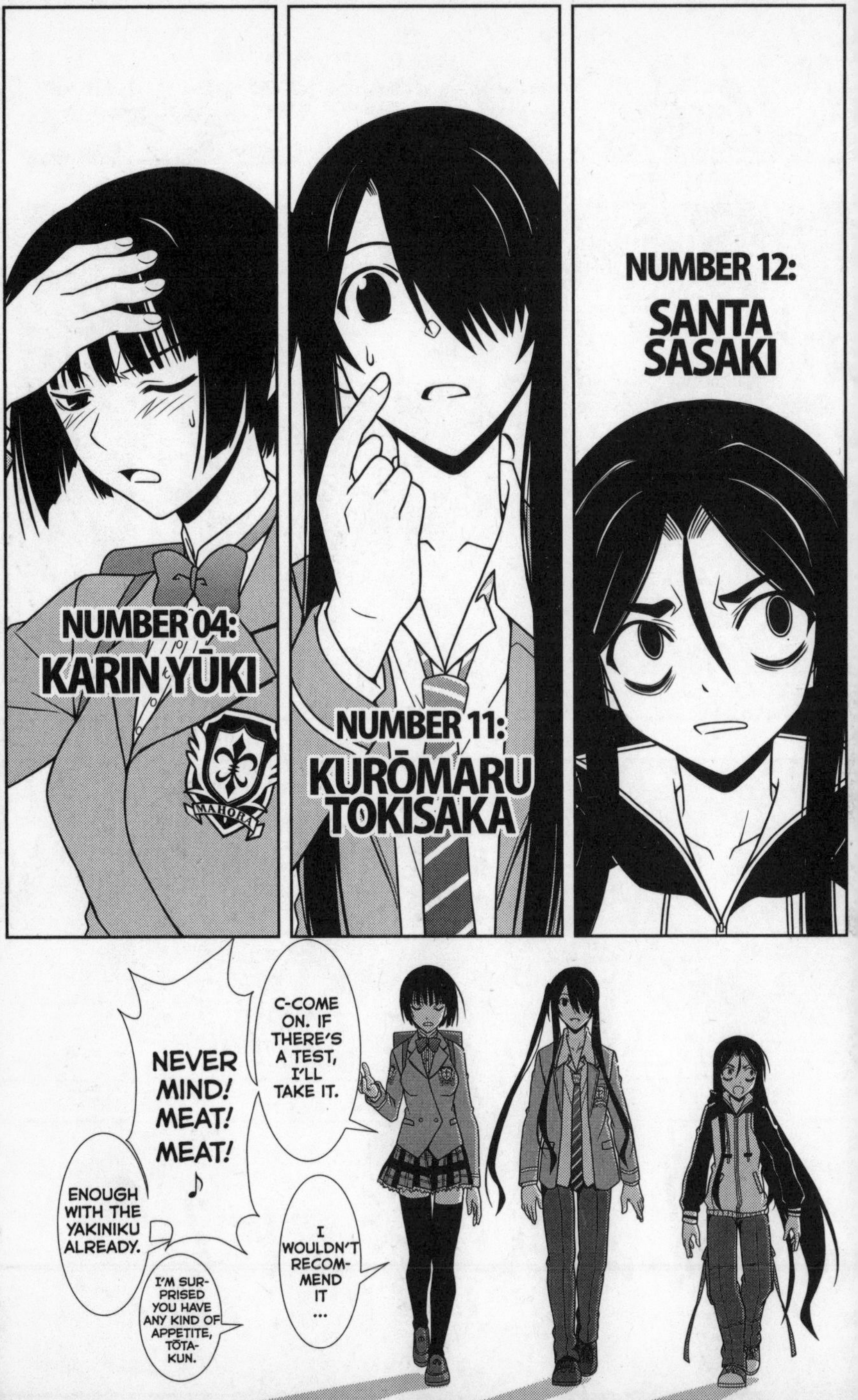
NUMBER 12:
SANTA SASAKI
NUMBER 11:
KURŌMARU TOKISAKA
NUMBER 04:
KARIN YŪKI
C-COME ON. IF THERE'S A TEST, I'LL TAKE IT.
NEVER MIND! MEAT! MEAT! ♪
I WOULDN'T RECOMMEND IT ...
ENOUGH WITH THE YAKINIKU ALREADY.
I'M SURPRISED YOU HAVE ANY KIND OF APPETITE, TŌTA-KUN.

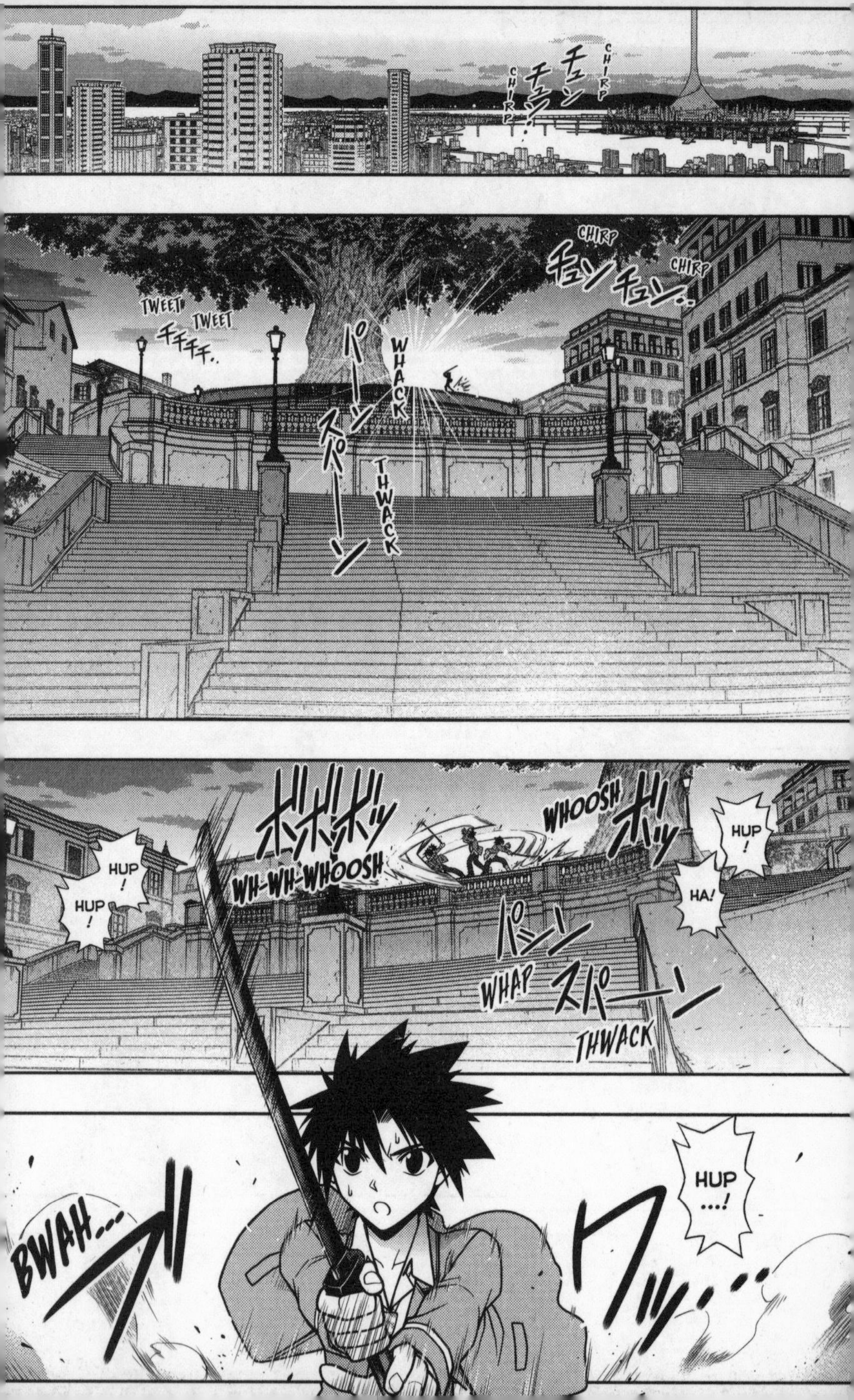

CHIRP
CHIRP
チュン チュン…
CHIRP
CHIRP
チュン チュン…
WHACK
パーン
THWACK
スパーン
TWEET
TWEET
チチチチ…
HUP!
HA!
WHOOSH
ボッ
WHAP
パシン
THWACK
スパーン
WH-WH-WHOOSH
ボボボッ
HUP!
HUP!
HUP ...!
BWAH...

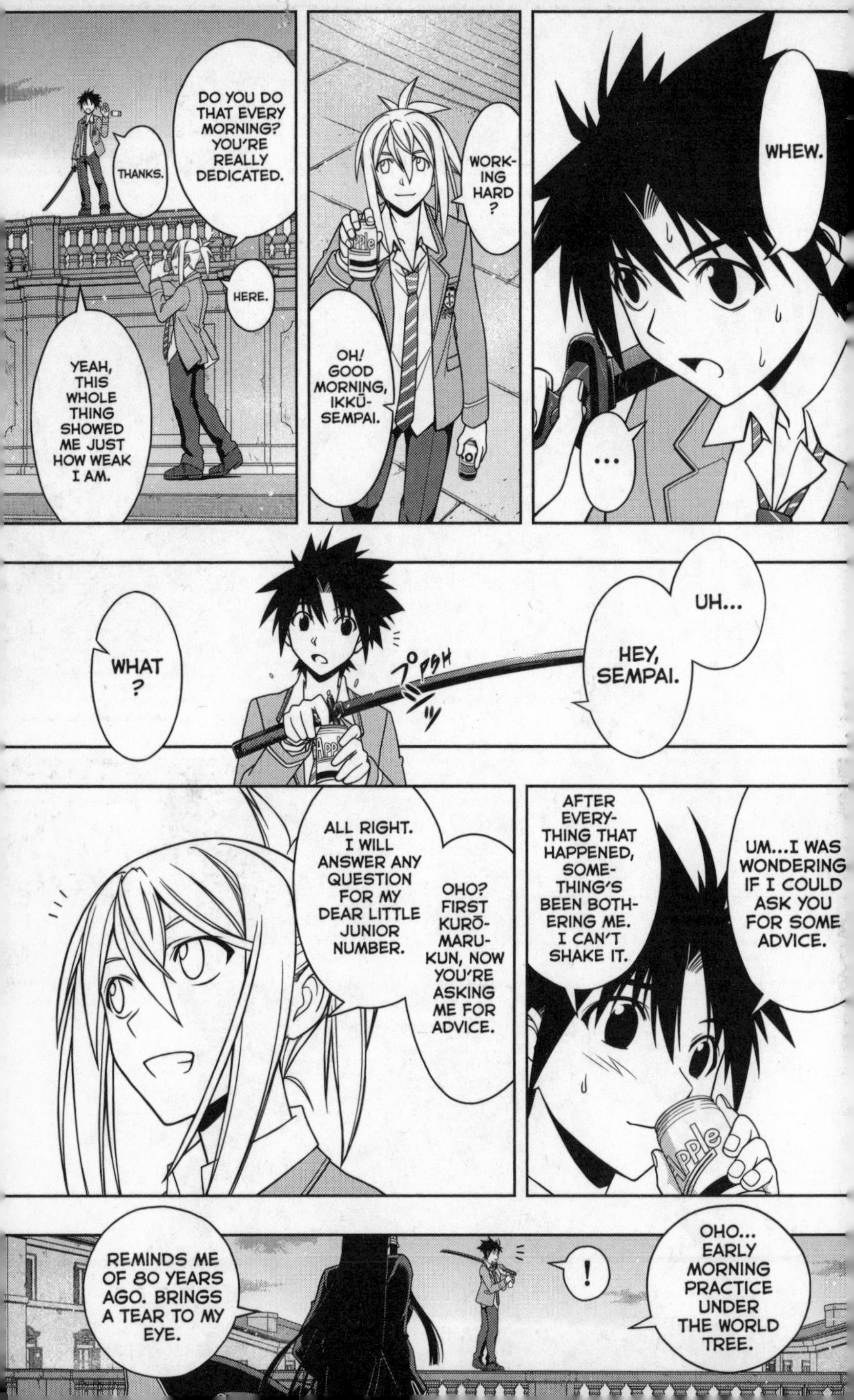
WHEW.
...
WORKING HARD?
OH! GOOD MORNING, IKKŪ-SEMPAI.
DO YOU DO THAT EVERY MORNING? YOU'RE REALLY DEDICATED.
THANKS.
HERE.
YEAH, THIS WHOLE THING SHOWED ME JUST HOW WEAK I AM.
UH...
HEY, SEMPAI.
POPSH
WHAT?
UM...I WAS WONDERING IF I COULD ASK YOU FOR SOME ADVICE.
AFTER EVERYTHING THAT HAPPENED, SOMETHING'S BEEN BOTHERING ME. I CAN'T SHAKE IT.
OHO? FIRST KURŌMARU-KUN, NOW YOU'RE ASKING ME FOR ADVICE.
ALL RIGHT. I WILL ANSWER ANY QUESTION FOR MY DEAR LITTLE JUNIOR NUMBER.
OHO... EARLY MORNING PRACTICE UNDER THE WORLD TREE.
!
REMINDS ME OF 80 YEARS AGO. BRINGS A TEAR TO MY EYE.

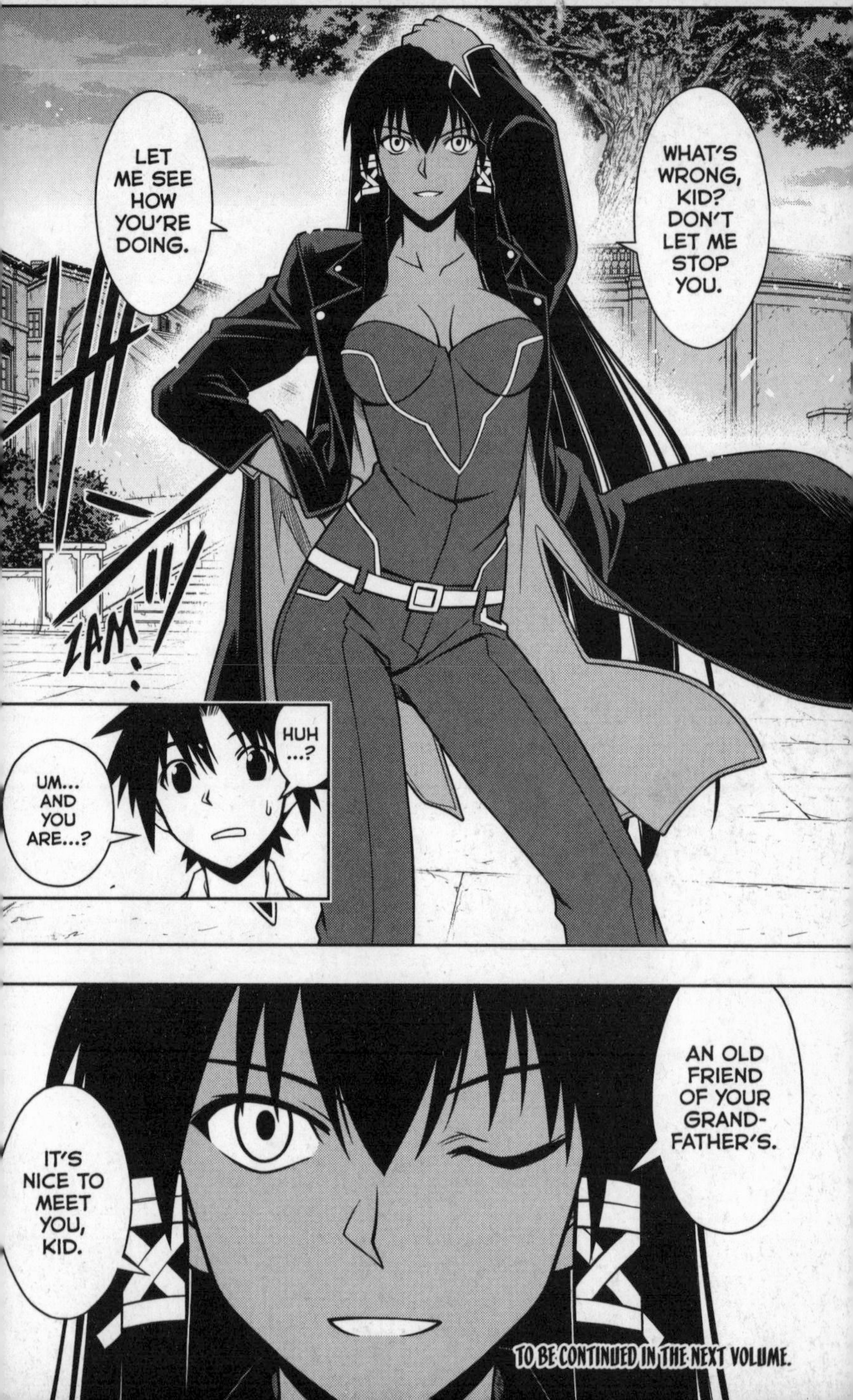
WHAT'S WRONG, KID? DON'T LET ME STOP YOU.
LET ME SEE HOW YOU'RE DOING.
ZAM!!
HUH ...?
UM... AND YOU ARE...?
AN OLD FRIEND OF YOUR GRAND-FATHER'S.
IT'S NICE TO MEET YOU, KID.
TO BE CONTINUED IN THE NEXT VOLUME.

UQ HOLDER!

STAFF

Ken Akamatsu
Takashi Takemoto
Kenichi Nakamura
Keiichi Yamashita
Tohru Mitsuhashi
Susumu Kuwabara
Yuri Sasaki

Thanks to Ran Ayanaga

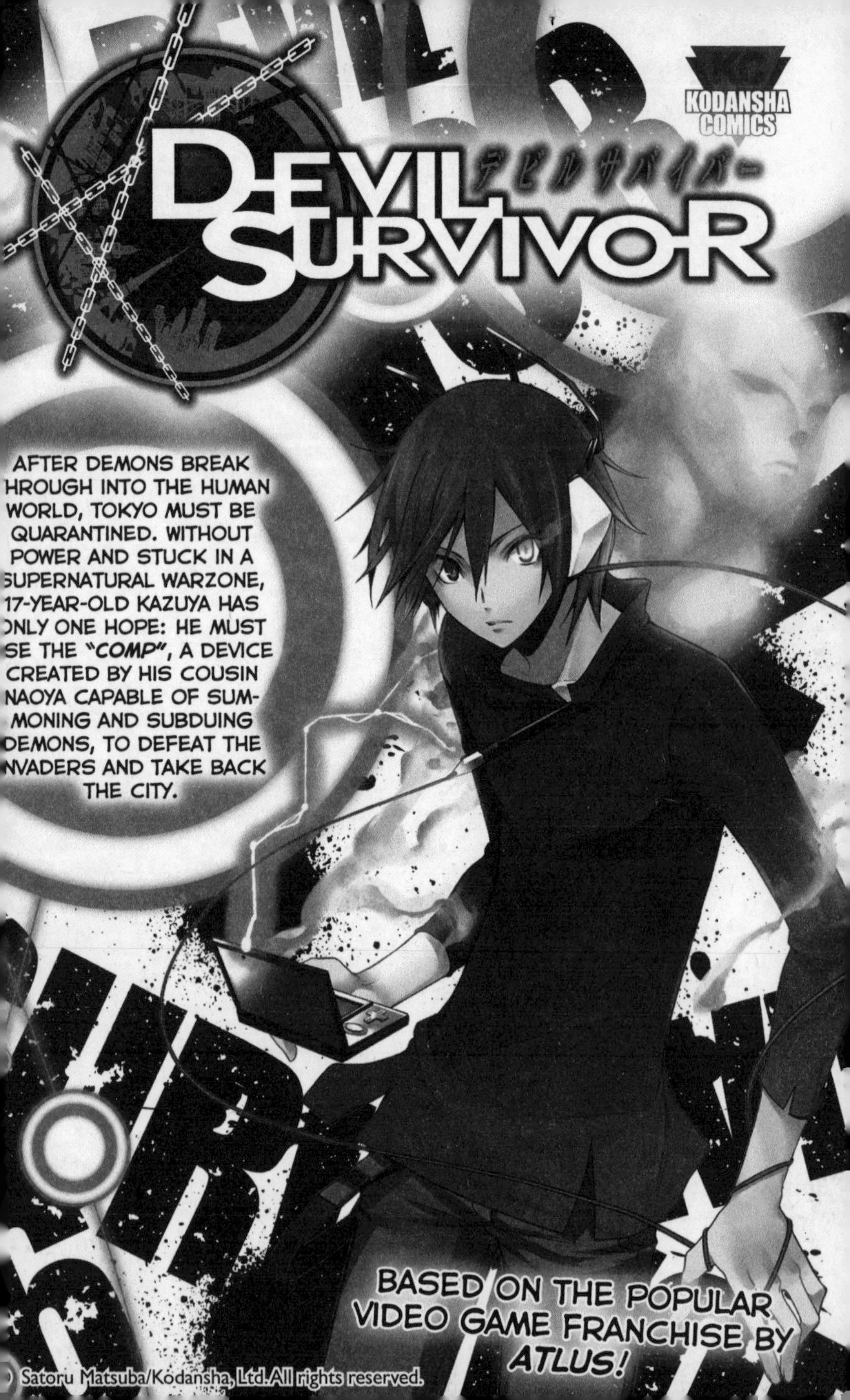
KODANSHA COMICS
DEVIL SURVIVOR
デビルサバイバー
AFTER DEMONS BREAK HROUGH INTO THE HUMAN WORLD, TOKYO MUST BE QUARANTINED. WITHOUT POWER AND STUCK IN A SUPERNATURAL WARZONE, 17-YEAR-OLD KAZUYA HAS ONLY ONE HOPE: HE MUST SE THE "COMP", A DEVICE CREATED BY HIS COUSIN NAOYA CAPABLE OF SUMMONING AND SUBDUING DEMONS, TO DEFEAT THE NVADERS AND TAKE BACK THE CITY.
BASED ON THE POPULAR VIDEO GAME FRANCHISE BY ATLUS!
Satoru Matsuba/Kodansha, Ltd. All rights reserved.

UQ HOLDER! VOLUME 6 IS A WORK OF FICTION. NAMES, CHARACTERS, PLACES, AND INCIDENTS ARE THE PRODUCTS OF THE AUTHOR'S IMAGINATION OR ARE USED FICTITIOUSLY. ANY RESEMBLANCE TO ACTUAL EVENTS, LOCALES, OR PERSONS, LIVING OR DEAD, IS ENTIRELY COINCIDENTAL.

A KODANSHA COMICS TRADE PAPERBACK ORIGINAL

PUBLISHED IN THE UNITED STATES BY KODANSHA COMICS, AN IMPRINT OF KODANSHA USA PUBLISHING, LLC, NEW YORK.

PUBLICATION RIGHTS FOR THIS ENGLISH EDITION ARRANGED THROUGH KODANSHA LTD., TOKYO.

FIRST PUBLISHED IN JAPAN IN 2015 BY KODANSHA LTD., TOKYO.

ISBN 978-1-63236-119-6

PRINTED IN THE UNITED STATES OF AMERICA.

WWW.KODANSHACOMICS.COM

9 8 7 6 5 4 3 2 1

TRANSLATOR: ALETHEA NIBLEY AND ATHENA NIBLEY
LETTERING: JAMES DASHIELL